THE
COLUMBIA
SOURCEBOOK
OF MUSLIMS
IN THE
UNITED STATES

THE
COLUMBIA
SOURCEBOOK
OF MUSLIMS
IN THE
UNITED STATES

EDWARD E. CURTIS IV
Editor

COLUMBIA UNIVERSITY PRESS
NEW YORK

Columbia University Press
Publishers Since 1893
New York   Chichester, West Sussex
Copyright © 2008 Columbia University Press
All rights reserved

Library of Congress Cataloging-in-Publication Data
The Columbia sourcebook of Muslims in the United States / Edward E.
Curtis IV, editor.

p. cm.

Includes bibliographical references and index.

ISBN 978-0-231-13956-4 (cloth : alk. paper)

1. Muslims—United States—History—Sources.   2. Muslims—United States—
Social conditions—Sources.   3. Islam—United States—History—Sources.
4. United States—Ethnic relations—Sources.   5. United States—Religion—
Sources.   6. United States—Religious life and customs—Sources.   I. Curtis,
Edward E., 1970–   II. Title: Sourcebook of Muslims in the United States.

E184.M88C65   2008

973.088′297—dc22

2007018968

Columbia University Press books are printed on permanent and durable acid-free paper.
This book is printed on paper with recycled content.
Printed in the United States of America

c 10 9 8 7 6 5 4 3 2 1

To my parents,

Susan Saffa Curtis and Edward E. Curtis III

Contents

FIVE

American Muslim Politics and Civic Engagement After 9/11 264

SIX

American Muslim Spirituality and Religious Life 336

Introduction to an
American Muslim Panorama

After 9/11, talk of Islam and Muslims became as commonplace in America as discussion about the baseball season, at least in some circles. Books by Islamic studies scholar Bernard Lewis appeared on the *New York Times* bestsellers list, and a rash of other volumes followed. Bookstores couldn't keep the Qur'an on their shelves. AM-radio shock jocks were full of views about Islam, and concerned citizens wrote in to their local papers. Presidential candidates and Christian preachers discussed Islamic theology on the Sunday morning talk shows and in the pulpit. On television, Muslims were asked whether they condemned terror. Mosques held information sessions. High schools and colleges invited guest speakers. More people than ever attended interfaith dialogue groups and many checked to make sure that their Muslim friends were safe.

Muslims in the United States became the subject of genuine curiosity, deep compassion, increased government surveillance, and great fear. Some Americans called American Muslims the "enemy" inside the country. Others countered that Muslims were neighbors, friends, husbands, sisters, coworkers, doctors, and artists. Many Americans acknowledged their ignorance about the two to eight million Muslims in the United States—even the experts disagreed about how many Muslims there were. They wanted to learn more. Who are these Muslims? Where are they from? What do they believe? What are they like?

This sourcebook is written for all those who seek a fair-minded, balanced, and human portrait of Muslim history and life in the United

States. It is the first volume to tell that story using largely first-person Muslim documents from every period of American Muslim history. Though no book is truly comprehensive, this one adopts a wide lens in portraying the American Muslim experience; it looks not only at Islamic religion but also at the everyday activities and concerns of Muslims. Readers will encounter an American Muslim panorama. The first half of the book focuses on the history of American Islam, and the second half examines contemporary issues including Islam and gender, American Muslim politics, and contemporary Islamic spirituality.

American Muslims are an incredibly diverse group who trace their ethnic and linguistic roots to every inhabited continent and nearly every country on the planet. They are a microcosm of the Islamic world. Many scholars make a historical distinction between "indigenous" Muslims, who are mostly African Americans, and immigrant Muslims, who are largely South Asians and Middle Easterners. It is estimated that black American Muslims may constitute the single largest group of Muslims in the United States—certainly more than 25 percent of the total, though probably less than 40 percent. Or perhaps South Asian Muslims—those who trace their roots to India, Pakistan, and to a lesser degree Bangladesh— are the largest group. As many Americans might suspect, there are also large numbers of Arab American Muslims, those with historical ties to Arabic-speaking countries from Morocco to Iraq. They may represent a quarter of the total. While African Americans, South Asian Americans, and Arab Americans are the three dominant ethnic groups, any inclusive story of Islam in the United States must also include the voices of whites, Hispanics, Iranians, Turks, Indonesians, Bosnians, Albanians, Afghanis, Somalis, Nigerians, and many, many others.

American Muslims are not only diverse by ethnic and racial background, but also by religious ideology, belief, and practice. In the aftermath of the 2003 war in Iraq, many Americans are becoming more familiar with the religious split in Islam between Sunni and Shi'a Muslims, a sectarian division with historical roots in the question over who should lead the Muslim community in the absence of the Prophet Muhammad. While that historically important divide also exists in the United States, it is often less significant in American Muslim communal relations than whether one is a conservative or a liberal. Like some socially conservative American Christians and Jews, socially conservative Muslims often condemn what they believe to be the moral failings of America, including the overabundance of sex and violence in popular culture, the right to have an abortion, and the legalization of gay marriage. American Muslim liberals, on the other hand, are often far more concerned with the struggle against poverty, racial and ethnic discrimination, and gender inequality, like many of their liberal Christian and Jewish compatriots. Despite differences between conservative and liberal Muslims, most American Muslims do have some religious traits in common: they often rely upon what are heartfelt understandings of their sacred texts and religious traditions in coming to understand their moral and ethical obligations as people of faith.

Of course, there are some American Muslims who are neither conservative nor liberal, neither Sunni nor Shi'a. Their voices are here as well. The result is that in weaving together a narrative of American Muslim life, we do not have one story, but many—or perhaps we have an epic in which the characters share the same historical space but do not always meet or know one another. In fact, some practicing Muslims in the United States may not recognize themselves in the words of other Muslims in this volume. That's inevitable. Because the book includes first-person voices from so many different people, there is bound to be disagreement and divergence. This is a sign of Islam's vitality in the United States. There is no American Muslim monolith.

But while this anthology contains many American Muslim stories— narrative fragments that sometimes have very little to do with one another—it also shows when and where these different stories collide and connect. The histories of indigenous and immigrant Muslims have never been entirely separate, and one of the distinguishing features of this book is that it seeks to show where Muslims of different racial and ethnic backgrounds have made contact across important social boundaries and influenced one another. Some scholars and practicing Muslims consider the history of black Muslims to be entirely separate from the history of immigrant Muslims; the charge is sometimes made that many African American Muslims are not "real" Muslims. This book does not make such judgments. When someone calls himself or herself a Muslim, this work's immediate reaction is curiosity: what does it mean for that person to be Muslim? By listening closely, we can better understand the distinctions between various kinds of Muslims and how they may or may not be related to one another.

The book is similarly inclusive when it comes to the question of who is an "American" Muslim. In deciding this question, some observers make a distinction between Muslims *in* America and American Muslims. According to this more narrow view, American Muslims are generally defined as naturalized citizens of the American nation-state or Muslims who were born on American soil. In general, most of the American Muslims mentioned in this volume are people who have lived in the United States for years. But the voices of Muslim permanent residents (green-card holders), visitors, and even guests are also included at times, since they have played an important role in shaping American Muslim life. American Muslim identity and culture are not delimited by the political borders of the United States. Some of the people whom I call American Muslims might reject such a label—not just Muslim visitors from other countries, but also some American-born Muslims who do not consider themselves American. Still, they, too, are an important part of the scene, and their voices are included. If a Muslim sets foot in the United States, this sourcebook considers what that person's effect may have been on other American Muslims' history and life.

The book also includes a number of different literary genres—speeches, interviews, editorials, stories, song lyrics, books, articles, autobiographies, and Web sites. They shed light on the major ideas, trends, and groups in American Islam, and they illuminate minority perspectives as well. Some are well-known sources that have been influential in the American Muslim community itself. For example, Amina Wadud's book *Qur'an and Woman* is an oft-quoted text among many American Muslims and a jumping-off point for many discussions about the status of women in the Muslim community. Other documents are quite rare and appear here for the first time in print. For example, we encounter the oral history of Mary Juma, a Syrian immigrant who left the Middle East over a hundred years ago to become a sodbuster in North Dakota and help establish the town of Ross as a Muslim outpost on the Great Plains. Other documents are politically provocative, like Capital D's rap about the culture of terrorism, and still others are nostalgic, like Imam Vehby Isma'il's children's story about Muslim life in Albania.

Roughly half of the documents uncover the history of American Muslims. While 9/11 focused new public attention on Muslims in the United States, Muslims are nothing new in America. The book begins with the stories of an African Muslim who came to the United States as a slave and wrote his autobiography in Arabic. Chapter 1 also includes an essay written by one of the first prominent white American converts to Islam and the comments of a famous African American intellectual who praised what he called the salutary effect of Islamic religion on black persons. In addition, this chapter contains a history of the Shriners, an American fraternal organization that would interest thousands of American males in Islamic signs and symbols, contributing to the eventual flowering of Islam among both blacks and whites.

Chapter 2 includes coverage of Muslim immigrants from the Middle East, South Asia, and Europe who arrived in the United States from World War I to the 1960s. The reader will encounter the famous Muslim mystic and musician Pir Inayat Khan and the amazing stories of Toledo barkeepers who used their profits to build one of North America's most famous mosques. However, even more attention is devoted to the rise of Islam among African Americans during a period of American Muslim history characterized by personal contact and communal divergence. Some black American forms of Islam bore little resemblance to the Islamic expressions of Muslim immigrants from the Afro-Eurasian landmass. Other forms of African American Islam were the products of the encounter between African American Muslims and Muslim immigrants. In still other instances, African Americans converted to the forms of Islam practiced by the immigrant communities and formed interracial American Muslim communities. Tracing those genealogies is an essential task in telling the story of American Muslims.

After 1965, when President Lyndon B. Johnson signed an immigration reform bill permitting more nonwhite persons to immigrate to America, African and Asian Muslims arrived in even greater numbers in the United States. The ethnic diversity of the American Muslim community exploded, and developments in Muslim-majority countries had more immediate effects on the life of Muslims in the United States. Teachers, preachers, ideas, and books arrived from newly independent nations struggling to overcome the legacy of European colonialism and to resist superpower intervention in their domestic affairs. In the age of Vietnam, the civil rights movement, and Watergate, some American Muslims developed a more explicitly political view of Islam sharply critical of the American government. Others called for a moral renewal along the lines of "old-fashioned" social conservatism. Still others sought peace and harmony in mystical movements. American Islam echoed the spirit of the age, and as more whites, blacks, and Hispanics became Muslim, they not only borrowed traditions from immigrant Muslims but created their own forms of American Muslim religious practice. That trend, the subject of chapter 3, continues today.

The second half of the anthology highlights issues of great concern to contemporary American Muslims—and many non-Muslims, too. Chapter 4 examines controversies about the status of women, gender identity, and sexuality in Islamic religion and the American Muslim community. Documents from African American, Middle Eastern, South Asian, and white American Muslim women show that while few American Muslim women think that Islam is an oppressive religion toward women, many think that women are oppressed by Muslim culture. We also hear from an American Muslim lesbian who struggles for acceptance in her family, as well as the story of an HIV-positive woman who attempts to educate other Muslims about AIDS. Finally, there are several points of view presented on the question of whether there should be female prayer leaders and preachers in American mosques.

Chapter 5 examines the ways that American Muslims engage American political ideas, the U.S. government, and American society more generally. It is bound to be a charged topic after 9/11, and this book attempts to take a broad-minded, balanced, and inclusive view. The documents include a study of anti-Muslim hate crimes and a critique of the Bush administration's policies on Muslim charities. There is also the plea agreement of an American Muslim who conspired against America with the Taliban—and an American Muslim *fatwa*, or religious ruling, against all forms of terrorism. One document sets out a plan for dialogue among persons of different faiths in America; another urges all Americans to convert to Islam. Muslim law professor Khaled Abou El Fadl argues that democracy is the best form of Islamic government available today. Some social workers discuss the difficulties faced by Somali political refugees trying to find a place to live.

The concluding chapter portrays the contemporary religious practices and the spiritual life of American Muslims. It includes documents, as one might expect, about the Qur'an, daily prayer, and fasting, but it also looks at Islamic financing for home purchases, Islamic medical ethics, American whirling dervishes, and Islamic hip-hop. There is no one form of Muslim spirituality or religious practice in America, and like the rest of the volume, the final chapter seeks to capture the diversity of the American Muslim experience. In doing so, it recapitulates many of the book's themes, including the idea that religion is never completely separate from the rest of human life. The social, cultural, economic, and political identities of religious persons inevitably color their religious activities. The result, as we see, is a faith that responds to the exigencies of life, reflecting all the beauty, failings, and promise of humanity.

My hope is that this book will be of interest to readers of all kinds—those browsing the shelves of their local bookstore as well as students of U.S. history, Islamic religion, and contemporary American culture. To make it as "good a read" as possible, I have chosen to eliminate footnotes, and I have tried to speak plainly—not always easy for a college professor. Those interested in reading the academic books and articles that have informed my approach to these topics will find them listed in the Further Reading section. For readers unfamiliar with Islam, Islamic terms absolutely essential to this volume have been generally italicized and then briefly defined in brackets. At the end of the book, there is also is a glossary of Islamic terms and a pedestrian pronunciation guide. To avoid confusing the reader, I have also taken the liberty of standardizing as much of the spelling as I can. Now more than ever, many scholars of religion are reaching out not only to their colleagues and students, but also to the public at large—sometimes to anyone who will listen—in an attempt to nurture dialogue and understanding among people of different faiths. This volume is a humble contribution toward that larger effort.

THE
COLUMBIA
SOURCEBOOK
OF MUSLIMS
IN THE
UNITED STATES

Whispers and Echoes

American Muslims Before World War I

FROM colonial times to the present day, many Americans have been alternately allured and repulsed by images of the Muslim Orient, which was often associated with political despotism, sexual excess, and cultural backwardness. This understanding of Islam, Muslims, and the Orient, called "orientalism" by scholars, often said much more about non–Muslim American fears, interests, and cultures than it did about actual Muslims and Islamic religious traditions. But orientalism has been an important if little understood part of American culture. In the 1800s, a significant number of American men journeyed to the Christian Holy Land in Palestine, recording their impressions of Middle Eastern Muslims and Muslim holy sites in popular travelogues. For some men, the chance to travel to the Middle East was an opportunity to affirm their male identities. Their writings contained wild fantasies about Muslim harems, and some even dressed up like Turkish sultans, imagining themselves as potent men who dominated exotic Oriental women at will. In the 1870s, Muslim signs and symbols were incorporated into the ritual acts of an American fraternal organization, the Ancient Arabic Order of the Nobles of the Mystic Shrine, or the "Shriners." Thousands of white and, later, African American males eventually joined the Shriners, which traced their lineage to the "Grand Shaykh" of Mecca and to Sufism, the mystical branch of Islam. They attended lodges named after important Arab-Islamic places such as the "Kaaba" and "Medina," and they wore red Turkish fezzes. Today, the Shriners remain active, known to many Americans as the folks who drive tiny cars in American street parades and who render significant service to a number of charities, especially hospitals.

In the 1800s, many Americans saw Islam and Muslims not only as a source of the exotic but also as a sign of the devil. Some Christian Americans depicted Islam as a misguided religious tradition, a Christian heresy, and even a sign of the Antichrist. In so doing, Americans reproduced centuries-old stereotypes of Islam that emerged in Christian Europe at the time of the Crusades. The Prophet Muhammad was the object of much of this prejudice. For example, Dante, the great Italian author of the *Inferno*, placed Muhammad in the ninth circle of hell, where he was punished by being split from his anus to his chin in perpetuity. While such violent images of the Prophet did not always consume the American Christian imagination, Muhammad was nevertheless considered to be violent, oversexed, and a spiritual charlatan. At various points in the 1800s, images of Islam and its false prophet became important to those Christians who expected the imminent return of Christ. For some, the demise of Ottoman Turkish power in the 1800s was viewed as a sign of the Second Coming.

Other Americans adopted a more sympathetic stance toward Islam and Muslim persons. West Indian–born Edward Wilmot Blyden (1832–1912), an African American Presbyterian missionary, studied Arabic and Islamic history and conducted fieldwork in West Africa so that he could better understand the growth of Islam in that region. In his classic *Christianity, Islam, and the Negro Race* (1887), Blyden openly praised and defended Islam as a positive force among black Africans, shocking his British and American audiences by presenting a harsh critique of Western imperialism and missionary Christianity.

Though nineteenth-century America may have been saturated with images of Islam and the Muslim Orient, it is striking that actual human contact between Muslims and non-Muslims in the United States was rare. One important exception was the interaction of Muslim slaves with some non-Muslim slaves, slaveholders, politicians, and eager ethnographers in the antebellum United States. Most of the Muslims who first came to the Americas during the colonial period were West African slaves. While it is difficult to estimate the number of slaves who were Muslim, some scholars believe as many as 10 to 20 percent of all slaves brought to the Americas practiced some form of Islam. It makes sense that at least some slaves were Muslims, since Islam was a vital component of many West African cultures during the time of the slave trade. Some of these Muslims were urbane and literate merchants, peripatetics, and *marabouts*, or mystics. Some had memorized the Arabic Qur'an by heart. In the Americas, these persons maintained their Arabic literacy by reading Arabic New Testaments given to them by Christian missionaries and by purchasing expensive supplies of paper to practice their writing. Muslims from Yoruba in Bahia, Brazil, used Arabic as a secret language in planning the revolt of 1835.

How many black Muslims continued to practice Islam in British North America and the United States, however, is difficult to know. In general, historians have uncovered more evidence of Muslim practices in places where slaves lived in predominately black or isolated areas, or where there were more first- or second-generation African Americans. In these places, there was a greater chance that certain African traditions would be preserved or perpetuated. For example, in the 1900s, oral historians collected tales of several Muslims who continued to practice some form of Islam on the islands off the Georgia coast. Sahih Bilali of Saint Simons Island, for example, was known to have fasted. Bilali Mohamed of Sapelo Island used a Muslim prayer rug and wore a fez. And the names of Gullah children sometimes bore Muslim influence.

One of the greatest records of early African American Muslim history in the United States is the 1831 autobiography of Omar ibn Sayyid (c. 1770–1864), a North Carolinian slave originally from Futa Toro on the Senegal River. Like other educated West Africans, he was literate in written Arabic, the language of the Qur'an and a lingua franca in West Africa. In his memoir, Omar ibn Sayyid claimed to have been a baptized Christian for some years, but for some reason he dedicated his work not only to God but also to the Prophet Muhammad. Whether he was hiding his true Muslim identity or had combined his Islam with his Christianity is unknown. But it does indicate the continued influence of Islam on his consciousness well after his conversion to Christianity.

The autobiography is a rare document. On the whole, there is little direct evidence in North America of the large-scale practice of Islam among slaves. While some slaves may have brought Islamic religion with them to North America, the meaning and function of their Islamic religious practices may have changed once they landed on American soil. For example, the use of amulets, so important to the West African practice of Islam, certainly continued, but most who valued these charms probably did not think of them as "Islamic" objects. The American descendants of African Muslims most likely refashioned their religious traditions into new African American religious traditions, as they did with many of the African traditional religions practiced in North America. These traditions did not lead in most cases to the perpetuation of a self-consciously defined Muslim identity.

But in the 1880s, a new group of Muslims came to American shores. From that decade until World War I, hundreds of thousands of people from the Ottoman Empire immigrated to the Americas. Many who came to the United States were Arabs from what is today Syria and Lebanon. Most were Christian but at least some were Muslim. In 1902, for example, twenty identifiably Muslim persons settled in Ross, North Dakota, where they adopted American dress but continued to practice fasting during Ramadan, traditional wedding celebrations, and Syrian foodways. Many of the first immigrants were single men who, like others who immigrated to the United States during the Gilded Age, sought economic opportunity, often hoping to make a small fortune and return home. Many began humbly as peddlers, selling wares and Arab foodstuffs along railroads and rivers. Others were unskilled laborers. In Quincy, Massachusetts, some were dockworkers. And in the Plains states such as the Dakotas, they became dry-goods salesmen. By 1907, some immigrants were working for Henry Ford in his automobile factory in Highland Park, Michigan, and in 1916, Ford's sociological department counted 555 Arab men as employees. This link to the burgeoning automobile industry in Michigan established an immigration pattern that continues to this day; in fact, one of the largest Arab American communities in the United States is in Dearborn, Michigan.

During this period, at least some white persons became attracted to Islam, as well. In 1893, for example, the World Parliament of Religions invited a Muslim to represent Islam at their Chicago, Illinois, assembly. Their choice was Mohammed Alexander Russell Webb, a white American convert to the faith. Many Christian missionaries in attendance at the World Parliament did not seek a true religious dialogue of equals. Instead, they hoped to learn about other religious traditions so that they could convert non-Christians to Christianity. Still, Webb's very presence represented the attraction of at least some Americans to Islam and to the "mysterious" and "spiritual" religions of the East. At the time, his voice was but an exotic whisper—but it was a voice that would echo into the 1900s, as more and more Americans, especially African Americans, came to call themselves Muslims.

1. Omar ibn Sayyid,
The Autobiography of Omar ibn Sayyid (1831)

Omar ibn Sayyid, a slave from North Carolina, was an urbane and educated man. Like other religious Muslims in West Africa, Omar had been trained in the religious sciences of Islam and had learned the Arabic language of the Qur'an. In 1831, many years after he had been enslaved and forcibly removed from his homeland, he still remembered enough of his training to write his memoirs in Arabic. Though Omar ibn Sayyid's remarkable autobiography was cited by slaveholders as evidence that slavery could be benign and beneficial, one reading of this remarkable document casts doubt on such assertions. The text begins with Omar's quotation of verses from Surat al-Mulk, *the sixty-seventh chapter of the Qur'an, which emphasizes God's ownership of the heavens and the earth. Perhaps Omar was surreptitiously asserting, in an environment where antislavery sentiments were best expressed privately or in secret, that no human being could rightfully own another. It is also possible that while Omar claimed to have converted to Christianity, he continued to practice Islam. Certainly, the reader will note Omar's citation not only of Qur'anic verses but also his use of Islamic references in naming God, such as when Omar describes God as the "Lord of the worlds" (Qur'an 1:2). At the same time, one might conclude that Omar ibn Sayyid had developed a religious orientation that combined elements of both his new and old confessions, producing a pluralistic faith that was African, Muslim, and American.*

In the name of God, the merciful the gracious. God grant his blessing upon our Prophet Mohammed. Blessed be He in whose hands is the kingdom and who is Almighty; who created death and life that he might test You; for he is exalted; he is the forgiver (of sins), who created seven heavens one above the other. Do you discern anything trifling in creation? Bring back your thoughts. Do you see anything worthless? Recall your vision in earnest. Turn your eye inward for it is diseased. God has adorned the heavens and the world with lamps, and has made us missiles for the devils, and given us for them a grievous punishment, and to those who have disbelieved their Lord, the punishment of hell and pains of body. Whoever associates with them shall hear a boiling caldron, and what is cast therein may fitly represent those who suffer under the anger of God. Ask them if a prophet has not been sent unto them. They say, "Yes; a prophet has come to us, but we have lied to him." We said, "God has not sent us down anything, and you are in grievous error." They say, "If we had listened and been wise we should not now have been suffering the punishment of the Omniscient." So they confess they have sinned in destroying the followers of the Omniscient. Those who fear their Lord and profess his name, they receive pardon and great honor. Guard your words, (ye wicked), make it known that God is all-wise in all his manifestations. Do you not know from the creation that God is full of skill? That He has made for you the way of error, and you have walked therein, and have chosen to live upon what your god Nasur has furnished you? Believe on Him who dwells in heaven, who has fitted the earth to be your support and it shall give you food. Believe on Him who dwells in Heaven, who has sent you a prophet, and you shall understand what a teacher (He has sent you). Those that were before them deceived them (in regard to their prophet). And how came they to reject him? Did they not see in the heavens above them, how the fowls of the air receive with pleasure that which is sent them? God looks after all. Believe ye: it is He who supplies your wants, that you may take his gifts and enjoy them, and take great pleasure in them. And now will you go on in error, or walk in the path of righteousness. Say to them, "He who regards you with care, and who has made for you the heavens and the earth and gives you prosperity, Him you think little of. This is He that planted you in the earth, and to whom you are soon to be gathered." But they say, "If you are men of truth, tell us when shall this promise be fulfilled?" Say to them, "Does not God know? and am not I an evident Prophet?" When those who disbelieve shall see the things draw near before their faces, it shall then be told them, "These are the things about which you made inquiry." Have you seen that God has destroyed me or those with me? Or rather that He has shown us mercy? And who will defend the unbeliever from a miserable punishment? Say, "Knowledge is from God." Say, "Have you not seen that your water has become impure? Who will bring you fresh water from the fountain?"

O Sheikh Hunter, I cannot write my life because I have forgotten much of my own language, as well as of the Arabic. Do not be hard upon me, my brother. To God let many thanks be paid for his great mercy and goodness.

In the name of God, the Gracious, the Merciful. Thanks be to God, supreme in goodness and kindness and grace, and who is worthy of all honor, who created all things for his service, even man's power of action and of speech. . . .

You asked me to write my life. I am not able to do this because I have much forgotten my own, as well as the Arabic language. Neither can I write very grammatically or according to the true idiom. And so, my brother, I beg you, in God's name, not to blame me, for I am a man of weak eyes, and of a weak body.

My name is Omar ibn Seid [Sayyid]. My birthplace was Fut Tur, between the two rivers. I sought knowledge under the instruction of a Sheikh called Mohammed Seid, my own brother, and Sheikh Soleiman Kembeh, and Sheikh Gabriel Abdal. I continued my studies twenty-five years, and then returned to my home where I remained six years. Then there came to our place a large army, who killed many men, and took me, and brought me to the great sea, and sold me into the hands of the Christians, who bound me and sent me on board a great ship and we sailed upon the great sea a month and a half, when we came to a place called Charleston in the Christian language. There they sold me to a small, weak, and wicked man called Johnson, a complete infidel, who had no fear of God at all. Now I am a small man, and unable to do hard work so I fled from the hand of Johnson and after a month came to a place called Fayd-il [Fayetteville, North Carolina?].

There I saw some great houses (churches). On the new moon I went into a church to pray. A lad saw me and rode off to the place of his father and informed him that he had seen a black man in the church. A man named Handah (Hunter?) and another man with him on horseback, came attended by a troop of dogs. They took me and made me go with them twelve miles to a place called Fayd-il, where they put me into a great house from which I could not go out. I continued in the great house (which, in the Christian language, they called *jail*) sixteen days and nights. One Friday the jailor came and opened the door of the house and I saw a great many men, all Christians, some of whom called out to me, "What is your name? Is it Omar or Seid?" I did not understand their Christian language. A man called Bob Mumford took me and led me out of the jail, and I was very well pleased to go with them to their place. I stayed at Mumford's four days and nights, and then a man named Jim Owen, son-in-law of Mumford, having married his daughter Betsey, asked me if I was willing to go to a place called Bladen. I said, Yes, I was willing. I went with them and have remained in the place of Jim Owen until now.

Before [after?] I came into the hand of Gen. Owen a man by the name of Mitchell came to buy me. He asked me if I were willing to go to Charleston City. I said "*No, no, no, no, no, no, no,* I not willing to go to Charleston. I stay in the hand of Jim Owen."

O ye people of North Carolina, O ye people of S. Carolina, O ye people of America all of you; have you among you any two such men as Jim Owen and John Owen? These men are good men. What food they eat they give to me to eat. As they clothe themselves they clothe me. They permit me to read the gospel of God, our Lord, and Saviour, and King; who regulates all our circumstances, our health and wealth, and who bestows his mercies willingly, not by constraint. According to power I open my heart, as to a great light, to receive the true way, the way of the Lord Jesus the Messiah.

Before I came to the Christian country, my religion was the religion of Mohammed, the Apostle of God—may God have mercy upon him and give him peace. I walked to the mosque before day-break, washed my face and head and hands and feet. I prayed at noon, prayed in the afternoon, prayed at sunset, prayed in the evening. I gave alms every year, gold, silver, seeds, cattle, sheep, goats, rice, wheat, and barley. I gave tithes of all the above-named things. I went every year to the holy war against the infidels. I went on pilgrimage to Mecca, as all did who were able. My father had six sons and five daughters, and my mother had three sons and one daughter. When I left my country I was thirty-seven years old; I have been in the country of the Christians twenty-four years. Written A.D. 1831.

O ye people of North Carolina, O ye people of South Carolina, O all ye people of America—

The first son of Jim Owen is called Thomas, and his sister is called Masa-jein (Martha Jane?). This is an excellent family.

Tom Owen and Nell Owen have two sons and a daughter. The first son is called Jim and the second John. The daughter is named Melissa.

Seid [*Sayyid*, or Master] Jim Owen and his wife Betsey have two sons and five daughters. Their names are Tom, and John, and Mercy, Miriam, Sophia, Margaret and Eliza. This family is a very nice family. The wife of John Owen is called Lucy and an excellent wife she is. She had five children. Three of them died and two are still living.

O ye Americans, ye people of North Carolina—have you, have you, have you, have you among you a family like this family, having so much love to God as they?

Formerly I, Omar, loved to read the book of the Koran the famous. General Jim Owen and his wife used to read the gospel, and they read it to me very much, the gospel of God, our Lord, our Creator, our King, He that orders all our circumstances, health and wealth, willingly, not constrainedly, according to his power. Open thou my heart to the gospel, to the way of uprightness. Thanks to the Lord of all worlds, thanks in abundance. He is plenteous in mercy and abundant in goodness.

For the law was given by Moses but grace and truth were by the Jesus the Messiah.

When I was a Mohammedan I prayed thus: "Thanks be to God, Lord of all worlds, the merciful the gracious, Lord of the day of Judgment, thee we serve, on thee we call for help. Direct us in the right way, the way of those on whom thou hast had mercy, with whom thou hast not been angry and who walk not in error [Qur'an 1:1–7]. Amen." But now I pray "Our Father" [here Omar writes out the Protestant version of the Lord's prayer] in the words of our Lord Jesus the Messiah.

I reside in this our country by reason of great necessity. Wicked men took me by violence and sold me to the Christians. We sailed a month and a half on the great sea to the place called Charleston in the Christian land. I fell into the hands of a small, weak and wicked man, who feared not God at all nor did he read (the gospel) at all nor pray. I was afraid to remain with a man so depraved and who committed so many crimes and I ran away. After a month our Lord God brought me forward to the hand of a good man, who fears God, and loves to do good, and whose name is Jim Owen and whose brother is called Col. John Owen. These are two excellent men. I am residing in Bladen County.

I continue in the hand of Jim Owen who never beats me, nor scolds me. I neither go hungry nor naked, and I have no hard work to do. I am not able to do hard work for I am a small man and feeble. During the last twenty years I have known no want in the hand of Jim Owen.

2. Mohammed Alexander Russell Webb,
Islam in America (1893)

Mohammed Webb (1846–1916) was born in Hudson, New York, and raised a Presbyterian Christian. A journalist by trade, he worked as a writer and editor for the Missouri Republican *and* St. Joseph Gazette *before being appointed by*

President Grover Cleveland as United States Consul to the Philippines in 1887.
He was already a religious seeker when he arrived in Manila, where he studied
the teachings of Islam under the guidance of Budruddin Abdulla Kur, a Mus-
lim from Bombay, India. After converting to Islam, Webb resigned his post and
set out, with the financial support of Hajj Abdulla Arab, a merchant from Me-
dina, Arabia, to be a Muslim missionary in America. Webb's writings about
Islam challenged the stereotypical views of Muslims that were so much a part of
American popular culture at the time. His defense of Islam as a rational, scien-
tific, and progressive religion reflected the influence of his Asian mentors, who
had fashioned a modern interpretation of Islam meant to combat the claims of
Christian missionaries in British India and other colonized lands. Webb's
Islam in America thus rejected images of Islam as the religion of the sword,
defended the status of women in Islam, and sought to clarify the significance of
polygamy to the average Muslim; in fact, Webb presents Islamic religion as
perfectly compatible not only with the ethical principles that he views as com-
mon to all Abrahamic religions but also with Victorian norms of propriety and
cleanliness, as well. Webb's introduction to "orthodox Islam," as he called it,
features an explanation of the five pillars of practice, including the profession of
faith, prayer, alms, fasting, and pilgrimage, and a summary of Muslim beliefs
in God, angels, revelation, the prophets, the Day of Judgment, and God's omni-
science. But Webb also indicates that these "exoteric" aspects of Islam are only
part of the religion, suggesting that for him, the "esoteric" or philosophic as-
pects of Islam are equally important.

I have been frequently asked why I, an American, born in a country which
is nominally Christian, and reared, "under the drippings" of an orthodox
Presbyterian pulpit, came to adopt the faith of Islam as my guide in life.
A reply to this question may be of interest now to that large body of independent thinkers, who are manifesting a desire to know what the Islamic
system really is. I am not vain enough to believe that I am the only American in this vast and progressive country capable of comprehending the
system taught by the inspired Prophet of Arabia, and of appreciating its
beauty and perfection. Nor do I believe that I am so deficient mentally as
to accept, as truth, a religion which no one else in this country would be
foolish enough to accept. But whether those who do accept it are wise or
foolish in the estimation of their fellow men, I feel quite confident that at
least a few may be benefited by my experience.

I was not born, as some boys seem to be, with a fervently religious strain in my character. I was emotional in later years, but not mawkishly senti-mental, and always demanded a reason for everything. I will not even go so far as to assert that I was a good boy, such as fond and prejudiced mothers sometimes point out as shining examples for their own sons. I attended the Presbyterian Sunday school of my native town—when I couldn't avoid it—and listened with weariness and impatience to the long, abstruse dis-courses of the minister, while I longed to get out into the glad sunshine, and hear the more satisfying sermons preached by God Himself, through the murmuring brooks, the gorgeous flowers and the joyous birds. I lis-tened incredulously to the story of the immaculate conception; and the dramatic tale of the vicarious atonement failed to arouse in me a thrill of tearful emotion, because I doubted the truth of both dogmas. Of course the narrow-minded church Christian will say at once, that the scriptural bogey-man, Satan, had me in his clutches as soon as I was born.

When I reached the age of twenty, and became, practically, my own master, I was so weary of the restraint and dullness of the church that I wandered away from it, and never returned to it. As a boy I found nothing in the system taught me in church and Sunday-school calculated to win me to it, nor did I find it any more attractive in later years, when I came to investigate it carefully and thoroughly. I found its moral ethics most com-mendable, but no different from those of every other system, while its su-perstitions, its grave errors, and its inefficiency as a means of securing salvation, or of elevating and purifying the human character, caused me to wonder why any thoughtful, honest and intelligent person could accept it seriously. Fortunately I was of an enquiring turn of mind—I wanted a reasonable foundation for everything—and I found that neither laymen nor clergy could give me any rational explanation of their faith; that when I asked them about God and the trinity, and life and death, they told me either that such things were mysteries, or were beyond the comprehension of ordinary mortals.

After trying in vain to find something in the Christian system to satisfy the longings of my soul and meet the demands of reason, I drifted into ma-terialism; and, for several years, had no religion at all except the golden rule, which I followed about as closely as the average Christian follows it.

About eleven years ago I became interested in the study of the Oriental religions, beginning with Buddhism, as students of the Eastern systems usually do, and finding much to interest me in the Theosophical litera-ture, which was not easy to be obtained in this country at that time. So intensely absorbed did I become in my studies and experiments, that I devoted four and five hours a day to them, often taking for that purpose time that I really needed for sleep. My mind was in a peculiarly receptive, yet exacting and analytical condition, absolutely free from the prejudices of all creeds, and ready to absorb the truth, no matter where it might be found. I was intensely in earnest in my efforts to solve the mysteries of life and death, and to know what relation the religious systems of the world bore to these mysteries. I reasoned that if there was no life beyond the grave, no religion was necessary to mankind; while if, as was claimed by many, there was a post-mortem life of far greater duration than the earthly existence, the nature and conditions of which were governed by our life on this globe, then it was of the greatest importance to know what course of life here would produce the most satisfying results in the next world.

Firmly materialistic, I looked at first to the advanced school of materialistic science, and found that it was just as completely immersed in the darkness of ignorance concerning spiritual things, as I was. It could tell me the name of every bone, muscle, nerve and organ of the human body, as well as its position, and (with one exception) its purpose or function; but it could *not* tell me the real difference between a living man and a dead one. It could tell me the name of every tree, plant and flower, and designate the species to which each belonged, as well as its apparent properties or attributes; but it could not tell me how and why the tree grew and flower bloomed. It was absolutely certain that man was born of woman, lived a brief period, and died; but whence he came, and whether he went were riddles which it confessed itself utterly unable to solve.

"Those matters belong to the church," said a scientist to me.

"But the church knows nothing of them," I replied.

"Nor do I, nor does science," was the helpless, hopeless way in which he dismissed the question from the conversation.

I saw Mill and Locke, and Kant and Hegel, and Fichte and Huxley, and many other more or less learned writers, discoursing, with a great show of wisdom, concerning protoplasm, and protogen, and monads, and yet not one of them could tell me what the soul was, or what becomes of it after death.

"But no one can tell you that," I fancy I hear someone say.

That is one of the greatest errors that poor, blind humanity ever made. There are people who have solved this mystery, but they are not the blind, credulous, materialistic followers of materialistic creeds.

I have spoken thus much of myself in order to show the reader that my adoption of Islam was not the result of misguided sentiment, blind credulity or sudden emotional impulse, but that it followed an earnest, honest, persistent, unprejudiced study and investigation, and an intense desire to know the truth.

After I had fully satisfied myself of the immortality of the soul, and that the conditions of the life beyond the grave were regulated by the thoughts, deeds and acts of the earth life; that man was, in a sense, his own savior and redeemer, and that the intercession of anyone between him and his God could be of no benefit to him, I began to compare the various religions, in order to ascertain which was the best and most efficacious as a means of securing happiness in the next life. To do this it was necessary to apply to each system, not only the tests of reason, but certain truths which I had learned during my long course of study and experiment outside the lines of orthodoxy, and in fields which priest and preacher usually avoid. . . .

There is no religious system known to humanity that is and has been, for centuries, so grossly misrepresented and thoroughly misunderstood by so-called Christians as that taught by the Prophet of Islam. The prejudice against it is so strong among the English-speaking people of the globe, that even the suggestion that it may possibly be the true faith and at least, worthy of a careful, unprejudiced investigation, is usually received with a contemptuous smile, as if such a thing was too palpably absurd to be considered seriously. It is this stubborn, unreasoning prejudice that prevents Europeans and Americans, who visit the East, from acquiring any accurate knowledge of Mohammedan social and religious life, or of the true doctrines of Islam. The air of superiority and self-sufficiency which they usually carry with them, repels the better and more enlightened classes of Mussulmans, and what is acquired from the lower classes cannot be taken as in any sense reliable. And yet it is this class of information that furnishes the inspiration for the magazine articles and books upon Mohammedan social life and beliefs which circulate in Europe and America.

Before covering in detail the Islamic system, let me say that my study and observation among the Mussulmans of the East have led me to confidently believe that it is the most perfect system of soul-development ever given to man, and the only one applicable to all classes of humanity. It is founded upon that eternal truth, which has been handed down to man

from age to age by the chosen prophets of God, from Moses to Mohammed. It is the only system known to man that is strictly in harmony with
reason and science. It is free from degrading superstitions, and appeals
directly to human rationality and intelligence. It makes every man individually responsible for every act he commits and every thought he thinks,
and does not encourage him to sin by teaching him a vicarious atonement. It is elevating and refining in its tendencies, and develops the higher,
nobler elements of humanity when it is faithfully, wisely and intelligently
followed.

I am aware that this declaration will cause some of those Christians
who are broad-minded enough to read this book, to smile and ask, if, in
my extensive intercourse with Mohammedans of all classes in the East, I
discovered much striking evidence of the exalting, ennobling influences
of Islam. Of course the wise Christian will refrain from asking this question, but it is probably the first one that the mentally blind churchman
will ask after he has duly questioned me concerning polygamy, that great
bugbear, which Christians almost universally consider the first and most
important article of faith with the Mussulman.

If we are to judge a religious system by the moral and social character of
many of its professed followers, Christianity will be so thoroughly condemned that it will speedily pass out of existence. Take a professed Mohammedan and compare him with a professed Christian of the same
intellectual caliber, the same education and the same opportunities for obtaining secular knowledge, and I am confident that the Mohammedan will
show a cleaner moral record and higher spiritual perceptions than the
Christian. Some of the most wretchedly degraded and fanatically superstitious people I have ever met in my life, called themselves Christians. Of
course they were *not* Christians, nor did they have even the remotest conception of the true teachings of Jesus of Nazareth, but they believed, or
claimed to believe, in the Christian dogmas. Now every Mohammedan
knows that it requires something more to make a true Mohammedan than
the parrot-like repetition of certain words of sentences. Because a man *says*
he is a Mohammedan, it does not follow that he comprehends, or lives up
to the spirit of, the teachings of the Prophet. If he does not do so he cannot
properly be taken as an example of the effects and tendencies of Islam. No
religious system can fairly be judged by the acts and expressions of all of its
professed followers; its plainly and fully established fundamental teachings and tenets only should guide us in forming an opinion of it.

And here let me assure the reader that there is nothing in the Islamic system that tends to immorality, impurity of thought, social degradation, superstition or fanaticism. On the contrary it leads on to all that is purest and noblest in the human character, and when we see a professed Mohammedan who is unclean in his person and habits, who is untruthful, cruel, intolerant, irreverent or fanatical, we may at once conclude that he is not a true follower of Islam, and, that he fails utterly to grasp the spirit of the religion he professes.

Let us consider briefly some of the salient principles—the most prominent features of this religion, viz: the unity of God, cleanliness, prayer, fasting, fraternity, pilgrimage and almsgiving. These may be said to form the foundation of the system, and I believe that an understanding of them is all that is necessary to commend it to any intelligent person.

Islam means, literally, resignation to the will of God, and the Islamic prayer is an aspiration to the higher spirit which is with and within every man. The Bible teaches that the Kingdom of Heaven is within us; the Koran teaches that God is nearer to every man than his jugular vein. The word Islam, by which every Mussulman designates his religion, carries with it the idea of an effort to become purer, better and more worthy to worship and submit to the will of the one true God. . . .

Anyone who will analyze the teachings of Mohammed will find that, in their ethical aspect, they are exactly in harmony with the ethical teachings of Moses, Abraham, Jesus and every other truly inspired prophet known to history. The system he promulgated differs quite materially from that previously given to the world, because his mission was to present a thorough and complete code, the general purpose of which was to correct the abuses and destroy the errors that had grown about the doctrines taught by his prophetic predecessors. His manifest purpose was to win mankind from idolatry, and to present a series of rules or laws which, if followed faithfully and intelligently, would draw men closer to God and make them purer and cleaner, mentally as well as physically, and better in every respect. He accomplished this mission fully, and was not called hence until he had seen the Islamic system firmly established in the hearts and minds of his followers.

Of course, at this time, we can consider the Islamic system only in its popular or exoteric aspect. As before stated, it has a deeper, more philosophic aspect than is apparent at a first glance. But its chief beauty, viewed superficially, is its perfect adaptability to the spiritual needs of all classes of humanity, from the humblest laborer to the most advanced thinker and man of letters. There is nothing in it that does violence to reason or common sense, or that is in any degree contrary to the natural instincts of justice and mercy. It requires no belief in the supernatural, nor the adoption of any absurd superstitions nor impossible theories. Purity of thought, word and deed, perfect mental and physical cleanliness, and steady, unwavering aspiration to God, coupled with pure, unselfish fraternal love, are the principal ends sought, and the means are as perfect as it is possible for man to conceive.

The Prophet forcibly declared that prayer was the corner stone of religion, and he laid greater stress upon this than upon any other feature of his system. In order to show the solemnity and importance of prayer more plainly, as well as to secure the carrying out of another principle, the "Woozoo [*wudhu*]," or ablution, was ordered. It was his evident intention to impress upon his followers the idea of cleanliness in such ways as were the most effective and permanent, and in the rule of ablution, as well as in other rules, we readily see that he understood and appreciated the force of habit. No Mussulman, who prays the required number of times daily, ever thinks of praying without thinking also of his "Woozoo," and thus he is reminded five times a day, at least, that he should have clean hands, face and feet, and in responding to the calls of nature, he is cleanly to the last degree; far more so than the average man of any other faith. Thus he acquires habits of personal cleanliness, which he cannot break away from without breaking away from his religion. All the evidence at hand, bearing upon the subject, tends to show that the Prophet not only intended that the hands, feet, face and other parts of the body, and the clothing should be clean when the face was turned toward the Kaaba, and the heart toward God.

No intelligent physician will deny that personal cleanliness, regular habits, and simple diet are conducive to the health of the body. The spiritual philosopher insists that late hours, irregular habits, dissipations of various kinds, and devotion to physical comfort are deleterious to the physical, as well as the moral health.

In the Islamic system, the times for prayer are irrevocably fixed. The first prayer must be said just as the first rays of the sun are gilding the Eastern horizon. After sunrise it must not be said until the time for the noon prayer. Thus the devout Mussulman must arise before daylight. The time for the second prayer is between 12 and 2 o'clock; the third between 4 and

5 o'clock; the fourth just as the sunlight has died away in the West; and, the fifth just before retiring at night. It is considered very meritorious to arise at midnight and pray, but it is not obligatory, before each of these five prayers, the worshipper washes his hands, arms, face, mouth, nostrils, ears and feet in running water.

It will be seen at once that the tendency of this perfect system of prayer is to cultivate habits of healthful regularity and cleanliness; to say nothing of its moral effects.

Man is a creature of habit; and, as a rule, when he once drops into a groove he rarely gets out of it without an unusual effort, unless he does so in order to follow something a little nearer to the earth. If he acquires the habit of praying five times a day, it will cling to him until he dies, and his prayer will increase in earnestness and soulfulness, as his knowledge of the fundamental principles of his religion increases.

One of the wisest provisions of the Islamic system is the rule relative to congregational prayer. The Mussulman is taught that he should always pray in company with others when it is possible for him to do so. Now there are several very good and sufficient reasons for this rule which can only be discussed under the head of Islamic Philosophy; we can only look, now, at its outward aspect. In the first place it is calculated to break down caste distinctions, and place the servant and his master upon a common level before God, in whose presence all men are equal; the beggar, the merchant, the shopkeeper, mechanic, millionaire, and the professional man, all stand elbow to elbow as brothers in the mosque at the time of prayer. And when a number of Mussulmans come together anywhere at the stated hours, they are bound to cast aside social distinctions and pray together. It is also the duty of the Mussulman to pray wherever he may happen to be when the hour of prayer arrives; or if the place is unsuitable, to seek a better one. . . .

It is generally admitted that a man may call himself a Mussulman if he simply declares his belief in the Unity of God and the inspiration of the Prophet. But he certainly cannot be called a true follower of Islam unless he prays from the very depths of his heart, and make the purpose of his prayer to bring his soul nearer to God. . . .

[T]he essence of the true faith of Islam is resignation to the will of God, and its corner stone is prayer. It teaches universal fraternity, universal love, and universal benevolence, and requires purity of mind, purity of action, purity of speech and perfect physical cleanliness. It is the simplest and most elevating form of religion known to man. It has no paid priest-hood, nor elaborate ceremonial, admits no vicarious atonement, nor re-lieves its followers of any of the responsibility for their sins. It recognizes but one God, the Father of all things, the divine spirit that dwells in all the manifestations of nature, the one omniscient, omnipotent, omnipresent ruler of the universe, to whom its followers devoutly pray, and before whom all stand upon a platform of perfect equality and fraternity. The devout Mussulman, one who has arrived at an intelligent comprehension of the true teachings of Our Holy Prophet, lives in his religion and makes it the paramount principle of his existence. It is with him in all his goings and comings during the day, and he is never so occupied with his business or worldly affairs that he cannot turn his back upon them, when the stated hour of prayer arrives, and present his soul to God. His loves, his sorrows, his hopes, his fears, are all immersed in it; it is his last thought when he lies down to sleep at night and the first to enter his mind at dawn when the voice of the Muezzin [the prayer caller] rings out loudly and clearly from the minaret of the mosque, waking the soft echoes of the morn with its thrilling solemn, majestic monotones: "Come to Prayer! Come to Prayer! Prayer is better than sleep! Prayer is better than sleep!"

3. Edward Wilmot Blyden, "Islam in the Western Soudan" (1902)

Edward W. Blyden (1832–1912) was born in the Dutch West Indies, traveled to the United States in 1850, and then immigrated to Liberia, where he became a Presbyterian missionary, a classics professor, president of Liberia College, am-bassador to Great Britain, secretary of state, minister of the interior, and one of the most noted black authors in the English-speaking world. Blyden, who explored firsthand the indigenous Muslim cultures of West Africa, or what was called the Western Sudan, became a harsh critic of white Christian mis-sionary activities. White missionaries did not save black souls as much as they helped to enslave black bodies and minds, he said. For Blyden, who was well versed in the scientific racism of the nineteenth century, it seemed that whites were, by their very nature, prone to imperialism. Unlike white missionary Christianity, he argued, Islam promoted human equality and encouraged the development of indigenous culture. It helped to build black nations, educate black minds, mold the black character, foster industry and philanthropy, and

protect black persons from genocide. Blyden's audacious comments upset his
audiences both white and black. But his arguments were remarkably pre-
scient: they foreshadowed many of the themes that later became central to the
flowering of Islamic religion among African Americans in the United States.

Civilization has its advantages and disadvantages, its privileges and its
burdens; the White Man's Burden and the Black Man's Burden. To the African, forced to come into contact with it, the religion of Islam furnishes
the greatest solace and the greatest defence. To him it is *praesidium* as well
as *dulce decus*. The foreigner never fails to respect him when he presents
himself with the badge of the faith of Mohammed.

The religion of Arabia has this feature—that it has been preached to,
accepted by, and become the abiding faith of members of all the known
races—Caucasian, Mongolian, Negro. Shem, Ham and Japheth [figures
in the Hebrew Bible representing, respectively, Semites, black Africans,
and Europeans] all unite under its banner and speak its language. Christianity has never been able thus to unite distinct and dissimilar races.
Ham and Shem have never found cordial and unqualified welcome in its
fold, whether Roman, Anglican, or Puritan. Yet its Japhetic professors
have assumed that all races outside its fold should not only enter, but are
anxious to enter. When, however, through special efforts made to secure
them strangers come "from many an ancient river, and from many a
palmy plain," they are assigned a back seat. They are not allowed to share
in the brotherhood and equality promised. "Hitherto shalt thou come
and no further" is the practice, if not the law of religion. . . .

Islam, on the other hand, makes room for all. If a Muslim Negro from
Soudan or a Malay from India, or a Chinaman from Pekin, is competent
he can be sent on any—the most important mission—in connection with
his religion, and he will be invited to lead the prayers in any mosque in Europe, Asia, Africa, or America. A Negro Muslim from Sierra Leone has
lately been leading the devotions of English Muslims in the mosque at
Liverpool. The Sheikh-ul-Islam of England, Abdullah Quilliam, an En-
glishman, whose nationality does not debar him from holding that high
position in the Mohammedan community, delivered by his faith from racial prejudices and restrictions, has named one of his sons after an African slave—BELAL: a name which, Mr. Townsend tells us, though that of
a Negro, is in Asia, through his connection with Islam, better known than
that of Alexander the Great. Sultans and Pashas will take their places in

the ranks at the time of prayer behind the black or brown Imam, if only he is qualified to lead or stand before them, as the word means. Mr. Bryce, in his *Romanes Lecture*, a few months ago, confessed to the inability of Christianity on this subject as compared with Islam. "Christianity," he said, "with its doctrine of brotherhood, does not create the sentiment of equality which Islam does." This is not the fault of Christianity but of the earthen vessel in which the treasure is contained. An Imperial race is incompetent to maintain the simplicity of the Nazarene, and diffuse His teachings as He gave utterance to them. It is not the business of Imperialism to make men but to create subjects, not to save souls, but to rule bodies.

It must have a certain repulsiveness. On its moral side, it must be imperious, with pronounced self-confidence, a certain unsympathising straitness—a pride in itself and an inevitable ignorance of others. It is deficient in spirituality and therefore cannot impart it. Its most successful work for aliens must be on its material side. Well regulated police supervision, technical and industrial schools, hospitals and dispensaries, are its proper and most effective instruments for civilizing and building up backward races.

Islam is the most effective educational force in Negroland. A system of common schools prevails throughout Islamic Africa by which every child is taught to read the Koran in the original and to commit to memory what has been taught. Thousands learn the Koran in this way and thus acquire a familiarity with an immense number of Arabic words, which serve as a bond of union and produce a solidarity of views and of interests which extends from the Atlantic to the Red Sea, and from the Mediterranean to the Equator. And when it is considered that five times a day millions in those latitudes and longitudes repeat in their devotions the same words, it will be seen what a mighty force they form on the continent—Mandingoes, Foulahs, Jalofs, Hausas, Yorubas, and all the vast variety of tribes whose names are not known to Europe, speak each its own vernacular, but when they meet all prostrate themselves before the great Creator with the same words of adoration and self-extinction—*Allahu akbar*, and grasp each other by the hand with the same language of salutation, in the spirit of the watchword of the Koran. *Almumimuna Ikhwaiun*. "All believers are brethren." How is Christianity, bearing on its back the burden of its caste prejudices, the liquor traffic, and its ethical intolerance, ever to make way among these people?

African Muslims live only for Islam. The wealthy ones—and there are seldom any paupers among them—use their means for the promotion of intellectual and spiritual education. I was present in 1894 at the dedication of a magnificent mosque erected at Lagos at an expense of £5,000 by a wealthy native Mohammedan. The Governor of the Colony, Sir Gilbert Carter, presided, and there was present the Sheikh-ul-Islam, Quilliam, appointed by His Majesty the Sultan, Abdul Hamid Khan, to represent him at the ceremony and to invest with a Turkish Order the devoted and patriotic builder.

Six months ago, during a visit which I made to the French colony of Senegal, I saw numerous evidences of the practical interest which the Native Muslims take in Education. One of the largest and most important of the mosques in St. Louis, a two story stone building, 60 by 48 feet, with tiled roof, was erected, I was informed, by private beneficence. Prayers are held in the lower story. The upper story is used for literary gatherings, lectures and discussions. It is surrounded by nine small comfortable dwelling houses, constructed of similar materials, of one story, erected by the same liberal builder of the mosque for the poor, where respectable indigent persons too poor to own or rent houses are given shelter for life. The benefactor, whose name is Ahmad Gouray, I did not have the pleasure of seeing. He had left a few weeks before my arrival on pilgrimage for the second time to Mecca.

The skill of these people in the Arabic language and literature is often marvelous. They not unfrequently surpass in culture their Oriental co-religionists. I have seen Arabs and Moors sit in perfect amazement and as outsiders while listening to the reading and exposition of Arabic books—not excepting the Koran—by Natives of West Africa. . . .

Islam in Soudan is propagated by self-supporting missionaries without supervision or emolument from any recognized or directing centre. I have often seen these missionaries in remote and sequestered pagan towns and villages, away from the public eye, earnestly teaching and preaching the Unity of God and the Mission of His Apostle, and teaching children and youth. What these men do never appears in any newspaper, foreign or local, to be brought back to them either in terms of eulogy or of dispraise. There is a spiritual impotentiality, so to say, which cannot be trusted away from conventional incentives and supports. Every mite which it drops into the treasury of the Lord must be inscribed with the name of some individual or sect and heralded to the world. Not so the missionary of Islam in Africa who, strong in his belief in the doctrines he promulgates, acts everywhere on his own initiative; his only support being the words of the Koran, *Ajri ind Allahi*, "My reward is with God." No human praise elates and no human censure depresses him. "Why don't you send reports of your successes to the local papers?" I asked one of the active Muslim missionaries at Lagos. "We report to God" was the laconic but significant reply. . . .

Every one will remember the fervent appeals of the Bishop of Western Equatorial Africa against the liquor traffic. It is clear to all acquainted with the conditions that, unless Christian missionaries can induce the nations whose citizens they are to suppress the export of liquor to Africa, their labours on this continent will be those of the Danaides, and Islam, keeping immeasurably in advance in its influence, will finally absorb the whole of the intellectual and physical strength of the country.

With Islam Africa is safe at least from physical destruction: with popular Christianity it might share the fate of the North American Indians, Sandwich Islanders, [and] New Zealanders.

4. George L. Root, *The Ancient Arabic Order of the Nobles of the Mystic Shrine* (1903, revised 1916)

The Ancient Arabic Order of the Nobles of the Mystic Shrine, a white fraternal organization, was established around 1872 in New York City by Dr. Walter Fleming, a physician, and Billy Florence, an actor. Fleming, who was a Freemason, reportedly composed the ceremonial rites of initiation with the help of another Mason familiar with "Oriental" subjects. Like other Masonic organizations, the Shriners, as they came to be known, offered their members an extensive social network, opportunities for public service, and secret, esoteric knowledge about the nature of the universe. They incorporated Islamic names, symbols, historical figures, and themes into their founding mythologies, ceremonies, and Moorish-style temples. At Chicago's Columbian Exposition of 1893, African Americans formed their own version of the Shriners, the Ancient Egyptian Arabic Order of the Nobles of the Mystic Shrine. George Root's 1903 history of the white Mystic Shrine, revised in 1916, may surprise some readers with its explicit and thorough use of Islamic history to justify and explain the existence of an American fraternity. Even if one considers his narrative a burlesque, a playful act of the imagination that shrouds the fraternity in mystical and exotic genealogical garb, it is remarkable that so many American men came to embrace these particular images of the Orient. In so doing, George Root insisted, they were embracing not the religion of Islam but the universal values that it, like all true religion, represented, including the values of civilization, science, reason, and the brotherhood of all humankind.

The Order of the Nobles of the Mystic Shrine was instituted by the Mohammedan Kalif Alee [Caliph Ali] (whose name be praised!), the cousin-german and son-in-law of the Prophet Mohammed (God favor and preserve him!), in the year of the Hegira 25 (AD 644) at Mecca, in Arabia, as an Inquisition, or Vigilance Committee, to dispense justice and execute punishment upon criminals who escaped their just deserts through the tardiness of the courts, and also to promote religious toleration among cultured men of all nations. The original intention was to form a band of men of sterling worth, who would, without fear or favor, upon a valid accusation, try, judge, and execute, if need be, within the hour, having taken precautions as to secrecy and security.

The "Nobles" perfected their organization, and did such prompt and efficient work that they excited alarm and even consternation in the hearts of the evil doers in all countries under the Star and Crescent.

The Order is yet one of the most highly favored among the many secret societies which abound in Oriental countries, and gathers around its shrines a select few of the best educated and cultured classes. Their ostensible object is to increase the faith and fidelity of all true believers in Allah (whose name be exalted!). The secret and real purpose can only be made known to those who have encircled the Mystic Shrine according to the instructions in "The Book of the Constitution and the Regulations of the Imperial Council."

Its membership in all countries includes Christians, Israelites, Moslim [sic], and men in high positions of learning and power. One of the most noted patrons of the Order was the late Khedive of Egypt (whose name be revered!) whose inclination toward Christians is well known.

The Nobles of the Mystic Shrine are sometimes mistaken for certain orders of the dervishes, such as those known as the Hanafeeyeh, Rufaeeyeh, Sadireeyeh, and others, either howling, whirling, dancing or barking; but this is an error. The only connection that the Order ever had with any sect of dervishes was with that called the Bektash. This war-like sect undertook to favor and protect the Nobles in a time of great peril, and have ever since been counted among its most honored patrons.

The famous Arab known as Bektash, from a peculiar high white hat or cap which he made from a sleeve of his gown, the founder of the sect named in his honor, was an imam in the army of the sultan Amurath I, the first Mohammedan who led an army into Europe, AD 1360 (in the year of the Hegira, 761). This sultan was the founder of the military order of the Janizaries (so called because they were freed captives who were adopted into the faith and the army), although his father Orkhan began the work. Bektash adopted a white robe and cap, and instituted the ceremony of kissing the sleeve.

The Bektash Dervishes are numbered by many hundred thousands, and they have several branches, or offshoots, which are named after the founder of each. Among the most noted are those which have their headquarters in Cairo, in Egypt; Damascus and Jerusalem, in Palestine; Smyrna and Broosa, in Asia Minor; Constantinople and Adrianople, in Turkey in Europe; Teheran and Shiraz, in Persia; Benares and many other cities in India; Tangier, in Morocco; Oran, in Algeria; and at Mecca, in Arabia, at which latter city all branches and sects of dervishes are represented at the annual meeting, which is held during the month of pilgrimage.

The Bektasheeyeh's representative at Mecca is a Noble of the Mystic shrine, is the chief officer of the Alee [Ali] Temple of Nobles, and in 1877 was the Chief of the Order in Arabia. The Chief must reside either at Mecca or Medinah, and, in either case, must be present in person or by deputy at Mecca during the month of pilgrimage.

The Egyptian Order of Nobles of the Mystic Shrine has been independent of the Arabian, excepting the yearly presence of the Deputy in Mecca, since the expedition of Ibraheem Pasha of Egypt in 1818, when the Wahabees [Wahhabis] were conquered.

The Wahabees were a fanatical sect, who threatened to over-ride all other power in Arabia. Since Ibraheem's conquest they have continued only as a religious sect, without direct interference with the government. They are haters and persecutors of all other sects, and are especially bitter against all dervishes, whom they denounce as heretics and the very essence of heresy and abomination. In this conduct they violate a strict and oft-repeated saying of the Prophet Mohammed (God favor and protect him!) which is, "He who casts on a believer the slur of infidelity is himself an infidel."

All Mohammedans respect every one who has made a pilgrimage to Mecca, and who will repeat the formula of the creed, "There is not Deity but Allah," without reference to what his private belief may be, for they have a maxim, "The interior belongs to God alone."

The Nobles of the Mystic Shrine are eminent for their broad and catholic toleration. The Noble who holds to a belief in a Supreme or Most High is never questioned as to any definition of that belief. The finite cannot define the infinite, although it may be conscious of its existence.

The character of the Order as it appears to the uninitiated is that of a politico-religious society. It is really more than such a society could be; and there are hidden meanings in its simplest symbols that take hold on the profoundest depths of the heart. We may illustrate by an example. There are rays of light about the Sphinx and Pyramid. Each ray is numbered and has its appropriate signification. In general, Light is the symbol of intelligence. Through intelligence the world is governed, and the spread of knowledge renders crime and meanness unprofitable, and, through the scheme of the Order, impossible for the criminal to escape just punishment.

Among the modern promoters of the principles of the Order in Europe, one of the most noted was Herr Adam Weishaupt, a Rosicrucian (Rose Cross Mystic), and professor of law in the University of Ingolstadt, in Bavaria, who revived the Order in that city on May 1, 1776. Its members exercised a profound influence before and during the French Revolution, when they were known as the Illuminati, and they professed to be teachers of philosophy; to ray forth from their secret society the light of science over all mankind without fear or favor; to diffuse the purest principles of virtue; in short, restating the teachings of Aristotle, Pythagoras, Pluto, Confucius, and other philosophers. From the central society at Ingolstadt branches spread out through all Europe. Among the members there are recorded the names of Frederick the Great, Mirabeau, a Duke of Orleans, many members of royal families, literary, scientific and professional men, including the illustrious Goethe, Spinoza, Kant, Lord Bacon, and a long list besides, whose works enlarge and free the mind from the influence of dogma and prejudice.

Frequent revolutions in Arabia, Persia and Turkey have obscured the Order from time to time, as appears from the many breaks in the continuity of the records at Mecca, but it has as often been revived. Some of the most notable revivals are those at Mecca and Aleppo in AD 1698 (AH

1110), and at Cairo in AD 1837 (AH 1253), the latter under the protection of the Khedive of Egypt, who recognized the Order as a powerful means of civilization.

Among the renowned patrons of the Order in Arabia was the Imam, or Shayk Abu il-Barakat Abd-Ullah Ibn Ahmad Alnasafi, well known among scholars by his title of Hafizuddeen, and who died AD 1330 (AH 731).

Arabic writers say of him that he was "the scientific and learned Imam, the lord of the ingenuous and the gifted prince, the support of the excellent, a rare example of manly virtue in the ages, our eyes never beheld his equal, our lord the teacher and guardian of our Order."

The poet, Hafiz, is honored in Persia as Byron is in England, and their works are similar in many respects, treating of wine and women with an unequalled richness of vocabulary and ideality. Strict Mohammedans reject the writings of Hafiz as too suggestive, but yet he is more widely read than any other writer in the East, by members of the Order, who alone can fully appreciate many secret allusions in his verse.

In the year AD 804, during a warlike expedition against the Byzantine emperor Nikephorus, the most famous Arabian Kalif, Haroon al-Rasheed, deputed a renowned scholar, Abd el-Kared el-Bagdadee, to proceed to Aleppo, Syria, and found a college there for the propagation of the religion of the Prophet Mohammed (God favor and preserve him!). The work and college arose, and the Order of Nobles was revived there as a part of the means of civilization.

Nearly three centuries after the death of the great Kalif and patron of learning, the Order of Nobles was revived at Bagdad by Abd el-Kader Ghilanee, a noted Persian, an eminent doctor of the Soofi [Sufi] sect, AH 555 (AD 1160).

Among the traditions of the Order occurs this very significant record: "In no single instance has the government in any country ventured openly to oppose the silent secret workings of the 'Nobles,' although the secret agents of the government are always present and exercise a careful surveillance in every 'Mystic Temple.'"

The leading spirits of the Order are found in every circle of the higher classes, even including the functionaries of government, and exert an influence in proportion to their position, dangerous to the vicious, beneficial to the virtuous.

The Order of Nobles of the Mystic Shrine in *America* does not advocate Mohammedanism as a sect, but inculcates the same respect to Deity here as in Arabia and elsewhere, and hence the secret of its profound grasp on the intellect and heart of all cultured people.

The ritual now in use is a translation from the original Arabic, found preserved in the archives of the Order at Aleppo, Syria, whence it was brought, in 1860, to London, England, by Rizk Allah Hassoon Effendee, who was the author of several important works in Arabic, one of which was a metrical version of the Book of Job. His "History of Islam" offended the Turkish government because of its humanitarian principles, and he was forced to leave his native country. He was a ripe scholar in Arabic poetry and the general literature of the age, and his improvements in the diction of certain parts of the ritual of the Shrine are of great beauty and value.

In the year 1698 the learned Orientalist, Luigi Marracci, who was then just completing his great works, "The Koran in Latin and Arabic, with Notes," and "The Bible in Arabic" at Padua, in Italy, was initiated into our Order of Nobles, and found time to translate the ritual into Italian. The initiated will be able to see how deeply significant this fact is when the history of the Italian society of the "Carbonari" is recalled. The very existence of Italian unity and liberty depended largely on the "Nobles," who were represented by Count Cavour, Mazzini, Garibaldi, and the king, Victor Emanuel.

Although Marracci was confessor to his Holiness, Pope Innocent XI, for several years, yet he was censured by the College of the Propaganda at Rome for having aided and abetted the work of a secret society, and the book was condemned to be burnt. A few copies were saved and one is still preserved in the library of the Synagogue which stands just inside the ancient Roman gate of the city of Babloon, called by the Arabs Fostat, in the Middle Ages, and now known as Old Cairo.

In making the present version, the translator has had the benefit of the work of Alnasafi, of Marracci, and of Hassoon. The rendering is literal where the idiom permitted, except where a local reference required the substitution of American for Oriental names of cities.

The work was perfected in August, 1870, under the supervision of Dr. Walter M. Fleming, 33°, Sovereign Grand Inspector General, A.: A.: S.: Rite, and Past Eminent commander of Columbian Commandery No. 1, Knights Templar, New York, who received his instructions and authority from Rizk Allah Hassoon Effendee, who had competent jurisdiction for America.

The Ritual is known in Arabia as "The Pillar of Society," which is an honorary title given only to persons of very great distinction in the service of truth, justice and mercy, and the support of learning and culture, and was by courtesy attached to this work as originally written by the renowned Alnasafi the Hafiz, the Persian poet.

The salutation of distinction among the faithful is: "Es Salamu Aleikum!" ("Peace be with you!"), to which is returned the gracious wish, "Aleikum es Salaam!" ("With you be peace!")

The jewel of the Order is a crescent, formed of any substance. The most valued materials are the claws of the royal Bengal tiger, united at their bases in a gold setting which includes their tips, and bears on one side of the center the head of a sphinx, and on the other a pyramid, urn and star, with the date of the wearer's reception of the Order, and the motto:

> Arabic—"Kuwat wa Ghadab."
> Latin—"Robur et Furor."
> English—"Strength and Fury."

The crescent has been a favorite religious emblem in all ages in the Orient, and also a political ensign in some countries, such as in modern Turkey and Persia. The ancient Greeks used the crescent as an emblem of the universal Mother of all living things, the Virgin Mother of all souls, who was known as Diana, Artemis, Phoebe, Cynthia, and other names, varying with the character of her attributes in different localities. The chief seat of the Diana cult and worship was at Ephesus, and the great temple built in her honor at that city was the pride and glory of the Greeks.

The secret knowledge symbolized by the crescent has always had its devotees, in every age, in all civilized countries, and it is yet the master key to all wisdom. The Greek philosopher Plato, when asked the source of his knowledge, referred to Pythagoras. If we consult the writings of Pythagoras, we shall find that he points to the far East, whence he derived his instruction. In imitation of the humility of the wisest of mankind, we look to the East for light, and find placed there the beautiful emblem of new-born light—the crescent.

This is yet only a symbol, and refers to a higher and purer source, the great fountain of light, the sun, which is also an emblem of the Great First Cause, of light and intelligence. Thus do we lead the mind of the initiate, step by step, from the sterile and shifting sand of the desert, which typifies ignorance and darkness, into the halls of science, the chambers of culture, until he stands in the presence of the emblem of light and intelligence in possession of the key that will open to the diligent inquirer every truth in nature's wide domain.

For esoteric reasons we hang the horns pointing downward, representing the setting moon of the old faith at the moment of the rising sun of the new faith in the brotherhood of all mankind—the essential unity of humanity as of one blood, the children of one fatherhood.

5. WPA Interviews with Mary Juma and Mike Abdallah (1939)

During the era of the Great Depression, the Works Progress Administration (WPA), a child of President Franklin Roosevelt's New Deal, oversaw the creation of the Federal Writers' Project. This government program not only supported starving playwrights and the authors of now classic American fiction, but also sustained a national effort to collect the oral history of what many observers saw as the disappearing ethnic cultures of America's immigrant populations. Among the ethnic groups interviewed were the "Syrians" of North Dakota. These immigrants arrived in North Dakota in the early 1900s, before the modern nation-states of Lebanon and Syria were founded. Because greater Syria was then ruled by the Ottoman Empire, Syrian immigrants were often classified as "Turks." But as the reminiscences below show, they called themselves Syrians. While most of the immigrants who arrived on both South and North American shores were Maronite, Orthodox, and Melkite Christians, North Dakota's Syrian population had an unusually high percentage of Muslims, estimated by some scholars who have done careful analysis of census data and land-ownership records to be around 30 percent of the total. These "sodbusters" were homesteaders who applied for and received a free forty-acre tract of land from the U.S. government in the first decade of the 1900s. On the prairie, they continued to observe the fast of Ramadan and celebrated the feast at the end of this month of dawn-to-dusk fasting by visiting one another's homes. By the late 1920s or early 1930s, they constructed a mosque—a "half basement building of cement with a shallow gabled roof"—and established a Muslim cemetery, the latter of which still exists today. The interviews excerpted below, which are based on a common questionnaire used by the WPA interviewer, describe the transitions of two remarkable North Dakotans, one male and one female, who left what they often described as the temperate climate of Syria and Lebanon for the harsh winters of the American Great Plains.

County—Mountrail
Field worker—Everal J. McKinnon
Address—Ross, North Dakota
Informant—Mrs. Mary Juma
Interpreter—Mr. Charles Juma
Address—Ross, North Dakota
Section—23-156-92
Place of interview—Farm home

I was born in Byria, Rushia, Syria. I don't know my exact age, but according to my naturalization papers, I am sixty-nine years old. I am sure that I am at least seventy-five years of age, however.

My home in Syria was a large, one-story, stone house. The floors were made of logs (about the size of our telephone poles), and the space between the poles was filled with smaller poles. Branches were used to fill small unfilled parts. A mixture of wet clay and lime was spread over the poles and branches, packed in hard, and smoothened by running a heavy roller over the floor. This was allowed to dry, and the result was a hard floor looking like cement. The roof was made in the same way.

Our village was located in a valley, and the land surrounding the village was level, extending two miles on each side of a river meeting rougher and more rolling land.

My religion in the Old Country was Moslem. We attended services every Friday, the same as we do here.

I received no education, as our people figured that it was a waste of time and money to teach a girl to read and write. There were no schools in our village, and those that were taught to read and write, were taught by a tutor.

Being a woman, I knew nothing about labor conditions, wages, renting, taxes, nor about farming methods. I know that everything was done the hard way. We didn't have machinery to farm, and used oxen on a walking plow. Seeding, harvesting, and threshing was done by hand.

Parties were given only to celebrate such an occasion as a wedding. The kind of party given would depend on the financial condition of the family giving it. If the people were well-off, they would prepare for many and invite the people from the nearby villages, and there would be much feasting and dancing. The table was set all the time and people ate whenever they felt like it. When dancing, everyone danced alone, not in couples. There was one dance where many joined hands and danced in a circle, a great deal like our square dances here. These parties [lasted] for days sometimes.

A wedding in the Old Country was just the same as a Moslem wedding anywhere. There is no courting before the wedding. When a boy decides to marry a certain girl, he goes to her parents and tells them about it. If he is not of age, he tells his own mother and she goes to see the girls' parents.

They then have a private discussion as to whether or not they should marry. The girl is not consulted at all. She, in most cases, is but a young miss of only eleven or twelve years of age. The outcome of the decision depends on the financial status of the prospective groom. An agreed amount of money is to be put aside by the groom in case of a separation. The separation must not be culminated through the fault of the bride if she is to receive that dowry. This amount varies. After the preliminary agreements are made, the date of the wedding is set. If the family of the groom is wealthy, the people from all the neighboring villages are invited to the ceremony and a feast is prepared. The bride names two witnesses for the ceremony, and then all is ready. The bride goes to an enclosure away from the ceremony and her father acts in her place. He clasps the hand of the groom and a handkerchief is draped over the clasped hands, and thus the vows are exchanged. After the ceremony, the feasting and celebrating begins.

My husband's farm was very small. I don't know the number of acres, but it wasn't enough for us to but barely exist on. The people in our vicinity were migrating to America and kept writing back about the riches in America. Everyone wanted to move and we were a family of the many that contemplated leaving. We sold all our possessions and borrowed two-hundred dollars from a man, giving our land as a collateral.

A big farewell party was given in our honor, as there were twelve of us coming to America from that one village. It was a sad farewell as our relatives hated to see us leave. We feasted, danced, and played games at the party. The games were for men, which were feats of strength and endurance.

We left two daughters in the Old Country with relatives. One of the girls has died since, and the other one still lives there.

We went to Beirut, which was about thirty miles from our home, and caught a boat to France. It took us about three weeks to travel through France. I do not remember the name of the boat we took from there to America. It took us three weeks to come from France to Montreal, Canada.

We moved further inland and started to travel over that country with a horse and cart as peddlers. We stayed there only a few months, and then moved to Nebraska, in the United States. We traveled through the entire state in a year. We never had trouble making people understand what we wanted while peddling, but many times we were refused a place to sleep. We suffered the same conditions as the pioneers, and at times were even more uncomfortable.

We were in Canada in 1900, and in Nebraska in 1901. In 1902, we came to western North Dakota where we started to peddle. It was at the time when there was such an influx of people to take homesteads, and for no reason at all, we decided to try homesteading too.

We started clearing the land immediately, and within a year, had a horse, plow, disk, drag, and drill. We also had some cattle and chickens. When there was a very little work to do on the farm, my husband traveled to Minnesota and eastern North Dakota to peddle.

In 1903, my son, Charles, was born. He was the first Syrian child born in western North Dakota. We were the first Syrians to homestead in this community, but soon many people from that country came to settle here.

Our home has always been a gathering place for the Syrian folk. Not many parties or celebrations were held, except for occasions like a wedding or such. Before we built our church [mosque], we held services at the different homes. We have a month of fasting, after which everyone visits the home of another, and there was a lot of feasting.

I am pretty old now, and am confined to this wheel-chair because of my leg which was amputated two years ago. I miss my work, both indoor and outdoor, but still enjoy life.

We were always able to make a very good living by farming and raising livestock, until the death of my husband in February of 1918. My son then took over the management of the farm, and I have lived with his family since. The depression has made living hard, but I don't worry.

Charles went to school in Ross until my husband died, and was not able to even complete the eighth grade.

We always speak in our native tongue at home, except my grand-children who won't speak Syrian to their parents. They do speak in Syrian to me because I cannot speak nor understand English. My grand-children range from fourteen months of age to eight years, and there are four of them. . . .

I can't read at all, neither in English nor Syrian. My son and daughter-in-law tell me the news they think might interest me.

We don't have any recreation; we only work. Sometimes friends stop in to talk for awhile, and then we attend services every Friday too, but that is all. I sew a little occasionally, and like to hold the baby.

Our farm home is a low three-room house, with furnishings that are old and worn as a result of hard times and rough usage by children. The outside of the house has never been painted. Within, it is clean but shabby-looking. The barn is quite large with a hip roof, and is painted red.

The thing that sets this farm apart as a Syrian-American home is that all the buildings are located close to the house, and all the chickens and sheep come close, even to the doorstep of the house. . . .

There is too great a comparison to say much about America and my native land. This country has everything, and we have freedom. When we pay taxes, we get schools, roads, and an efficiency in the government. In the Old Country, we paid taxes and Turkey took all the money, and Syria receiving nothing in return. We were repaid by having Turkey force our boys to join her army. The climate in the Old Country was wonderful, but we [Americans] have such a climate down south.

If I had my life to live over, I would come to America sooner than I did. I would have liked to visit the people in Syria five or ten years ago, but now that I am helpless, I wouldn't care to go. I don't ever want to go back there to live.

County: Mountrail
Name of Field Worker: Everal McKinnon
Address: Ross, No. Dak.
Name of informant (person interviewed): Mike Abdallah
Place of interview: Farm Home
Sec 28-157-92
Address: Ross, No. Dak.

I was born in Rufage, Rushia, Syria. I don't remember the date, nor the month but I believe that it was in 1886. (People in the Old Country did not keep track of their age or birth date because of the Turkish rule and they forced our boys into military service when they were of a certain age.) The village that I was born in had a population of about four hundred people. The land on the east of the village was level farm land and on the west at a short distance was mountains. My home was a one story six room stone building, about thirty by forty. The floor was made like all the other homes in the Old Country, poles about six inches in diameter were laid side by side on the ground. Then we mixed clay with water till it made a very thick mud, this was packed in between the poles and on top of the poles with a very heavy roller, then lime that we found was spread on the top of the clay while the clay was still wet and then the heavy roller was used some more until the lime was worked into the clay. When this became dry it would harden like cement. The floors for the second story of a two story house we made the same way.

I went to school one year. It wasn't a school like in this country. Father paid a man, living in our town to write and read our Bible [Qur'an]. That was my education.

Father was a farmer and until I was a full grown man, I worked at home for father. When I was old enough to work out for others, I received about twenty-five cents a day.

Taxes in the Old Country was much different from here. Taxes there were figured according to what your crop produced. For instance, for every ten bushels that the farmer got from the crop, the government took one bushel.

For seven years, I farmed for myself in the Old Country. I farmed about forty acres, with a team of oxen, wooden plow equipped with an iron lay, the rest of the farm work such as seeding, reaping and threshing, I had to do by hand. I had one cow and about a dozen chickens, but no goats or sheep as most people had.

We had church services every Friday. I belonged to the Moslem church in the Old Country the same as I do in this country. We didn't have any thing like confirmation.

For recreation we had parties, dances, and feasts. The parties were mostly like celebrations in this country, and would consist of competitive games and feats of athletics and strength. The sword-dance (as described to the field-worker was much the same as fencing in this country except that it was done to music and they danced among the crowd. The dance continued until such time as blood was drawn by one of competitors. A scratch of a finger would be enough. This dance was done by only certain men trained for the dance, it wasn't everyone that could do it.)

When dances for everyone were held, the people did not dance in couples but danced single. Then there was a dance where a group would clasp hands and dance much similar to the square dance in this country.

After all arrangements for the wedding were completed, such as the consent of the girl's parents, [an] amount of money set aside to provide for the bride in case the marriage proves a failure because of some fault of the groom, or desertion by the groom; this amount is set according to the financial condition of the groom. Then a feast is prepared for the crowd that is invited, the table remains set with all the food during the whole time of the celebration and the people can and do eat whenever they want to. A man, or boy, may make arrangements for the wedding whenever he sees a girl that he wants as his wife, the agreement is made between the man and the parents of the girl, or if the man is not of age the boy will tell his parents that he desires a certain girl and then his parents will make the arrangements with the parents of the girl. This agreement is sometimes made when the girl is only a few years old. When the ceremony takes place the bride goes to a room by herself and remains there alone until after the ceremony, she has named witnesses to act in her behalf. The father of the bride then clasps the hand of the groom and a cloth is draped over the clasped hands. The ceremony is then read from the Koran (our Bible). Then there is dancing and feasting for sometimes many days and nights.

In the old country I only had forty acres to farm and only one cow so it was very hard to make a living. A man couldn't make a living by working out. Quite a few people from our town had already come to America and their letters told of lots of work for which they got big pay, free land to farm and live on, and much freedom. We didn't have any freedom in the Old Country as we were under the Turkish rule and we even had to be very careful what we said and the taxes we paid were taken by Turkey and we never got anything back for the taxes we paid. Our roads were terrible. Then the Turkish government made our men and boys serve in their army for sometimes many years.

When I left for America, I gave my land and things to my mother and sister, my father was dead. I borrowed seventy-five dollars besides the money I had saved, to make the trip. I brought only some clothes and enough food to last until I got to France. There were fifteen of us that left from our town at that time. H. A. Juma and Alley Farhart were in the group. I don't remember the names of the rest. We left from Beirut the spring of 1907 and sailed to Naples, Italy, on a cattle boat, from there we traveled through France by train and took a boat to Liverpool, England. I can't remember sailing from England to Montreal, Canada. It seems to me that I was only on a boat two times on the whole trip. (Field Worker's Note: Mrs. Abdallah tried to convince the informant that he must have crossed the ocean on a boat, but he could not recall it.)

I stayed in Montreal for one month and then came to Fargo, N.D., by train. I tried to peddle for about three months but I couldn't make a living at that, so I took the train to Ashley, N.D. There were other Syrians already there and I went to work on a farm; worked on farms there for three years, making from twenty-five to thirty dollars a month. In 1911, I came to Ross. I worked out for four years and during threshing I got $1.25 a day. When working by the month I got $30. In 1915, I filed on a homestead sec. 12–157–92. I lived on my homestead for two years and then lived with Frank Osman for a year. I got my Naturalization papers Oct. 2, 1916. In 1918, I moved to New Rockford, N.D. I stayed in New Rockford for five months and worked in the section crew. In 1919, I moved to Detroit, Michigan, and worked in the factories for two and a half years. In 1921, I moved back to Ross, N.D., as I got married in 1920 and had to settle down and make a home. I have lived around Ross ever since. I rented three farms and in 1927, I bought the farm we are now living on.

When I first came to America, I thought America was pretty funny. The way people done things seemed funny. The people were always in a hurry and when they got done there didn't seem to be any reason for the hurry. When they went someplace they were in a hurry; everything in the Old Country was much slower and people weren't in a hurry. I didn't like it for the first two years I was in America and many times I felt like I wanted to go back to the Old Country.

I couldn't talk or understand the American language when I came here and when I was peddling I had to talk to people by motions and when I wanted to tell anyone the price of a thing, I would take money from my pocket and show them the amount of the price. When I wanted to ask for a place to sleep, I had to lay down on the floor and play that I was asleep and then they knew what I wanted. Nearly everyone felt sorry for me because I couldn't talk their language. I remember one time when a bunch of people wanted to know what nationality I was so a man asked me if I was Jewish, and I nodded my head no. So he asked me if I was a sheeny [an archaic epithet for Jews]. It sounded enough like "Syrian" so I nodded my head meaning yes. Everyone laughed very hard. It took me about two years to learn enough English to get along good.

I was attracted to my first American residence by other Syrians living in that community and an opportunity to make a living. That was at Ashley, N.D. Hassyn Murray and Frank Osman live there in a Russian settlement. I guess my real first residence was on my homestead at Ross, N.D., as before that I only worked for others. I lived there to prove up my homestead. The Syrians living at Ashley came from the Old Country.

When I first started farming in this country I had a plow, harrow, and binder. I farmed 100 acres when I started and in 1924 I farmed 240 acres. Now I farm 160 acres. My best crop was in 1925, I had a real good crop that year. I believe, in fact my steadiest income has been from cattle and sheep. Until 1934 we depended mostly on the cattle, since it was so dry we have depended more on the sheep. I have 106 head of sheep, 9 cows, and 7 horses. I have more machinery now and do all my farming with horses. In 1934 I was forced to sell 39 head of cattle to the government because I didn't have feed for them.

I have not been able to make anything farming since 1929. I belong to the Agricultural Conservation Association. If it weren't for this there wouldn't be any money in trying to raise a crop. I don't think we live any different now than we did before there was a depression. If we can't eat good there wouldn't be any use living. It was hard to have to sell my cattle to the government for so little money but they would have starved if had tried to keep them. I think the depression was because of the war.

My wife was born in Rufage, Rushia, Syria. We don't know the date of her birth but it was in the year 1886. (Field Worker's Note: Mrs. Abdallah told as a joke: there are several of the Syrians here that don't know their age, and they never get to be over 55 or 60 years old. I guess I am like the rest of them. Because of military reasons nobody in the old country kept track of their age and they still don't know. I am sure that some of them can't tell within 15 or 20 years of their correct age.) Mrs. Abdallah was married and had two children in the old country before coming to America. One of these was a girl and she remained in the old country and is married, the other also a girl born in 1910 in Rufage, Rushia, Syria. Her name is Nozema, now married. Sarah [was] born at Medina, N.D., born in 1914 (date of birth can be found in write-up on Allay Omar, as she is now Mrs. Omar). She completed the eighth grade in Ross Public School. Alley born July 4, 1915, at New Rockford, N.D. completed 6th grade. . . .

We (meaning Syrians) have a religious belief concerning the butchering of meat. We believe that an animal should not be shot or hit in the head to kill it. It should be bled to death. We think that when an animal is shot or hit in the head, the evil and sins remain in the meat and it is a sin to eat this meat. We also know that when an animal is butchered our way the blood drains from the meat better and in this way the meat is a lighter color and it will keep much longer. There is another old country belief that to pass a comment when looking at a newly born baby, such as saying that the baby is good looking, etc., will make the baby become sick. We also have a Syrian way of blessing and saying thanks for our food on the table before eating even one bite. We believe that it is a sin to eat without saying this (cannot give it in English).

[We don't have much recreation] besides going to town, listening to the radio, the children try to play the mouth organ and the guitar. Sometimes we go to the neighbors to visit but most times we have work enough to keep us busy. The boys do a lot of trapping and hunting here in these hills and they like the sport of it and the cash they get out of it. My wife does a lot of sewing and the girls also do some of this.

[Field Worker's Note] There was nothing about the farm or the home to set it aside as a Syrian American home. One frame barn, and one straw barn, a few small frame sheds and a frame house. All the buildings are badly in need of paint. The house consists of three large rooms and an attached coal shed downstairs, upstairs there are two rooms. I can say that this is an exceptionally clean and well managed house. I ate dinner with the family and for dinner we had chicken that had been cooked with a stew, but served separate. The stew contained potatoes, onions, and a number of other vegetables cooked with tomatoes and well seasoned. Then there was a large platter of fried potatoes, a plate of home made cheese (made from sweet milk), Syrian bread (much the same as lefse), home-made cookies and cake and plum sauce and tea (green). The table was set the same as other peoples table with salt, pepper, sugar, butter, etc. . . .

I suppose that the Old Country has changed a lot since I left there but at that time the work was very hard, as everything had to be done by hand, while in this country the work was really very easy as most of it was done by machinery even at that time. In the Old Country the climate is much better than here and it seemed to make old people feel young. You could work hard all day and go to bed real tired and when you wake up in the morning you feel as if you had never worked, while here a night's sleep doesn't make you feel that good. It sometimes snows a foot or more over there but still the people go bare-footed and the water under the snow feels as warm as though it had been warmed on the stove for about fifteen minutes. The water on the top of the ground is always too warm to drink and be good. I think that is the only way that the old country is better. In this country we get improvements for our tax money and we can think and say what we think while in the Old Country we could think what we wanted but we didn't dare say it.

In the Old Country we planted our winter wheat in August and planted our spring crop in April. Our harvest came in June.

If I had my life to live over again, I'd likely do about the same things only I'd come to America when I was younger and I settle down and stay there. I'd maybe settle in the state of Michigan or in No. Dak. I would get married younger and try to save for my old age. I wouldn't try to raise much crop if I was on a farm; I'd go into cattle and sheep. I can't really say that I am sorry that I lived the way I have because I have always enjoyed life.

Contact and Divergence

Immigrant and African American Muslims from World War I to 1965

AFTER World War I began, emigration from the Ottoman Empire and other Muslim-majority lands slowed. While immigration resumed after the war ended, the number of Muslim immigrants was severely curtailed by the Johnson-Reed Act, passed by the U.S. Congress in 1924. This law virtually banned immigration from Asia, southern and eastern Europe, and the Middle East, instituting a quota system that strongly favored white immigrants from "Nordic" stock. Though first-generation Muslim immigrants, like other non-Nordic people, continued to arrive on American shores, this period of American Muslim history was shaped as much, if not more, by second- and third-generation Muslim Americans, who ensured the continuity of American Muslim institutions and communities. Many Muslim immigrants had become citizens of the United States and were determined to become fully American while also preserving their religious and ethnic identities.

During this period, there is evidence that Muslims from Albania and Turkish *mevlevis*, the so-called whirling dervishes, settled in Detroit, among other American cities. After Albanian independence from the Ottoman Empire in 1912 and the subsequent invasion by Greece, the number of Albanian immigrants to the United States increased, and by 1945, they had established the Albanian American Moslem Association in Detroit. By the early 1950s, members of the Detroit community, with help from Albanians around the country, formed a mosque and a Bektashi *tekke*, a Sufi lodge where a spiritual and religious master, the Baba, conducted Muslim prayers, initiation ceremonies, and *dhikr*, or the remembrance and praise of God and the prophet. While hoping to preserve certain aspects of their ethnic Albanian traditions, most of these immigrants proudly proclaimed their American identity and saw the United States as a haven for the practice of Islamic religion.

Albanians constituted only one of the several Muslim groups—both indigenous and immigrant—that made the Motor City a center of Muslim American activity. In 1919, for example, Lebanese immigrant Muhammad Karoub helped to construct a mosque in the Detroit area. His brother, Husain, reportedly served as *imam*, or prayer leader. Both Sunni and Shi'a Muslims from Lebanon and Syria moved in large numbers to Detroit and nearby Dearborn, which remains a hub of Arab American activity to this day. In 1920, hundreds of Turkish Muslims from the Balkans and Anatolia also established a Detroit chapter of the Red Crescent, the Muslim equivalent of the Red Cross, and purchased grave plots so that they could bury the community's departed in accordance with Islamic law.

The Ahmadiyya, a South Asian Islamic group, also put down roots. After World War I, missionaries from this group appeared in the United States, ready to spread Islam across America. The Ahmadiyya had been established in the late 1800s in the Indian Punjab, where some followers of a man named Ghulam Ahmad proclaimed him to be a prophet, a messianic figure meant to lead the Muslim community toward peace and justice. Though many other Muslims thought that the followers of Ahmad were heretics, they pressed ahead with their missionary efforts, becoming one of the most successful Muslim missionary groups to non-Muslims in modern times. Known for mass distributing English translations of the Qur'an, the Ahmadiyya established a center in Chicago. Traveling around the country, head missionary Muhammad Sadiq praised Islam as a religion of peace and reason. He also targeted African Americans for conversion, promising that Islam offered them equality and freedom. He argued that Arabic was the original language of black people and said Islam had been their religion, stolen from them during slavery. This message attracted hundreds if not thousands of African Americans to the movement. And the Ahmadiyya seemed to practice the equality they preached. In 1920s St. Louis, Missouri, for example, African American P. Nathaniel Johnson, who became Shaikh Ahmad Din, led a local Ahmadiyya group that included immigrant Muslims, blacks, and whites.

Some African Americans who joined the Ahmadiyya were migrants from the American South. During the years between World War I and World War II, over a million and a half black persons moved from rural areas in the South to cities in the North. Those who came as part of this Great Migration, as the event is known, lived near and sometimes worked with Muslim immigrants from the Middle East. As the conversion of African Americans to Ahmadiyya Islam shows, these black American migrants were now part of an dynamic cultural environment where the ideas and culture of Asian immigrants were beginning to influence African American religious culture, and vice versa.

African American Muslims, however, were not simply joining Asian immigrant groups. They were also creating their own forms of Islam. The first to do so was Timothy Drew (1886–1929), a native of North Carolina who had traveled to New Jersey as part of the Great Migration. While living in Chicago in the 1920s, Drew attracted hundreds if not thousands of black Americans to his Moorish Science Temple, the first indigenous African American group to claim that blacks were both biologically and historically Muslims. Creating a complicated historical genealogy based on scriptures in the Hebrew Bible, Drew argued that black people were racially linked to Asiatic peoples, whose natural religion was Islam. He took the title of Noble Drew Ali and became known as a prophet. His *Holy Koran of the Moorish Science Temple* (1927), a document entirely different from the Qur'an revealed to the Prophet Muhammad of Arabia, preached the importance of moral behavior, industrious work habits, and social solidarity, and promised that the secrets of Moorish Science would bring earthly and divine salvation to persons of African descent. Many of the Islamic symbols that Drew adopted, including his fez and his title of "Noble," came not from the Islamic culture of immigrants but from the black Shriners, discussed in chapter 1. The Moorish Science Temple was more a child of black fraternal organizations and African American popular culture than it was of Afro-Eurasian Islamic traditions.

And yet the Moorish Science Temple is central to understanding the development of Islam in the United States, since it was the first indigenous African American organization to propagate the idea that black people were, by nature, Muslims. It was an idea that Elijah Muhammad and the Nation of Islam would spread around the country. The Nation of Islam, the best-known African American Muslim organization in the history of the United States, began around 1930 in the Detroit area, where W. D. Fard

Muhammad, a mysterious peddler, promoted the idea that Islam was the original religion of the "Blackman." One of his followers was Elijah Poole, a black migrant from Georgia. By 1934, Fard had disappeared, apparently leaving Poole in charge. Poole, who became known as Elijah Muhammad, believed Fard to be God, or Allah, in person; he thought himself to be His Messenger.

The Honorable Elijah Muhammad, as he was addressed by his followers, taught that blacks must seek economic and political independence from white America, return to their original religion of Islam, and abandon immoral "slave behaviors" like eating pork, drinking liquor, and fornicating. In addition to a message of black nationalism and strict moral discipline, Elijah Muhammad offered his followers an apocalyptic myth that explained black suffering and promised black redemption. Called "Yacub's history," the myth taught that blacks were the original people of earth, living a glorious existence until a mad scientist named Yacub betrayed them by genetically engineering a white man. The white man was by nature violent, and he eventually overpowered and enslaved the black man, who had weakened himself by abandoning the true religion of Islam. But God would not leave his chosen people helpless. Appearing in the person of W. D. Fard, God commissioned the Messenger to mentally resurrect the "so-called Negro" and prepare him for the end of the world, when God would destroy whites and restore the black Islamic nation to its original place of glory.

These teachings came to the nation's attention during the civil rights era, when black middle-class leaders like the Rev. Dr. Martin Luther King Jr. argued that the Nation of Islam and other "black nationalist" groups were products of poor race relations and inequality. In 1959, Mike Wallace of CBS News made similar arguments in a television documentary about the Nation of Islam entitled *The Hate That Hate Produced*. In addition to introducing the Nation of Islam to the American public, this program featured the attractive, articulate, and righteously angry Malcolm X (1925–1965), who was one of Elijah Muhammad's most effective organizers and representatives.

Because many scholars of African American Islam have focused their research on the Nation of Islam, much less is known about the thousands of African Americans who converted to and practiced other forms of Islam, including Sunni Islam, as early as the 1930s. Groups like the First Cleveland Mosque, guided by an African American Muslim convert named Wali Akram (d. 1994), often focused their attention on the five pillars of Islam and on the Qur'an. Other examples of early black Muslim communities include the Adenu Allahe Universal Arabic Association in Buffalo, New York, and Jabul Arabiyya, a Muslim communal farm also located in New York State. By the 1940s, Sheik Daoud Ahmed Faisal, an immigrant from the Caribbean island of Grenada, had established the Islamic Mission of America in Brooklyn, New York, arguably the most successful of the early African American Sunni Islamic mosques. Over time, this religious leader, reportedly the son of a Moroccan father and a Jamaican mother, came to provide religious guidance to a community of both indigenous and immigrant Muslims, stressing the importance of what he characterized as Islam's opposition to the allure of the material world. The presence of all these groups shows that the practice of Islam in the African American community was characterized by religious diversity from the time of its inception, and further, suggests that the very diversity of Islamic communities may have been one factor in its continuing growth among black Americans.

As more and more African Americans came to identify themselves as Muslims, the number of Muslims in the United States also rose, due to a wave of visitors, students, and immigrants from the Islamic world. After World War II, many of the former European colonies in Asia and Africa declared their independence from the European powers. In the wake of these political revolutions, those Muslims who were perceived to be too close to the former occupiers or who were viewed, for one reason or another, as opponents of the new regimes were often dispossessed. In the case of Israel, which declared its independence in 1948, many Palestinian Arabs lost their homes and livelihoods, and some sought refuge in the United States. After the 1952 revolution in Egypt, Egyptians who lost favor with the regime of Gamal Abdel Nasser also fled. These immigrants joined other Muslim Americans who were, by this time, starting to organize on a national scale. In 1952, Muslim Americans formed the Federation of Islamic Associations in the United States and Canada, a network of more than twenty mosques in North America.

During the 1950s, students from the newly independent states in Africa and Asia also started to attend American universities in larger numbers. In many instances, they criticized what they saw as the assimilation of immigrant Muslims into American culture. Many of these students were also influenced by the rise of Islam as a vehicle of social and political protest against often oppressive socialist and nationalist regimes in the "old country." In 1963, some of these students formed the Muslim Student Association at the University of Illinois, Urbana-Champaign. Among the founders were representatives of Egypt's Muslim Brothers, a political party and religious movement that opposed the Nasser regime in Egypt and called for the abandonment of Arab socialism in favor an Islamically oriented political system. Their message would continue to grow in popularity in the United States and abroad, especially after Nasser's defeat in the 1967 war with Israel.

These newly arrived students sometimes clashed with older Muslim Americans who had adopted some of the characteristics of non-Muslim American religionists. In the Toledo Islamic Center, for example, mosque members were known for their liberal interpretations of Islam. Many of the younger members of the mosques drank alcoholic beverages at public parties, and men and women performed the *dabka*, the popular Arab line dance, together. Some scholars would attribute such behavior to "Americanization." Indeed, that the mosque performed functions similar to those of churches and other American "voluntary organizations" does seem to reflect larger trends in American religious history, as a late 1950s ethnographic study of Muslims in Toledo suggests. But the idea that a Muslim could pray and fast—and drink and dance—is *not* distinctively American; these are, among Muslims throughout the Old World, typical behaviors.

During the early 1960s, African American Muslim leader Malcolm X also renounced the teachings of Nation of Islam leader Elijah Muhammad, rejecting the claim that all white people were blue-eyed devils. He set out in 1964 on his famous *hajj*, or pilgrimage, to Mecca and shared the news with folks back home that he had felt spiritual kinship with some Muslims who happened to be white. Later that same year, he was invited back to Mecca to be trained as a Muslim missionary by the Muslim World League, a missionary organization supported by Saudi Arabia that promoted Islamic education and outreach in both the Islamic world and the West. Malcolm's continuing commitment to black liberation even after his pilgrimage—an aspect of his story sometimes forgotten—put him at odds with many of his fellow Muslim missionaries. His debates with them symbolize a longstanding tension in the American Muslim community between many, but not all, immigrants and African Americans. Even after discarding Elijah Muhammad's racial view of Islam, Malcolm X refused to abandon the fight for black liberation, saying he felt his first duty was to help persons of African descent achieve full equality. Until his death in 1965, he proudly proclaimed his religious identity as an "ortho-dox" Muslim and as a black revolutionary.

After Malcolm X's death, black Muslims interpreted his call for both political and religious liberation in different ways, incorporating more and more Islamic traditions learned from immigrant and foreign Mus-lims into their religious practice while also articulating a political and so-cial program that had relevance for black America. Like some fellow Muslim activists across the seas, at least a few African American Muslims separated themselves from mainstream society and formed vanguards that strictly followed the precepts of *shari'a*, or Islamic law and ethics. For example, a predominately African American group of believers broke away from Shaikh Daoud's Islamic Mission of America to form the Ya-Sinn mosque. Criticizing the lax religious practices of some assimilated Muslims, they insisted on more literal adherence to *shari'a*. Other African American Muslims, however, focused on more active community involve-ment and on building a multiethnic Islam. In the late 1960s, Sheik Tawfiq, an African American from Florida, founded the Mosque of the Islamic Brotherhood in Harlem, New York. Stressing the call of Islamic universal-ism, the idea that Islam crossed all racial barriers, African Americans, Hispanics, and others prayed together, established housing and education programs, and ran small businesses in the heart of the United States' larg-est city. Such groups blurred the important social distinctions between immigrant and indigenous by emphasizing common religious roots.

Despite or perhaps because of the diversity of American Muslim groups and persons during this era, one can safely conclude that by this time, Is-lam was no passing fad in the American religious landscape. From World War I to 1965, Americans established "Islam," however one defined it, as an institutional presence and a vital aspect of American culture and soci-ety. The simultaneously entangled and separate histories of indigenous and immigrant Muslims sparked its growth and insured its relevance.

1. Pir Inayat Khan, "America: 1910–1912" (c. 1925)

Inayat Khan (1882–1927), a musician and modern mystic from British India, visited the United States from 1910 through 1912 and again during the 1920s

for a lecture tour. During his stay in the United States, the pir, a title meaning
master, met and married his wife, Ora Ray Baker, who was a relative of the
famous Mary Baker Eddy, the mother of Christian Science. Inayat Khan
settled in Europe, but his philosophies also took root on American soil. The
founder of the Sufi Order in the West, he taught his followers to challenge
religious exclusivism and form cross-cultural, cross-confessional communi-
ties in search of beauty and harmony. He encouraged them to meditate, to
treat others always with dignity, and to hear the sounds of the Divine in the
world around them. His philosophies revealed a number of civilizational
influences—in his words one hears ancient Greek, Islamic, Indian, and mod-
ern Euro-American voices. Such ecumenism found a ready audience among
religious liberals and seekers in the United States who had already been
exposed to Asian religious traditions through various movements like the-
osophy and American Orientalist literature. The Sufi Order of the West,
now Sufi Order International, continued after the pir's death, headed by
his son, Vilayat Inayat Khan, and later his grandson, Zia Inayat Khan.
Other American Sufi organizations to follow in Inayat Khan's footsteps in-
clude Sufi Ruhaniat International and the International Sufi movement. In
this passage from his memoirs, Inayat Khan looks back fondly on his 1910–
1912 stay in America but also offers criticisms of American racism, capital-
ism, and the fast pace of American life.

I was transported by destiny from the world of lyric and poetry to the
world of industry and commerce, on the 13th of September 1910. I bade
farewell to my motherland, the soil of India, the land of the sun, for
America the land of my future, wondering: "perhaps I shall return some
day", and yet I did not know how long it would be before I should return.
The ocean that I had to cross seemed to me a gulf between the life that
was passed and the life which was to begin. I spent my moments on the
ship looking at the rising and falling of the waves and realizing in this rise
and fall the picture of life reflected, the life of individuals, of nations, of
races, and of the world. I tried to think where I was going, why I was going, what I was going to do, what was in store for me. "How shall I set to
work? Will the people be favorable or unfavorable to the Message which I
am taking from one end of the world to the other?" It seemed my mind
moved curiously on these questions, but my heart refused to ponder upon
them even for a moment, answering . . . one constant voice I always heard
coming from within, urging me constantly onward to my task, saying:

"Thou art sent on Our service, and it is We Who will make thy way clear." This alone was my consolation.

This period while I was on the way, was to me a state which one experiences between a dream and an awakening; my whole part in India became one single dream, not a purposeless dream, but a dream preparing me to accomplish something toward which I was proceeding. There were moments of sadness, of feeling my self removed further and further from the land of my birth, and moments of great joy, with the hope of nearing the Western regions for which my soul was destined. And at moments I felt too small and little for my ideals and inspirations, comparing my limited self with this vast world. But at moments, realizing Whose work it was, Whose service it was, Whose call it was, the answer which my heart gave moved me to ecstasy, as if I had risen in the realization of Truth above the limitations which weigh mankind down.

When our ship arrived in the harbor of New York, the first land of my destination, I saw before me the welcoming figure of the statue of Liberty, an idol of rock, which I felt was awaiting the hour to turn into an ideal, awaiting the moment to rise from material liberty to spiritual liberty. Its wings suggested to me that it wanted to spread from national liberty to world liberty.

My first impression of New York, the city of modern grandeur, was that of a world quite other than those I had seen or known before. The grand, high buildings, the illuminations in all the shops, people moving about in crowds, conveyances running on three levels: tramways, subway, and elevators running overhead, people running at the station, each with a leather bag in his hand, and a newspaper. Everything seemed moving, not only the trains but even the stations, every moment filled with the rush of activity, calling to every sense, on the ears and on the eyes. It was removed from the land I had come from by a distance as wide as the expansion of the vast ocean which separated these two lands.

I soon began to try to get accustomed to the people, to the atmosphere, and to the country. And as I came of that people whose principal characteristic is adaptability, it was not too difficult for me to attune myself to the people and the conditions there. As the Message I brought was the Message of unity, it was natural that I should give proof in my own life of unity with people and conditions, however different and far removed. I saw in the people of America the sum-total of modern progress. I called it "the Land of the Day"; that for which Rumi [the famous medieval poet] has used in the *Masnavi* the word "Dunya", the worldly life, to which the word "Samsara" is equivalent in Hindi, I found there in its fullness. The first opportunity I had of making the acquaintance of some people in America, was in the studio of Mr. Edmund Russell, who gave a reception where I met with some people among whom I found some responsive persons. I came to America with the Sufi Message, but the only means which I had to carry out my mission was by music, my profession, in which my cousin Ali Khan and my two brothers Maheboob Khan and Musheraff Khan assisted me. But my music which was most valued and admired as science and art, was put to a hard test in a foreign land, where it was as the old coins brought to a currency bank.

Now before me there was the question: how to set to work and in what direction? For the Message the time was not yet ripe, as I was at that time rather studying the psychology of the people than teaching. In a busy place like America where in the professional world already great competition exists, to have an opening for concerts or an opportunity to sing at the Opera seemed for the moment an impossible thing. I met with the well-known singer Emma Thursby who, being a great artist herself, became interested in our music.

My first address to the people of America was arranged at Columbia University in New York by Dr. Reebner, and there I found a great response. Dr. Reebner, the Head of Music at the University was most interested in Indian music and we became friends. Among the audience was Miss Ruth St. Denis who invented Indian dances of her own and was making a speciality of it, and for whom our music became as a color and fragrance to an imitation flower. She tried to introduce the Indian music on the program of her performance, which was to me as a means to an end. We had an interesting tour together throughout the States, and yet for the public, which was for amusement, our music became merely an entertainment. This was an amusement for them, and therefore painful for us. Also it was not satisfactory to combine real with imitation. However it helped to keep the wolf away from our door.

I once visited the house of Miss Ruth St. Denis after a long time and saw to my surprise that all the Indian things that were in her room as a decoration, had been removed altogether and in their place Japanese things were placed, which amused me. She then entered the room, in a Japanese kimono, which surprised me still more. I said to her, "Now I have found out the reason why you have not seen us for a long time. It seems you have forgotten India altogether." She said, "I am trying to forget it, though I find it difficult to forget. For now that I have to produce a Japanese dance, I do not wish to think of India any longer." It explained to me what influence the power of concentration makes upon one's life and work, that when the whole surrounding is inspiring a person with one particular idea, it creates in his soul the spirit of the desired object, and in this lies the mystery of life. I found Miss Ruth St. Denis an inventive genius, and I was struck with a witty answer she gave upon hearing my ideas about human brotherhood, uniting East and West. She said, "Yes, we, the people of the Occident and Orient may be brothers, but not twins."

Before ending our tour in the States I spoke at the University of Los Angeles, and to a very large audience at the Berkeley University of San Francisco where I met with a very great response, and where my lectures on, and my representation of Indian music and the presentation of its ideal met with a great interest.

At the end of my tour through the United States, when I arrived at San Francisco, I found the meaning of the scheme of Providence, that I was meant to come to San Francisco, a land full of psychic powers and cosmic currents, and begin from there the work of my Message. It is here that I found my first *mureed* [student] Mrs. Ada Martin.

I was welcomed by Swami Trigunatita and his collaborator Swami Paramananda, who requested me to speak on Indian music to their friends at the Hindu temple, and was presented with a gold medal and an address.

I saw among the audience a soul who was drinking in all I said, as the Hamsa, the bird of Hindu mythology, who takes the extract from the milk leaving the water. So this soul listened to my lecture on music and grasped the philosophical points which appealed to her most. She thanked me, as everybody came to show their appreciation after the lecture. But I saw that there was some light kindled there in that particular soul. Next day I received a letter near to my time of departure from San Francisco, saying that this lady was immensely impressed by the Message, though it was given under the cover of an address on music and would most appreciate some further light on the path. I knew that she received the call, and wrote her that I regretted very much that I was leaving, but yet I could be seen at Seattle, a city at a considerable distance from San Francisco. I had a vision that night that the whole room became filled with light, no trace of darkness was to be found. I certainly thought that there was some important thing that was to be done next day, which I found was the initiation of

Mrs. Ada Martin, the first *mureed* on my arrival to the West and, knowing that this soul will spread light and illuminate all those who will come in contact with her, I initiated her and named her Rabia after the name of a great woman Sufi saint of Basra, about whom so much is spoken in the East. Since her initiation she has entirely devoted her life to spiritual contemplation and the service of humanity.

After my return from San Francisco to New York, I stayed a while to be able to do some work and gave a few lectures at the Sanskrit College where I made the acquaintance of Baba Bharati, who preached the love of Krishna to the Americans. I made there the acquaintance of Mr. Bjerregaard, who afterwards wrote on my request the book called "Sufism and Omar Khayyam". He was the only student of Sufism known in New York, and he helped me to have access to the Sufi literature in the Astor Library, of which he was the head.

Ralph Perish, Miss Genie Nawn and Mrs. Logan were made *mureeds*, and later Miss Collins and Mrs. Eldering and also Mrs. Morrison. Among them there was a *mureed* who showed no end of respect, devotion and interest in the Cause, and yet there was something in him which voiced to me his hidden insincerity. He followed me for a considerable time, till his patience was exhausted. In the end he gave way to his weakness, admitting he could not go on any longer. I then found out that he had been sent by some society which collected the teachings of different secret orders, where initiations were given, its members entering somewhere or the other in every order of inner cult. It made me very sad, more for him than for me, to think how he wasted his time for nothing. He came, trying to steal something which can never be stolen. Truth is not the portion of the insincere ones. Sincerity alone is the bowl that can hold Truth. I then called Mrs. Martin, who had by then progressed wonderfully—which consoled me—to whom the robe of Murshida was given; and the care of a grain of the Message, which was cast in the soil of America, was entrusted to her before I left the United States for Europe. She represented the Sufi Message at the religious congress in San Francisco at the Panama Canal World Fair.

During my stay in America for more than two years there was not much done in the furtherance of the Sufi Movement. From my stay in America I began to learn the psychology of the people in the West and the way in which my mission should be set to work. If I can recall any great achievement in America, it was to have found the soul who was destined to be my life's partner.

With the liberal idea of freedom in all directions of life and in spite of Abraham Lincoln's liberal example and reform, there is still to be found in America a prejudice against color which is particularly shown to the Negroes who were for a long time in slavery, and since their freedom the prejudice has become still greater. It seems almost impossible to think that in a country which is most up-to-date in civilization, there should be a population so looked down upon. Yes, in India there are *shudras*, lower castes who are called untouchable. Yet there have been scientific reasons, from a hygienic point of view, for not touching them, and the attitude of the high caste towards them has never been that of hatred. The men and women of that pariah class in India are called by others *mehter*, which means master. Yes, the people in America have their reason for it. They think Negroes are too backward in evolution to associate with. But to me it seems that the coming race will be the race of Negroes; they are show-ing it from now. In whatever walk of life they find an opportunity, they come forward in competition. Not only in wrestling or boxing, but also on the stage the Negroes show their splendor, and the most surprising thing to me was that, conscious of all the prejudice against the Negro from all around, he does not allow his ego to be affected by it. In every po-sition of outward humiliation he is put to, he stands upright with a mar-velous spirit, which I only wished the man in the East had, who has become as a soil worn-out after a thousand harvests. The spirit in the East seemed to me deadened, being weighed down by autocratic influences, tramped upon by foreign powers, crucified by high moral and spiritual ideals, and long starved by poverty.

An ordinary man in America confuses an Indian with brown skin with the Negro. Even if he does not think that he is a Negro, still he is accus-tomed to look with contempt at a dark skin, in spite of the many most un-clean, ignorant and ill-mannered specimens of white people who are to be found there on the spot. I did not find so much prejudice existing in America against a Japanese, of which so much has been said. Still in an-swer to the unchristian attitude of theirs, the government of Japan has all along threatened them with the Mosaic law, and is ready to return the same when the Americans visit Japan. Indians, when insulted abroad, can do nothing but bear it patiently. The color prejudice in some nations of Eu-rope is even more, but it is often hidden under the garb of politeness and not so freely expressed as in America; the difference is between a grown-up person and a child in his expression of prejudice.

An American as a friend is very agreeable and desirable and most sociable. One feels affection, spontaneity in his feelings, although the business faculty is most pronounced in him, yet together with it he is most generous. The American readily responds to the idea of universal brotherhood. He is open to study any religion or philosophy, although it is a question if he would like to follow a certain religion long enough, because freedom, which is the goal, by many in America is taken as the way, and therefore, before starting the journey towards spiritual freedom, they want the way also to be a way of freedom, which is impossible. I have seen among Americans people of a thorough good nature and their life itself a religion, people of principle and gentleness. The broad outlook of the people in America gave me a great hope and a faith that it is this spirit which in time must bring the universal idea to the view of the world. It is most admirable for a great nation to bring forward the idea of world disarmament, when many other nations are fully absorbed in covetousness, and submerged in their own interests. This idea of disarmament brought out by President Harding, was responded to by the public there. This shows the bent of their mind. Besides, to friends or enemies, in their trouble, whenever the occasion has arisen, America has most generously come first to their rescue.

With all the modern spirit in America I found among the people love for knowledge, search for truth, and tendency to unity. I found them full of life, enthusiasm, and goodwill, which promises that this modern nation, although it is now in its childhood, will become a youth who will lead the world towards progress.

2. *Moslem Sunrise*, "I Am a Moslem" (1921),
"True Salvation of the 'American Negroes': The Real Solution of
the Negro Question" (1923), "Crescent or Cross: A Negro May Aspire
to Any Position Under Islam Without Discrimination" (1923),
and "Living Flora—And Dead" (1924)

The Ahmadiyya movement has converted persons around the globe to its interpretation of Islam. While Ahmadi practitioners constitute a minority of Muslims in the United States, their strong missionary presence in the 1920s left an indelible mark on the shape of American Muslim thought and practice. The history of Ahmadiyya in the United States proves that from the very beginning, some American Muslim communities were multiracial and multiethnic. At the same time, the writings below help us understand how the Ahmadiyya influenced the development of Islam among black Americans in particular. The South Asian publishers of the paper promoted Islam as a religious tradition that offered equality and brotherhood to all, regardless of skin color, but also depicted Islam as a tradition particularly well suited for building black unity and Afro-Asian cooperation. The Ahmadi emphasis on Islam as a vehicle of black manhood, self-reliance, and self-determination both recalled Edward Blyden's claims and anticipated Elijah Muhammad's philosophies. Such interpretations of Islam also indicated that the Ahmadiyya were attempting to cooperate and/or compete with Marcus Garvey's popular Universal Negro Improvement Association (UNIA), a pan-Africanist movement of the 1920s that advocated black capitalism, political independence, race pride, and emigration to Africa.

The last article excerpted here, P. Nathaniel Johnson's "Living Flora—and Dead," gives an additional explanation for the attraction of African Americans to Islam. For Johnson, an African American convert and Ahmadi leader who took the name Ahmad Din, the revelations of God in the Qur'an expressed timeless truths and even divulged secret knowledge about the nature of the universe. Shaikh Ahmad, a religious seeker who experimented with many religions before coming to Islam, viewed Prophet Muhammad of Arabia as a master spiritualist who bridged the divide between God and humankind through the revelation of the Qur'an. His view that God was not only transcendent but also imminent—that human beings could experience the presence of God more deeply through Islam—represented a synthesis of Islamic thought and American metaphysical religion, a product of the transnational encounter between Americans like Johnson and South Asian Ahmadi missionaries.

I Am a Moslem (1921)

I am a Moslem. And do you know what a Moslem is? Is it the name of some particular exclusive nationality? No, a Moslem belongs to all. He knows no difference of nations as all the nations are his own. Does he belong to any one country? No. On his Map of the Globe there are no border lines. Is he white or is he colored? He knows no such distinctions, which are only skin deep. The Moslem eye looks at the heart and not at the outer shape. He concerns the Dwellers in the tent and not the tent. Is Moslem Male or Female? He knows no gender in the uplift of the soul. Men and women all are children of God, all come from Him and all return to Him. A Moslem is one who has resigned his will to God. A Moslem is he or she who belongs to God and God alone. A Moslem is one who sympathizes with all and hurts none. The Moslem enjoys his love for God. He is always ready to sacrifice his desires for the sake of God and His people. In and out he is one and the same. He practices what he preaches. He is sincere in his promises. His one goal is his Creator, his Provider and his God—God of Infinity towards whom he continues soaring higher and higher in Infinity. His progress is ever onward and onward as his Beloved One is Infinite. He is in Union with God and he is in Communion with Him. Abraham was a Moslem, Moses was a Moslem, David was a Moslem, Jesus was a Moslem, Ahmad was a Moslem, but Muhammad was the greatest Moslem that the world has ever seen. A Moslem is an Abraham, and a Moslem is a Christ and a Moslem is a Muhammad as he loves, follows, and imitates all the great Teachers from Allah. Be a Moslem and join the Universal Brotherhood.

True Salvation of the "American Negroes": The Real Solution of the Negro Question (1923)

My dear American Negro, As-Salaam-o-Alaikum. Peace be with you and the mercy of Allah. The Christian profiteers brought you out of your native lands of Africa and in Christianising you made you forget the religion and language of your forefather—which were Islam and Arabic. You have experienced Christianity for so many years and it has proved to be no good. It is a failure. Christianity cannot bring real brotherhood to man, especially to a fallen and downtrodden nation. So now leave it alone. Join Islam, the real faith of universal brotherhood which at once does away with all distinctions of race, color, and creed. The holy Quran is the true book of God. You need a religion which teaches manliness, self-reliance, self-respect, and self-effort. Islam does not teach you the vicarious sacrifice, nor does it teach you that all human nature is corrupt and thus make you suffer needlessly. Islam frees you from all sorts of debasing associations and idolatry. Mohammed does not tell you not to live a full life here in this world; he tells you the world is good, therefore you must make the most of it. Islam does not say sell all you have, it says get all the good you can out of this life and make it a good start for the life to come for our future is to be shaped on our present. It is not a bad world we live in. Moreover you can be good Moslems in America as well as in Asia, Europe, and Africa. Join Islam in the Ahmadia Movement founded by Ahmad of India, the Prophet of the day, and be blessed. For further particulars address all communications to the undersigned.

Muhammad Din.
Ahmadia Movement
4448 So. Wabash Ave.
Chicago, Ill. U.S.A.

Crescent or Cross: A Negro May Aspire to Any Position Under Islam Without Discrimination (1923)

The Teaching of the Prophet Is Being Profitably Imbibed—With Millions of Moslems the World Over Pressure Can Be Brought to Solve the Race Question.

Apart from a confederation of the African tribes or peoples of African origin, the possibility of which is an awful nightmare to the white man, he lives in fear and trembling that El Islam may become the religion of the Negro. And why should it not be? "El Islam" would be a wonderful spiritual force in the life of the colored races, uniting us in a bond of common sympathy and interest. We could then add to our motto of one God, one aim, one destiny, the words one language, and that language would be Arabic. It could easily be made the universal language of Negroes and would remove the barriers which now face us in the intercommunication of the different tribes in Africa. Arabic is already spoken by millions of Negroes.

Most white missionaries in order to keep up and encourage contributions to their foreign mission fund sometimes draw upon their imagination when they speak of the number of converts to Christianity, and would have us believe that the poor heathen is anxious to see more white men leading them to peace and happiness. The majority of the converts to Christianity in India and Africa are of the lower caste, people who have nothing to lose by changing their religious views and practices, but who expect in the new order of things to become the social equal of their superiors. They belong to that type which toadies to the white man and tamely submits to segregation and discrimination, believing that the white master is good, holy, just and meek.

In spite, however, of the desperate efforts being made by the "other fellow" to convert the African to Christianity in order to make his enslavement and exploitation easier and more secure, the African is slowly but surely realizing that under the Crescent he will be better able to reach the goal of his ambition than under the Cross. British administrators sometimes inadvertently admit that the Mohammedan natives are far superior in intelligence, morals and fighting spirit to the Christian native.

El Islam teaches its followers to be manly, self-respecting, charitable and ambitious, and, unlike his Christian brother, who waits for the good white man to restore him his rights, the follower of the prophet is always ready to draw his sword in defense of sacred right and honor.

Within recent years 53,000,000 natives have been converted to Mohammedanism in Africa. In Southern Nyasaland, where in 1900 you could not meet one native Mohammedan, there are mosques all over the country. In the region between Durba[n] and the Cape 1,000,000 natives were converted to Mohammed . . . last year. Under Islam a Negro may aspire to and attain any position in mosque or state, and Islam knows nothing of segregation and discrimination.

Yes, El Islam is spreading fast, and spreading not only in Africa but also in these United States. Within three months over 100 converts have been made to the cause of Mohammedanism in America. The spreading of El Islam cannot help but benefit the U.N.I.A. for they are desperately engaged in preparing for That Day—that day that we of the Universal are also preparing for.

Living Flora—and Dead (1924)

In the field of religious literature Mohammed's Koran is the healthiest plant with the hardiest stalk, produces the sweetest bloom and yields the more wholesome fruit.

The soil which gave to it healthy growth was rich beyond comparison. Allah's abundance made its foliage green, its blossoms beautiful, and its yield so heavy that whosoever reaps has but to enjoy an everlasting harvest.

This plant of which I speak, grew from the true seed to maturity; no grafting on of other plants, no artificial irrigation, no pruning to make it trim was necessary, this plant—QURAN!

Other plants in the field of religious literature? Let us review them. Their seeds were true but ah! look at them now! How sad! Much deliberate meddling has been done.

Perusing a certain Holy Book I found it to be a plant withered, barely being kept alive by artificial watering not at all green—dying! This book, The Torah—Talmud of Judaism. I perused another Holy Book and it was found to be a plant faded, green stems and a few green leaves from true vines grafted on to give it the appearance of life. This book, The Vedas of Hindoos. The perusal of another Holy Book found it to be a plant already dead from too much pruning. This book, The Gospels. Besides these, some others I perused, finding them all decadent Al Quran excepted.

The Sun of Tradition glowed dimly down through the clouds of Mythology, the atmosphere was dry, the rainbow hung westward on the horizon signifying also that the life-giving rains had passed. Blasted Gardens! But the Prophet's Quran stood as a lone apple tree among the other trees of the garden. Consider the Holy Prophet and his Koran. Take the sent One all in all, what he was, what he accomplished, and the good he inspired others to do. Compare him with all other poets, law-givers, prophets, sons of God, statesmen, etc.; and the son of Abdallah alone stands above all other men that mankind has called "GREAT."

Other bibles are mostly the works of an aggregation of poets, prophets, prophetesses, statesmen and lawgivers, historically covering thousands of years, crammed full of conflicting statements. The Koran comes straight from the mouth of the man who proves himself to be the "MASTER MIND" of the earth.

The Quran is a poem, a code of laws, a prayer book, and the world's best bible combined. THE MAN UNIQUE! THE BOOK UNIQUE! As in a looking glass we behold the MASTER SPIRITUALIST of the world intoxicated with the gifts of God.

O, ye howlers and spillers of ink! Climb Mount Sinai and swim the river Jordan, baptize yourselves in pools of blood, rattle the dry bones in Ezekiel's valley, but the echo of it all is dead after all allowance is made.

Sheik Ahmad Din.

(P. Nathaniel Jo[h]nson)

3. Noble Drew Ali, *The Holy Koran of the Moorish Science Temple* (1927)

Much of the Holy Koran of the Moorish Science Temple, *a sixty-page scripture, was borrowed from other texts. Chapters 1 through 19 were taken from Levi Dowling's 1908* Aquarian Gospel of Jesus the Christ, *a kind of modern gospel that depicted Jesus as a spiritual peripatetic who wandered around the ancient world teaching others to master their own higher spiritual powers. Chapters 20 through 44 were copied from a Rosicrucian ethics manual that was published as* Unto Thee I Grant *and* The Infinite Wisdom. *But the excerpts reproduced below, which are derived from an early version of the text available through the FBI file on the Moorish Science Temple (MST), seem to be from the hand of Prophet Noble Drew Ali himself. In these passages, the popular black nationalist Marcus Garvey, founder of the Universal Negro Improvement Association, is understood as a forerunner to Noble Drew Ali. Noble Drew, the text explains, is a prophet chosen by God to lead the Moorish nation in America (that is, black people) to confess and practice their original religion of Islam. The text explains the complicated reasons why African Americans forgot their true identity, emphasizing that, because the end of the world is imminent, the time for a return to their roots is now. The scripture strongly rejects the idea that there is a "negro, black, or colored race," instead emphasizing that blacks are members of the Moorish nation, the Asiatic race, and the Islamic religion. The establishment of racial harmony and world peace is possible, Noble Drew promises, if each group of humans will gather unto itself and cease amalgamation with other races, nations, and creeds. Though Noble Drew was killed in 1929, his movement continued to grow, establishing lodges across the United States by the 1940s. The popularity of the MST declined as the Nation of Islam rose to prominence after World War II, but various claimants would keep Noble Drew's legacy alive, offering new interpretations of Moorish Science.*

Chapter XLV

THE DIVINE ORIGIN OF THE ASIATIC NATIONS

1. The fallen sons and daughters of the Asiatic Nation of North America need to learn to love instead of hate; and to know their higher self and

lower self. This is the uniting of the Holy Koran of Mecca, for teaching and instructing all Moorish Americans, etc.

2. The key of civilization was and is in the hands of the Asiatic nations. The Moorish, who were ancient Moabites, and the founders of the Holy City of Mecca.

3. The Egyptians who were the Hamathites, and of a direct descendant of Mizraim, the Arabians, the seed of Hagar, Japanese and Chinese.

4. The Hindoos of India, the descendants of the ancient Canaanites, Hittites, and Moabites of the land of Canaan.

5. The Asiatic nations of North, South, and Central America; the Moorish Americans and Mexicans of North America, Brazilians, Argentineans and Chileans in South America.

6. Columbians, Nicaraguans, and the natives of San Salvador in Central America, etc. All of these are Moslems.

7. The Turks are the true descendants of Hagar, who are the chief protectors of the Islamic Creed of Mecca; beginning from Mohammed the First, the founder of the uniting of Islam, by the command of the great universal God-Allah.

Chapter XLVI

THE BEGINNING OF CHRISTIANITY

1. The foundation of Christianity began in Rome. The Roman nations founded the first Church, which crucified Jesus of Nazareth for seeking to redeem His people from under the Roman yoke and law.

2. Jesus himself was of the true blood of the ancient Canaanites and Moabites and the inhabitants of Africa.

3. Seeking to redeem His people in those days from the pressure of the pale skin nations of Europe, Rome crucified Him according to their law.

4. Then Europe had peace for a long time until Mohammed the First came upon the scene and fulfilled the works of Jesus of Nazareth.

5. The holy teaching of Jesus was to the common people, to redeem them from under the great pressure of the hands of the unjust. That the rulers and the rich would not oppress the poor. Also that the lion and the lamb may lay down together and neither would be harmed when morning came.

6. These teachings were not accepted by the rulers, neither by the rich; because they loved the principles of the tenth commandment.

7. Through the tenth commandment the rulers and the rich live, while the poor suffer and die.

8. The lamb is the poor people, the lion is the rulers and the rich, and through Love, Truth, Peace, Freedom, and Justice all men are one and equal to seek their own destiny; and to worship under their own vine and fig tree. After the principles of the holy and divine laws of their forefathers.

9. All nations of the earth in these modern days are seeking peace, but there is but one true and divine way that peace may be obtained in these days, and it is through Love, Truth, Peace, Freedom, and Justice being taught universally to all nations, in all lands.

Chapter XLVII

EGYPT, THE CAPITAL EMPIRE OF
THE DOMINION OF AFRICA

1. The inhabitants of Africa are the descendants of the ancient Canaanites from the land of Canaan.

2. Old man Cush and his family are the first inhabitants of Africa who came from the land of Canaan.

3. His father Ham and his family were second. Then came the word Ethiopia, which means the demarcation line of the dominion of Amexem, the first true and divine name of Africa. The dividing of the land between the father and the son.

4. The dominion of Cush, North-East and South-East Africa and North-West and South-West was his father's dominion of Africa.

5. In later years many of their brethren from Asia and the Holy Lands joined them.

6. The Moabites from the land of Moab who received permission from the Pharaohs of Egypt to settle and inhabit North-West Africa; they were the founders and are the true possessors of the present Moroccan Empire. With their Canaanite, Hittite, and Amorite brethren who sojourned from the land of Canaan seeking new homes.

7. Their dominion and inhabitation extended from North-East and South-West Africa, across great Atlantis even unto the present North,

South, and Central America and also Mexico and the Atlantis Islands; before the great earthquake, which caused the great Atlantic Ocean.

8. The River Nile was dredged and made by the ancient Pharaohs of Egypt, in order to trade with the surrounding kingdoms. Also the Niger river was dredged by the great Pharaoh of Egypt in those ancient days for trade, and it extends eastward from the River Nile, westward across the great Atlantic. It was used for trade and transportation.

9. According to all true and divine records of the human race there is no negro, black, or colored race attached to the human family, because all the inhabitants of Africa were and are of the human race, descendants of the ancient Canaanite nation from the holy land of Canaan.

10. What your ancient forefathers were, you are today without doubt or contradiction.

11. There is no one who is able to change man from the descendant nature of his forefathers; unless his power extends beyond the great universal Creator Allah Himself.

12. These holy and divine laws are from the Prophet, Noble Drew Ali, the founder of the uniting of the Moorish Science Temple of America.

13. These laws are to be strictly preserved by the members of all the Temples, of the Moorish Science Temple of America. That they will learn to open their meeting and guide it according to the principles of Love, Truth, Peace, Freedom and Justice.

14. Every subordinate Temple of the Grand-Major Temple is to form under the covenant of Love, Truth, Peace, Freedom and Justice; and create their own laws and customs, in conjunction with the laws of the Holy Prophet and the Grand Temple. I, the Prophet, Noble Drew Ali, was sent by the great God, Allah, to warn all Asiatics of America to repent from their sinful ways; before that great and awful day which is sure to come.

15. The time has come when every nation must worship under its own vine and fig tree, and every tongue must confess his own.

16. Through sin and disobedience every nation has suffered slavery, due to the fact that they honored not the creed and principles of their forefathers.

17. That is why the nationality of the Moors was taken away from them in 1774 and the word negro, black and colored, was given to the Asiatics of America who were of Moorish descent, because they honored not the principles of their mother and father, and strayed after the gods of Europe of whom they knew nothing.

Chapter XLVIII

THE END OF TIME AND THE FULFILLING
OF THE PROPHESIES

1. The last Prophet in these days is Noble Drew Ali, who was prepared divinely in due time by Allah to redeem men from their sinful ways; and to warn them of the great wrath which is sure to come upon the earth.

2. John the Baptist was the forerunner of Jesus in those days, to warn and stir up the nation and prepare them to receive the divine creed which was to be taught by Jesus.

3. In these modern days there came a forerunner of Jesus, who was divinely prepared by the great God-Allah and his name is Marcus Garvey, who did teach and warn the nations of the earth to prepare to meet the coming Prophet; who was to bring the true and divine Creed of Islam, and his name is Noble Drew Ali: who was prepared and sent to this earth by Allah, to teach the old time religion and the everlasting gospel to the sons of men. That every nation shall and must worship under their own vine and fig tree, and return to their own and be one with their Father God-Allah.

4. The Moorish Science Temple of America is a lawfully chartered and incorporated organization. Any subordinate Temple that desires to receive a charter; the prophet has them to issue to every state throughout the United States, etc.

5. That the world may hear and know the truth, that among the descendants of Africa there is still much wisdom to be learned in these days for the redemption of the sons of men under Love, Truth, Peace, Freedom and Justice.

6. We, as a clean and pure nation descended from the inhabitants of Africa, do not desire to amalgamate or marry into the families of the pale skin nations of Europe. Neither serve the gods of their religion, because our forefathers are the true and divine founders of the first religious creed, for the redemption and salvation of mankind on earth.

7. Therefore we are returning the Church and Christianity back to the European Nations, as it was prepared by their forefathers for their earthly salvation.

8. While we, the Moorish Americans are returning to Islam, which was founded by our forefathers for our earthly and divine salvation.

9. The covenant of the great God-Allah: "Honor they [sic] father and they [sic] mother that thy days may be longer upon the earth land, which the Lord thy God, Allah hath given thee!"

10. Come all ye Asiatics of America and hear the truth about your nationality and birthrights, because you are not negroes. Learn of your forefathers' ancient and divine Creed. That you will learn to love instead of hate.

11. We are trying to uplift fallen humanity. Come and link yourselves with the families of nations. We honor all the true and divine prophets.

4. Shaikh Daoud Ahmed Faisal, *Al-Islam: The Religion of Humanity* (1950)

Shaikh Daoud Ahmed Faisal (d. 1980) was an African American Muslim missionary devoted to converting all Americans to what he considered to be the only true religion of humankind. This spiritual head and founder of the Islamic Mission of America successfully converted perhaps thousands of African Americans to a Sunni interpretation of Islam. His publications, which often borrowed, with acknowledgement, from other Muslim missionary tracts, sought to inform the American public on the basics of Islamic religion. His books described the holy cities of Mecca and Medina, reproduced large excerpts from the Qur'an, taught believers how to make the salat, *or daily prayers, and detailed and praised contemporary Muslim heads of state. While his adventuresome spirit led him to establish a short-lived Muslim village in rural New York state, he achieved his greatest success as leader of the State Street mosque in Brooklyn. As a New Yorker, Sheikh Daoud came to know Muslims who traveled to the city from various countries. In* Al-Islam: The Religion of Humanity *(1950), he acknowledged the assistance not only of his wife, Khadijah, but also M. A. Faridi of Iran, Bashir Ahmed Khan of Pakistan, and others from Afro-Eurasia. The sheikh was also pictured in this volume wearing light-colored Arab robes, sitting cross-legged on a prayer rug or oriental carpet. In his hands he held the Qur'an, deeply contemplating its contents in the manner of an Old World Islamic scholar. In the excerpts below, he argues that for the sake of their own salvation, Jews and Christians must convert to Islam. His criticism of Jews and Christians is grounded both in an Islamic critique of Jewish and Christian religious claims and in his experience as an African American in New York. Shaikh Daoud's religious thought is both local and international. He simultaneously asserts the truth of basic Sunni Islamic doctrines while also criticizing white supremacy, discrimination against blacks among some American Jews, and the violent history of European Christian expansion and imperialism.*

For the assurance of everlasting *Peace* and *Security,* the people and the nations of the world must accept "Al-Islam," the *Religion of humanity,* revealed by "Allah," the "Almighty God," unto His chosen Prophets, as the *Religion of humanity* in which to worship Him as their *Religion.* And they must also adopt and put in execution its Principles and its Laws as revealed by "Allah," the Lord of the worlds, unto His Holy Apostle Mohammed, for the one world government of the *brotherhood* of all humanity, as decreed by God, so that all men shall worship and be of one *God,* one *Religion* and one *Law.*

For The Benefit Of Humanity, "Al-Islam" is the Religion of the Peace of God, the Reward or the Attributes of obedience to the Commandments and the Laws of "Allah," the "Almighty God." "Al-Islam" is the *Religion of humanity.* It is the reward, the gift from "Allah" to all who bowed down their will in *submission* to the (*Will*) of "Allah," the (one) God, in obedience to His Laws, His Commandments, His Prophets and what He hath revealed for the government and guidance of humanity, and as the Religion and the *Faith* in which to worship Him.

All the people and the nations of the world should know that "*Islam,*" the *Religion* of "Allah," the "Almighty God" is the *only* Religion of humanity. They should also know that "Islam" is the Religion of all the *Prophets* and *Messengers* of God, including Abraham, Isma'il, Isaac, Jacob, the Tribes, Moses, David, Jesus and Mohammed, and the Prophets of God were not Jews but *Muslims.* No one has Religion, and neither can any one worship God, unless he bows down his will in submission to the *Will* of "Allah," the "Almighty God," the Lord of the worlds, in obedience to His Laws, His Commandments, His Prophets and what He hath revealed for the benefit of humanity.

The Islamic Mission of America, Mosque and Institute, established in the name of "Allah," the "Almighty God" according to His own Divine revealed laws in the promotion of the highest human interest in the worship of "Allah," the (one) true God, designed especially for the propagation, teaching and defending "Al-Islam," the Religion of humanity, which "Allah," the Lord of the worlds, hath revealed unto His Chosen Prophets, as the Religion and the Faith in which all humanity shall worship Him. It appears to me as though the people of the Western parts of this world have no knowledge of the Religion of their Lord. Their constant *laughing* and *mocking* the *Muslims'* manner of worshipping God clearly proves this, because it is only fools who laugh and mock at things of which they have no knowledge. They have never been made to know that prostration is the proper manner of worshiping God. Prostration signifies humility and meekness of oneself before his or her creator. Muslims are the true believers who have never deviated in the slightest degree from "Islam," the Religion of God and His Prophets and mankind. We are in strict accordance and obedience with the laws of our Lord as revealed and as prescribed by His Holy Prophets.

It is deceiving and shameful on the part of the leaders of the Jews, the Catholics and the Protestants, to proclaim the so-called three Faiths at a time like this, to an enlightened and troubled world, to people who are seeking for the truth, peace, security and the brotherhood of man.

Faith is to believe in the oneness of God, obedience to His Commandments, His Laws, His Prophets and what He hath revealed. All who believe in the oneness of God, Who created the universe, His commandments and His Laws are of (one) Faith. The Jews know better because their religion is of the religion of Abraham. They are only leading the Christians on who are using the books of Moses, the law giver, and, a prophet of the Israelites. This is no way to establish brotherhood. Human brotherhood is a reality, because we are one human family. The brotherhood of man must be established in obedience to the Commandments and the laws of the (one) God of Abraham, which is a different thing all together. "Islam," our religion, mine and yours, is the Religion of humanity. The so-called three Faiths must find a different name for unification. But to call yourselves the three faiths when you believe in the one and the same God is deception in the highest degree. The Jews must return to "Islam," the religion of Abraham, and the Christians must accept "Islam," the Religion of humanity; that is if they hope to bring about peace and the one universal brotherhood of man.

It is my desire that the Christian people should know that I am not an enemy of theirs, but a friend of humanity, a lover of truth and humanity, and a heralder of the truth as revealed by the "Almighty God." And should you find knowledge, guidance, peace, the blessings and the forgiveness of God through the pages of this book then I will have accomplished more than my object. I beg of you to read this book very carefully and then make a fair comparison of what you read and what you have been taught to believe. However, there are certain things you must know in relationship with your God before you die.

Christianity is not your Religion, and it is not the Religion of God, and it has no relationship with God, because its teachings and its philosophy are contrary to the revelations and the laws of the Almighty God and the teachings of His Holy Prophets. But "Islam" is your Religion, and unless you surrender your will to the WILL of "Allah," the Unity in the one God, in obedience to His commandments and His laws and observe the teachings of His Prophets, which will automatically make you a Muslim, the gates of Heaven and Paradise will be closed to you, because none goes to Heaven but Muslims who observe the Commandments and the Laws of their Lord.

We are asking the Christian people to stop making fools of themselves, because it is only fools who laugh and mock at things of which they have no knowledge. Why laugh at the Muslims, when the Muslims are the only true believers whose Religion has always been the Religion of God and His Prophets. The religious laws, habits and culture of the Muslims are in true accord with the revealed laws of God.

"They Were Not Jews but Israelites"

For over nineteen hundred years, the so-called Christians with the aid of the Jews and the Scripture of the Israelites' Prophet Moses, have falsified to humanity, misled and misguided them in the name of Jesus, misrepresenting God's Holy Scripture and His Holy Prophets. According to the Holy Quran, a lie is sometimes more dangerous than murder. The greatest injustice that has been committed to humanity, was the willful withholding of the true and most important Revelations of God from the people by both the Jews and the Christian leaders.

Every Jewish and Christian leader knows or should know that "Obedience" to the Holy Laws of "God," as Revealed unto His Holy and chosen Prophets is "Islam," the Religion of humanity. From Genesis to Revelation, the Books Revealed by our Lord unto Moses and David, never once was the name Jews mentioned, because there were no Jews during the Advent of the Holy Prophet Moses, David and Solomon. They also know that the word Jew does not apply to a nationality, but a religious cult, whose followers worshiped idols-gods and they also know that the idol-worshiping cult of Judea was not established until after the death of Solomon by Jereboam, who rebelled against Rehoboam Solomon's son and rightful heir and ruler over the Kingdom of his father whom he succeeded because he refused to recall the exile of his wise father from Egypt. Why do the Jews and the Christians withhold this most important revelation of God from the people and why do they not teach their children to know who the children of Israel are and what their Religion is and what the Religion of the Prophets of God was? Why are they withholding these facts from humanity if they were of the true God?

Moses and the children of Israel were Muslims and not Jews and so were all the Prophets and Messengers of God. There were no Jews during the Advent of the Prophets Moses, David and Solomon and the people of God whom Moses helped to escape from Egypt by the Will and the help of God, known as the Flight or the Exodus, were not Jews but Israelites, of the seed of Abraham, Isaac and Jacob and of their generations. The Jews were not God's chosen people but the Israelites. Anyone can become a Jew, but anyone can not become an Israelite. Israelites as I stated before are the seed of Abraham, the descendents of the generations of Isaac and Jacob and their nationality was known as Hebrew and they spoke Hebrew and they were dark skinned, their skin was like polished bronze and their hair was like lambs' wool.

The Hebrews more or less are the dark skinned people of the world and they are not proud because they are people of God. Righteous and wise people are not proud because they know that they are servants of God in the service of humanity. The Jews of America are the proudest of all the people, if by chance a man of colour would move into their neighborhood they would raise such a rumpus which would give one cause to believe that that one person had committed murder, although that coloured person is supposed to be of their own Religious Faith. This proves that the American and European Jews of today are not related by blood with the Israelites and the Hebrew of the Scripture of Moses.

Do you desire to see the original Jews who had turned away from the Religion of Abraham, Isaac, Jacob, Moses, David, Solomon and Rehoboam of the Holy House of David, the keeper of the Covenant of God who are the true seed of Jacob, Isaac and their father Abraham. Then take a trip to the Saharah to East and North Africa to Yemen, to Ethiopia and you will see dark Jews by the hundreds of millions, they are of all shades and colors, but they are not proud of the color of their skin. The only member of the human family who are proud of the color of their skin is the White-man, known as the Northern Barbarians; the Gentiles who now call themselves Christians and who during the Advent of the Prophet Jesus, whom they now worship as their personal God and saviour, was not even recognized nor considered other than a crazy harmless man. These African and Arabian Jews today called themselves Orthodox Jews, instead of Israelites because they have changed their Religion from "Islam," the Religion of Abraham to Idol worshiping.

It must also be remembered that it was not until after the flight from Egypt, that God Revealed unto Moses the Holy Scripture with the Laws for the government and guidance of the children of Israel and as a protection for them from evil. They were abandoned at the hands of the Philistines for forty years, due to their disobedience to God and His Holy Prophets. There were not Jews even then. These people were Israelites and their tongue was Hebrew and their Religion was "Islam," the Religion of Abraham, which is "Obedience" to the Holy Laws of God.

He who disclosed the truth as revealed by God in His Holy Books unto the people has none to fear but his Lord and he is a true friend of humanity and his Lord "Allah", is his inspiration, his protector, provider, and guide and his friend. But he who withheld and concealed the Truth, which is the Word of God and as Revealed by Him for the benefit of humanity is the real aggressor, a true agent of evil, an enemy of God and humanity. The aggressors call out aloud, murder, murder even before he is hurt because he serves no good purpose and therefore he expects nothing good in return and he tries to involve everyone in his aggressiveness, his evil experiences and miseries. Such is the enemy of humanity, yours and mine.

They shall continue to write, to speak and to teach falsehood until they learn to know the truth and no one knows the truth but the Muslims and the true believers who accept all the Prophets of God as equal and all the true Books Revealed by God in the Holy Quran, which contains the complete Revelations of "Allah," the "Almighty God," the Lord of the worlds with the complete Laws for the government and guidance of humanity and as a protection for us from evil. The Criterion of all Laws is enclosed in the Holy Quran.

"Those Who Laugh and Mock"

It is only fools who laugh and mock at things of which they have no knowledge, they were never taught to love and respect their human brothers, other than those of their own tribes. Truth is something they know nothing about. Fools as a rule are slaves to the ideology of their influential leaders, they were made to believe certain things and deny and hate certain things and certain people. They were never given the chance to think and reason for themselves. That is why we have slaves. It is not the body that is enslaved, but the spirit, the mind and the will by subjective means. The spirit is broken, the mind is subdued, and the will to do is denied. There are other kinds of fools; they are the ones who know that you are right and they are wrong, but they cannot afford to let their followers know, for fear of losing prestige which would hurt their pride. But they have no fear of God and the loss of their souls. They would laugh and encourage others to laugh and mock at people who are doing the right thing merely to cover up their own wrong doings.

Christianity is not the religion of God nor humanity, yet the Christian leaders who know that Christianity is not the Religion of God nor of humanity, but a society trying their best to make the people of the world believe otherwise. This in itself is transgression against God, because the Religion of our Lord is "Islam," the Religion of the Prophets, the Laws and the commandments of the one God of Abraham. It is submission to the Will of God, in obedience to His Laws and His commandments, and in obedience to His Prophets. Christianity is not the Religion of humanity, but "Islam." Christianity is but a social order, a philosophy, based on certain principles of White Supremacy, that White people are superior to their human brethren who are not White.

Originally Christianity was not intended to be a religion in which to worship God. It was a society for the unification of the followers of the teachings of Jesus, not a Religion nor the Religion of Jesus because the Religion of Jesus was the Religion of Moses whose laws he came to confirm. Jesus' Religion was "Islam," the Religion of the Prophets and humanity; Christianity was advocated by the Emperor Nero and other European rulers as a social and political organization, as an instrument of conquest.

Their motives were to conquer, subjugate, suppress and oppress all people and nations other than their own Tribes and Christian nations. Christianity, as a European organization, was designed especially to conquer and enslave the people and the nations of the East; especially Africa, Arabia, India and China, and as a matter of fact they were more than successful. They did not only conquer, suppress and oppress the unfortunate people, but they also sold them in public markets for a price, bidding for them as they would bid for horses or dogs. Could you consider these people civilized or righteous? Are they worthy to be considered as leaders of humanity, after considering the treatment they have inflicted upon their unfortunate suppressed and conquered slaves? Christianity as a social and political organization served well the purpose of the European Kings, Emperors, Czars, Queens, Dukes, Princes, Counts and other Christian rulers. The religious lives of the people were influenced by those of their ruler; for instance if a certain King happened to be a Catholic, all of his subjects had to be Catholics; if he happened to be a Protestant who disliked the Catholics, his subjects had to be Protestants. This was by force of law and not by choice of faith. In those early days the Christian people did not worship God, for they knew not God, nor His Religion, nor His Laws, nor His commandments, they could neither read nor write. They were not only subjects to their Kings and Lords, but their slaves; they worshipped their rulers as something sacred and holy as though they were gods, even up to these enlightened times some of them still worship their rulers as their God. Christianity did not help the people to know and to worship God; it made them believe that Jesus, son of Mary, the Messenger of God, was God and the son of God and his mother, Mary was the mother of the Almighty God. People became so bewildered and confused that they decided not to believe in any kind of God but to get all that life can afford. This is what brought on communism in Russia, Spain, France, Rome and all over the wide world today: falsification and deception. Every Christian leader knows today that Jesus is not God nor the son of God, and they also know that Mary, the mother of Jesus, is not the mother of God, but a woman just like your mother and mine. Nevertheless, they have kept up their pretense. In the early days of Christiandom the European rulers did not worship God, they worshipped their power and glory, while pretending to be worshipping God, which they knew not, selling the name of God or a conquered slave for whatever price it would being.

Christianity must make way for "Islam," the Religion of Humanity.

Thanks to Mohammed and other inspired good and faithful servants today, through the propagation of "Islam," the true Religion of humanity has reached the four corners of the earth; its knowledge and its wisdom are now driving the enemies of God, truth, peace, love and justice into the open where they must give a true, just and fair account of all their deceptive practices. The Christian social organizations have served their usefulness, and now they must make way for the true Religion of "Allah," His prophets and mankind to serve humanity. The Christian leaders are now in frantic despair; they are trying to find a way to make Christianity, which is only an organization, serve as the Religion of humanity. But they are too late; they have falsified too long and have fooled too many too long. The time has come that truth has revealed itself. "Islam," the Religion of humanity, shall now be the Religion in which to worship god, not Jesus nor his mother, but "Allah," the Almighty God, the Lord of the worlds, the God of Abraham, Isma'il, Isaac, Jacob, Moses, David, Jesus and Mohammed.

5. Imam Vehby Isma'il, "Our Prophet, Muhammad" (1959)

The first Albanian mosque in the United States was organized in Detroit in 1949. In addition to functioning as a place for the performance of prayers, the mosque served as a space for the making of Albanian American social networks and the celebration of Albanian nationalism. Many of those Albanian Americans associated with the mosque were anticommunists who had fled Albania for political reasons after World War II. While they embraced their newfound American identities, they also worried that their children might forget about Islam, or even worse, become atheists. In 1949, the Albanian American Moslem Society invited Imam Vehby Isma'il (b. 1919), an Albanian religious leader who had received training in Egypt, to come to the Detroit area. The imam conducted funerals and weddings for the community, oversaw the Friday prayers, and encouraged the participation of community members in the two Islamic holidays marking the end of Ramadan and the hajj. *He also edited the journal* Albanian Moslem Life, *which contained articles in both English and Albanian. The children's story by Imam Vehby excerpted below depicts an Old World encounter with a friend and the friend's daughter. The story conveys nostalgia for the old country while also expressing hope that a strong Muslim identity will be forged among the community's American children.*

Fatima was the only daughter of Hasan and Nadira.

Nadira had graduated from girls' high school in Scutari, Albania. Later she became a nurse. She worked in the largest hospital in Tirana, the capital of Albania.

Hasan had finished his high school studies in General Medrese in Tirana. This was the only Moslem Seminary in Albania. He was a religious teacher in one of the elementary schools of Tirana.

Good luck or bad, you may say as you wish, made Hasan ill. He was cared for in the largest hospital of Tirana. This was the same hospital where Nadira was working. It became Nadira's turn to nurse several of the patients. Among them was Hasan. Thus it was that Nadira saw him several times a day. She took his temperature and gave him medicine prescribed by the doctors.

At first, Hasan's heart was full of respect and sympathy towards his nurse for she gave him the best of care. With her angelic smile she seemed to relieve his pain. With the passing time, his respect and sympathy was replaced with a deep love. This love found its mate in Nadira's heart. Thus after Hasan was well again and released from the hospital, no time was lost and this love was crowned by their marriage.

After the passing of one year during which existed a happy and harmonious atmosphere, Hasan and Nadira were blessed with a girl whom they named Fatima, remembering that this was the name of our prophet's daughter.

Hasan was my friend as we were classmates in the General Medrese, and therefore, I was an invited guest at his wedding. It was there that I was introduced to his wife. A few days later, I left Tirana and as Hasan and I were very good friends we wrote often. He wrote me, among other things, about the arrival of his daughter. For thirteen years, however, the opportunity did not arise that we should meet.

Then, one cold wintry night, I was in Tirana and decided to visit my old friend Hasan. His joy when he saw me was very great. We embraced as though we were brothers. Later we sat near the hearth telling each other of events which had occurred during those long thirteen years and of the many things which we had only slightly mentioned in our letters.

It was not long—at least it did not seem as though much time had passed. Then a glance at my watch revealed that several hours had elapsed. Then there was a knock at the door of the sitting room. The door opened and Nadira entered with her daughter.

Fatima, even though she had just celebrated her twelfth birthday, looked as though she might have been fifteen. She was quite tall. Her eyes were large and black like olives, her complexion was white as snow, and her hair was the color of chestnuts. When she spoke, her lips would yield an angelic an attractive smile. After she greeted me she sat next to her father and said:

"Dad, as Mother and I were returning from the market, I saw that the minarets of Et'hem Bey and Vjeter mosques were decorated and shone with brilliant green lights. I have never seen them illuminated like that. What is the occasion that they were so lustrous?"

"My dear," her father answered, "tomorrow is the Birthday of our Prophet Muhammed, peace and blessings of God be upon him. For that reason the mosques have been decorated with lights. Tomorrow night we are going to the mosque together at 7 o'clock to hear the Mevlud which is chanted in all mosques and Moslem homes throughout the world."

"What is Mevlud?" asked Fatima.

"The word 'Mevlud' is Arabic and it means 'Birth,'" answered her father. "We in Albania and other Moslem and non-Arab countries use this word for the celebration of the birthday of the Prophet Muhammed. When we say that the Mevlud is being sung, we mean that the life of the Holy Prophet is chanted in verses. It is sung every year and naturally each country sings it in its own language."

"Dad, would you tell me something about the life of the Holy Prophet Muhammed whose birthday you mentioned is tomorrow?" asked Fatima.

"As you see, Fatima, tonight we have company and I would like to chat with my friend and speak about our old times, but I promise you that beginning next Saturday, I will tell you, little by little, about the life of our Prophet, Muhammed—peace and blessings of God be upon him."

Fatima then rose and bade us goodnight and she went to her room.

Hasan and I stayed together until late at night. We recalled the sweet days of our youth which we spent together in school. As we parted, I asked Hasan if I could visit him every Saturday so I could hear him tell his daughter of the Prophet's history. And so it was that I went to Hasan's home every Saturday until he finished the story.

In the pages which follow are compiled the history which Hasan told Fatima. I wrote it just as I heard it. Here I have printed it for you, where I hope, my dear friends, you will be pleased with it just as Fatima was. Pray to God to guide all of us in the right path, the path which was preached by our Prophet, Muhammed, peace be upon him.

The First Night: Arabia

Muhammed, my dear child, was born in Arabia, and before I tell you about his life, I see it proper to speak tonight a little on Arabia. Next week

I will tell you about the Arabs, and thus you will be able to understand and better evaluate our Prophet Muhammed.

If you glance at a map of the world, you will see a peninsula is a portion of land whose three shores are surrounded by water and the other is united with land. This peninsula is located in Asia Minor which is linked to Africa. It is called Arabia. Arabia is surrounded by the Black Sea, the Arabian Sea and the Indian Ocean.

Arabia is a rather large peninsula. The land does not have many rivers, but it has many deserts full of sand, stones and bare hills. Even so, some parts of Arabia are very fertile. In those places there is sufficient water and the climate is good. Here wheat, corn, dates and grapes are grown. Coffee is planted in a province of Arabia called Yemen. Coffee from Yemen is the best in the world.

The largest province of the peninsula is owned by royalty. It is called "Saudi Arabia" and it is ruled by King Saud. It is very famous for its many oil wells near Dhahran. They are used by an American Company. This oil is making "Saudi Arabia" a prosperous country and it will be someday one of the most progressive parts of Asia.

In "Saudi Arabia" there is a section called "Higaz." Higaz has two large famous cities which are well known throughout the world. One is Mecca, which is a Holy City for all Moslems. Each Moslem turns his face towards it at prayer time. In Mecca there is a large Mosque and in the center of its courtyard is a cube which is called "Kaba." Moslems believe that "The Kaba" was first built by the Prophet Abraham with the help of his son, Ismael. Those Moslems who are financially able, from all corners of the world go each year to visit the Kaba at the time of Kurban Bayram [the ritual sacrifice at the end of pilgrimage]. Here they fulfill their religious duty of the pilgrimage. About this pilgrimage, Fatima, you will learn more in your religious Sunday School. Those who visit Kaba take the title "Haji" and when they return to their homes, this title is placed before their name.

The second largest and famous city in Higaz is Medina and this is also a Holy City for Moslems. The Prophet Muhammed emigrated from his birthplace, Mecca, and lived in Medina for more than ten years. Medina was a Moslem capital for a long period. There Muhammed died and was buried. Over his tomb was built a building which is called a mausoleum. Every Moslem who performs the pilgrimage to Mecca also may visit the mausoleum of the Holy Prophet, Muhammed—peace and blessings of God be upon Him—in Medina.

Arabia is noted for its camels and horses. Camels are used mostly as they are good desert travelers. They can live a long time without water; because, as you know, in the Sahara it is difficult to find water. Therefore, camels are used for riding and burden. Camels are adaptable for their hoofs are flat so they walk lightly on the sands of the Sahara. Camels are a necessity in all places similar to Arabia, sandy and without water. Many writers have called them "Boats of the Sahara." Arabs enjoy eating camel meat, with its fur they make clothes. Camel fur is very soft, but the clothes made from it are very durable and of high quality.

Arabs love horses very much; perhaps as much as their children. Arab horses, even though of small stature, are world famous for their speed. For this reason, most racing horses in modern times are selected from the Arab breed and are costly.

Arabs take great care in horse breeding. Before he buys one, the Arab must know every little detail about it. For example, he must know its pedigree and the reputation to tell the history for its parents and its parents' ancestors. He is proud of his distinguished horses.

Long ago, horses played an important part in the wars, because then wars were fought with swords. Perhaps this is one of the important reasons why Arabs are so fond of their horses; as most of their time, before Prophet Muhammed, was spent in battle. I will tell you more of this later.

"That is enough for tonight, Fatima," Hasan said to his daughter. "It is time for bed. Next week I will tell you about a few of their customs. Good night and God bless you."

"Thank you father. Good night." Fatima left and went to sleep as it was nearing midnight.

6. Abdo Elkholy, *The Arab Moslems in the United States* (1966)

Abdo Elkholy, an Egyptian Muslim sociologist who taught at Northern Illinois University, penned one of the classic ethnographies of Arab American Muslim life. Comparing Muslims in Detroit and Toledo, Elkholy argued that there was a strong correlation between Muslim religiosity and "Americanization." His research, conducted in 1959 and supported by the Dodge Founda-

tion, showed that those Muslims who participated actively in the life of their
mosques were more likely to assimilate into mainstream (white) American
culture than those who did not participate in mosque life. Such findings chal-
lenged the assumptions of some social scientists, who believed that identifica-
tion with a "foreign" religion might prevent strong identification with
American values and beliefs. The following excerpts from his book focus only
on the Toledo community, which he viewed as more successfully integrated
than the Detroit community. Elkholy saw the practice of Islam in Toledo as a
vibrant response to the exigencies of American life, and he heralded the par-
ticipation of Toledo's Muslims in the city's economy and culture.

The first Moslem family settled in Toledo in 1915, after eight years of wandering in the United States. There were two waves of migration to Toledo:
from 1945 to 1949, and from 1952 to 1955. The great majority of the Toledo
members did not come directly from the old country, as was the case in
Detroit, but from within the United States itself. They were mainly attracted to the city by the liquor business which one Moslem family was
said to have entered. This family imported relatives from other states and
employed them to meet the business expansion, securing maximum profit
with minimum cost in paying wages. But those business-minded relatives
very quickly realized the attractive net profits, and thus branched out in
the same business direction, helped by the first family. The relatives
brought others with them to start the same cycle; the news was spread,
and in less than twenty years the Moslems owned 127 of the city's 420 bars,
or about 30 per cent, in addition to liquor stores, carry-out businesses,
and restaurants with liquor licenses. Some Moslems today have two or
three bars. Many retire but keep the bars, either running them through
hired workers or subletting them with the reservation of license ownership. Some with high status occupations also indulge in bar ownership,
hire help, and invest their outside working hours in the business.

It has become well known in and around Toledo that the city's liquor
business is almost monopolized by the Moslems who had actually started
this trend by chance, and continued it by profit-orientation, cohesive relationships, and natural jealousy among the relatives to imitate the successful members. The cost of a liquor license has risen in the last ten years
from $600 to $20,000 and more on the black market. One of the inter-
viewees said: "Liquor is the most profitable business we have ever experienced. You never lose on it or bear any waste by contamination. To give

you just one example, last year I sold in my restaurant whiskey for $11,000. The net profit was $9,000."

The Toledo community represents a pattern of selectivity: its members, due to their long period of exposure to the American culture before establishing the community, had internalized to a high degree the American values, and they planned Toledo as an American-Moslem community.

The members did not come directly from the old country to gather haphazardly in one area where the traditional values are preserved: they migrated to the community from other American states where they had lived among Americans. The occupational pattern of liquor is strong evidence of such Americanization. The purpose of establishing the community was to preserve the Islamic religious identification in support of their social status as American middle class. That social-religious decision was taken after realizing the psychological commitment of establishing their life permanently in America.

Thus the intention to settle permanently in America was made early by the Toledo first generation because of their economic success. This decision helped them to adjust to the new environment. The deceptive attitude of, "when we go back to the old country, our children will learn a lot about their religion" did not emerge among them. The Toledo first-generation members realized their new minority status in the new environment. Having committed themselves to a permanent settlement, they accepted and welcomed the inevitable associate factor of being American. But being American, they saw, does not mean being without religion; rather, good Americans are in favor of religious affiliation. The first-generation members conveyed to the second the common ethical values of America and the old country in terms of religion and they accepted from the second generation the new American norms, mores, and social habits. This reciprocity between the two generations permitted the joining of the two cultural streams and resulted in an integral American Moslem community. The traditionalistic sectarian values which separated Sunnis from Shi'as in the old country disappeared, at least from public view.

Many secular elements have penetrated religion in the Toledo community. On Sunday, when the first- and second-generation parents bring their children to Sunday school at the mosque, most of them pray without ablution. This habit is not institutionalized, however, for the parents do not proclaim it as a principle that ablution must be avoided; they explain the practice this way:

> Ablution was introduced to the nomadic communities in the absence of hygienic habits and instructions. But now, under the sanitary conditions of our day in this country, everyone is supposed to be clean—thus ablution has lost its function as a precondition for prayer.

Also, among the second generation in both communities, 82 per cent do not even know that a bath is religiously required after sexual intercourse. Rationalizations of these changes encourage the congregation to participate fully in the religious practices without hidden restrictions. This kind of secularization conforms to the American religious patterns in which tradition often gives way to rationalization.

Leadership in the Toledo community's social activities as well as the religious teachings is held mainly by the American-oriented, second-generation females. In their relations with the other religious groups as well as teaching their younger generation, they stress the social and religious ethics and religious tolerance of Islam. "To be a good Moslem you have to be a good American and vice versa," this writer heard a young woman tell her Sunday school class. "Islam acknowledges and respects the other heavenly religions. It came to abolish human inequality on the basis of language, nation or race. It preaches human brotherhood."

This religious moderation and orientation of the Toledo second generation has Islamic self-identification compatible with Americanism. The social changes in the family and community relations between the Toledo first and second generations have taken the American direction, where the older generation plays a guiding, but not a leading role. The Toledo first-generation parents adjusted themselves to the more American role of providing affection in a conjugal family rather than of acting as the authority. This adjustment in the family has made it possible to build community solidarity with a minimum of revolt or deviation by the younger generation. . . .

The social religious role of the Toledo community is played so much by the women that the fine Toledo mosque may be attributed to the efforts of the women of the community.

These women participate in a variety of activities to support the mosque institution. One of their more popular fund-raising activities is selling tickets and serving dinners of Middle Eastern dishes in the basement of the mosque. Another activity is baking Middle Eastern pastries, which they sell for maintaining the mosque. They also arrange picnics during the summer for the families of the community, and they have joint activities with the Youth Club. Their branch, called the American Moslem Society Ladies Auxiliary, has 60 active members who meet frequently at the mosque to discuss social affairs. Many decisions of the main American Moslem Societies are delegated to this Ladies Auxiliary. The women are the sole teachers in Sunday school. Even in their religious lectures at the mosque and at other churches and social organizations, the women are very active and speak with authority and intelligence about Islam.

Had it not been for the activities of the women of Moslem communities, it may be truly said that the Moslem religious movement in America would not be as steady and strong as it is now. The social religious activities of these women is the product of the Western influence and of their assimilation achieved by the women in both communities. More assimilated to the Western environment, the women in the Toledo community are more active in the mosque affairs than the women in the Detroit community who still hold the tradition that the mosque is the community of males. . . .

In contrast to Detroit, Toledo second-generation members have [also] played an active role in promoting their children's religious status and in teaching them to be good Moslems and good Americans. Despite the large number of Toledo's first-generation immigrants, these elders have yielded the position of social and religious leadership to the second-generation members who have carried over moderately and very skillfully. After all, they know the different conditions of their present environment and the universal characteristics of their religious heritage. "Islam is not a national religion," said a young second-generation social leader. "It is, rather, international by its unique principles which coincide with general human morals and stress the welfare of society. And," he added, "its details and applications are left to be shaped and reshaped to suit the particular time and place. Islam in America, with its principles, has to take into account the particular features of the American culture, it has to be a living thing in our everyday life and it has to contribute its shares to the culture surrounding us." Right or wrong in his philosophical religious view, he represents the view of his generation.

Having felt the psychological problems of their children who are looking for something to identify themselves with, the small Moslem community of Toledo in 1955 contributed $80,000 to build one of the newest and most beautiful mosques in the United States. The second generation started the campaign to which the first generation generously contributed.

Since 1955, many second-generation Moslems have moved with their families to Toledo because of the mosque. A young second-generation member bore a heavy loss to move with his family from Virginia to Ohio after the mosque was erected. He said that he wanted his children to be religious and used to send them to church every Sunday in Virginia. Religion to him, springing from a psychological need, helps to solve many everyday problems that are beyond the individual's capacity to solve. In addition, as said before, religion in Toledo is one of the most cherished social values of the middle class, to which the majority of the community belong. The erection of the mosque solved many problems of the second-generation members, especially in providing the necessary religious training for their children.

Being merchants and having wandered through so many states before permanently settling in Toledo, the old-generation members developed a moderate attitude toward sharing the responsibility of community affairs with the second generation. They also accepted the principle of religious coexistence which turned out to work for the best of their interest. As their children expressed the desire to marry Americans, they first advised them to marry from their own people. But when they saw the persistence of their children, they accepted the mixed marriages on the condition that the spouses familiarize themselves with the community affairs, customs, and religion. By this means, the spouse was introduced to the community and studied its religion objectively; and the community, besides keeping its own children, gained new members. It often happened that the American spouses, observing the community's tolerant attitude, converted to Islam and became very active members. By this attitude, the community seems to have violated the traditional religious doctrines which forbid a Moslem girl to marry a non-Moslem. However, there is no explicit prohibition in either the Quran or true tradition against a Moslem girl marrying a follower of a "heavenly Book." It is, however, against the traditions and customs of the old countries that a Moslem girl marry a non-Moslem. The reserved acceptance of Toledo community, therefore, represents a deviation from tradition, tending toward assimilation of the American culture.

The most religiously active members in the Toledo community married outside the faith. They and their spouses have contributed a great deal to the social and religious life of the community. It may be that they have wanted to show the good will and true faith which an ordinary born-Moslem does not need to show. It is also worth mentioning that the Islamic Associations in the United States and Canada, are the product of the mixed-marriage children.

In conversation with a score of those Moslems who adopted Christianity in both communities, the writer was told that the majority of those who became Christians were mostly women in Detroit. They converted out of frustration, having been slighted by the Moslem men who left them to marry Americans. Thus they were forced to marry outside their community and found themselves rejected by their relatives and the entire community. Because of that rejection, they moved away spiritually as well as physically. The Toledo community overcame this problem by absorbing the outsiders into the community.

The high degree of religiosity of the Toledo third generation supports the sociological theory of religious regression. But this regression should not be taken as a general condition for all third generations. Rather, it should be looked at in the light of Merton's "middle range theories," which provide that when the second-generation members carry out the social and religious leadership to bridge the gap between the third and first generations, the third generation then develops a favorable regressional attitude toward the religion of the old generation. Despite this regression, however, the religion of the third generation differs in kind and degree from that of the first.

The religion of the first generation is also associated with nationalistic sentiments. This is the case in Detroit. For this reason, the non-Arab Moslems are not accepted in the community as fully as they are in Toledo. The president of the Youth Organization in Toledo is an Indian Moslem student who is treated and looked upon as a full member of the community. The religious leader is a Yugoslav graduate of al-Azhar University. He is highly respected and fully accepted as a member of the community.

Having searched a very long time for a scholarly religious leader, Detroit was offered the services of that highly educated Toledo religious leader. He was rejected on the grounds of being non-Arab. In his correspondence with the writer, the president of the Detroit community said, "The colony here is trying to contact the Toledo community's sheikh [after he left

Toledo]. But the majority, and I am one of them, would rather have a sheikh from Cairo for reasons one of which is [Arab] nationalism."

The Toledo community is, first of all, a *Moslem-American* community. Moslem-oriented, the community recognizes that Islam means more than Arab. It encloses many nations. The religious leader is a non-Arab Moslem. Some Indian students are accepted as full members of the community. The community's sentiment for Egypt or Libya is not a religious sentiment, equal to their feeling toward Indonesia and Pakistan. The horizon of the Toledo community has become as international as Islam itself and not, as in Detroit, confined to Arab nationalism. Being more assimilated into their new environment and farther removed from their old traditions, the members of the Toledo community differentiate between Islam as an international religion and Arab nationalism as a regional political ideology. . . .

At a formal meeting of the American Muslim Society of Toledo, held at the new mosque, the president proposed to the committee the introduction of the bingo game at the mosque as a possible source of support. Although the proposal did not pass, its very introduction indicates the direction in which the community is moving as well as its degree of assimilation of certain values of the host culture.

That most of the Toledo male members are owners of bars, alcoholic beverage stores, and liquor-licensed restaurants is another evidence of assimilation. Although within the realm of religious practice the people are firm on abstinence from drinking, they have made an occupational shift from traditional values to a new set of values. During Ramadan, the writer often had interviews with members of the community at their bars while he found them fasting. The beautiful mosque, the most striking religious institution in the community, is built from liquor money. Paradoxically, the shift in occupational values has helped to sustain the religious institution.

Could it be that the subconscious religious guilt is sublimated by generous material support to the religious institutions? While satisfying their religious conscience, the Toledo members also show the surrounding Moslem communities how religiously well the liquor trader's community is. As businessmen have no limited ceiling on their earnings, the members of the Moslem community in Toledo believe that the more they give for the support of their religious institutions, the more they will earn and their earning will become blessed and purified from the sin of its means.

It is a kind of religious reconciliation with the deity, in which flourishing social functions are associated with the process of assimilation. Religious movements throughout history have owed a great deal to the consciousness of sin, perhaps even more than to the feeling of piety. The pious man very often lives on the secular contribution offered by the sinner. . . .

Sunday is not the only active day in the Toledo mosque. There are many activities every day: at least one religious group comes daily from different religious faiths and institutions to acquaint themselves with their Moslem fellow citizens; there are occasional meetings and parties; certain times one is always sure to meet the religious leader of the community in the mosque. Nevertheless, Sunday is the most active day of the week in the regular life of the mosque. It is the day of Sunday school and practically every family brings its children to the school to learn about their religion. There are about 150 students enlisted in the school, ranging in age from 4 to over 15. . . .

The curriculum is very well organized and harmonized by the religious leader who arranges the lessons weekly and meets with the teachers beforehand to instruct them on how to conduct the lessons. Toward the end of the year, these lessons are collected to be followed in Sunday school in the years to come. The teachers are exclusively second-generation young women, some of whom are the product of mixed marriages.

The four small classes start in the basement from 10:00 am until 11:30; the fifth, conducted by the sheikh, is held upstairs from 11:30 to noon. This arrangement is to give the religious leader a chance to supervise the classes. In return, it gives the teachers and older children a chance to hear lectures about Islamic ethics. All the classes and lectures are given in English. About noon, all the attendants, from three generations, are engaged in the Sunday noon prayer, lining up behind the religious leader in a traditional way; females are at the end of the group. After the classes and lecture, there is a collection. This collection has the function of teaching the youth how to support their mosque. It is also a borrowed element from the American churches.

Chanting the prayer loudly at Sunday noon is a kind of adjustment to the American environment. Its practical function is to teach the youth how to perform prayer. Sunday noon prayer itself, as it is done in the Toledo community, represents a kind of over-all religious integration with the American environment. It fills the religious vacuum in the spirit of those youths who see their friends and schoolmates belonging and going to a church of which they are proud. Now, they too have a God to fill their entity, to Whom they bow and kneel, and from Whose unlimited power they derive their power to conquer problems of everyday life. The mosque institution plays a vital role in the life of the entire community, for religion's vital psychological functions integrate the individual personality with that of the surrounding society.

7. Piri Thomas, "God, Ain't You for Everybody?" from *Down These Mean Streets* (1967)

Born in 1928 in Spanish Harlem, writer and poet Piri Thomas was the son of Puerto Rican and Cuban parents. After becoming involved in a life of drugs and gang warfare, he was convicted of assault and attempted robbery in 1950 and served over five years in prison. In 1967, Alfred A. Knopf published his first book, a memoir entitled Down These Mean Streets, *which subsequently received critical acclaim. In addition to describing his life on the streets of Spanish Harlem, the memoir depicted the harsh realities of Comstock Prison, where Thomas met followers of Elijah Muhammad during a formative decade for the Nation of Islam. These Muslim believers repeated Elijah Muhammad's teachings about the white devil and the need for clean living. But they also read at least parts of the Qur'an and the* hadith, *the sayings and deeds of the Prophet Muhammad and an important source of Islamic religious traditions. Eventually, these Muslims taught him the* salat, *or prescribed Islamic prayers. They instructed Thomas on how to say the* adhan, *or call to prayer, and insisted that he learn the* wudu, *or the ablutions to be performed before prayer. Thomas became a convert to Islam and learned at least some of the prayers in Arabic, although he did not continue to practice Islam once released from prison.*

One night I was sprawled out on my bed in my cell hearing something that I had been hearing for a long time every night. But tonight I just listened to it harder:

> Allahu Akbar, Allahu Akbar,
> Allahu Akbar, Allahu Akbar,
> Allahu Akbar, Allahu Akbar,
> Allahu Akbar, Allahu Akbar.

I heard the chanting coming from the cell somewhere below. I knew it was Chaplin, who would rather be called Muhammad. I had heard him often enough telling cons who had addressed him as Chaplin not to call him by his given Christian name, since he was a Muslim. I knew from what I had been reading that the religion Muhammad was following was the religion of Islam and was what the Arabs believed in. I knew there were a lot of colored people in Harlem who believed in this Arab religion, but I wondered if the cats in this jailhouse were really serious about this religion, or was it just a prison fad to help while away long years.

I got a chance to find out what was shaking one Sunday afternoon out in the prison yard. I saw Muhammad sitting Indian-style with four or five guys in a circle. He was reading to them out of a book. I walked over to them and sat just close enough to be noticed. Muhammad looked up and smiled a Christ-like smile and said, "Like to sit in, friend?" I couldn't help thinking that his English was as smooth as Mr. Prissy's. I nodded a "Yeah" and the circle opened enough for me to become a part of it.

"We are reading from the Holy Quran. As you may know, we are followers of the religion of Islam." I nodded understanding and he went on to introduce those in the circle. "This is Ben Jussaf, and this is Hussein," and his finger pointed out the owners of these funny-sounding names, "and this is Jamal, Nassum, Ali—and I am Muhammad." He went on, perhaps because the look on my face was saying how come you guys give up such easy-saying names like Jones and Smith for such hard-sounding ones. "These are the believers' names we have chosen for ourselves or were given to us when we embraced the religion of Islam. The names on our birth certificates, if we had one, are what the white devil has fostered upon us. Many of us simply have an X for a last name."

"Are you the pastor?" I asked. There was a little bit of smiling in his voice as he replied, "No, we don't have pastors or reverends. We have what are called imams—er—teachers, and that's what I am. What is your name?"

"Piri."

"Piri what?"

"Piri, number 18193." I smiled.

Muhammad's gentle-like face ignored my punch line and went on: "Are you interested in the religion of Islam?"

"I'm interested in anything that will get the cockroaches of confusion outta my head. I've heard you praying in another language a lot of times. It sounded like Alla-hu Actbarr or something—"

"It was the opening words of the Adhan, or the call to prayer. 'Allahu Akbar—Allahu Akbar, Allah is the Greatest.'"

I nodded to the book in his hands. "Is that your Bible?"

"What the Bible is to the Christian, the Holy Quran is to the followers of Islam, only more so," he answered.

"I've heard of Moslems before," I said, feeling uncomfortable for not having read more and for having to feel half-blank like now.

"We are not Moslems. Moslem is the way the Western world pronounces it. We are Muslims."

Again my head went up and down in understanding. Another Negro walked up to the group. I heard him say what sounded like "Asalamaleecum." The others in the circle replied, "Waa-lee-kum-salam." "Our brother Albert X has just greeted us. 'As-salamu alaikum' means 'Peace be on you,' and 'Wa-alai-kum-salam' means 'And on you be peace.'"

I thought of the Jews in Harlem and how close this sounded to the "Sholom" I'd heard them greet each other with once in a while. I lit a cigarette and felt a staring of eyes. I excused myself for not sharing my pack around. They all shook their heads in polite refusals—and Muhammad the imam explained, "A true Muslim does not smoke, drink intoxicating beverages, nor eat pork, among other things."

"Sounds like my momma's religion."

"Oh, is she a true believer?"

"She was a Seventh-Day Adventist. She's dead now."

"Oh, that's not quite like being a Muslim, although Christianity has many things in common with the true religion of Islam."

I thought inside my head that so far it was a clean-living religion. I'd seen these Muslim cons around a lot and I had never heard them curse or seen them eat pork when it was given out in the mess hall. I never once saw them take off on pills or dug them high from prison home-brew. "So where's the difference?" I asked.

"Christianity is the white devil's religion. God or Jehovah is the white man's God and he's used his Christianity as a main weapon against the dark-skinned inhabitants of the world. What his blood-letting or slaughter did not destroy, his Christianity ably conquered. Even though Abraham is called the father of the faith, there's where it ends as far as we Black Muslims are concerned."

I opened my mouth to say something, but Muhammad gently cut me off. "You and I will speak further some other time. If you will bear with us, I will teach from the Quran to my brothers."

I sat there and listened as Muhammad read first in Arabic and then in English. I later found out he was also teaching the followers how to read, write, and speak Arabic. I got to know Muhammad pretty well in the next few years. He was a light-skinned Negro, slightly built with built-in deep thoughts.

A few days later, I ran into Muhammad in the recreation hall. He was sitting at table poring over a book. I greeted him, "As-salamu alaikum." "Wa'alai-kumu-s-salam," he answered without looking up, and then looking up and seeing me, he said softly, "Only believers greet each other this way; any other way it's like blasphemy." I mumbled an "Excuse me" and added, "I'd like to know more."

"About what?" he motioned for me to sit down.

"I've been thinking if maybe the reason for this jumping of Negroes to become Muslims is on account of maybe Allah is a black man's god."

"One doesn't have to be a Negro to be a Muslim. There are many Caucasians that are Muslims."

"Where?"

"In the Far East, where our religion was born."

"I've never heard of any in Harlem," I said.

"If there are," answered Muhammad, "they are rare. The white devil in this country had his chance to be our brother. His chance is lost. His rule is at an end. His time is running out. His rule is almost buried under six feet of dirt decorated with his famous cross. We, the Black Muslims, are coming into our own."

"Lotta black humans are Christians," I pushed.

"That's the worst mistake the black man made, in allowing his brain to be Christianized." Muhammad's face was getting tight. I nodded, thinking about my hang-ups with Muhammad's white devils. Muhammad closed his book and went on. "When the black man ate the poison of Christianity, he finally was where the white man wanted him. First he took away the black man's freedom, then his dignity and pride, then his identity. In return, he gave him a secondhand sense of values—a concept of nonexisting dignity by putting him in a certain place, like low man in anything, then taught him about Christianity and how, as a Christian, he could bravely stand the pain of his slavery, all the time softly purring into his eyes, 'No matter how much you lose here on earth, Jesus loves you and you'll get it all back in heaven.'" Muhammad somehow reminded me of Brew and me. I listened: "The white devil has kept chanting 'All men are brothers,' while all the time he meant 'if they're white.'"

Muhammad's face had totally lost all of its gentleness. He was still speaking low, but the voice was tense, angry, and curling with the hate that millions of white devils had helped so well to cultivate.

"Christianity—white man's style isn't for the black man. Christianity is only first-class salvation for the white devil, the salvation of overabundance of good living wrung out from stripped backs and millions and millions of knees bended in the prayer of black slavery." Muhammad shook his head in disgust, and mine became a companion also. "Christianity—Christianity," Muhammad spoke the name like a curse, "it's the power of good living reality for them and reality of pain, hunger, despair, and degradation for us black men. The white devil has claimed to have given the black man all that he has. He's right. And it's all been bad. He's exploited every source the black man could provide—his strength, his labor, his dignity, his woman, his spirit—and has done all he could to exploit even his soul."

Muhammad asked me softly, "You said you've seen Muslims in Harlem?"

"A-huh," I nodded a yes. "A lot of them wear something called a fez on their heads, others wear hats made outta Persian wool, and most of them wear a mustache and a beard, but not all. Their women don't paint themselves."

"Yes, but what else did you notice about our Black Muslims?"

"Uh, they don't smoke, drink liquor, or curse, and they dress well, like neatly pressed all the time."

"Yes, but what else?" Muhammad pushed. Before I could think of something else, Muhammad himself answered, "They all walk with dignity and quiet pride. We are a united people, and only Allah, through his beloved prophet Elijah Muhammad, could have brought this about. We are educating ourselves, not as the white devil would have it but in a superior way. We have learned that our heritage is a great one. We are of a mighty race of people. We are superior in whatever we undertake, be it science, art, music, sports—name it, and we excel. The white devil's time of keeping us living in a lie is over. He's afraid now, because he knows his time is up now. He knows it isn't a white world alone any longer. He'd like a chance for us to get along like brothers. Well! the white man is not our brother. He doesn't know how to be one. All he knows is how to be a slave master, and now that he sees the black man coming into his own, he's afraid. And with good reason, for what cruel slave master would look forward to the day that he would be slave to his former slave. His conscience itself frightens him at the thought that he may be treated as he himself once treated. Yes, he'd like for us to be brothers now.

"Our leader is right when he said, 'White man, for two thousand years you've been on top of us like this.'" Muhammad turned the two palms together like in an attitude of prayer, and went on: "He wants us to be even-Stephen, he says—to walk side by side in sameness . . . like brothers. But he's not our brother. We weren't brothers from way back then and we're not gonna be brothers from here on out. He's a white devil and no matter what he does to try to expiate his guilt—it's no good. It's going to be like this . . . " Muhammad turned his palms still together back on their side, only this time the hand representing the black man was on top. Muhammad's voice was now almost gentle again as he went on: "White man—for two thousand years you've been on us—and now we're going to be on you. We want a piece of this world and we're going to get it, even if we have to take it all away from you."

He didn't say another word. I didn't say one either.

The bugle blew and we each made it to our lines for the trip back to our cells.

Muhammad and I became friends, and after a time we became brothers. But first he gave me books to read on the religion of Islam and one of them was the . . . Muslim prayerbook.

"Read the prayerbook first," he said, "and learn the one called The Adhan. As I told you it is the call to prayer."

I nodded and began to peel through the pages.

"But before you say them, learn the Wudzu, or Ablution, on page eight."

I looked at the page and it was in English, the words were hard to pronounce, and I told Muhammad so.

"Don't worry," he said, "just learn the Wudzu and we will hold classes for all the rest."

That night in my cell, I tried to memorize the Wudzu. It went like this:

Before saying prayers it is necessary to wash those parts of the body which are generally exposed. This is called *wudzu*, or ablution. The ablution is performed thus:

1. The hands are cleansed, washing them up to the wrists.
2. Then the mouth is cleansed by means of a toothbrush or simply with water.
3. Then the nose is cleansed within the nostrils with water.
4. Then the face is washed.
5. Then the right arm, and after that the left arm, is washed up to the elbow.
6. The head is wiped over with wet hands, the three fingers between the little finger and the thumb of both hands being joined together.
7. The feet are then washed up to the ankles, first the right foot and the left.

But if there are socks on, and they have been put on after performing an ablution, it is not necessary to take them off; the wet hands may be passed over them. They should be taken off, however, and the feet washed once in every twenty-four hours. The same practice may be resorted to in case the boots are on, but it would be more decent to take off the boots when going into a mosque.

A fresh ablution is necessary only when a man has answered a call of nature or has been asleep.

In case of intercourse between husband and wife, *ghusl* or washing of the whole body is necessary.

When a person is sick, or when access cannot be had to water, what is called *tayammum* is performed in place of *wudzu* or *ghusl*. *Tayammum* is performed by touching pure earth with both hands and then wiping over with them the face and the backs of the hands.

I got up from my bed and tried out the ablution, and then after a few tries at it, I decided to write out the Adhan. The following words are spoken as one faces toward the East (Mecca):

Allahu Akbar, Allahu Akbar,
Allahu Akbar, Allahu Akbar.
"Allah is the Greatest" (*repeated four times*).
Ashhadu an la ilaha illa-llah,
Ashhadu an la ilaha illa-llah.
"I bear witness that nothing deserves to be worshiped except Allah"
    (*repeated twice*).
Ashhadu anna Muhammadan Rasulu-llah, Ashhadu anna
    Muhammadan Rasulu-llah.

"I bear witness that Muhammad is the messenger of Allah"
    (*repeated twice*).
Hayya ala-s-sala,
Hayya ala-s-sala.
"Come to prayer" (*repeated twice, turning the face to the right*).
Hayya ala-l-falah,
Hayya ala-l-falah.
"Come to success" (*repeated twice, turning the face to the left*).
Allahu Akbar,
Allahu Akbar.
"Allah is the Greatest (*repeated twice*).
La illaha illa-lah.
"Nothing deserves to be worshiped except Allah."

There was more, but for now this was enough. In the weeks that followed, sitting in the small circle with Muhammad as the imam, I learned the pronunciation and the ceremonies that went with prayers. Then one day I was invited to join the brothers as a follower of the true religion of Islam. I accepted, and after a short ceremony I took the hand of brotherhood and was given the name of Hussein Afmit Ben Hassen. I learned to pray in Arabic. I learned the respect for the Holy Quran by never holding it with my left hand, which was only to cleanse myself after making ca-ca.

I learned many things, because it involved me. I became curious about everything human. Though I didn't remain a Muslim after my eventual release from the big jail, I never forgot one thing that Muhammad said, for I believed it too: "No matter what a man's color or race he has a need of dignity and he'll go anywhere, become anything, or do anything to get it—anything."

8. Elijah Muhammad, "What the Muslims Want" and "What the Muslims Believe," from *Message to the Blackman in America* (1965)

The Nation of Islam's platforms were published on a weekly basis throughout the 1960s and 1970s, often on the back page of the Muhammad Speaks *newspaper. While many of Elijah Muhammad's numerological theories, doctrines of the apocalypse, and interpretations of the Bible and the Qur'an were difficult to comprehend without study, these documents presented some of the basic teach-*

ings of the Nation of Islam in an easy to understand format. Sharply dressed men wearing suits and bow ties hawked Muhammad Speaks *on the streets of black America and even door to door, spreading the good news of this program to mentally resurrect the "so-called Negro" in the wilderness of North America. Whether one's concern was religious, political, economic, or social, one of these positions was bound to be appealing. And while the Nation of Islam rejected the Christian civil rights movement led by Martin Luther King Jr., these statements make clear that the Nation of Islam understood well the battle cry for freedom and the hope for black enfranchisement during this era of American history.*

What Do the Muslims Want?

1. We want freedom. We want a full and complete freedom.

2. We want justice. Equal justice under the law. We want justice applied equally to all, regardless of creed, or class, or color.

3. We want equality of opportunity. We want equal membership in society with the best in civilized society.

4. We want our people in America whose parents or grandparents were descendants from slaves, to be allowed to establish a separate state or territory of their own . . . either on this continent or elsewhere. We believe that our former slave masters are obliged to provide such land and that the area must be fertile and minerally rich. We believe that our former slave masters are obligated to maintain and supply our needs in this separate territory for the next 20 to 25 years . . . until we are able to produce our own needs.

Since we cannot get along with them in peace and equality, after giving them 400 years of our sweat and blood, and receiving in return some of the worst treatment human beings have ever experienced, we believe our contributions to this land and the suffering forced upon us by white America, justifies our demand for complete separation in a state or territory of our own.

5. We want freedom for all Believers of Islam now held in federal prisons. We want freedom for all black men and women now under death sentence in innumerable prisons in the North, as well as the South.

We want every black man and woman to have the freedom to accept or reject being separated from the slave-masters' children and establish a land of their own.

We know that the above plan for the solution of the black and white conflict is the best and only answer to the problem between two people.

6. We want an immediate end to the police brutality and mob attacks against the so-called Negro throughout the United States.

We believe that the Federal government should intercede to see that black men and women tried in white courts receive justice in accordance with the laws of the land, or allow us to build a new nation for ourselves, dedicated to justice, freedom and liberty.

7. As long as we are not allowed to establish a state or territory of our own, we demand not only equal justice under the laws of the United States, but equal employment opportunities—NOW!

We do not believe that after 400 years of free or nearly free labor, sweat and blood, which has helped America become rich and powerful, that so many thousands of black people should have to subsist on relief or charity or live in poor houses.

8. We want the government of the United States to exempt our people from ALL taxation as long as we are deprived of equal justice under the laws of the land.

9. We want equal education—but separate schools up to 16 for boys and 18 for girls on the condition that the girls be sent to women's colleges and universities. We want all black children, educated, taught and trained by their own teachers.

Under such schooling systems we believe we will make a better nation of people. The United States government should provide, free, all necessary textbooks and equipment, schools, and college buildings. The Muslim teachers shall be left free to teach and train their people in the way of righteousness, decency and self respect.

10. We believe that intermarriage or race mixing should be prohibited. We want the religion of Islam taught without hindrance or suppression.

These are some of the things that we, the Muslims, want for our people in North America.

[What Do Muslims Believe?]

1. We believe in the One God Whose proper Name is Allah.

2. We believe in the Holy Qur-an and in the Scriptures of all the Prophets of God.

3. We believe in the truth of the Bible, but we believe that it has been tampered with and must be reinterpreted so that mankind will not be snared by the falsehoods that have been added to it.

4. We believe in Allah's Prophets and the Scriptures they brought to the people.

5. We believe in the resurrection of the dead—not in the physical resurrection but in mental resurrection. We believe that the so-called Negroes are most in need of mental resurrection; therefore, they will be resurrected first.

Furthermore, we believe we are the people of God's choice, as it has been written that God would choose the rejected and the despised. We can find no other persons fitting this description in these last days more than the so-called Negroes in America. We believe in the resurrection of the righteous.

6. We believe in the judgment. We believe this first judgment will take place in America.

7. We believe this is the time in history for the separation of the so-called Negroes and so-called white Americans. We believe the black men should be freed in name as well as in fact. By this we mean that he should be freed from the names imposed upon him by his former slave-masters. Names which identified him as being the slave of a slave-master. We believe that if we are free indeed, we should go in our own people's names—the black people of the earth.

8. We believe in justice for all whether in God or not. We believe as others that we are due equal justice as human beings. We believe in equality—as a nation—of equals. We do not believe that we are equal with our slave master in the status of "Freed slaves."

We recognize and respect American citizens as independent people and we respect their laws which govern this nation.

9. We believe that the offer of integration is hypocritical and is made by those who are trying to deceive the black people into believing that their 400-year-old open enemies of freedom, justice and equality are, all of a sudden, their "friends." Furthermore, we believe that such deception is intended to prevent black people from realizing that the time in history has arrived for the separation from the whites of this nation.

If the white people are truthful about their professed friendship toward the so-called Negro, they can prove it by dividing up America with their slaves.

We do not believe that America will ever be able to furnish jobs for her own millions of unemployed, in addition to jobs for the 20,000,000 black people as well.

10. We believe that we who declared ourselves to be righteous Muslims should not participate in wars which take the lives of humans. We do not believe this nation should force us to take part in such wars, for we have nothing to gain from it unless America agrees to give us the necessary territory wherein we may have something to fight for.

11. We believe our women should be respected and protected as the women of their nationalities are respected and protected.

12. We believe that Allah (God) appeared in the Person of Master Fard Muhammad, July, 1930—the long-awaited "Messiah" of the Christians and the "Mahdi" of the Muslims.

We believe further and lastly that Allah is God and besides HIM there is no God and He will bring about a universal government of peace wherein we all can live in peace together.

9. Malcolm X, Interview with *Al-Muslimoon* (1965)

One of Malcolm X's last press interviews was given to Al-Muslimoon, *a journal published by the Islamic Center of Geneva, Switzerland. Responding to a written questionnaire, he completed his answers to the journal's questions on February 20, 1965, one day before his assassination. The interview appeared in the journal first in Arabic translation and then in an English-language edition in September 1965. Malcolm had visited the Islamic Center's director, Said Ramadan, in 1964, the year of Malcolm's famous pilgrimage to Mecca and his training as a Muslim missionary by the World Muslim League. Ramadan, son-in-law of Muslim Brothers' founder Hasan al-Banna, was one of several people who helped to establish the league with the support of Saudi Arabia. Like other members of the Muslim Brothers, Ramadan strongly asserted the view that Islam was both a religion and a state, the solution to all of humanity's economic, cultural, and political problems, including the oppression of black persons in the United States. In his written questions to Malcolm X, Ramadan challenged Malcolm's focus on black racial identity and liberation, asserting that the conversion of Americans to Islam would solve such problems. Malcolm X disagreed and insisted that while he would always be a devout Muslim, his first duty in life was to work for the political liberation of all*

African Americans in the United States. The interview also explains the origi-
nal mythologies of the Nation of Islam, doctrines that are considered heretical
by most other Muslims in the United States and the world, and Malcolm offers
what many scholars would dub a very partisan history of Elijah Muhammad's
Nation of Islam. Finally, Malcolm asks for more financial support of Muslim
missionary efforts in the United States, calls for education reform and women's
uplift in the Muslim world, and criticizes Zionism, the modern movement to
establish and support a Jewish national home in Palestine.

QUESTION: The Black Muslim Movement is one of the most controversial
movements in the United States. Having been for a considerable period
its main organizer and most prominent spokesman, could you kindly
give us some concise firsthand picture of the background of this movement, its history, its main ethics, and its actual strength?

MALCOLM X: The Black Muslim movement (which calls itself officially
the Lost-Found Nation of Islam) was founded in 1930 in Detroit, Michigan, by a Mr. Fard Muhammad, who claimed he had been born in
Mecca, and that he had come to America for the sole purpose of teaching the supreme secrets of Islam to the Black Americans exclusively,
who he said were actually the people referred to in the Old Testament
of the Christian scriptures as the "lost sheep." Elijah Muhammad was
one of the first to be converted from among these "lost sheep," and
Elijah taught us to refer to him as "the first begotten," or the "lamb of
God." Elijah also taught us that Mr. Fard was Allah in the flesh, and
that this Mr. Fard (God in person) had been born in Mecca for the sole
purpose of coming to America and teaching this secret supreme wisdom of Islam to the American Blacks, and by this he meant that this
secret wisdom of Islam had been hidden even from the eyes and ears of
the wisest and holiest men in Mecca and had been preserved specifically to be revealed by Allah himself in person to the American Blacks
at the "end of time." Elijah said that the real supreme of devils had been
artificially created by a mad Black scientist [Yacub] six thousand years
ago. They would rule the world for six thousand years and then be destroyed at the "end of their time" by the Blacks. He said the whites were
devils by nature and the Blacks were gods, and Judgment Day means
only that at the "end of time" the gods (Blacks) would destroy the entire white race (devils) and then establish a paradise (nation) on this
earth ruled forever by the Blacks (gods).

Elijah taught us that Mecca was a symbol of heaven itself. He said that since whites were devils by nature they could not accept Islam, and therefore no whites could be Muslims. He taught us that Mecca was forbidden to all nonbelievers, and because [of that] whites could never enter the paradise (heaven) that would be established by the gods (Blacks) here on this earth after the destruction of the whites. He taught that "doomsday" refers to the "doom of the white race."

Mr. Fard taught in Detroit from 1930 until 1934 and then he disappeared. It was only after Fard's disappearance that Elijah then began teaching that Fard was Allah himself, that he had returned to heaven, but would come back again to destroy the white race and America and then would take all the American Negroes (lost sheep) who had become Muslims back to heaven (Mecca) with him, and that we would then rule the entire world from there with an iron hand. He never did teach us that we would return to Africa. He shrewdly ridiculed the culture and the features of the Africans.

From 1934 until 1952 Elijah could only gather a handful of people who would follow him, which by 1952 numbered less than four hundred, most of whom were old people whose education was limited. No Arab or Asian Muslims were ever permitted in his temples or places of worship. In fact, his doctrine is as anti-Arab and anti-Asian as it is anti-white.

Until 1963 his followers practiced iron discipline, mainly because all of us believed in the infallibility and high moral character of Elijah himself, but when his own son Wallace Muhammad exposed Elijah Muhammad as a very immoral man who had deceived and seduced seven of his young secretaries, fathering at least ten illegitimate children by them, the moral discipline of the entire movement decayed and fell apart.

From 1952 until 1963 over one million American Blacks have accepted Elijah's distorted version of Islam. But today he has less than five thousand actual followers. Despite the fact that many have left him, no matter how disillusioned they have become even after learning the truth about his personal moral weakness and the fallacies of his doctrine, still they never return to the church, they never return to Christianity.

QUESTION: What were the reasons behind Elijah Muhammad being against you immediately after the assassination of Kennedy, and then behind your breakaway from the movement as a whole?

MALCOLM X: Elijah Muhammad allowed himself to become insanely jealous of my own popularity, which went even beyond his own followers and into the non-Muslim community, while his own prestige and influence was limited largely among his immediate followers. While I was still in the movement and blind to his faults by my own uncompromising faith in him, I always thought the jealously and envy which I saw constant signs of was stemming mainly and only from his immediate family, and it was quite shocking to me whenever members of his own family would warn me that it was their father (Elijah Muhammad himself) who had become almost insane with jealously.

When Elijah learned that his son Wallace had told me how his father had seduced his teenage secretaries (by telling them that he was the prophet Muhammad, and making each of them think she was to be his favorite and most beautiful wife Aisha), Elijah feared that my position of influence in the movement was a threat to him and his other children who were now controlling the movement and benefiting from its wealth. Because they feared my popularity with the rank-and-file Muslims, they were careful about any immediate or open move to curtail my authority without good cause, so they patiently waited until they felt that my statement about the late President Kennedy's assassination would give them the proper public support in any kind of action they'd take to curtail or remove me.

At the time they announced I was to be suspended and silenced for ninety days, they had already set in motion the machinery to have me completely ousted from the movement, and Elijah Muhammad himself had already given the order to have me killed because he feared I would expose to his followers the secret of his extreme immorality.

QUESTION: Should these differences be of a basically ethical nature and on essential matters of faith? What, in your opinion, are the prospects of radical reform within Elijah Muhammad's followers now or in the future?

MALCOLM X: No, Elijah Muhammad himself will never change. At least I doubt it. He's too old, dogmatic, and has already gone too far in teaching that he is a greater prophet than Muhammad Ibn Abdullah. He is too proud to confess to his followers now that he has deliberately taught them falsehood. But as his well-meaning followers become exposed to the true religion of Islam, they themselves will leave him and practice Islam as it should be. This is why it is so important for centers to be established immediately where true Islam can be taught. And these centers should be located at this time primarily in Black communities, because at this particular time the American Blacks are the ones showing the most interest in true religion.

QUESTION: Have any of Elijah Muhammad's followers left the movement with you, and do you think that your breakaway from the movement has affected its main body in any considerable way?

MALCOLM X: Yes, many of Elijah's followers could not go along with his present "immorality," and this opened their eyes to the other falsities of his doctrine. But we have not been able to regroup and reorganize them as we should. It takes finance, and we left all treasuries and properties with Elijah, and he uses this wealth that we amassed for him to fight us and keep us from getting organized. He is fanatically opposed to American Negroes hearing true Islam, and has ordered his own well-meaning followers to cripple or kill any one of his followers who wants to leave him to follow true Islam. He fears that true Islam will expose and destroy the power of his false teachings.

QUESTION: Do you plan to just stop at voicing your opposition against Elijah Muhammad and his group or do you have any course of action in mind towards establishing some new organization in the field? If so, on what basis and for what specific near or distant goals?

MALCOLM X: With what little finance we could raise, we have founded the Muslim Mosque, Inc., with headquarters here in Harlem. Our sole interest is to help undo the distorted image we have helped spread about Islam. Our mosque also is for those who want to learn how to live the life of a true Muslim.

However, since we live as Black Americans in a white racist society, we have established another organization which is non-religious, known as the Organization of Afro-American Unity (OAAU), and which is designed to unite all Black Americans regardless of their religious affiliation into a group that can fight against American racism and the economic, political, and social evils that stem from white racism here in this American society. With the Muslim Mosque we are teaching our people a better way of life, and with the OAAU we are fighting on an even broader level for complete respect and recognition as human beings for all Black Americans, and we are ready and willing to use any means necessary to see that this goal is reached.

QUESTION: What have you been actually doing since you broke away from Elijah Muhammad's movement?

MALCOLM X: I have traveled to the Middle East and Africa twice since leaving Elijah Muhammad in March of 1964, mainly to get a better understanding of Islam and the African countries, and in turn to give the Muslim world a better understanding of problems facing those of us here in America who are trying to become Muslims. Also, in Africa to give our people there a better understanding of the problems confronting black Americans in our struggle for human rights.

QUESTION: Is it true that even after your breakaway from Elijah Muhammad you still hold the Black color as a main base and dogma for your drive under the banner of liberation in the United States? How could a man of your spirit, intellect, and worldwide outlook fail to see in Islam its main characteristic, from its earliest days, as a message that confirms beyond doubt the ethnological oneness and quality of all races, thus striking at the very root of the monstrosity of racial discrimination. Endless are the texts of the Qur'an [Koran] and prophetic sayings to this effect and nothing would testify to that more than the historic fact that heterogeneous races, nations, and linguistic entities have always mingled peacefully in the homeland.

MALCOLM X: As a Black American I do feel that my first responsibility is to my twenty-two million fellow Black Americans who suffer the same indignities because of their color as I do. I don't believe my own personal problem is ever solved until the problem is solved for all twenty-two million of us.

Much to my dismay, until now the Muslim world has seemed to ignore the problem of the Black American, and most Muslims who come here from the Muslim world have concentrated more effort in trying to convert white Americans than Black Americans.

(*Note by Malcolm X to* Al-Muslimoon *editors*: I had arrived back in the States from London at 4:30 p.m. on February 13, and had worked until 12:30—just after midnight—on the above. I got very tired at midnight, decided to leave the above pages in the typewriter and finish early in the morning. I retired at 12:30 and exploding bombs that were thrown into my home by would-be murderers rocked me and my wife and four baby daughters from sleep at 2:30 a.m. Only Allah saved us from death. This is only one of the many examples of the extremes to which the enemies of Islam will go to see that true Islam is never established on these shores. And they know that if I was so successful in helping to spread Elijah Muhammad's distorted version of Islam, it is even easier for me to organize the spread of true Islam.)

There are two groups of Muslims in America: (1) those who were born in the Muslim world and migrated here, and were already Muslims when they arrived here. If these total over 200,000, they have not succeeded in converting 1,000 Americans to Islam. (2) American-born persons who have been converted to Islam are 98 percent Black Americans. Up to now it has been only the Black American who has shown interest even in *Sunni* Islam.

If a student of agriculture has sense enough to concentrate his farming efforts on the most fertile area of his farm, I should think the Muslim world would realize that the most fertile area for Islam in the West is the Black American. This in no way implies discrimination or racialism, but rather shows that we are intelligent enough to plant the good seed of Islam where it will grow best; later on we can "doctor up" or fertilize the less-fertile areas, but only after our crop is already well planted in the heart and mind of these Black Americans who already show great signs of receptiveness. Was it not Bilal, the Black Ethiopian, who was the first to receive the seed of Islam from the prophet himself in Arabia 1,400 years ago?

QUESTION: Now that you have visited and revisited many Muslim countries, what are your major impressions regarding Islam and Muslims both in the present and in the future?

MALCOLM X: We are standing at the threshold of the nuclear age. Education is a must, especially in this highly technical era. In my opinion, Muslim religious leaders have not stressed the importance of education to the Muslim communities, especially in African countries. Thus when African countries become independent, the non-Muslim areas have the higher degree of educated Africans who are thus the ones best qualified to occupy the newly created positions in government. Muslim religious leaders of today need a more well-rounded type of education and then they will be able to stress the importance of education to the masses, but ofttimes when these religious leaders themselves have very limited knowledge, education, and understanding sometimes they purposely keep their own people also ignorant in order to continue their own personal position of leadership. They keep the people narrow-minded because they themselves are narrow-minded.

In every Middle East or African country I have visited, I noticed the country is as "advanced" as its women are, or as backward as its women. By this I mean, in areas where the women have been pushed into the background and kept without education, the whole area or country is just as backward, uneducated, and "underdeveloped." Where the women are encouraged to get education and play a more active role in the all-around affairs of the community and the country, the entire people are more active, more enlightened, and more progressive. Thus, in my opinion, the Muslim religious leaders of today must reevaluate and spell out with clarity the Muslim position on education in general and education in the Muslim world. An old African proverb states: "Educate a man and you educate an individual; educate a woman and you educate an entire family."

QUESTION: Africa seems to have captured most of your attention and eager concern. Why? And now that you have visited almost every part of it, where do you think Islam actually stands? And what, in your opinion, could be done to save it from both the brainlessness of many, or rather most of those who are considered to be champions of its cause, and from the malicious, resourceful alliance of Zionism, atheism, and religious fanaticism against Islam?

MALCOLM X: I regard Africa as my fatherland. I am primarily interested in seeing it become completely free of outside political and economic influence that has dominated and exploited it. Africa, because of its strategic position, faces a real crisis. The colonial vultures have no intention of giving it up without a fight. Their chief weapon is still "divide and conquer." In East Africa there is a strong anti-Asian feeling being nourished among the Africans. In West Africa there is a strong anti-Arab feeling. Where there are Arabs or Asians there is a strong anti-Muslim feeling.

These hostilities are not initiated by the above-mentioned people who are involved. They have nothing to benefit from fighting among themselves at this point. Those who benefit most are the former colonial masters who have now supplanted the hated colonialism and imperialism with Zionism. The Zionists have outstripped all other interest groups in the present struggle for our mother continent. They use such a benevolent, philanthropic approach that it is quite difficult for their victims to see through their schemes. Zionism is even more dangerous than communism because it is made more acceptable and is thus more destructively effective.

Since the Arab image is almost inseparable from the image of Islam, the Arab world has a multiple responsibility that it must live up to. Since Islam is a religion of brotherhood and unity, those who take the lead in expounding this religion are duty-bound to set the highest example of brotherhood and unity. It is imperative that Cairo and Mecca (the Supreme Council of Islamic Affairs and the Muslim World League) have a religious "summit" conference and show a greater degree of concern and responsibility for the present plight of the Muslim world, or other forces will rise up in this present generation of young, forward-thinking Muslims and the "power centers" will be taken from the hands of those that they are now in and placed elsewhere. *Allah can easily do this.*

THREE

American Islam After 1965

Racial, Ethnic, and Religious Diversities

IN 1965, President Lyndon B. Johnson signed a new immigration bill that reversed the 1924 law severely restricting nonwhite immigration to the United States. As a result, thousands of people from Latin America, Asia, and Africa began to arrive in the United States. Between 1965 and 1990, more than 800,000 people would come from South Asia alone. Many of the South Asian Muslim immigrants were successful doctors, engineers, and academicians. They changed the face of American Islam, becoming one of the most financially successful immigrant groups in the history of the United States. Moving to the suburbs, many of these South Asian American Muslims, along with immigrants from the Middle East, established their own mosques and schools, far away from the inner-city mosques frequented by many African American Muslims. There are many exceptions, but one might argue that in the period after 1965, American Muslims, like American Christians, remained divided by both class and race, living in segregated neighborhoods, attending segregated schools, and marrying persons of the same racial and class group.

But as we have seen already, social division in religious communities need not dampen their vitality and creativity. Indeed, by any quantitative measure—the number of Islamic organizations, mosques, and schools—institutional Islam grew by leaps and bounds. American Muslim artists, writers, and thinkers became better known, and Muslims began to make an impact on American society as successful businesspeople, philanthropists, and increasingly, politicians. The number of practitioners increased. In addition to all the new Muslim immigrants, more indigenous Americans than ever were practicing Islam. Some white American converts were attracted to what they saw as Islam's rational theology, many liked the mystical elements of Islam, and still others, especially women, became Muslim after marrying an Arab or South Asian immigrant. On the East and West coasts and in the Southwest, Mexican Americans and Puerto Rican Americans joined the ranks of the believers. Many felt that in becoming Muslim, they were reclaiming a part of their heritage, stolen when the Roman Catholic monarchs of Spain banned Islam in Iberia and their Latin American possessions after 1492. By this time, African Americans were not only converting to Islam; they were also raising their children to be Muslims. Islam was the only faith that some of these second- and third-generation African American Muslims had ever known.

The varieties of Islamic religion practiced in the United States during this period reflected the remarkable racial and ethnic diversity of the American Muslim community. It was during this time, for example, that Shi'a (or Shi'i) Islam became institutionally established in America. Shi'a Muslims constitute approximately 10 to 15 percent, perhaps more, of Muslims worldwide. They trace their origins to an historical disagreement over the question of who is entitled to lead the Muslim community in the absence of the Prophet Muhammad. Generally emphasizing the right of the *family* of the Prophet Muhammad to lead Muslims, most Shi'a believe that Ali, the son-in-law and cousin of the Prophet Muhammad, was the Prophet's rightful heir. Shi'a Muslims refer to these leaders, all of whom must be descendants of the Prophet Muhammad through the line of Ali, as Imams (which, in its generic form, means "leader" or the "one in front"). The largest group of Shi'a Muslims in the world are the Twelver (or Ithna 'Ashari) Shi'a, who generally believe that the twelfth of these Imams went into hiding in 873 AD but remains on earth and still secretly guides his followers. Many also posit that this Imam will reappear at the end of the world to rule with peace and justice.

While at least some Shi'a Muslims had arrived in America decades before as part of the first wave of Syrian-Lebanese migration, the period after 1965 saw a dramatic increase in the number of Shi'a Muslims, many of whom were professionals and students from Iran and Lebanon. Other Shi'a Muslims arrived as refugees. During the long Lebanese civil war from 1975 to 1990, and later, during the Gulf War of 1990–1991 and the Iraq War of 2003, many Shi'a Muslims sought to escape the violence and turmoil of their home countries. They were a diverse group. The Iranian Shi'a were generally Persian speakers, and some of them were completely secular Muslims. The Lebanese and Iraqis were generally Arabic speakers, though their ethnic and linguistic identities also set them apart from one another. Moreover, the Shi'a Muslim community was divided by political ideology. After the Iranian revolution of 1979, in which the Ayatollah Khomeini seized power from the U.S.-backed Shah, many American Shi'a expressed solidarity with his goals. Others wanted nothing to do with Khomeini and what they feared would be a backlash against them because of the conflict between the Iranian and U.S. governments. During this time, as refugees continued to arrive in various American cities, especially around Detroit, mosques sometimes split and new mosques were created to accommodate the increased number of believers and their differing ideologies.

Sufism, the mystical branch of Islam, also grew and became more diverse during this period. Though Sufis had been a part of the American Muslim scene since Turks, Albanians, and Punjabis immigrated to the United States, a larger number came after 1965. Sufi orders, called *tariqas*, became more numerous and popular. For example, Sri Lankan Sufi master M. R. Bawa Muhaiyaddeen, who had been trained in a Sufi *tariqa* called the Qadiriyya, arrived and established a community of followers in Philadelphia, Pennsylvania. A number of white Americans began to turn to Sufism as a religious path. Some of those who claimed to be Sufis did not label themselves Muslims. Others, however, sought to follow Sufi ideas in tandem with foundational Islamic practices of piety like the daily prayers and fasting during Ramadan. Bawa Muhaiyaddeen, for example, slowly led his followers in Philadelphia toward the five pillars of Islamic practice. According to one follower, he first emphasized the spiritual nature of Islamic religion and the teachings of Sufism. Then he discussed the need to observe the basic rituals of prayer and fasting.

By the turn of the millennium, American Sufism was a cross-class and multiethnic phenomenon. Some Sufi masters created their own organizations, as Pir Inayat Khan, founder of Sufi Order in the West, had done decades before. Samuel L. Lewis, for example, was the inspiration behind Sufi Ruhaniat International, an organization that welcomed all religious seekers of inner truth—whether they found their inspiration in Muhammad, Christ, Buddha, or the Divine Mother. Other Sufi leaders arrived as representatives of older Sufi orders like the Naqshbandiyya and Mawlawiyah. All of these groups catered to a variety of tastes in the United States, and their memberships sometimes reified and at other times challenged the racial and class divisions of American Muslim communities. Many of Bawa Muhaiyyadeen's followers celebrated the interracial nature of their community, for example. But the Tijaniyya, a West African Sufi order central to Senegalese society, appealed mainly to African American Muslims, whom one might find at a Sufi lodge in Brooklyn, New York, engaged in the types of *dhikr*, rituals of meditation and praise for God and the prophet, practiced by their African brothers and sisters across the Atlantic.

The Sunni Muslim community became more diverse than ever. During the 1970s, for example, an increasing number of *imams* (prayer leaders) and preachers, trained and funded by the same missionaries who sponsored Malcolm X's second visit to Saudi Arabia, began to serve as leaders of various immigrant Muslim communities in the United States. As the price of oil rose after the 1973 and 1974 OPEC oil embargos, various Arab governments and Arab citizens also funded an increasing number of Muslim institutions and Islamic centers in the United States. These financial supporters were successful missionaries for a socially conservative form of Islam that bore a great deal of resemblance to what one might call "family-values" Christianity and Judaism. Some Americans called it Islamic fundamentalism.

Many of these missionaries and their followers were devoted to a Salafi interpretation of Islam. According to most scholars of religion, the Salafi movement, though at first glance "traditional," is a thoroughly modern and reformist version of Islam. While Salafi Muslims are a diverse group, they tend to believe that the practice of Islam has been corrupted since the time of the Prophet and the pious ancestors, or *salaf.* They wish to return to what they see as the original and uncorrupted teachings of Islam and therefore dismiss or question the legitimacy of many Islamic traditions. Some Salafi Muslims see Sufism as an impermissible addition to the corpus of Islamic thought and practice and often accuse Sufis of heresy. Furthermore, Salafis often reject on principle the notion that there can be several different interpretations of the *shar'ia*, or Islamic law and ethics; for many of them, there is only one straight path, clearly laid out in the Qur'an and the Sunna of the Prophet. Some Salafi Muslims are exclusivists—meaning in this case that they think they have a monopoly on religious truth—but it is important to note that many of them are peaceful exclusivists.

The American Muslims who were influenced by the missionaries and other Muslims devoted to a Salafi interpretation of Islam were a diverse lot. Salafi Islam was not only attractive to immigrants but also to indigenous Muslims. Some Salafi Muslims stressed the importance of personal piety; others advocated a political form of Islam that, following the philosophy of the Egyptian activist Sayyid Qutb, called for the establishment of Islamic political authority over all the earth. Salafi Muslims may have shared certain ideas, but they often differed on others. For example, Yahya Abdul-Kareem, an African American leader of the Sunni Islamic movement called Darul Islam, declared in the late 1970s that Muslims should avoid participation in American politics and eschew friendships with all Americans, non-Muslim and Muslim alike, if they did not practice the "correct" form of Islam. But his group never stressed the same degree of opposition to Sufism or traditional interpretations of Islamic law and ethics that some Salafis did.

Salafi Islam was not the only form of Sunni Islam in the United States that grew in the 1970s. In 1975, thousands of African American Muslims proclaimed themselves "orthodox" or Sunni Muslims after Wallace D. Muhammad (b. 1933) assumed the leadership of the Nation of Islam after the death of his father, Elijah Muhammad. Wallace D. Muhammad's "Second Resurrection" of the Nation led to a sudden realignment of thousands of black Muslims with Sunni Islamic tradition. Shortly after his ascension, Wallace Muhammad began to dismantle the racialist version of Islam that his father had worked so long to construct. He reinterpreted and ultimately rejected the teachings that W. D. Fard was God in the flesh and that white people were devils. Instead, he encouraged followers to practice the daily prayers, to make the *hajj* to Mecca, and to fast during the lunar month of Ramadan (rather than at Yuletide, as his father had instructed). He renamed the organization, calling it the World Community of al-Islam in the West and, eventually, the American Muslim Mission. He even introduced American flags into movement temples and established an American patriotism day. Finally, he decentralized authority in the movement, empowering local communities to chart their own course or, as some might put it, to fend for themselves.

Not all followers agreed with such dramatic changes, however. The most prominent was Minister Louis Farrakhan (b. 1933), the former national spokesman for Elijah Muhammad. In the late 1970s, he publicly stated his disagreements with the new leader and reconstituted a version of the old Nation of Islam. Minister Farrakhan positioned himself as the true heir to Elijah Muhammad and eventually purchased Elijah Muhammad's old mansion and other former Nation of Islam properties. In the 1990s, Minister Farrakhan incorporated more and more Sunni Islamic traditions into his new Nation of Islam and officially reconciled with Wallace Muhammad, but he also remained devoted to many of the old teachings of Elijah Muhammad. Just as noteworthy, Farrakhan, who has been strongly linked to anti-Semitism in the past, became a spokesperson for interfaith dialogue, interracial harmony, and social justice.

Other heirs to Elijah Muhammad's teachings included the Nation of Gods and Earths, also known as the Five Percenters. Begun by Clarence 13X around 1963, this group has become well known not only among urban African Americans but also among thousands of rap and hip-hop fans who can hear the group's themes in music by the Wu Tang Clan, Nas, Brand Nubian, Eric B. and Rakim, and others. Offering a variation on original Nation of Islam teachings, the Nation of Gods and Earths teaches that only 5 percent of humanity has true self-knowledge, namely that they are, or are like, Gods. In addition, the Five Percenters often stress the importance of black nationalism, economic self-determination, and patriarchy. Few Muslims would recognize the Five Percenters as a legitimate Islamic group, and many Five Percenters want nothing to do with Muslims. Still, the Nation of God and Earths evidences the powerful allure of Islamic symbols and themes within African American cultures.

The existence of the Five Percenters serves as a useful reminder that in attempting to present an inclusive vision of Islam and Muslims in the United States, this chapter cannot hope to interpret this period of American Muslim history by employing only one or two dominant lines of thought. To be sure, there were watershed moments in this period of American history that affected many, perhaps most, Muslims in the United States. Geopolitical events like the Iranian Revolution of 1979, the Gulf Wars, and above all 9/11 were crucibles in which images of Islam and Muslims lodged themselves into the imagination of non-Muslims. Many Muslims, especially those who "looked Arab," came under scrutiny, suspicion, and surveillance. But as important at these developments were in affecting in how most non-Muslim Americans viewed Islam and Muslims, even they do not tell the whole story of Muslims in the United States from 1965 until the present. There is no lens large enough to capture the sheer variety of American Muslim life in these decades. Instead, this chapter embraces the religious, ethnic, and racial diversity of American Muslim communities after 1965, giving voice to white, black, and brown Muslims, to Sunnis, Shi'as, Sufis, the Nation of Islam, and Five Percenters alike.

1. Muhammad Raheem Bawa Muhaiyaddeen, "The Inner Qur'an," from *Islam and World Peace* (1987)

In 1971, M. R. Bawa Muhaiyaddeen, a Sri Lankan Muslim mystic, established a Sufi fellowship in Philadelphia, Pennsylvania. The ethnically diverse group catered not only to Muslim immigrants but to all religious seekers interested in "contemplating the truth and unity of God." Muhaiyaddeen, who died in 1986, gradually introduced his non-Muslim students to the Qur'an, the hadith, *and Sufi understandings of the Divine. In 1981, he directed his followers to begin observing* salat, *the prescribed prayers recited five times a day. The leader, whose followers live in the United States, Great Britain, and other countries, was a tireless advocate for peaceful coexistence and religious pluralism, affirming the essential goodness of all mainstream religious traditions. He insisted the Islamic idea of jihad could never justify the killing of others for personal or nationalistic gain; "real holy war," he said, "is an inner war" against "the darkness of the mind and the veils within the innermost heart." Real peace, he said, could be found only in God. In the excerpt below, the shaikh offers a mystical reading of the Qur'an that views the book not only as an ethical guide for one's life, but also as the light of God, meant to be fully imbibed through deep contemplation. To have an intimate relationship with God, said the Sufi leader, one must realize this inner meaning of the Qur'an.*

I seek refuge in Allah from the evils of the accursed Satan.

In the name of Allah, Most Merciful, Most Compassionate. May all the peace, the beneficence, and the blessings of God be upon you.

Brothers and sisters in Islam, no matter what changes occur throughout the ages, the Qur'an is one thing that never changes. It is immutable. It offers an explanation appropriate for every period of time and for every level of understanding. All the meanings it contains could not be written down even if all the oceans of the world were made into ink and all the trees were made into pens.

To comprehend the Qur'an, first we must establish our absolute faith, certitude, and determination; then we must acquire wisdom; and finally we must delve deep inside and study it from within. If we look into the depths of the Qur'an, we will find the complete never-ending wealth and grace of Almighty God. We will find the light of Allah, the resplendence of Allah. We will not find racial or religious prejudices, battles, or fighting of any kind. We will find only the benevolence of all the universes.

The Qur'an appeared as the beginning, the emergence of creation . . . , as the eternal life, the emergence of the soul . . . , as the food, the nourishment for all creations . . . , as the innermost heart . . . , as the beauty of the face which is a reflection of the beauty of the heart . . . , and as the plenitude, the light which became completeness within Allah and then emerged.

The Qur'an is a treasure which continually speaks to our faith. Its verses were sent to Muhammad one by one, according to the needs of the people, the difficulties they were undergoing, and the questions they asked. These verses and chapters were sent to bring clarity to man, from the time he appears as a fetus, from the *mim* [pronounced *meem*, the Arabic letter resembling a sperm] to the moment he reaches the shore of the hereafter. They cleanse man stage by stage. Whatever state he is in at one time of prayer, the Qur'an explains the state he should achieve by the next prayer time. In this way, the Qur'an lifts man up, causing his wisdom, his beauty, and his divine knowledge to grow little by little.

The Prophet said, "Even though I depart from the world, I leave you the Qur'an. That is your evidence. Please keep it close to you. The Qur'an will be a teacher and a learned one to the innermost heart." That is why its verses were sent to mankind. Step by step the Qur'an elevates man; chapter by chapter, it cuts away all the things within him that need to be discarded. That is the purpose of the Qur'an—to eliminate the four hundred trillion, ten thousand degenerate qualities and actions which oppose the truth of God, and to show man how to develop, how to beautify and improve himself. The Qur'an has the capacity to cut away this birth, to cast out arrogance, karma, illusion, and the sexual energies of the three sons of illusion. It can dispel man's love for earth, sensual pleasures, and gold. It can drive away lust, anger, miserliness, attachment, bigotry, envy, theft, murder, falsehood, and the effects of intoxicants.

To rid himself of these evil qualities, a true human being must sacrifice and purify his heart for Allah. He must perform the ritual sacrifice called *qurban* [here meaning the ritual sacrifice of one's inner "animal"] for the sake of truth and justice, for the sake of righteous action, duty, equality, peacefulness, unity, and for the love of the one human family. If he does this, he will acquire the qualities, actions, and beauty of Allah. This is the state which the Qur'an depicts, the path of perfect purity. This is Allah's kingdom, and He is the only One who protects it, conducts its affairs, and rules over it with total justice. Anyone who acts according to that justice and understands Allah in completeness becomes His slave. Such a man owns nothing of his own, and so Allah protects him and looks after all his needs.

If a man progresses to this state of purity, if he succeeds in cutting away all these evil qualities, then he becomes a true believer, living for nothing other than Allah, and having nothing other than Allah in his thoughts or intentions. He does not concern himself with seeing or hearing others, because no one else exists for him. He sees nothing other than Allah. He speaks to no one other than Allah. He has closed himself off to the sight and sound of everything but Allah. That is why he is called an *ummi*, an unlettered one. And because he has no words of his own, Allah's words and sounds come through him. He becomes the *hadith* which explains the inner and outer aspects of Allah's revelations. In that state, his body or form is the holy book and his innermost heart is the *Umm al-Qur'an*. What does *Umm* mean? It means mother. The mother who raises the true believer is the *Umm al-Qur'an*, the mother of justice and faith, the mother of man's wisdom. The *Umm al-Qur'an* is the essence of the Qur'an, the eye of the Qur'an.

If man will only open that eye, he will know Allah, and knowing Allah, he will hear only His sounds and His words. This was the state of the Prophet, *Muhammad al-Ummi*. He was unlearned, and therefore, the words that he received could only have come through God's revelation. Allah explained to Muhammad the meaning of *Iman-Islam*, prayer, worship, and everything He had revealed to the earlier prophets. Through Muhammad, His final Prophet, Allah clarified everything for mankind.

Of all the prophets, only Moses and Muhammad attained the state where they met and spoke directly to God—Moses on Mount Sinai, when God revealed Himself as a resplendent light, and Muhammad once face to face during his mystical journey to heaven, and also in the many direct revelations he received.

Moses and Muhammad also shared another distinction. They were the only two prophets whose names began with the letter *mim*. The *mim* was what Allah created first, and from it He made all of His creations. The letter *mim* covers the universes of the primal beginning, this world, and the hereafter. It penetrates the essence and the manifestation, as well as good and evil. All creations begin with *mim*, and as long as they continue to appear, that *mim*, the pearl of creation, will exist. It is endless.

Through that *mim* Allah gave Moses the Ten Commandments and the explanations of the Torah, showing him what was permissible and forbidden according to God's law, and what was good and evil. With the grace of that *mim*, Moses was able to perform miracles and to deliver his people from Pharaoh. And it was to the *mim* in Muhammad that Allah revealed the 6,666 verses of the Qur'an.

The Sufis say that it is impossible to give a complete explanation of the *mim*; it can only be grasped by those who search deeply with perfect faith and an open heart. How then is it possible to explain who Muhammad truly is? How can we say when Muhammad was created or when he appeared? Only if we understand the real Qur'an completely can we understand Muhammad. Until a man reaches that state, he will continue to say that Muhammad is the son of Aminah and 'Abdullah. The Sufis call Muhammad the light or the innermost heart. In Tamil *muham* means face and *aham* means heart. When the Ahmad, the state of the heart, becomes Muhammad, then the light of the innermost heart is revealed in the beauty of the face.

The Sufis also say that only when man comes to a realization of himself and dives deep within the inner Qur'an, drinking from its essence, will the truth of Muhammad be revealed to him in his meditation. Only when he reaches the state where he speaks to Allah alone, can he be said to truly exist in Islam. When he attains that state of communion with Allah, he will understand that the Qur'an and the holy books are his body, the inner mystical form of a human being. Such a man will understand the inner meaning of *al-hamdu lilla*, which is the praise of the inner form of man. Understanding the history of the One who is all praise, he will glorify Him alone. Only then can he see this history as one continuous study, an endless ocean of divine knowledge. Otherwise each book he reads will then refer him to yet another book. As long as he continues reading only those outer books, he will never reach his freedom.

My brothers, we must consider how the Qur'an came from Allah, and we must delve deep within it. In order to understand its true meaning, we must be in the same state as that original Qur'an was when it emerged from Allah. It came as a resplendence, a radiance, resonance, and a grace. Then it came as a light to Gabriel. And when it came to Muhammad, the Messenger, it came as the grace and attributes of Allah. Next Muhammad brought it to us as a revelation. Then the sound of these revelations was transformed into letters and formed into words. What was revealed in those words ultimately became public knowledge and part of history. The interpretations of this knowledge later gave rise to religious differences, divisions, and bigotry, which in turn gave rise to prejudice, fighting, and wars. This is the state the world has come to.

We, however, must delve into the depths of the Qur'an; we must experience each step of the way as it originally came from Allah. As we look deeper and deeper, we will see the Messenger of God, and once we see him, we will know how Gabriel came to him and how he received that grace. We will see the light, and if we look through that light we will experience the resonance of Allah within the Qur'an. As we understand that resonance, we will understand our life and our death; we will understand the Day of Judgment, the Day of Questioning, and the ninety-nine attributes of Allah.

Once we have this understanding, we will see that all men are our brothers just as the Qur'an teaches us. To truly see all people as our brothers is Islam. If we see anyone who is in need, we must offer him the water of the mercy of all the universes, the water of absolute faith, and the affirmation of that faith, the *kalima* [there is no god but God, Muhammad is the Messenger of God]. That water must be given to everyone who is hungry or thirsty. We must embrace them lovingly, quench their thirst, and wash away their dirt. We must offer them love, compassion, patience, and tolerance, just as the Prophet did. This is what will satisfy their needs and dispel the darkness in their hearts.

My brothers and sisters in Islam, if we offer peace, then justice will flourish. Love will cut away all enmity. Compassion will cause God's grace to grow in this world, and then the food of faith and the mercy of all the universes can be offered. When that food is given, hunger, disease, old age, and death will be eliminated, and everyone will have peace.

Allah and the state of a true human being are right here within us. It is a great secret, hidden within our hearts, within the *Umm al-Qur'an*. Only if we can study this divine knowledge can we attain our freedom. All who have faith must reflect upon this, understand it, and teach it to those who have less wisdom, to those who have no clarity of heart, to those whose minds oppose us, and to those who have no peace of mind. We must teach them these qualities, give them this food, this beauty, and this nourishment of grace and absolute faith. Every human being in the community of Islam, everyone who has faith, all those who are learned and wise, all the leaders of prayer and the teachers, all those who know the Qur'an—all must understand this. This is what I ask of you.

Amen. Allah is sufficient unto us all.

2. W. D. Mohammed, "Historic Atlanta Address" (1978)

Born Wallace Delaney Muhammad to parents Elijah and Clara in 1933, W. D. Mohammed grew up a member of the Messenger Elijah Muhammad's "royal family." From the 1950s through the 1970s, Mohammed served on and off as a minister in his father's Nation of Islam, but he drifted in and out of favor as he questioned the Islamic legitimacy of his father's teachings. Even so, when Elijah Muhammad died in 1975, this prodigal son emerged as the movement's leader. He radically altered the official religious doctrines of the Nation of Islam, instructing members to observe the traditional five pillars of Islamic practice. During this period, perhaps W. D. Mohammed led more African Americans toward Sunni Islam than any other person in history, before or after. He became known as mujaddid, *or a renewer of religion; later, he would encourage his followers simply to call him "Imam Mohammed." As the Imam led his followers toward Sunni Islam and away from his father's black religious separatism, he also insisted that African American Muslims continue to work for improvement in the quality of black life, to take pride in their ethnic heritage, and to interpret Sunni Islam in light of African American historical circumstances. He also initiated dialogues with Jews and Christians, especially under the auspices of the Roman Catholic Focolare movement, and he built strong ties to other Muslim leaders both in the United States and abroad. In 1992, he became the first Muslim to offer the opening prayer before a session of the U.S. Senate. In this excerpt from a 1978 address to followers in Atlanta, Imam Wallace Deen, as he was also known, outlines some of the principles that he consistently followed in leading his community of Sunni African American Muslims in the last quarter of the twentieth century. He condemns immorality, reminds his believers about proper rules of Islamic etiquette, and reaffirms his commitment to perennial themes of black uplift. In so doing, Imam Mohammed appeals to the imams of his various communities, asking for their loyalty and their submission to the God of Abraham, the God of Muslims, Christians, and Jews.*

All praise is due to Almighty God, the guardian evolver and sustainer of all the worlds. The blessings and peace be upon Muhammad, the Messenger of Allah to us all.

O Allah, guide us, forgive us our faults, and grant us the blessing of faith. I bear witness there is no deity except Allah and I bear witness Muhammad is His Servant and His Messenger. Peace be upon him, his descendants, his companions, the righteous servants, all of them, and upon us in America and throughout the world:

I shouldn't have to ask anybody to propagate the work and spirit of our community. Once I say something, it should be readily accepted by every member. If it's not readily accepted, I should get a quick rebuttal. That's how we progress.

If the leader invites you to do something or asks something from you and you feel it is not right, challenge him right away. But, if it is right, if it is good, and in the light of the Quran and in the life of Prophet Muhammad and in the conscience of good people of the society, what right have you to hesitate?

Right away you should support it!

I've been a follower since I was a little child. In fact, I've never known a time when I wasn't a follower. The environment that I came up in produced followers.

I was a follower of the Honorable Elijah Muhammad; I was a follower of the teacher, and principal, the one who taught me most of what I learned in elementary and high school, Sheikh James Abdul Aziz Shabazz.

I was a follower of Captain Raymond Sharif and the captain before him. I followed the leaders and even when they were wrong, I didn't disrespect them. I just didn't follow them in the wrong.

When they became so wrong that I thought they weren't qualified to be leaders, I began to protest. This is the way!

Some people don't want to be followers. They want to be individuals without following anything. That's not a Muslim.

Allah tells us to obey God, obey His apostle and obey those charged with authority over you. We should love leadership. Leadership is the hope of a civilized people. Without leadership they have no hope.

Our priorities haven't changed and if you go along with me they will never change until Judgment Day.

Number one, is education. Number two, is jobs for the husbands and the fathers. Not for the pimps, for husbands and fathers. For men who still value the family and want to marry and have children. These are the people we want to see with jobs because they have more responsibility. Number three, is moral excellence.

If we just keep these three priorities in mind—education, jobs for the husbands and fathers and moral excellence. We shouldn't tolerate any moral diseases in our community. If we find a moral disease, get to work on it right away. Under these priorities, we have many things going for us.

I'm very proud of the leadership that I've given to you, and I know that without God, it couldn't have been done. You couldn't have given me the support I needed and I couldn't have given you the faith you needed because I would only have been a weakling.

I'm not an educated man with a doctorate or a master's degree, not even a bachelor's degree. I received most of my education in the school established by Dr. Fard Muhammad and made a reality for us by the Honorable Elijah Muhammad.

The school was hardly recognized by the Board of Education but they sure turned out a pretty good high school product in me.

I wanted to find out just how I rated with the public school so I took the GED test and rated high nationwide.

We must get the Imams, not some of you, all of you, to support and promote American patriotism—sober, intelligent patriotism, and also to support our call for the common people to respect and work to dutifully preserve the government.

Recent developments have been turning the people away from civilization and government to anarchy, savagery and orgiastic forms of life.

Thanks to Almighty God, with a President like Jimmy Carter and the support he's getting from the members of his staff and the good people in government throughout the United States, and with the voice of one in the ghetto as one in the wilderness saying, "come back to civilization, come back to respect for human dignity," we have turned the tide of moral decadence, savagery, filth and vulgar permissiveness.

We have turned around. There is a new spirit in America today. The sun is rising on the human being and going down on the brute and the filthy savage.

Our Imams must support our movement for interfaith cooperation to create a common religious front to fight the evils of our society.

The people of the Torah, the Gospel and the Quran are a family from one common patriarch, Abraham, who is called "our father" in Judaism, in Christianity and in Al-Islam. And, we are called people of the Book.

I think we can all unite on those strong points and fight the common enemies.

Religion won't survive unless we come together. We need help. As the majority of people today are leaving the strong, healthy, good things that civilization has established, don't you know we will all be run over and trampled under the feet of those wild animals unless we unite and preserve all that we cherish?

We can't look at each other as Christians or Jews, we have to look at each other as people believing in One God.

"Oh, Chief [Minister], they don't believe in our God." Well, I can prove something quite different, dear Sister and Brother.

Our Imam Council has to accept the responsibility of promoting and preserving the religion of Al-Islam for the World Community of al-Islam in the West [the reformed version of the Nation of Islam]. They have to preserve the Islamic spirit of this community.

We should say, "As-Salaam-Alaikum," "Wa-Alaikum-As-Salaam." We shouldn't pass by and ignore each other. We shouldn't come in on a group of Muslims and say nothing or walk away from a group of Muslims and say nothing, even from one Muslim. Give the greeting when you come in or leave.

The rule is the smaller group is to speak to the larger group. They are obligated to greet the larger group and the one who comes in later is obligated to greet those who are already in. Most of us love this, it's just a few having the problem.

The Imams have to be pledged to work for the human dignity of the individual. Your Brother and your Sister are our equals in Al-Islam. There are no class distinctions, no respect for your degrees or your muscles. The only recognition in Al-Islam is for your being a decent human being— that's what we respect.

In the eyes of God, he who is best is the one most careful of his duty to the Almighty.

The majority of our Imams have no problem. Those of you yet to come around, we are begging you, Brother—we need you and you need us.

I've done my best to foster in us a spirit of healthy, sober, intelligent patriotism as Americans, and a healthy, intelligent attitude toward human dignity over the past three and one half years, and I hope none of you will let me down.

Let us have a Patriotism Day Parade every year. Let us show all American people we were brought here as slaves and treated like work animals or worse. We were invited to come into the mainstream of American life and the law of the land rose up and said, "We will protect the black, the African-American just as we protect any other citizen."

We accepted it and we're proud of it and we'll hold the American Flag high, we'll fight for it, we'll die for it. We're not going to put our burden on another citizen; I accept the burden. I accept the responsibility.

As religious people, as Muslims, we have to be of service to all peoples. We can't just serve Muslims, we have to serve all peoples.

When we walk out of our door we see people; all were created by the same God, and whatever God has revealed for one He has revealed for all.

If they are not Muslim now, that's God, He's the judge of that. Almighty God says that you will be differing even up to Judgment Day. But at the same time, He says go you all together as in a race toward all that is good.

Not only Muslim with Muslim, but Muslim with Jew, Muslim with Christian. Let us all go together.

Allah is the prefect being. Allah is all righteous, truthful—no imperfections in Allah. Allah is Supreme and Perfect without any imperfections.

O Allah. Make us of those who purify themselves and of those who repent, and guide us in your path. Amen.

Peace be to you
Your brother in service to Allah
Wallace Deen Muhammad

3. Nation of Gods and Earths, "What We Teach," "Allah," and "Supreme Mathematics" (1992)

For the most part, the religious teachings of the Nation of Gods and Earths, or the Five Percenters, do not utilize the Qur'an and the Sunna of the Prophet Muhammad of Arabia as sources of wisdom and guidance. The numerological and linguistic theories of the Five Percenters instead recall the traditions of black Masonic organizations and modern African American vernacular traditions. The readings below suggest that the Nation of Gods and Earths might also be seen as a new religious movement, one with its own founder, sacred texts, symbols, and rituals. The attraction of hip-hop artists and rappers to the Five Percent Nation is no coincidence. Whether believers in Five Percent theology or not, all of these persons see hidden meanings, wisdom, and power in the use of human language. Language becomes a moral guide for one's life and its proper deployment results in personal and collective liberation. Five Percenters are also devoted to numerology, the study of the spiritual and secret meaning of numbers. Improvising on themes introduced in Elijah Muhammad's Nation of Islam, Five Percent leaders developed their own version of the "Supreme Mathematics," a secret knowledge originally taught only to those who were fully initiated into Elijah Muhammad's group. Like the Nation of Islam, the Nation of Gods and Earths also espouses a form of religion that is synonymous with black liberation and nationalism. The articles below are excerpted from The Word, *a movement newspaper.*

What We Teach

1. We teach that black people are the original people of the planet earth.
2. We teach that black people are fathers and mothers of civilization.
3. We teach that the science of supreme mathematics is the key to understanding man's relationship to the universe.
4. We teach Islam as a natural way of life; not a religion.
5. We teach that education should be fashioned to enable us to be self sufficient as a people.
6. We teach that each one should teach one according to their knowledge.
7. We teach that the Blackman is God and His proper name is Allah: Arm, Leg, Leg, Arm, Head.
8. We teach that our children are our link to the future and they must be nurtured, respected, loved, protected and educated.
9. We teach that the unified black family is the vital building block of the Nation.

Allah was born Clarence Smith on Friday, February 22, 1928 in Danville, Virginia. His parents (Louis and Mary) gave birth to seven children, six boys and one girl, of which he was the fifth son. As a baby his mother affectionately named him "put" and this is what he was called throughout his early childhood years.

In the 1940s Allah's mother moved to New York to seek employment. Arriving in New York she settled in Harlem, where she rented an apartment. In 1946 Allah came to the North to join his mother and older brother. Once in New York his nickname "put" was mistaken for "Puddin," and this is what he would be known as. Not long after arriving in New York Allah would meet a beautiful young lady by the name of Willieen Jowers with whom he would produce two sons, A-Allah and Be-Allah. This relationship would be short lived. Allah's heart would eventually be captured by a beautiful blackwoman by the name of Dora, whom he would ask to marry him, and from this bond came the birth of Christine, Debra, Clarence and Perry. Unreconcilable differences would unravel the marriage between Allah and Dora but they would always remain close throughout the years. Allah's seventh child, a son, was given the name of Allah by his mother (earth), Gevasia, a poor Righteous Teacher of the Nation of Gods and Earths.

In 1950, Allah joined the Army and was sent to fight in the Korean War. While he was away his wife became a Muslim and became a member of the Nation of Islam under the leadership of the Honorable Elijah Muhammed. When Allah returned home, he too accepted the teachings of Islam and joined her at Mosque No. 7, under Minister Malcolm X.

It was in the Mosque that Allah met Justice, then named Arkbar, who would become his closes[t] confidant for many years to come. Allah's years in the Mosque began inauspiciously enough. His initial duty was an elevator operator in the Mosque, however, he was to rise through the ranks very quickly and soon he was promoted to the position of lieutenant with the responsibility of training the Fruit of Islam (F.O.I.), in the science of martial arts, which he had learned while in Korea. Members of the Nation of Islam are given (sparingly) lessons to study, Allah studied diligently and became proficient with their advocation. The mastery of this knowledge inspired within him a fiery wisdom that was unique to him, with his slow methodical cadence speaking style of stressing syllables not normally stressed, causing audiences to be held spell-bound in a trance-like state.

In 1963 Allah left the Mosque and went to the streets of Harlem to do God's work. God's work as he saw it was to teach the blind, deaf and dumb people and from them raise the 5% Nation. Allah began teaching Islam to the people in the community. The message he delivered to them was they had to clean themselves up in order to regain their long lost status of prominence in this world. He mainly focused his attention on [what he] realized was the link to the future and survival of the Black Nation. He developed the science of Supreme Mathematics as the basis of his teaching and the key to unlock the minds of the youth. The Supreme Mathematics are the ten principles which correspond to the nine numeric units and the zero in the number system. Using the Supreme Mathematics and the Supreme Alphabets (principles that Allah Justice created, corresponding with the twenty-six letters of the alphabet), he taught the youth how to break down and build profound relationships with significant life experiences. He took his message to the poor, delinquent and hard core street youths, many of whom were drug addicts, alcoholics, criminals and school dropouts. The incorrigible black youths that society had long since failed and had given up on.

Allah's first student he named Karriem, later Allah would rename him Black Messiah. Messiah brought other youths to be taught by Allah. Allah began the foundation of this nation that is now known as the Nation of Gods and Earths, by basically educating nine youths who were to become known as the "first nine born":

1. Karriem-Black Messiah
2. Al-Salaam
3. Al-Jabbar-Prince Allah
4. Nihiem-Bisme Allah
5. Arkbar
6. Kihiem
7. Bilal-ABG
8. Al-Jamel
9. Uhura

They called him "Father," because some were from families headed by mothers and this was the father they knew, loved and respected. He taught them that they were of the most high even though at present they were considered by some to be of the most low in the wilderness of North America. He taught them that they should not be anti-white pro-black, but that they should be anti-devilishment and pro-righteousness.

That they did not need guns, unless they had legal papers on them, because their tongues were their sword and that they could take more heads with the word than any army with machine guns ever could. He didn't teach them to fight fire with a flower, but he taught them not to try to pour out a fire with gasoline. Allah's first born became a very powerful and dynamic young man and brought hundreds of black youths into the knowledge of self. They became known as Allah's five percent or the Five Percenters.

These are the teachings of Almighty God Allah regarding our Supreme Mathematics.

The original Mathematics that were taught by the Hon. Elijah Muhammad (PBUH) were as follows:

> One = Wisdom
> Two = Knowledge
> Three = Understanding
> Four = Culture
> Five = Justice
> Six = Equality
> Seven = Islam

Allah taught me that when he and Shaheed (John 37x) left temple number seven [in Harlem, run by Malcolm X and then Louis Farrakhan], they argued for three days concerning the proper order of Mathematics and how it should be taught. This argument was based on which comes first Knowledge or Wisdom? On the third day, Shaheed bear witness that Knowledge comes before Wisdom. The Attribute Shaheed means: from who eyes the veil has been removed. Shaheed is the first one to bring the Knowledge of the reality of God to Patmos, thereby fulfilling prophecy. He is the one spoken of in the book of revelation chapter 1, verse 9.

Allah (The Father) taught me never to write the Supreme Mathematics or the Supreme Alphabets down on paper, that this language should be taught by word of mouth, however, he also taught us "that as time change you must change, or you are gonna die." And so out of necessity and to meet the challenge to rectify this crisis that we are faced with, it is now necessary for this Knowledge and Wisdom to be written to bring those who are in search of the true Knowledge of Allah and the Wisdom of our language into the pure light of Allah and his original teachings as revealed to me.

The original Supreme Mathematics as given and taught to me by Allah is as follows:

1 = Knowledge
2 = Wisdom
3 = Understanding
4 = Culture or Freedom
5 = Power, Justice or Refinement
6 = Equality
7 = God (Allah)
8 = Build or Destroy
9 = Born
0 = Cipher

The original Supreme Alphabets as given and taught to me by Allah is as follows:

A = Allah
B = Be or Born
C = See
D = Divine or Destroy
E = Equality or Evil
F = Father
G = God
H = He or Her
I = I
J = Justice
K = King
L = Love
M = Master
N = in or now
O = Cipher
P = Power
Q = Queen
R = Rule or Right
S = Savior or Self

T = Truth or Square
U = You
V = Victory
W = Wisdom
X = Unknown
Y = Why
Z = Zig, Zag, Zig (meaning understanding)

As it was in the beginning so shall it be in the end.
PEACE

4. Frances Trix, Prologue to *Spiritual Discourse: Learning with an Islamic Master* (1993)

In the course of her research on Bektashi Muslims in the United States, Dr. Frances Trix, a linguist and anthropologist, became the student of Albanian Sufi master Baba Rexheb. Baba Rexheb was the leader of the Albanian Bekstashi Tekke established in the Detroit, Michigan, area around 1953. As we have already seen, the Bektashi order is only one of many Sufi groups to put down roots in the United States. Located in a rural area, the Detroit community's tekke, or Sufi lodge, is used by its members not only as a place for daily prayers and festival celebrations but also as a space for the performance of certain Sufi rituals, such as the praising of God through the recitation of poetry. Trix studied with the spiritual leader of this community for over twenty years. As she explains below, Baba Rexheb was her murshid, or spiritual guide, and she did her best to be his talib, or student. The kind of master-disciple relationship that Trix established with the Baba exemplifies larger patterns in Sufism, the mystical branch of Islam. As the student seeks a guide toward greater knowledge of the truth and a closer relationship with God, he or she often relies on a spiritual guide, someone who is committed to helping the student with his or her religious quest.

*Prologue / in which the frustration of a student after
many years of study discreetly erupts*

"Baba, how did Selim Baba teach you?" In isolation an innocent enough question.

There I sat on my folding chair in the study room of Baba's *tekke*—a sort of "Muslim monastery." And there across from me sat Baba, the then eighty-four-year-old Muslim "monk" who was the head of the *tekke*.

The room we were in had probably been the dining room of a Michigan farmhouse that in the 1950s had been bought by a group of Albanian Muslims and converted into a Bektashi *tekke*. Were the former owners to return, no doubt they would have had difficulty recognizing their farmhouse, due to both additions to the building and changes in interior décor and use.

On one side of Baba's chair, where perhaps a tall cabinet of the farm's finest china had once stood, there was now a bed whose headboard and footboard were covered with prayer rags. Pillows were propped on the bed against the wall. And people would sit on the bed with their legs folded under them, much as they had sat on carpet-covered floors in the traditional guest rooms back in the Balkans.

On the other side of Baba's chair, and under the window, where the dining-room table had once stood, there was still a table, only it was piled high with books and papers. There was a six-volume set of encyclopedias, published in Constantinople in 1901 and written in the Arabic letters of the Turkish of that time. Scattered among the volumes were copies of *Dielli* ("The Sun"), an Albanian-American newspaper, as well as letters to Baba from Bektashis from all over the world. Toward the back of the table were several Qur'ans, along with the sixteenth-century commentary on the Qur'an by Husein Vaiz, and a nineteenth-century defense of Bektashism, the particular Sufi Order to which Baba belonged. And then of course there were the books of poetry. These were in Turkish and Persian by poets like Nesimi (fourteenth to fifteenth century), Fuzuli (sixteenth century), Pir Sultan Abdal (sixteenth century), and Niyazi Misri (seventeenth century). Besides books of collected works of individual poets, there were several anthologies of Turkish mystic poetry written in the Roman letters that have been used in Turkey since the 1920s. The anthologies had been sent as gifts from Bektashis in Turkey and were easier for me to follow. As for Baba, he reads Arabic, Persian, Turkish, Greek, Albanian, and Italian, and so is at home in several scripts; but he prefers the Turkish poetry in its original Arabic letters.

The walls at least had not changed in the *tekke* study room. They still had the stucco finish that had been such a popular embellishment of American home architecture in the twenties. But on the walls, where once perhaps a mirror and a placid landscape had hung, there was now a lunar calendar, with a small watercolor of Baba's native Albania obscuring half the calendar. Across from that hung a framed piece of Arabic calligraphy—a scarlet background with gold lettering of the first line of the Qur'an: "In the Name of God the Merciful, the Mercy-giving." Over the bed was a photograph of dry and dusty buildings that I was told were the shrine of Ali in Najaf, Iraq—hardly an inducement to pilgrimage. Behind Baba's chair was a large picture of mountains being scaled by two large rams with antlers, reminiscent of the sheep in Albania. No one was sure who had donated it—the *tekke* has been furnished with gifts, which accounted for the unusual assemblage—but I suspected some Albanian Bektashis who had gone to Alaska and who regularly sent Baba gifts including blankets depicting the midnight sun.

In stark contrast to all this is Baba's bedroom, where the only picture on the wall is a photograph of Selim Baba, Baba's spiritual teacher.

Also in contrast to the study room is the private ceremonial room of the *tekke*. This large room was the Bektashis' first addition to the farmhouse. The room is carpeted and without furniture. Its pale blue-washed walls are bare. All attention is thus focused on the *mihrab* or "prayer niche" where Baba sits, and on the steps of candles to his right. Back in the study room, Baba's high-back chair also has the place of prominence. And as we talked, Baba sat comfortably in his chair with one leg curled under him. His baggy pants seem made for sitting like that, but it is his flexibility that makes such sitting possible. No doubt the Muslim way of prayer, in which one kneels and then bows until the forehead touches the floor, facilitates such flexibility late in life. But it is the flexibility of Baba's talk that I would explore and the subtlety of the way he teaches.

When I asked Baba the question about how Selim Baba had taught him, I had been coming to the *tekke* for lessons, on a weekly basis, for twelve years. One would think that by then I would have known how my teacher had been taught. But I was not even sure, after all those years, how Baba taught me. There was no syllabus. Baba did not announce topics or even initiate talk. Instead it fell into my lap to begin lessons.

I found that initiating topics myself was uncomfortable, for clearly Baba had the greater authority. Baba is the head of the *tekke*. When people come to the *tekke* they always go first to greet him. This involves taking his hand, kissing the back of it, and putting it to their foreheads. Or if they are "inner members," they kiss the inside of Baba's hand and then kiss his heart as well. When people leave a room where he is, they back out, bowing in respect.

Behind these gestures is respect and love for Baba as one who took vows of dervishhood and vows of celibacy at age twenty-one, and who has since dedicated his life to serving God and his community. I am an American student from Michigan. How should I deign to initiate lessons?

And yet we have studied together all these years. But what have I learned? That too is problematic. The best answer I can give is that I have learned to come back. In other words, I have been learning a relationship. I have been learning how to be a *talib* (seeker) as the student of a *murshid* (spiritual guide) is known. This is no small undertaking, for the relationship of *talib* to *murshid* is a model of the relationship of human being to God. How is this relationship learned? That is the central question of . . . [my] study, and my approach is to assume that a description of our lessons will shed some light on this issue.

Most of our lessons have been spent talking with each other and reading Turkish *nefes* together. Nefes are the spiritual poems of the Bektashis. After all these years of study together, I should be able to follow these *nefes*, or at least Baba's explanations. Or, and perhaps this is the most important, if I do not follow I should be patient and trust that what is confusing will straighten out in time. Alas, this is not always so.

In fact, when I asked Baba how he had been taught by Selim Baba, it was precisely in the context of my own perplexity as a *talib*. Baba had explained a quatrain, I had been confused, I had asked for repeated explanation, and had been even more confused. After a third unsuccessful try, I had cried out in frustration, "Baba, how did Selim Baba teach you?" (In asking this I had hoped to discover how Baba had learned from his own *murshid*, and by extension what I was doing wrong.)

Baba answered my intent. That is, instead of answering how he had been taught, he answered how he had learned. Baba responded in the Turkish that was our common language: . . . "thus, by listening."

Baba then went on to respond to my impatience and frustration with myself for not being able to follow the explanation of the *nefes*: . . . "Many things you have learned from me. But how have you learned? By listening. . . . I talk as a friend, I speak. . . . As for you, you listen. It stands out in your memory."

Baba's kindness in suggesting I had learned much from him was salve to my dignity. He did not bother to confront me with the foolishness of my insistence on immediate understanding.

But all was not dismal. The very way I had expressed my frustration and called for help did show I had learned how to ask in a Bektashi frame. For, in asking how Baba's *murshid* had taught him, I had appealed to the basic relationship of the Bektashis.

5. Minister Louis Farrakhan, "Million Man March Address" (1995)

Born Louis Eugene Walcott in 1933 in the Bronx, New York, Minister Louis Farrakhan became an accomplished and well-known musician, singer, and violinist in Boston. When he converted to Elijah Muhammad's Nation of Islam in 1955, however, he gave up his career in music to spread the word of the Messenger, first as a local minister in Boston and eventually as minister of Harlem's Mosque No. 7 and as national spokesman for Elijah Muhammad. After W. D. Mohammed changed the direction and name of the organization in the mid-1970s, Farrakhan tried to support that change. When he could no longer do so, he left the organization, and during his international travels was inspired to rebuild the work of Elijah Muhammad. He has continued in his role as head of that Nation of Islam since 1978. The excerpt below is from what is arguably his most important speech, made in front of hundreds of thousands if not over a million black men who traveled to Washington, D.C., on October 16, 1995, for the Million Man March. The march sought to challenge the negative stereotypes of black men and communities as violent and troubled, and it also provided Farrakhan an opportunity to call for personal responsibility and racial reconciliation. Employing a numerological analysis that paid attention to U.S. history, the height of various Washington monuments, and Masonic images on the Seal of the United States, Minister Farrakhan suggested that the redemption of African Americans and America's atonement for the sin of slavery are necessary preconditions for the healing of the racial divide in the United States. The well-read preacher blended Muslim and Christian scriptures in calling for black men to take responsibility for any violent and immoral acts in their past. He asked participants to join a black political organization like the NAACP or the Urban League, and he suggested that all black men attend a church, mosque, synagogue, or any other house of worship that would help them lead a more moral life.

In the name of Allah, the beneficent, the merciful. We thank Him for his prophets, and the scriptures which they brought. We thank him for Moses and the Torah. We thank him for Jesus and the Gospel. We thank him for Muhammad and the Qur'an. Peace be upon these worthy servants of Allah.

I am so grateful to Allah for his intervention in our affairs in the person of Master Fard Muhammad, the Great Mahdi, who came among us and raised from among us a divine leader, teacher and guide, his Messenger to us the Most Honorable Elijah Muhammad. I greet all of you, my dear and wonderful brothers, with the greeting words of peace. We say it in the Arabic language, As-salam Alaykum.

I would like to thank all of those known and unknown persons who worked to make this day of atonement and reconciliation a reality. My thanks and my extreme gratitude to the Reverend Benjamin Chavis and to all of the members of the national organizing committees.

To all of the local organizing committees, to Dr. Dorothy Height in the National Council of Negro Women, and all of the sisters who were involved in the planning of the Million Man March. Of course, if I named all those persons whom I know helped to make this event a reality, it would take a tremendous amount of time. But suffice it to say that we are grateful to all who made this day possible.

I'm looking at the Washington Monument and beyond it to the Lincoln Memorial. And, beyond that, to the left, to your right, the Jefferson Memorial. Abraham Lincoln was the sixteenth president of these United States and he was the man who allegedly freed us. Abraham Lincoln saw in his day, what President Clinton sees in this day. He saw the great divide between black and white. Abraham Lincoln and Bill Clinton see what the Kerner Commission saw thirty years ago when they said that this nation was moving toward two Americas—one black, one white, separate and unequal. And the Kerner Commission revisited their findings twenty five years later and saw that America was worse today than it was in the time of Martin Luther King, Jr. There's still two Americas, one black, one white, separate and unequal.

Abraham Lincoln, when he saw this great divide, he pondered a solution of separation. Abraham Lincoln said he never was in favor of our being jurors or having equal status with the whites of this nation. Abraham Lincoln said that if there were to be a superior or inferior, he would rather the superior position be assigned to the white race. There, in the middle of this mall is the Washington Monument, 555 feet high. But if we put a one in front of that 555 feet, we get 1555, the year that our first fathers landed on the shores of Jamestown, Virginia, as slaves.

In the background is the Jefferson and Lincoln Memorial, each one of these monuments is 19 feet high.

Abraham Lincoln, the sixteenth president. Thomas Jefferson, the third president, and 16 and three make 19 again. What is so deep about this number 19? Why are we standing on the Capitol steps today? That number 19—when you have a nine you have a womb that is pregnant. And when you have a one standing by the nine, it means that there's something secret that has to be unfolded.

Right here on this mall where we are standing, according to books written on Washington, D.C., slaves used to be brought right here on this mall in chains to be sold up and down the eastern seaboard. Right along this mall, going over to the White House, our fathers were sold into slavery. But, George Washington, the first president of the United States, said he feared that before too many years passed over his head, this slave would prove to become a most troublesome species of property.

Thomas Jefferson said he trembled for this country when he reflected that God was just and that his justice could not sleep forever. Well, the day that these presidents feared has now come to pass, for on this mall, here we stand in the capital of America.

And the layout of this great city, laid out by a black man, Benjamin Banneker. This is all placed and based in a secret Masonic ritual. And at the core of the secret of that ritual is the black man, not far from here is the White House.

And the first president of this land, George Washington, who was a grand master of the Masonic order laid the foundation, the cornerstone of this capitol building where we stand. George was a slave owner. George was a slave owner. Now, the President [Clinton] spoke today and he wanted to heal the great divide. But I respectfully suggest to the President, you did not dig deep enough at the malady that divides black and white in order to effect a solution to the problem.

And so, today, we have to deal with the root so that perhaps a healing can take place.

Now, this obelisk at the Washington Monument is Egyptian and this whole layout is reminiscent of our great historic past, Egypt. And . . . look at the original Seal of the United States, published by the Department of State in 1909. Gaylord Hunt wrote that late in the afternoon of July 4, 1776, the Continental Congress resolved that Dr. Benjamin Franklin, Mr. John

Adams, and Mr. Thomas Jefferson be a committee to prepare a device for a Seal of the United States of America.

In the design proposed by the first committee, the face of the Seal was a coat of arms measured in six quarters. That number is significant. Six quarters, with emblems representing England, Scotland, Ireland, France, Germany, and Holland, the countries from which the new nation had been peopled. The eye of providence in a radiant triangle and the motto, "E Pluribus Unum," were also proposed for the face of the Seal. Even [though] the country was populated by so-called Indians and Black Slaves [who] were brought to build the country, the official Seal of the country was never designed to reflect our presence, only that of the European immigrants. The Seal and the Constitution reflect the thinking of the founding fathers, that this was to be a nation by white people and for white people. Native Americans, blacks, and all other non-white people were to be the burden bearers for the real citizens of this nation.

For the back of the Seal the committee suggested a picture of Pharaoh sitting in an open chariot with a crown on his head and a sword in his hand, passing through the divided waters of the Red Sea, in pursuit of the Israelites. And, hovering over the sea was to be shown a pillar of fire in a cloud, expressive of the divine presence and command. And raised from this pillar of fire were to be shown, beaming down on Moses standing on the shore, extending his hand over the sea, causing it to overwhelm Pharaoh.

The motto for the reverse was, "Rebellion to tyrants is obedience to God." Let me say it again. Rebellion is obedience to God. Now, why did they mention Pharaoh? I heard the President say today, "E Pluribus Unum—out of many, one." But in the past, out of many comes one meant out of many Europeans come one people. The question today is, out of the many Asians, the many Arabs, the many Native Americans, the many Blacks, the many people of color who populate this country. Do you mean for them to be made into the one?

If so, truth has to be spoken to justice. We can't cover things up. Cover them over. Give it a pretty sound to make people feel good. We have to go to the root of the problem. Now, why have you come today?

You came not at the call of Louis Farrakhan, but you have gathered here at the call of God. For it is only the call of Almighty God, no matter through whom that call came, that could generate this kind of outpouring. God called us here to this place. At this time. For a very specific reason.

And now, I want to say, my brothers—this is a very pregnant moment. Pregnant with the possibility of tremendous change in our status in America and in the world. . . .

We stand here today at this historic moment. We are standing in the place of those who couldn't make it here today. We are standing on the blood of our ancestors. We are standing on the blood of those who died in the middle passage, who died in the fields and swamps of America, who died hanging from trees in the South, who died in the cells of their jailers, who died on the highways and who died in the fratricidal conflict that rages within our community. We are standing on the sacrifice of the lives of those heroes, our great men and women that we today may accept the responsibility that life imposes upon each traveler who comes this way.

We must accept the responsibility that God has put upon us, not only to be good husbands and fathers and builders of our community, but God is now calling upon the despised and the rejected to become the cornerstone and the builders of a new world.

And so, our brief subject today is taken from the American Constitution. In these words, . . . toward a more perfect union.

Now, when you use the word more with perfect, that which is perfect is that which has been brought to completion. So, when you use more perfect, you're either saying that what you call perfect is perfect for that stage of its development but not yet complete. When Jefferson said, "toward a more perfect union," he was admitting that the union was not perfect, that it was not finished, that work had to be done. And so we are gathered here today not to bash somebody else. We're not gathered here to say, all of the evils of this nation. But we are gathered here to collect ourselves for a responsibility that God is placing on our shoulders to move this nation toward a more perfect union. Now, when you look at the word toward, toward, it means in the direction of, in furtherance or partial fulfillment of, with the view to obtaining or having shortly before coming soon, imminent, going on in progress. Well, that's right. We're in progress toward a perfect union. . . .

We responded to a call and look at what is present here today. We have here those brothers with means and those who have no means. Those who are light and those who are dark. Those who are educated, those who are uneducated. Those who are business people, those who don't know anything about business. Those who are young, those who are old. Those who are scientific, those who know nothing of science. Those who are religious and those who are irreligious. Those who are Christian, those who are Muslim, those who are Baptist, those who are Methodist, those who are Episcopalian, those of traditional African religion. We've got them all here today.

And why did we come? We came because we want to move toward a more perfect union. And if you notice, the press triggered every one of those divisions. You shouldn't come, you're a Christian. That's a Muslim thing. You shouldn't come, you're too intelligent to follow hate! You shouldn't come, look at what they did, they excluded women, you see? They played all the cards, they pulled all the strings.

Oh, but you better look again, Willie. There's a new Black man in America today. A new Black woman in America today. Now Brothers, there's a social benefit of our gathering here today. That is, that from this day forward, we can never again see ourselves through the narrow eyes of the limitation of the boundaries of our own fraternal, civic, political, religious, street organization or professional organization. We are forced by the magnitude of what we see here today, that whenever you return to your cities and you see a Black man, a Black woman, don't ask him what is your social, political or religious affiliation, or what is your status? Know that he is your brother. . . .

[Minister Farrakhan begins to describe eight steps necessary to the achievement of more perfect union with oneself and the world:] Pointing out fault, pointing out our wrongs is the first step. . . .

The second step is to acknowledge. . . . To acknowledge means to admit the existence, the reality or the truth of some reality. It is to recognize as being valid. Or having force and power. It is to express thanks, appreciation, or gratitude. So in this context, the word acknowledgement is to be in a state of recognition of the truth of the fact that we have been wrong. This is the second step.

Well, the third step is that after you know you're wrong and you acknowledge it to yourself, who else knows it except you confess it. You say, well, yeah, all right. But who should I confess to? And why should I confess?

And why should I confess? The Bible says confession is good for the soul. Now, brothers I know, I don't have a lot of time, but the soul is the essence of a person's being. And when the soul is covered with guilt from sin and wrongdoing, the mind and the actions of the person reflect the condition of the soul. So, to free the soul or the essence of man from its burden, one must acknowledge one's wrong, but then one must confess.

The Holy Qur'an says it like this: I've been greatly unjust to myself, and I confess my faults. So grant me protection against all my faults, for none grants protection against faults but Thee. It is only through confession that we can be granted protection from the consequences of our faults.

For every deed has a consequence. And we can never be granted protection against the faults that we refuse to acknowledge or that we are unwilling to confess. So, look. Who should you confess to? I don't want to confess. Who should you confess to? Who should I confess to? Who should we confess to? First, you confess to God. And every one of us that are here today, that knows that we have done wrong. We have to go to God and speak to Him in the privacy of our rooms and confess. He already knows, but when you confess, you're relieving your soul of the burden that it bears.

But, then, the hardest part is to go to the person or persons whom your faults have ill-affected and confess to them. That's hard. That's hard. But, if we want a perfect union, we have to confess the fault. Well, what happens after confession? There must be repentance. When you repent, you feel remorse or contrition or shame for the past conduct which was and is wrong and sinful. It means to feel contrition or self-reproach for what one has done or failed to do.

And it is the experiencing of such regret for past conduct that involves the changing of our mind toward that sin. So, until we repent and feel sick, sorry over what we have done, we can never, never change our minds toward that thing. And if you don't repent, you'll do it over and over and over again. But to stop it where it is, and black men, we got to stop what we're doing where it is. We cannot continue the destruction of our lives and the destruction of our community. But that change can't come until we feel sorry.

I heard my brother from the West Coast say today, I atone to the mothers for the death of the babies caused by our senseless slaughter of one another. See, when he feels sorry deep down inside, he's going to make a change. That man has a change in his mind. That man has a change in his heart. His soul has been unburdened and released from the pain of that sin, but you got to go one step further, because after you've acknowledged it, confessed it, repented, you've come to the fifth stage [of atonement]. Now, you've got to do something about it.

Now, look brother, sisters. Some people don't mind confessing. Some people don't mind making some slight repentance. But, when it comes to doing something about the evil that we've done, we fall short.

But atonement means satisfaction or reparation for a wrong or injury. It means to make amends. It means penance, expiation, compensation, and recompense made or done for an injury or wrong.

So, atonement means we must be willing to do something in expiation of our sins so we can't just have a good time today, and say we made history in Washington. We've got to resolve today that we're going back home to do something about what's going on in our lives and in our families and in our communities.

Now, we all right? Can you hang with me a few more? Now, brothers and sisters, if we make atonement it leads to the sixth stage. And the sixth stage is forgiveness. Now, so many of us want forgiveness, but we don't want to go through the process that leads to it. And so, when we say we forgive, we forgive from our lips, but we have never pardoned in the heart.

So, the injury still remains. My dear family. My dear brothers. We need forgiveness. God is always ready to forgive us for our sins. Forgiveness means to grant pardon for, or remission of, an offense or sin. It is to absolve, to clear, to exonerate and to liberate. Boy, that's something!

See, you're not liberated until you can forgive. You're not liberated from the evil effect of our own sin until we can ask God for forgiveness and then forgive others . . .

And then, that leads to the seventh stage . . . reconciliation and restoration. To restore, to reconcile means to become friendly, peaceable again, to put hostile persons into a state of agreement or harmony, to make compatible or to compose or settle what it was that made for division. It means to resolve differences. It can mean to establish or re-establish a close relationship between previously hostile persons. So, restoration means the act of returning something to an original or un-impaired condition. Now, when you're backed to an un-impaired position, you have reached the eighth stage, which is perfect union. And when we go through all these steps, there is no difference between us that we can't heal. There's a balm in Gilead to heal the sin sick soul. There is a balm in Gilead to make the wounded whole.

We are a wounded people, but we're being healed. But President Clinton, America is also wounded. . . . And so, the eighth stage is perfect union with God. And in the Qur'an, it reads, "Oh soul that is at rest, well-pleased with thy lord and well-pleasing" [89:28]. Oh, brothers, brothers, brothers, you don't know what it's like to be free. Freedom can't come from white folks. Freedom can't come from staying here and petitioning this great government. We're here to make a statement to the great government, but not to beg them. Freedom cannot come from no one but the God who can liberate the soul from the burden of sin. And this is why Jesus said "come unto me," not some who are heavy laden, "but all that are heavy laden, and I will give you rest" [Matt 11:28]. . . .

In the name of Allah the beneficent, the merciful, praise be to Allah the Lord of the world, the beneficent, the merciful master of the day of requital. Thee do we worship. Thine aid we seek. Guide us on the right path. The path of those upon whom you have bestowed favors, not the path of those upon whom wrath is brought down. Nor those who go astray [Qur'an 1:1–7].

Oh, Allah. We thank you for this holy day of Atonement and Reconciliation. We thank you for putting your spirit and your calm in Washington, D.C., and over the heads of this nearly two million of your servants. We thank you for letting us set a new example, not only for our people but for America and the world. We thank you, oh, Allah, for bringing us safely over the highways and we beg you to bring us safely back to our wives and our children and our loved ones, who saw us off earlier or a few days ago.

And as we leave this place, let us be resolved to go home to work out this atonement and make our communities a decent, whole, and safe place to live. And oh, Allah, we beg your blessings on all who participated, all who came that presented their bodies as a living sacrifice, wholly and acceptable as their reasonable service.

Now, "let us not be conformed to this world, but let us go home transformed by the renewing of our minds" [Romans 12:2] and let the idea of atonement ring throughout America. That America may see that the slave has come up with power. The slave is been restored, delivered, and redeemed. And now call this nation to repentance. To acknowledge her wrongs. To confess, not in secret documents, called classified, but to come before the world and the American people as the Japanese prime minister did and confess her faults before the world because her sins have affected the whole world. And perhaps, she may do some act of atonement, that you may forgive and those ill-affected may forgive, that reconciliation and restoration may lead us to the perfect union with thee and with each other. We ask all of this in your Holy and Righteous Name. Allahu akbar, Allahu akbar, Allahu akbar. That means God is great.

6. Jeffrey Lang, *Struggling to Surrender: Some Impressions of an American Convert to Islam* (1995)

Born in 1954 and raised a Roman Catholic in Connecticut, future University of Kansas professor of mathematics Jeffrey Lang ran into trouble his senior year in high school when he challenged his teacher's proof of the existence of God. Eventually, he abandoned his Catholic faith and embraced atheism: "I was the center of my universe: its creator, sustainer, and regulator," he wrote. It was, according to Lang, a lonely existence. During his graduate-school years, Lang became fascinated with other religions as he met various foreign students, especially a Middle Eastern Muslim woman who came to his office completely veiled one day. After graduating from Purdue University with a doctorate in math, Lang moved to San Francisco, where his conversion, the story of which is recounted below, took place. As we saw in the case of Malcolm X, Lang's conversion to Sunni Islam was influenced by the foreign Muslims with whom he came into contact. Their friendship was a key component in his journey to Islam. Lang's story also recounts in dramatic fashion the range of emotions he alternately endured and embraced as he converted to Islam—an experience that may feel familiar to many religious converts, whether Muslim or not. At the apex of his conversion, he narrates the personal and spiritual meanings of taking his shahada, or declaration of Islamic faith.

San Francisco was a chance to begin anew. New places provide new opportunities. You could do something different or unexpected because of your anonymity. My professors encouraged me to work elsewhere, but I chose the University of San Francisco. I was not sure why. It was not a research school, and I had never liked big cities. At the start of the semester, my personal life was already exciting and chaotic. I had decided to live for the moment and not to dwell so much on the future or past. It was wonderful to be earning a real living instead of the graduate student stipend I was used to.

I was about to begin my first lecture when this extremely handsome, regal looking Arab fellow walked in the rear door, or, I should say, made his entrance. He was tall, slim, and dressed in a style that reflected impeccable taste. The entire class turned to view him. I thought they might even stand! Everyone obviously recognized him, and he was acknowledging members of his audience with smiles and polite quips that had them laughing as he made his way to his seat. The mood had actually changed. My lecture had some relationship to medical research, and I asked the class if anyone had any insights to share. Who should raise his hand from the back of the room but the young man that I had assumed was a prince. In perfect English, with a slightly British accent and with great self-assurance, he elucidated the entire matter for the class.

"What's your name?" I asked. "Mahmoud Qandeel," he responded. "You seem to know quite a lot about medicine. Is that your area of study?" "No!" he replied, "I happened to read a magazine article on this subject the other day." "Well thank you for sharing it with us, but I think you should consider a career in medicine. Hereafter, I'll refer to you as Doctor Qandeel." He smiled graciously.

Mahmoud was five years younger than I and light years more worldly. He took it upon himself to introduce me to San Francisco. Everyone knew him (adored might be a better word): the mayor, police chief, rock stars, drug dealers, street people. He was excessively generous and could make the humblest person feel important. He was completely open and self-effacing. You did not have to hide things from Mahmoud, for he accepted you as you were. His greatest skill was people. He could discover your hurts and make you forget them, at least temporarily. He was charming, fun, and impossible to keep pace with. Women greeted him with kisses on the cheek everywhere we went, and we went everywhere! It was a world I had never seen before, one that consisted of the finest cars, clothes, delicacies, restaurants, rings, watches, yachts, dignitaries, diplomats, call girls, champagne and discotheques, where middle-aged wealthy women would ask you to come home for the night, "for breakfast" they would say. It glittered and glamored in every direction like ice! Conversations were cold, lifeless, and led nowhere. We were poor actors playing roles for which we were poorly suited. Everyone was desperately absorbed into having a good time, preoccupied with being "in" and "with it" and "exclusive." There was no joy or happiness—only laughter. I had never felt so much hurt in one place and at one time before. I did not fit in there, nor did I ever want to.

Although he had mastered the game, Mahmoud did not really belong there either. Intrinsically, he was a simple, humble, and generous man. His attraction was his innocence, his honesty, his boyishness, all of which miraculously had survived San Francisco only slightly tarnished. And I was not the only one who was missing something. He had his own agony. He could not have relieved so many others' pain if he did not. I hoped so badly that he would find what he had lost!

He introduced me to his family. It was not clear immediately who had adopted whom, but they surely gave more of themselves than I. Mahmoud was the oldest son, which is a position of responsibility in a Saudi family. His brother Omar was a very bright physics student at the University of California–Berkeley. He was tall and muscular and a second degree black-belt in Tae Kwon Do. His eyes were so intense that, when he was not smiling, you thought that he might be angry. But when he smiled, and he frequently did, it was the most gentle and comforting smile. His sister Ragia, also a student at the University of San Francisco, was pure goodness and kindness. Her large brown eyes were her whole story. They were caring, warm, penetrating and passionate. She was exotically and ethereally beautiful, difficult to define and impossible to forget. Hawazin was Mahmoud's pretty, young bride-to-be. She was intelligent, perceptive, witty, and loved to laugh. Mahmoud's father had died when they were children, and it was clear from their reminiscences that the emotional wounds still had not healed. His mother lived alone, with the exception of several servants, in Saudi Arabia.

The times we spent together picnicking and touring the Bay Area or eating dinner at their apartment were the best I had had in a long time. We did not discuss religion very much and, when we did, it was almost always in response to my questions. I did not push it, for I did not want it to interfere with our friendship. My understanding was that they felt the same way. And so I was astonished when I was given the Qur'an and some books about Islam. I knew they had an attachment to their faith, but their lives were not that religious and I had not seen them taking such an interest in anyone else. I wondered who thought of it. Omar certainly had the spirituality, Ragia the compassion, and, of course, Mahmoud knew me so well. Was it so obvious I was unhappy? In any case, I received it as a gift, a sharing of something personal. In return, I would read it and try to understand.

You cannot simply read the Qur'an, not if you take it seriously. You have either surrendered to it already or you combat it. It attacks tenaciously, directly, personally. It debates, criticizes, shames, and challenges. From the outset it draws the line of battle, and I was on the other side. I was at a severe disadvantage, for it became clear that the author knew me better than I knew Him. Painters can make the eyes of a portrait appear to be following you from one place to another, but what author can write a scripture that anticipates your daily vicissitudes? The Qur'an was always way ahead of my thinking. It was erasing barriers I had built years ago and was addressing my queries. Each night I would formulate questions and objections and somehow discover the answer the next day as I continued on in the accepted order. It seemed that the author was reading my ideas and writing in the appropriate lines in time for my next reading. I had met myself in its pages, and I was afraid of what I saw. I was being led, painting myself into a corner that contained only one choice. I had to talk to someone, but not the Qandeels! Someone who did not know me, so that there would be no expectations. That Saturday, while I was in Golden Gate Park and heading back to Diamond Heights after my daily walk, I settled on a solution: I would go to the local student-run mosque on Monday.

St. Ignatius Church, located at the peak of Golden Gate Boulevard, is a source of pride to the University of San Francisco. The university catalogue includes several shots of it from different angles. I have seen more majestic churches, but when the fog rolls in and descends over it, its steeples appear to be reaching into heaven. On this particular Wednesday afternoon, it was clear and breezy while I stood outside Harney Science Center, where my office was located, and stared at the church. Beneath and to the rear of the church was the mosque, which the Jesuits were letting the Muslim students use.

Contrary to my earlier plan, I had not yet visited the mosque. I was even beginning to wonder whether my decision to visit it had been too hasty. Finally, I decided to go ahead with my plan, reassuring myself that I was only going to ask a few questions. I rehearsed my introduction as I headed across the church parking lot. The stairway down to the mosque was up ahead and to the left of the statue of St. Ignatius. An American student had pointed it out to me several weeks earlier, jokingly: "The rumor is that they keep corpses down there!"

I arrived at the top of the stairs and eyed the door below. The writing on it was definitely Arabic. I could feel my heart racing as I stood there hesitating, allowing my anxiety to grow. I thought that I should ask somebody in the church if this was the right spot. I went around to the side entrance. It was quite dark inside, and the stained glass was sending down bold pillars of colored light. To the left of the altar I spied what had to be a janitor. As I darted over to him, I passed in front of the crucifix without genuflecting. It is amazing how these lessons get ingrained in you! "Can you tell me where the mosque is?" I must have looked as unbalanced as I felt, for his expression was a combination of surprise and indignation. I did not wait for an answer.

When I got outside, I drew a couple of deep breaths. What a relief it was to be out in the sun again! I needed to relax for a few minutes. I circled the church to see if there were any other possible entrances to the mosque. There was one, but the door was locked. And so I ended up where I began, in front of the stairs by the statue. I was anxious and a little nauseous as I started down the stairs. My chest tightened, and my heart was pounding midway to the door. I quickly turned around and climbed back up the stairs. "Wait a minute!" I scolded myself. "You go in and out doors every day at this university. There are only students in there, for goodness sake!" I took another deep breath and started back down the stairs. The midway point was worse this time. When I reached the bottom, I felt constricted and sick. My legs, which carried me seven miles every day on my walk, were weakening. I reached for the doorknob. My hand was shaking! I was shaking! I was sweating! I ran for the top of the stairs.

I froze there, with my back to the mosque. I did not know what to do. I felt embarrassed and defeated. I considered returning to my office. Several seconds passed. I was gazing at the sky. It was vast, mysterious, comforting. I had fought the urge to pray for ten whole years! But now my resistance was spent, I just let the feelings rise. "Oh God! If you want me to go down those stairs, please give me the strength!"

I waited . . . Nothing! . . . I felt nothing! I was hoping that the ground might shake, a bolt of light might surround me, at least goose bumps! I did not feel anything! I made a 180 degree turn, walked down the stairs, put my hand on the doorknob, and pushed open the door.

"Are you looking for something?" I had interrupted their conversation. They were standing directly ahead of me near the left wall. They both were barefooted and considerably shorter than I. One was dressed in what appeared to be traditional Eastern clothing with a round, white cap on his head. The other wore western clothing. I had forgotten my lines. "Is Omar, Mahmoud here?" I was getting nervous again. "What's their last name?"

The one without the cap looked suspicious. "Qandeel?" It did not help. "There's nobody else here. Just us." This was not going to work. "I'm sorry. I must be in the wrong place." I started to turn around. "Do you want to know about Islam?" called the one with the cap. "Yes! Yes! I would!" I took a step towards them. "Would you please take off your shoes? We pray here," he apologized. The traditional fellow was doing the talking. The other decided to merely observe something which was, judging from his expression, unusual.

We sat on the ground in the left-hand corner. They let me choose the place, and I positioned myself so that I was facing the door with my back to the wall. There was a small washroom off to my right and a closet-sized room for the ladies off to my left. Abdul Hannan, a student from Malaysia, was the young man with the white cap. Muhammad Yusuf, the other student, was from Palestine. I told them what I knew about Islam, and they were pleasantly surprised. We talked for about fifteen minutes. I asked some superficial questions, but nothing was as I had expected. Abdul Hannan began saying something about angels beating the souls of dead disbelievers and the tortures that they would be subjected to in the grave. I only pretended to listen. I said that I had an office hour to get to— I did not, but it always works—and I thanked them for their time.

I was about to stand up to leave when the doorknob turned. It was now late afternoon, and the setting sun was stationed somewhat behind the door. The lighting in the room was dim, so when the door opened the entrance was engulfed in light. Standing there was this silhouette of a man with a straggly beard, ankle-high robe, sandals, turban, and a cane. He looked like Moses returning from Mount Sinai. He was biblical and fascinating. I had to stay. He entered quietly and did not seem to notice us. He was whispering what must have been a supplication with his head raised slightly and his eyes almost shut. His hands were near to his chest, his palms turned upwards as if waiting for his share of something. When he finished, he asked Muhammad something in Arabic and then walked unassumingly into the wash room.

"That's brother Ghassan." They were revived and optimistic. "He's the imam. He leads the prayers." I knew from my reading that Muslims had no official clergy. "Anyone can lead," Muhammad offered, "Abdul Hannan, myself, anybody." A moment later Ghassan came into the room. His head was lowered meekly as he came over to us. He had a slight, Gandhi-ish kind of frame. His complexion was fair and his eyes and face were simultaneously peaceful and desolate, as if he had resigned himself to some great personal tragedy. As the other two students made room for him, he sat down next to me. He placed his hand on my knee. "What's your name?" He was the first to ask and, unlike Abdul Hannan and Muhammad, he wanted to talk casually at first, apparently to reduce the tension. I appreciated his attempt to put me at ease. His voice was low-toned and strong and had a certain special resonance that gave him an aura of inspiration. His accent told me he was from Arabia. He was somewhat shy and tried not to look straight into my eyes. "Jeff Lang." "Are you a student at USF?" he asked. I looked much younger than my age (earlier in the semester, I had been asked to leave a teachers' meeting because everyone thought that I was a student). "No, I'm a professor in the math department." His eyes widened and he glanced at the others. We spoke for a few minutes, and then Ghassan asked me politely if I would excuse them while they prayed the afternoon prayer. It was the first time I saw Muslims pray together. I used the break to stretch my legs, which by now were stiff from sitting on the floor.

We returned to our places when they were done. Ghassan resumed the conversation. "So how did you become interested in Islam?" I wondered if he knew the Qandeels. "I've been reading about it." Apparently, that answer sufficed. We continued on for a while discussing mostly technical matters, but we really were not communicating. I was running out of questions, and he was running out of comments. We were both disappointed and I thought of getting back to the math department.

"Do you have any other questions?" "No, not really." But then something popped into my mind. "I do have one question." I waited. I was not sure how to formulate it. "Can you tell me what it feels like to be a Muslim? I mean, how do you see your relationship with God?"

I could already see that Ghassan had the fantastic charisma and intuition so indispensable for a spiritual leader. I would later discover that he had a huge following both here and abroad. Like Mahmoud, he was acutely sensitive to your inner pain, but unlike Mahmoud, he would not let you ignore it. He would magnify it in front of you and force you to focus on it. This is a tremendous power that few possess. Every great religious leader must have it, however, and, along with it, the accompanying terrific responsibilities and dangers.

His eyes met mine and he did not answer immediately. Maybe he was surveying the source and the intent of the question. Then he lowered his head, as if praying, summoning his spiritual energy. Slowly moving his head from side to side, as people do when they want to indicate a negative response, he began to speak. The first word he said was both a prayer and a call: "Allaaahh!" He paused and took a deep breath. "Is so great!!! And we are nothing compared to Him, we are less than a single grain of sand." As he spoke, his thumb and index finger squeezed tightly a nonexistent speck of sand, which he lowered to the floor and then released to reveal nothing, making his symbol all the more effective. "And yet, He loves us more than a mother loves her baby child!"

He was fighting back his feelings. His eyes were nearly closed and his head still lowered. From this point on, until he finished his words, I would see the possession of a spirit that was burning with fear, hope, and desire. Each remaining sentence would be a wave of emotion, rising then receding.

"And *nothing* happens except by the will of Allah! When we breathe in," he put his hand to his chest, "it is by His will. And when we breathe out, it is by His will. When we lift our foot to take a step, it is by the will of Allah. And we would *never* be able to put that foot back on the ground, except by His command! When a *leaf* falls from a tree and twists and turns on its journey to the ground, no *segment* of that journey takes place, except by Allah's will. And when we pray and put our nose to the ground, we feel joy, a rest, a strength that is outside this world and that no words could ever describe. You have to experience it to know."

He remained quiet for several seconds, letting the words sink in. How much I wished that he and I could change places, if only for a few minutes, so that I could feel the desire, the passion, the anguish, the yearning for his Lord! I wanted to know the serenity and the torment, the trust and the fear, rising from insignificance, aspiring for surrender! I yearned to be resuscitated from this spiritual death!

"So would you like to become a Muslim?" His words cracked the air, exploding in my consciousness. Why did he have to say that! That was not why I had come here! I could see myself trying to explain it to my family, colleagues, and friends. I was working at a Jesuit university! What about my job? Faces and voices crowded my mind: my ex-wife, old acquaintances, a couple of them even dead, while I stumbled over excuses. I felt panicked again: my lower back and the back of my neck were hot, my palms were wet. What business was it of his anyway! Why not just leave it alone, let us both walk out of there! He was not going to lose anything! I did my best to conceal my anxiety and alarm. I suffocated all that turmoil and spoke calmly. "No, not today anyway, I really just wanted to ask a few questions."

How I hoped that that would end it. I needed to get to my office. What was I even doing here? My body was locked in tension, braced for the next attack. I knew I would have to be firmer this time. But a part of me was straining to hear him say it again. Groping! Reaching! Pleading! Begging! Praying! "Don't leave me, not after having come this far!"

Ghassan had been through this before and he knew better than to give up easily. He tried again softly. "But I think that you believe in it. Why don't you try?"

The voices and faces were gone. There was no need to get so upset. I did not owe anything to anybody—not to Ghassan, my friends, no one. The decision was mine alone. Then I remembered my parents and all of those lessons about being "German" that they had taught my four brothers and me—every culture has the same lessons that they identify as their own— and I remembered one in particular: if you feel that something is right, then pursue it, regardless of what other people think. "Follow your feelings," my mother would say. The first time I had applied that philosophy was when I had changed undergraduate majors. In retrospect, that was so comparatively easy. I looked at them all and nodded my head up and down. "Yes, I think I'd like to become a Muslim."

Their faces celebrated in jubilation and relief. They reminded me of NASA engineers after the successful moon landing. I wondered what was all the fuss about, you would think that *they* had converted to Islam. Anyway, I had not officially converted. I still had to make the profession of faith. The door knob turned again. There was another bolt of light, another silhouette, and another prophetic image standing at the door in a robe, turban, and beard. He was a little bigger and heavier than Ghassan.

"Mustafa!" Ghassan called. "This brother wants to become a Muslim!"

Mustafa's big, gentle, and fatherly face (he looked a little like Burl Ives) beamed gleefully. He ran over to hug me.

"Mustafa!" Ghassan interrupted. "He still has to say the *shahadah*!"

He retreated softly, as if he had discovered something fragile and precious. But Ghasan did not want to deprive him of his participation or excitement: "Teach the brother what to say, Mustafa."

Mustafa rehearsed the *shahadah* in English for me so that I would understand what I was about to say. His voice was hushed, as if he were talking to a newborn. He then pronounced the *shahadah* in Arabic, a word or two at a time, which I repeated after him.

"*Ashhadu*," said Mustafa. "*Ashhadu*," (I testify) I repeated. I was struggling with the pronunciation, trying to get it right. It was like learning how to talk again.

"*An la ilaha*," said Mustafa. "*An la ilaha*," (There is no god) I repeated. My entire adult life up to that day was a learning and confirmation of this fact. "There is no god." I had come to know firsthand the awesome truth of it and its terrible consequences and emptiness.

"*Illa*," said Mustafa. "*Illa*," (Except) I repeated. *Illa* is a conjunctive, pointing to something overlooked. A tiny word that had stood between me and the filling of that emptiness, the tremendous vacuum that was my life, that had distanced me from the reality I was always seeking.

"*Allah!*" said Mustafa. "*Allah!*" (God!) I repeated. The words were like drops of clear water being slowly dripped into the scorched throat of one who nearly died of thirst. I was regaining strength with each of them. I was coming to life again.

"*Wa ashhadu anna*," said Mustafa. "*Wa ashhadu anna*," (And I testify that) I repeated. I was joining a fellowship of prophets and followers throughout all history, races, and colors by extending my hand in discipleship to one who called us fourteen centuries ago.

"*Muhammadan*," said Mustafa. "*Muhammadan*," (Muhammad) I repeated. This was more than a mere acknowledgment: it was a commitment to a way, time-honored and universal, preached from the lips of the very first human message bearers and sealed in the revelation through Muhammad.

"*Rasul*," said Mustafa. "*Rasul*," (Is the messenger) I repeated. I felt protected, secure, and liberated. I could love again and be loved by One whose giving knows no limits. I collapsed into the mercy that flowed from the supreme love. I had come back home again!

"*Allah!*" said Mustafa. "*Allah!*" (God), I repeated.

7. Sally Howell, "Finding the Straight Path: A Conversation with Mohsen and Lila Amen About Faith, Life, and Family in Dearborn," in *Arab Detroit: From Margin to Mainstream* (2000)

In the 1998 interview excerpted below, scholar, documentarian, and curator Sally Howell explores the personal lives of two Shi'a Muslims from greater Detroit, Michigan. Hoping to present an intimate and human portrait of

Shi'a Muslims in Detroit, Howell asks Lila and Mohsen Amen, a married couple with children, to reflect on both the sacred and profane aspects of their lives. The picture that emerges sheds light on several larger themes in the story of Muslims in the United States. First, Lila and Mohsen's marriage is a product of cultural encounter—Lila was born in Michigan; Mohsen is an immigrant from Lebanon. As Howell notes, their union is an example of a larger trend in Arab Detroit, where immigrant and American Arabs "work, organize, worship, and frequently marry among each other." Their interactions reveal the interpersonal negotiations and personal transformations that take place as a result of such encounters. Their life histories also reflect the influence of events overseas on American Muslims. The 1979 Iranian Revolution, which was led by the Ayatollah Khomeini, inspired and fostered a religious revival among Shi'a Muslims all over the world, including in the United States. Their discussion of Islamic religiosity in Detroit begins to show how, even in one city, there is infinite variety in Muslim practice and thought. Finally, the issue of gender relations in American Muslim communities, a topic explored much more in the next chapter, is powerfully evoked in their descriptions of their life together. As Mohsen's commitment to Islam increases, Lila's frustrations with him do, too. But Lila, who was born a Sunni Muslim, eventually finds herself more deeply drawn to her Islamic faith, as well.

LILA: My name is Lila Amen, and I was born and raised in Dearborn, Michigan. I've been married for twenty-three years to Hajj Mohsen al-Amen, and I've got four children, Suehaila, nineteen, Shadia, eighteen, Bilal, sixteen, and Samira, who is going on fifteen. They're a product of the Dearborn public schools, where I'm currently working as a Public School Community Liaison for the Bilingual and Compensatory Education Program.

SALLY: Tell me about your family background. Where is your family from? What neighborhood did you grow up in?

LILA: Mom and Dad both came from Lebanon fifty years ago, around 1948. I was raised, in the first years of my life, on Roulo and Amazon Streets in Dearborn's Southend, and later on Evergreen in Detroit. Dad bought a combination house and store in Detroit, which Mom ran while raising us kids. We went to Leslie Elementary School, which is now the Malcolm X Academy. Then we moved back into Dearborn and I graduated from Fordson High School in 1972. My dad worked at Ford

Motor, at the Rouge Plant, steel division. He retired after almost thirty-six years. Mom was a housewife. They raised eight children.

SALLY: Would you fill me in a bit on your history as well, Mohsen?

MOHSEN: My name is Mohsen Amen. I came to the United States in 1970 when I was nineteen years old. I came to change my life and work in the factory, just like everybody else.

SALLY: Where did you come from?

MOHSEN: I came from southern Lebanon, from Ayat al Jabal. I brought with me here about thirty-six families so far. It turned out to be a big wave of immigration during the early 1980s. They all came to work in the factories. We lived on Dix in the Southend for a while, and we moved to east Dearborn, and I'm still there.

SALLY: So you came before the [Lebanese civil] war?

MOHSEN: Way before the war. . . .

SALLY: Well, tell me about growing up here. I'm especially interested in the religious life of your family. Which mosque were you a part of? How did you mature into the Muslim you are today?

LILA: At first there was the mosque on Dix [in Dearborn's Southend]. It's called the American Moslem Society. We attended that mosque on weekends. They had a weekend school, run by Imam Mohammed Karoub. He taught us kids how to do the Fatihah [the opening verses of the Quran] and how to pray and that sort of thing. We lived a conservative life. It wasn't as if Mom insisted on our wearing *hijab* [Islamic head covering, usually a scarf worn to conceal the hair and neck] or that sort of thing, and she herself never wore it, but it was conservative. It was very promotional, if you will. "This is Islam. These are the things that we do." We fasted at all times. We dressed conservatively. We left the Dix mosque when it changed hands, and Dad started driving us to Canada to attend the Muslim mosque built in Windsor.

SALLY: So your parents are Sunni? . . .

LILA: Sunni Muslim, yes. We attended the Canadian mosque for a couple of years. Then a mosque was built on Joy Road and Greenfield [in Detroit on the border of Dearborn] which is now the Islamic Center of America. It was run by Imam Mohammed Jawad Chirri. We started to attend there because it was closer and more convenient. At that time there was not a Sunni/Shi'a situation. Obviously, that wasn't the case if Dad was having us attend the mosque at Joy Road and Greenfield, because it was majority Shi'a. . . .

SALLY: I'd like to know how you felt about Islam. Did you feel you had a good knowledge of it when you were growing up? Did you ever feel out of place because you were a Muslim? How much a part of your identity was Islam when you were growing up?

LILA: I think being Arab American was more of an identity for me than being a Muslim. While growing up, there wasn't a big promotion of being a Muslim. People never said, "I am Lebanese. I am Palestinian." It was, "I am Syrian." That was the statement people would make. And, of course, during those years, Lebanon was considered a part of Syria. In some cases it still is today. So as a habit, people would refer to us as Syrians, not as Lebanese. Today it's far different, of course.

Being conservative the way we were, Mom and Dad didn't let us run around in a bikini. We would wear shorts and tops, but nothing like tank tops or things of that sort. Pretty much the whole lifestyle was conservative. It was very Arab American too, because everything we did socially had to do with our own people, whether they were relatives or friends. I spent a lot of time growing up, of course, with Americans. I have to say, whether it was just or not, a lot of the Arabs I had gone to school with actually made me feel annoyed with my own people. I am talking about some of the things the males did growing up. A lot of them even today, the same ones that I grew up with, are either in jail, or on drugs, or things of that sort, which hurts. When I met Mohsen, I used to joke about not being able to stand my own people, aside from the relatives and people that we socialized with. These kids that I'd gone to school with gave a bad name to the community. But it wasn't an Islamic thing at that time, it was an Arab thing. It was a "Syrian" kind of attitude.

SALLY: It was also the neighborhood you grew up in. It was a rough neighborhood back then.

LILA: Yes, it was.

SALLY: How old were you and Mohsen when you met?

LILA: I was nineteen. It was in 1973 that we met. In 1973 he asked me to marry him and in 1975 we got married.

SALLY: How did you meet?

LILA: Blame it on my sister. My sister introduced us to each other in November, and in December he asked me to marry him, and I laughed. I was like, "What? You're kidding!" It was only three weeks after we met. Then we got engaged in July of 1974 and we got married on June 14 of 1975.

SALLY: So tell me about your relationship. Did you date at all?

MOHSEN: Every time I took her out I had to drag her sister along.

LILA: You can consider that sort of a date. But my sister was always with us. Mom and Dad were conservative. Today it's different. When you get engaged, you actually get married in Islam.

MOHSEN: Culturally, if a woman gets pregnant out of wedlock, that's a big thing. Religiously, it's even bigger. So when the woman is married and she's still in her home, people tend to look at it like . . .

LILA: . . . like *ayb* [disgrace, shame].

MOHSEN: They do not understand Islam fully. Now, when they do *katib al-kitab*, they are married. That's it. People understand. Whatever happens, that's his wife. Now they understand more because now they look at it not through culture, but with regard to religion. Now there's more religious people around. They understand.

SALLY: I've also heard you talk about when you were dating, before you got married, how Lila wasn't *muhajiba* [did not cover her hair], you used to drink alcohol [which is forbidden in Islam]. At some point you both started to take your religion more seriously. I want to hear about your wilder days and what brought you back into the fold.

MOHSEN: I'll start before she starts. I came to America as a young man. I saw. I did. Whatever people did, I went along. I didn't know my religion. I came to this country eager to discover everything. And when you are a young man, you got . . . you know, peer pressure. Your friends, whatever they do you're gonna want to do. You want to show off. So we started on the wrong steps, which the others don't call wrong steps, they call them the "wild years." But to us, now, looking back, we did wrong. But this is part of growing up. We went to the bars. We drank. We did not drink to get drunk. We drank because you have to buy a drink when you go into the bar. And if you want to dance, you have to pay the consequences. So we drank a drink or two and danced. That's about it, really. We did not go overboard.

SALLY: This was the two of you?

LILA: No. This was him when he started out in Detroit.

MOHSEN: When I met my wife, she was still young. I went to the family and I told them, "I'm happy to see your daughter. I want to settle down. I want to get married." I wanted it to be known as . . . that. They agreed with that, and we read the Fatihah [the first chapter of the Qur'an].

This made it OK to an extent. She still had to be home at a certain time. If she wanted to go out somewhere, there had to be a third person, so they knew there would be no personal contact.

LILA: So they'd be comfortable with it.

SALLY: I understand that.

MOHSEN: There's got to be a third person to prevent you from doing the . . . the unmentionable. [Laughter]

MOHSEN: The taboo. Which is good. It's like we say, "Wherever there's a male and a female [alone together], the Devil is the third."

SALLY: He's right there in the middle. [Laughter]

MOHSEN: Because if we do something and have a baby, there will be a disaster, what if one of us changes his mind about marriage? The kid will be the one who suffers.

LILA: The kid will be without a name. Well, going back to those days, I never really used to go to nightclubs. I started doing that when I met him. Shame on you.

[Laughter]

LILA: Actually, shame on my sister, because she too used to go to nightclubs at that time! That's when we met, going to the clubs. Yes, we did drink. Yes, we did have a good time. We *dabkeed* [danced the traditional Arab line dance]. We even performed in a *dabkah* troupe for three or four years. I enjoyed that, but it was a folklore *dabkah* troupe, not just where you go to bars. We flew to Washington a couple of times and danced for organizations. It was beautiful. But we drank and we danced and we went places. We were no different than anybody else. Well, not everybody was that way. But we didn't drink to get drunk.

MOHSEN: We did it in a social way.

SALLY: Well, your community was more conservative than the mainstream was back in the 1970s, but it was less conservative than the Arab community is now in the 1990s. So you were like the majority of people your age?

LILA: Yeah. At that time.

MOHSEN: But they didn't know religion. They thought, this is sociable, so when you go over to somebody's house, you have a beer. Or when you go out, you have to pay for a drink. So you buy the drink.

SALLY: It was no big thing.

MOHSEN: It was no big thing.

LILA: You never had beer or things like that in your home. We never did in our home. I remember the only time we did was once we had a New Year's party. People brought their drinks and things like that in my home . . .

MOHSEN: We would go to the park and take a six-pack.

LILA: I think things started to change for us when I got pregnant. We were married in 1975, and I had Suehaila in 1979. We waited three-and-a-half years, at least. Mohsen's parents had twenty-one kids together, and Ammi [Lila's father-in-law] just couldn't deal with the fact that his son was not having a child. We put the poor man through some fears and let him think that his son couldn't have children, just so they'd leave us alone. You know the first thing that, I won't say Muslim parents . . .

MOHSEN: The parents.

LILA: . . . the Arab parents, say is like, "What's wrong, you're not pregnant yet?" First it's to the woman.

MOHSEN: Arab parents, they expect a child in the first year.

LILA: "What's wrong with her? She can't give you children?" So as much as this got on our nerves, we were struggling, paying bills. He was helping his family at that time too, so weren't able to save for ourselves and get on with our lives. We swore that we would not have children in an apartment. We would wait until we bought a house. Well, the only way to get them off of our backs was to say Mohsen couldn't have any children. His poor father. We never realized how much we'd hurt him. [General laughter]

SALLY: This is cruel.

LILA: We must have hurt him terribly. For months he didn't talk to us.

SALLY: So on top of the drinking and the dancing, you were lying. [More laughter]

MOHSEN: They told us to see a doctor. They offered me these tips on the village remedy.

LILA: How you have children . . .

MOHSEN: We used to laugh at all that, then we told them that we had to wait, to save some money at least. When we bought our home and we paid our bills and we relaxed, I said "It's time to have a family."

LILA: And we did, right away. We had Suehaila in 1979. Things started to roll in a positive direction. It was about in 1980 when Ammi, *Allah Yarhamu* [God rest his soul], Mohsen's father, started to really fall into the religion. There is a story behind that actually. That's when Sheikh Abd al-Latif came to town and started to introduce Islam on a different basis. And because they were from the same area in the *Janub* [south Lebanon], they went to him.

MOHSEN: Don't forget the revolution in Iran. That changed our perspective. . . .

LILA: First it was Sheikh Abd al-Latif. He lived over on Riverside and had a place there where everyone would meet. He also took a room at AC-CESS [the Arab Community Center for Economic and Social Services] and used it for Friday prayers. Then it started to grow, rapidly grow. This was in 1980, 1981. Of course, the Islamic revolution in Iran kicked off in 1979. I believe it was 1981 that Al Sayyed Mohammed Hussein Fadlallah came to town. Then, a whole group of people just woke up. It was very strange. He came to town. He was a very big figure from Lebanon. I'll never forget that they had this event out at a country club in Southfield, the Bonnie Brook. Hundreds of people went there. I think it was more out of curiosity. It was a political time.

MOHSEN: I will tell you a funny story about that. I learned religion when I was young, but it took somebody to shake it out of me and bring it out. One day my father came to me and said, "Hey, we are having a dinner. Do you want to come to it?" And, before I was away from the religious people, away from them, even in my own family. They used to call me the Americanized person in the family. So I told them, "I'll take two tickets." I took two tickets, not intending to go. It just so happened that on that Sunday, we had nothing whatsoever to do. I looked at my wife and said, "Do you want to go to that dinner?" And she said, "No. You go ahead." For the first time, I just drove myself to the Bonnie Brook. I didn't know where I was going. I just said, "Well I'm gonna go." And I went there and I saw six hundred people, seven hundred people there. Everybody that I knew was there. And I saw Al Sayyed Mohammed Hussein Fadlallah. I knew him since I was a little boy, cause he used to be a sheikh right in my neighborhood. He knew my father. I asked him if he remembered me. He said, "Yes. I do remember you. You are the son of so-and-so." And he reminded me of things I used to do when he was making sermons. For me, that was like I was sleeping and somebody woke me up from a dream. I came back home. I put the Quran in front of me and I started crying. I didn't know what to do. I had forgotten how to pray. I forgot everything. I didn't even know how to read the Fatihah. I forgot all about that. Then I start to read, read. And I start to do my *salah* [prayers], and I cried. My wife saw me. She said, "What the heck is wrong with that man? He goes to a dinner and he comes back like there is something wrong with him." [Laughter]

MOHSEN: And I took off from there. Like they say, I changed those clothes that I had on before and put on new clothes, with a new vision in front of me.

LILA: He's still a crazy man, though!

MOHSEN: Hey, I'm not a fanatic.

LILA: You don't go into the religion and stop living.

SALLY: You're talking to the daughter of a preacher.

MOHSEN: I'm not a fanatic.

SALLY: I know about being faithful and enjoying life at the same time. God doesn't say you are supposed to sit and pray twenty-four hours a day.

MOHSEN: Exactly. Islam came to save you, not to put you in misery. It came to help you throughout life. And when you understand Islam you will find out that you can have fun. You can live and you can get along with everybody. But . . .

LILA: You have your *wajibs*, obligations.

MOHSEN: You have obligations, like good manners, not making a fool of yourself. You don't have to be a joker to make somebody laugh. And you don't have to laugh out loud to make somebody notice that you are laughing. Everything with manners. Islam comes to teach you a way of life with good sense.

LILA: When Mohsen started to change, it was an annoyance to me. Because it wasn't just a change, a little-by-little, step-by-step thing. He went from one dinner to the next day. It was, in a way, frightening.

SALLY: Do you remember anything the sheikh said? Did he say anything specific that led you to this sudden change?

MOHSEN: It's not what he said. It's the sight, among all the people that I knew there, of this person who used to teach me when I was young.

LILA: The environment. To see all those people.

MOHSEN: And I looked at myself and said, "Where am I going?" I saw like a dead path with an obstacle, and I said, "Where am I going?" I didn't know where I was going. I go to work. I come home. I take care of the kids. Eat, drink, and go to sleep. And this is it. This is what? God did not make me just for that reason. There has got to be more to it. My subconscious started working. It was like somebody shook me and said, "There is a purpose for you here. You don't work, eat, sleep, and drink and have babies. We are not animals. There is a purpose for you. Go out and find what you can do." That's when Lila started to go through the misery with me because I was hungry to find out what lay ahead of me; the future, the religion, the hereafter. Now the kids. How are they going to be when they grow up? I started to look forward to everything. I started to look way ahead of me. I started learning about Islam. I started to inhale knowledge. I started buying books. Whenever there was a visiting imam [a Muslim teacher and scholar], I used to go and listen to what he had to say. A sermon about this, a sermon about that.

SALLY: Can I hear your side now, Lila? You said you were frustrated.

LILA: Yes. In the beginning, when Mohsen started, it was frustrating because we'd already had Suehaila and Shadia at the time, and I found that now this new thing in his life, this Islam, was taking him away from me and the kids. The time we had together on the weekends, he was preoccupied with going to these meetings, listening to sermons. In the evenings it was no longer playing cards until three or four o'clock in the morning, with his cousins—which is what I had problems with prior to that. Now he's going to listen to speeches through all hours of the night, and when they're done they go to his dad's house and have a cup of tea, forty men at a time. So I thought, "I can't deal with this sharing routine." I felt jilted, in a way, because I was working full-time, raising two kids, paying somebody to watch them while I worked to help him keep up with the bills. And on the weekends when we have time to do things together as a family, he doesn't have time for us. He only has time for himself. I began to hate what he was doing, which pulled me away from the religion.

A couple years later, in 1982, I was in a car accident while I was pregnant with my fourth. I had a difficult time, physically and emotionally, wondering if there's going to be something wrong with the child. *Al-hamdulillah* [praise be to God] she is healthy! Shortly afterwards, I was told that I either had tuberculosis, sarcoidosis, or lymphoma. Two out of these three are cancerous. This put me in a whole other light on life. "What is going on? What's going to happen next? I've got four children. Who's gonna take care of my kids? I'm gonna die. I know it. Maybe it's because I rejected what Mohsen was trying to teach me." These kinds of things were going on in my mind. It turned out to be sarcoidosis, an inflammation of the lymph nodes, which can shorten your life, but it wasn't as dangerous as lymphoma or tuberculosis. I did the operation. Then my gynecologist came and told me I had to take care of myself from now on. I had my tubes tied. No more kids. It was an agreed thing between us. Mohsen spoke to the sheikh about it, and the sheikh said, "If it's a life or death situation, you need to solve that. Your kids need a mom." So praise God, it worked out.

When I went in for the lymphoma tests, I did a *nidhar* [solemn vow], that if everything turned out OK, I would send Ammi and his wife on the pilgrimage to Mecca. Later, when I came out, and the results were OK, I did. I set aside four thousand dollars from the insurance money from the accident for them. Ammi didn't wind up going for various reasons. He had a heart attack. He had trouble raising the rest of the money he needed. But he gave his wife the permission to use his share from me, and she went.

In February of 1984, Hassan, Mohsen's brother, was killed in a robbery at a gas station in Detroit. That was the most fearful thing we ever dealt with in our lives, and it made me start to think differently. It turns out that it was his own two friends from our community that did it. One is still in jail. But the other was supposedly killed in an air raid in Lebanon, in Mashkara. I always say "supposedly," because at that time it was easy to buy off a name.

It was all of that, then, that woke me up. Mohsen's was seeing his friends make the change. Mine was seeing the things that happened in life.

8. Damarys Ocana, "Our Stories: A Leap of Faith," in *Latina Magazine* (2004)

In the 1960s, the number of American Hispanic or Latino/a converts to Islam began to increase. Several Puerto Ricans in New York City converted to Islam under the auspices of Elijah Muhammad's Nation of Islam. Since then, many more have converted to Islam through their exposure to various Sunni American Muslims. By the 1990s, Khadijah Abdelmoty, a Sunni convert to Islam, was missionizing among her Puerto Ricans brothers and sisters under the auspices of PIEDAD (Propagacion Islamica para la Educacion e la Devocion a Ala'el Divino). This group has distributed Spanish-language Islamic literature, acted as a mediator in the Muslim community, and provided support to the many Latina women who have converted to Islam. Chicanos, or Mexican Americans, have also converted to Islam. In 1997, the Latino American Dawah Organization, or LADO, was also established to promote da'wa, or missionizing, among Latino/a Muslims in the United States. LADO has published the Latino Muslim Voice *since 2002, and like other American Muslim groups, maintains an active presence on the Internet. In the article from* Latina Magazine *reproduced below, journalist Damarys Ocana recounts the story of three Latina Muslim converts and their struggles to honor their Hispanic heritage and families while remaining true to their new religious creed.*

Wearing a loose robe and veil that cover all but her face, Nylka Vargas glides into the mosque and takes her place in the middle of a row of solemn women. In unison with the others, she turns east, in the direction of Islam's holy city of Mecca, then touches her forehead and hands to the floor in submission to Allah. Some thirty feet in front of her, leading a row of men, the mosque's *imam*, or spiritual leader, chants a plaintive prayer in Arabic, his voice so clear and evocative that the nearby sounds of children playing and of rush-hour traffic grinding away seem to dissipate into the Union City, New Jersey, dusk. At the Imam's direction, Nylka joins the rest of her fellow worshippers and responds to his recitations from Islam's holy book, the Koran.

"Bismillahir rahmanir Rahim," she says in Arabic. In the name of Allah, the most gracious, the most merciful.

Growing up in her Peruvian-Ecuadorian home, Nylka said her prayers in Spanish and went to a Christian house of worship. Then, in 1995, as a 20-year-old college student, she became a Muslim—a decision that shocked her family at the time, even though it is becoming an increasingly common choice in the United States for Latinos. Although there are no official statistics on the number of Latino Muslims in this country (some estimates suggest there may be up to 75,000), over the past decade, Latino Muslim organizations have been cropping up across the country— Latino Dawah in New York City and Houston, and Propagacion Islamica para la Educacion e la Devocion a Ala' el Divino (PIEDAD) in Miami, are just two. There are also a growing number of Muslim Latino outreach programs, such as the one Nylka, now 30, heads at the Islamic Educational Center of North Hudson in Union City, New Jersey.

Since the terrorist attacks of 9/11, however, Latinos who convert to Islam are sometimes finding their decision met with grave concern, if not outright suspicion. Never mind that the Koran does not preach violence and that Muslims believe in the same God as Christians and Jews (though Muslims call him Allah). As the world's 1.2 billion Muslims celebrate Ramadan this month—which marks God's revelation of the Koran to the Prophet Muhammad—they do so against a backdrop in which being Muslim is often wrongly associated with being a terrorist. There are also more personal worries: When *mujeres* choose to wear *hijab*, the traditional Muslim covering, they are often defying furious families and friends who view conversion as a betrayal of their heritage.

What's ironic about this reaction is that there are few cultures to which Latinos are more connected than that of Islam. From the years 711 to 1492, Andalusia, Spain, flourished under the rule of the culturally advanced Islamic, or Moorish empire, which left its mark on everything from place and family names, like Cordova and Alameda, to people's facial features. Moorish architecture, so vividly preserved in Granada's Alhambra castle, also left its traces in some later cathedrals. Hundreds of Spanish words are derived from Arabic—the expression *ojalá*, for example, comes from *insha'Allah*, or "God willing," and *olé* is the Spanish adaptation of "Allah." Even *chaperonsa*, the dreaded *abuelitas* or *tias* who have supervised many a Latino on dates, have Islamic counterparts. "We can't deny the legacy of Islam in Latinos—you can scratch the surface of our skin and it's there, a *flor de piel*," says Juan Suquillo, an imam at the Union City mosque. "And that, combined with the fact that Islam offers a very logical, simple message that doesn't require people to give up most of their biblical beliefs, makes Latinos feel *en casa* (in the Muslim world)."

Other aspects of Islam are less easy for many Latinos to understand, such as the religion's strict guidelines for women. At a mosque, for example, women worship in a segregated section, which sometimes partitions off by a curtain. When a woman menstruates, she is prohibited from praying or touching the Koran, and, of course, women are expected to cover their hair with *hijab*. What, then, is Islam's appeal for so many *mujeres*? Like faith itself, the answer is a highly intimate matter. For *la espanola*, Diana Mariam Santos, conversion went hand in hand with a discovery of her true heritage; for Kathy Umaya Espinoza, a Chicana, it helped awaken her from a deep spiritual slumber. And for Nylka, it was about finally finding a place where she felt she belonged.

Who Am I?

Leaning over a sink in the bathroom at the Union City Mosque, Diana douses her hands, arms, mouth, nose, ears, feet, and hairline three times, the required preparation for prayer. "All this is *costumbre*," says the 25-year old social worker and teacher's aide. "Muhammad established (the ritual of ablution) not only as a preparation to pray, but for hygiene. In Islam, there is always a reason behind everything you do."

The study of Muslim customs is no mere history lesson for Diana, who was born in Seville and raised in Cadiz, both in Spain's Andalusia region. When Diana began looking into her family's history as a 19-year-old living in New York City, she discovered that—like many other Muslims living through the Spanish Inquisition during the 1400s and 1500s—her mother's ancestors had publicly converted to Christianity in order to hold on to their property and avoid being expelled. As it turned out, the maternal last name Diana knew as Calderon was actually Al Calderon. Diana, who had never felt at home with Catholicism (as a child, she was actually suspended from Catholic elementary school in Cadiz for asking too many questions), was "very angry, learning what they had to go through. They had to lose their identity."

At the time, Diana was already Muslim—in name, at least. She had converted years before, after learning about the religion from Moroccan neighbors back in Cadiz, but had never practiced. What really put her on the path to Islamic faith was seeing how the religion affected her Turkish Muslim bosses at the New York City gourmet market where she worked. "They were so peaceful," says Diana, who adds that although most of her family's has accepted her conversion, she's estranged from a few cousins because of it. "I was always very stressed. You see them and you are like, Oh my God, I wish I could have that light they have." She enrolled in Islamic classes and started reading the Koran. And although she took comfort in finding similarities between the Koran and the Bible she had grown up with (both holy books are against praying to graven images, for example, and the Bible's First Epistle to the Corinthians, like the Koran, urges women to cover their hair), she also found some of Islam's teachings—such as Jesus being a prophet instead of the son of God—easier to believe. As soon as she made her *shahadah*, the Muslim declaration of faith, Diana, who had suffered from depression in her teens, says she felt a light within her too.

Her newfound faith was severely tested during the September 11 attacks, when Diana, who was at work near the World Trade Center, walked the length of Manhattan in order to get home. Diana, who at the time didn't wear *hijab* because she didn't feel it was crucial to her faith . . . remembers clutching her purse in fear that someone would see her Koran and attack her. "Please let it not have been Muslims, because we wouldn't be very secure in this country if Muslims did this," she recalls silently praying. "I was so afraid." When she did find out the terrorists were Muslims, Diana says she was shocked—but is quick to add that they were extremists who do not represent the mainstream Muslim world. "You cannot control their sick mind," she says of the attackers. "You cannot blame the whole religion." Soon after the attacks, Diana came to the defense of a Muslim woman and girl who were being hassled on a Manhattan street for wearing *hijabs*. The incident led her to start wearing the scarf herself, as a tangible testament to her faith. "I was thinking, I'm an educated woman with a college degree," she says. "So when people come up to insult me or try to berate me, I will talk to them."

Since then, Diana occasionally runs into people who want to "liberate" her from Islam by telling her, "in this country you are free." Her response? "I just tell them that's exactly why I wear my *hijab*—because I am free to do so." She also draws strength from the mostly supportive response she receives from non-Muslim Latinas, who don't seem to doubt her cultural ties. "When they hear you speak Spanish," she says, "they know where you come from; they know who you are."

A Mother's Struggle

Stella Espinoza sat frozen in her chair. At the invitation of her daughter Kathy, she had come to a Muslim poetry slam in Irvine, California, hoping to reach a greater understanding of her daughter's new religion. But when a young man took the stage and started angrily criticizing Catholics and U.S. foreign policy, Stella's worst fears were confirmed. "I find the religion to be a bit political," says the retired secretary, who lives in River-side, California. "I was disturbed."

She might as well be talking about the way she felt that day in April 2001, when Kathy, then 22, told her she had converted to Islam. Growing up with her Mexican American mother, Kathy had been active in a Cath-olic youth group, even traveling to Denver one summer to hear Pope John Paul II speak. And when her older brother, Michael, strayed from the church after high school, it was Kathy who helped rekindle his faith; years later she served as an example when he applied to join the church's Do-minican Order of Preachers. "When you're a strong believer in your faith and you've tried to raise your children to the best of your ability," Stella says, her voice trailing off. "I never gave it a thought that one of my kids would want to go into another direction."

It was just this kind of assumption, however, that sent Kathy, now 26, a social worker who lives in San Jose, California, on her initial spiritual search. "We were kind of taught to not really question Catholicism—that we had to believe in it and have faith and that it's the truth," Kathy says. Then, while she was at San Jose State University, her two Muslim room-mates introduced her to Islamic principles such as the emphasis on a di-rect, priest-free relationship with God. "The fact that the Koran has not been changed in all these years, while the Bible has many versions—that was big to me," she says.

After finding peace in the Koran's teachings, Kathy now finds herself having to explain them to others who believe that being a Muslim means being a terrorist. "I'm constantly having to come up with passages in the Koran that show killing is wrong, and what is permissible in times of war and what is not," she says. "People see images of Muslims with (weapons), and that's what gets into their heads."

Then there are the questions she faces about what many view as Islam's oppression of women. The Muslim ban on women touching the Koran and performing the five daily prayers during their period is "about com-ing to God pure," Kathy says, noting that anyone with an unwashed open wound—be it man or a woman—is forbidden to touch the Koran. "When the prophet Muhammad came, women got their rights to own property and get an education," she says. "That was back in the 600s. In America, women couldn't even vote until the 1900s. Honestly, I'm sick of addressing it—it's frustrating (to have to defend the religion) you know so clearly and that is so beautiful." She does, however, share the alarm of people who read about women's lives in places like Afghanistan, where—prior to the 2001 U.S. overthrow of the religiously conservative Taliban regime— women were forced to cover themselves from head to toe and were not allowed to go to school or have jobs. Then there's Saudi Arabia, where women are not allowed to drive and cannot travel without written permission of a male relative. "My teachers have told me that is not Islam," Kathy says. "And there's a whole historical reason that folks in Saudi are the way they are. And I know Islam in its true form does not oppress women."

It's a shame that people see those cases and condemn all of Islam, she adds. "Islam is a monolith in that we believe, no matter who you are, that there is one God and that Muhammad is the last messenger of God," Kathy continues. "But you do have different people, different cultures. One thing that one of my teachers makes clear is that we are American Muslims, and our experience is not going to be the same (as Muslims overseas)."

There is a least one person, however, to whom Kathy is defending herself less and less: her mother, Stella, who is—slowly—coming around. Earlier this year the two attended a Muslim wedding, and these days, when Kathy comes over for family barbecues, Stella will take the meat Kathy brings—bought from a shop that prepares meat in accordance with Islamic *halal* guidelines, which state that animals must be killed in a way that minimizes their suffering—and cooks it in a separate grill. "My philosophy is that it's very important to be respectful. You have to let your kids go and do what they think is right," Stella says. "I love my pope—but I also love my daughter very much."

At Home in the World

Nylka steals a look at her imam, who is explaining the Islamic prayer calendar to a class of ten Latinas at the Union City Mosque, then quietly opens a small photo album. Stuck behind cellophane protectors are pictures of her before her conversion to Islam. There she is, blowing out birthday candles; kicking out a bare, leg, Rockettes-style, while dancing arm in arm with friends; and wearing a short-sleeved white lace dress and gloves, with her thick, jet-black hair sloping over her shoulders. "That's me at a wedding when I was 16," she says.

The change is remarkable. In accordance with strict Islamic principles that insist women dress modestly—both to honor Allah and to protect themselves from the lustful gaze of men—Nylka now wears loose clothes that cover her skin from neck to wrists to ankles. Her hair has disappeared behind her *hijab*, and because Muslim women are permitted to dance only when men aren't present, she no longer dances in public. But Nylka doesn't measure her transformation in terms of what she has left behind; she measures it terms of what she has gained: the spiritual fulfillment she always longed for, even as she was confirmed. As a child growing up Catholic, Nylka never felt in tune with church rituals like crossing herself with holy water or confessing to a priest, or paying money to light a candle and pray to a saint. Family visits to the religious services of other Christian denominations were equally baffling; during trips to a Pentecostal church, "I would see people jump up and dance, and I was never comfortable with that," she says. "I was always questioning, 'What are we doing here?' 'What's the reason?' My entire life, I couldn't find answers."

That changed while she was a student at Penn State University, where she formed friendships with several Muslims, who introduced her to the Koran. Nylka found the book's teachings intriguing, such as the concept of a direct link to God, as well as an easy-to-follow code. "Islam gives you specific guidelines for everything—hygiene, relations with your husband, how to play sports," she says. "It's not just about religion; it's a way of life." Simply put, she says, "Islam just made sense to me. It was natural."

Explaining that to her six siblings and mother, all Catholics, hasn't been easy. In the first few years after Nylka's conversion, her resistant mother would keep up a normal routine and cook Peruvian delicacies during the month of Ramadan—which requires Muslims to fast from sunrise to sunset—and heap it onto a plate that she served Nylka. "Sometimes I would have to hide it and pretend that I was eating," she says. "I tried to understand her point of view and not disrespect her."

The *hijab* was another battle. "For my mother and sisters, I'm in my youth, so I should be more glamorous," Nylka says. "It was hard for them to walk with me sometimes; hard for them to understand that Muslim women have to cover themselves to protect our charms from men." The *hijab* can seem "like a double standard," Nylka says, "but it's about modesty." Besides, she points out, "men have as much of an obligation to look away when they see a woman, whether she's wearing a *hijab* or not."

Fortunately, there is one place Nylka can go when she feels the need for understanding: her mosque. Although she still lives with her mother and plans to go to graduate school, she spends most of her time these days working as an assistant at the mosque, organizing Latino-Muslim get-togethers, and helping with an educational-outreach program, thus furthering her own study of the Koran. With the evening's prayer class ended, Nylka takes one final look around the mosque and nods. "This," she says, "is my home."

9. *Islamic Horizons,* "Matrimonials" (2005)

One way to measure the increasing prominence of South Asian Muslims from India and Pakistan on the American Muslim scene is to take stock of the matrimonials that appear in Islamic Horizons, *the official magazine of the Islamic Society of North America (ISNA). Though ISNA was initially an organization dominated by Arab American Muslims, it has become increasingly staffed and guided by South Asians. The magazine appeals to a wide audience, but most of the marriage advertisements reproduced below are from South Asian men or women, often parents seeking mates with an Indian or Pakistani background. To be sure, South Asian American Muslims are not the only Muslims in the United States who use marriage advertisements to meet potential mates. African American and other American Muslims do the same. For South Asians, however, endogamous marriage (that is, in-group marriage) reveals the importance of a diasporic identity shared by many South Asian immigrants who came to the United States after 1965, whether Muslim or not. While the break-up of British India after World War II created separate national identities among Indian, Pakistani, and eventually Bengali Muslims, South Asian immigration to the United States has led many Muslims from the Indian subcontinent to emphasize their common historical memories and roots. There is another factor at play in the preference for in-group marriages among South Asians, as well. Many of the advertisements express the desire for professional mates, especially those in the medical professions. Such preferences reveal the central role that class also plays in the selection of mates and in the creation of South Asian American identity more generally. South Asian Americans are, according to one census estimate, the wealthiest foreign-born immigrant group in the United States.*

And of His signs is this; He created for you spouses
from yourselves that you might find peace in them,
and He ordained between you love and mercy.
Lo, herein indeed are signs for people who reflect.
(Qur'an 30:21)

Seeking Husband

Sunni Muslim Indian parents invite correspondence for their U.S. born and raised daughter (25, medical student) from medical doctor or professional, 26–28 years old.

Sunni Muslim Indian parents invite correspondence for their U.S. born/ raised daughter (2nd year medical resident, wears hijab [veil]) from a medical doctor.

Sunni Muslim Pakistani parents invite correspondence for their U.S. born/ raised daughter (25, slim, attractive, 4th year medical student) from a born/raised medical doctor/lawyer/engineer/CPA/any educated professional, 24–32 years old. Please send resume/photo.

Pakistani parents living in U.S. invite correspondence for their daughter (26, medical resident in Pakistan) for suitable match, preferably Pakistani origin, U.S. citizen or permanent resident.

Professional woman moderately religious with character, strong values, principles, healthy, wants to meet like-minded Muslim gentleman between 55–60 for life partner. No strictly religious or already married individual needs to respond.

Sunni Muslim parents invite correspondence for their daughters (28-year-old, MD/resident and 25-year-old MPH/PharmD student) from professional gentlemen.

Pakistani parents invite correspondence for their U.S. born/raised daughter (beautiful, 24 years old, tall, college graduate) from professional MD/ Engineer/businessman, 24–30 years old. Send biodata w/photo.

Muslim Sunni parents invite correspondence for their daughter (U.S. citizen, beautiful, MS from U.S.) from MD or MS, Indo-Pak origin, 24–29 years old.

Muslim Indian parents of beautiful, U.S. born and raised daughter (21) invite correspondence from professional (24–30). Please respond with photo and bio/data.

Pakistani Punjabi parents, both physicians, invite correspondence for their 31-year-old daughter (MD in final year of residency at prestigious university hospital) from MD of similar background.

Respectable Sunni Indian educated family invite correspondence for daughter (born, raised, and settled in Saudi Arabia, 27 years old, physician) from religious, humble 28–33 year old, preferably naturalized Saudi citizen. Please contact U.S. relative.

Sunni Pakistani parents invite correspondence for their daughter (25, religious, wears hijab, slim/attractive, BSc computer science) from religious, well-educated professional.

Relative invites proposals for his two beautiful sisters (in Pakistan, single, educated, younger look, pray 5 daily prayers) from Sunni Muslim Pakistanis under 60, also for a brother age 48 who seeks Pakistani wife.

Muslim Pakistani parents invite correspondence for their U.S.-raised daughter, 2nd year family practice resident, from a medical doctor in NJ and surrounding states.

Pakistani parents seeking U.S. raised, well-educated professional, 25–32, for U.S. born, raised daughter, 25, 5'-6", attractive, practicing Muslim, BA/MA from top university.

Sunni Hyderabadi parents invite correspondence from U.S. for non-hijabi daughter, 25, 4th year medical student from U.S. born/educated MD, 25–29 years old.

South Asian parents invite alliance for U.S. born final year medical student, sincere, beautiful, Stanford educated, 26, from practicing Muslim professional (26–33) raised in U.S. or Canada.

Seeking Wife

Sunni Hyderabadi parents invite correspondence for son (born in U.S. 8/80, graduating from New York medical school 5/95) from U.S., religious, hijab-wearing, muslimah, 21–23 years old, in medical, dental, or pharmaceutical fields.

Sunni Hyderabadi parents invite correspondence for U.S. born son (fourth year medical student, 25 years old) preferably from medical student.

Sunni Hyderabadi parents invite correspondence for 28-year-old son (physician/second year resident) from medical student or resident.

Pakistani parents of 29-year-old son (U.S. born, neurology resident) seeking practicing Sunni muslimah with professional education.

10. Asra Q. Nomani, *Standing Alone in Mecca: An American Woman's Struggle for the Soul of Islam* (2005)

Growing up as the child of Indian immigrants who came to the United States after 1965, Asra Nomani (b. 1965) was acutely aware of her multiple identities as a South Asian Muslim American woman. As the passage below indicates, she spent much of her childhood, adolescence, and early adulthood negotiating the tensions between these identities, searching to integrate them into a unified whole. Her struggle to be both Muslim and American, authentic and independent, reflects the feelings of many other post-1965 Muslim immigrants, especially women. A former reporter for the Wall Street Journal, *Nomani has also become well known for her vision of a progressive, feminist, and pluralistic Islam. An unwed mother, she took her son on the pilgrimage to Mecca, claiming full membership in the community of Muslims in spite of her "sin"—and then she wrote about it. When her friend and colleague, reporter Daniel Pearl, was abducted in Pakistan in 2002, she helped Pearl's spouse, Mariane, lead an investigation into his disappearance and murder. Her revulsion of such acts led her to protest publicly and loudly against all social injustice committed in the name of Islam. In 2003, Nomani protested discrimination against women in her Morgantown, West Virginia, mosque by insisting on praying in the male-only main hall. In 2005, she organized a mixed gender congregational prayer in New York City that attracted international media coverage and the attention of American Muslim activists, whose reactions are further chronicled in chapter 4.*

Allahabad, India—One hot winter afternoon, I was lost in India on the banks of the Ganges, a river holy to Hindus. I was meandering with an American Jewish friend on a road called Shankacharaya Marg. By chance, my path intersected with the spiritual leader of Tibetan Buddhists, the Dalai Lama, inside an ashram, and he set me off on my holy pilgrimage to the heart of Islam.

It was January 2001, and I was, quite fittingly, in the city of Allah-abad, "the city of Allah," the name by which my Muslim identity taught me to beckon God. In Islam, Allah is our Arabic word for God. Born about a thousand miles westward along the Indian coastline in Bombay, India, I had evoked God with this name from my earliest days.

Although a Buddhist, the Dalai Lama, like millions of Hindu pilgrims, was in a dusty tent village erected outside Allahabad to make a holy pilgrimage to the waters there of the Maha Kumbha Mela, an auspicious Hindu festival. He joined the chanting of a circle of devotees dressed all in white. When they had finished, I followed the Dalai Lama to a press conference in a building surrounded by Indian commandos and his own bodyguards. Religious fundamentalism and fanaticism are wreaking havoc throughout the world, and in India they are redefining Hindu and Muslim communities that used to coexist peacefully. The demolition of a sixteenth-century mosque called Babri Masjid sparked one of India's worst outbreaks of nationwide religious rioting between Hindus and the Muslim minority; two thousand people, mostly Muslims, were killed. The cycle of hatred continued until that day when the general secretary of the sectarian World Hindu Council, Ashok Singhal, called Islam "an aggressive religion." At the press conference an Indian journalist raised his hand. "Are Muslims violent?" he asked.

My stomach tightened. This question reflected a stereotype of the people of my religion, but, alas, the national flag of Saudi Arabia, the country that considered itself the guardian of Islam's holiest cities—two historical sites called Mecca and Medina—includes the sword.

The Dalai Lama smiled. "We are all violent as religions," he said. After pausing, he added, "Even Buddhists."

We all smiled.

"We must stop looking at the past," he continued, "and look at the present and the future."

I sat near the back, my usual spot at press conferences, and pondered his words. I had spent a lot of my life trying to understand my past. My mother and father, Sajida Zafar Nomani, were children of India when it was still under British colonial rule. I was born in Bombay in 1965, after the country had won liberation. My parents left for America when I was two so my father could earn his PhD at Rutgers University in New Brunswick, New Jersey. My brother, Mustafa, my only sibling, and I stayed with my father's parents until we boarded a TWA jet in 1969 to JFK Airport in New York to be reunited with our parents. I became a journalist, landing my first job at the age of twenty-three with the *Wall Street Journal*. Despite my apparent success, I had difficulty expressing my voice. I wanted to raise my hand, but even though I had been a successful staff reporter for one of the most powerful newspapers in the world for over a decade, I could barely muster the courage to ask questions at press conferences. To justify my fears, I accepted the rationale passed on to me once by a senior journalist at the *Wall Street Journal*: "Don't ask any questions at press conferences," she had told me over the phone as I reported from the scene of a United Airlines plane crash. "That way, nobody will know what you're thinking."

Inviting and beaming, the Dalai Lama triggered something. All of a sudden, I wanted to let others know what I was thinking. I realized I had a responsibility to speak up. As long as I called myself a Muslim, I had to try to bridge the schism between my religion and others. I tentatively raised my hand. To my surprise, the Dalai Lama gestured eagerly at me. I began to speak my thoughts, marking a turning point in my life as I did so.

"Through personal meditation we can transcend ego and power in our own lives," I said. "What is it that our leaders can do to transcend the issues of power that make them turn the people of different religions against each other?"

He looked at me intently and said: "There are three things we must do. Read the scholars of each other's religions. Talk to the enlightened beings in each other's religions. Finally, do the pilgrimages of each other's religions."

I nodded my head in understanding. I, a daughter of Islam, was in the midst of the Hindu pilgrimage. I had grown up with a mocking understanding of the deities to which Hindus bow their heads, but sitting in a retreat colony amid simple devotees like an elderly Indian Hindu woman named Mrs. Jain, I understood that the spiritual intention of a polytheist is no different from that of a monotheist who prays in a synagogue, church, or mosque.

Just months earlier, I had climbed into the Himalayas at India's border with China and joined about twenty thousand Buddhists in a pilgrimage led by the Dalai Lama. On the last day I had tried to resuscitate an elderly Nepali Sherpa who had gotten caught in a stampede by pilgrims rushing to witness a holy religious sand creation called a mandala. He literally died resting in my hands, and I knew at that moment the universal phenomenon of faith that defines all religions. I had just spent two years speaking to the scholars of the faiths and reading their texts. I had read the teachings of the Buddha. I had read the Bible. I had sat at the feet of a pandit, a Hindu scholar who comes from the upper Brahmin caste of Hinduism. As a woman, I was trying to grasp the role of women in the faiths. I learned that sacred goddesses were integral to early civilizations, such as the Indus civilization from which India sprang.

These societies honored matriarchy and emphasized the power rooted in women. But they mostly evolved into patriarchal cultures in which men are considered more important than women. Most of the principles of goddess worship have disappeared from modern society.

I had not been able to understand my role as a woman in my religion of Islam. When I was a child of seven or eight in Piscataway, New Jersey, I asked my Islamic Sunday school teacher, a kind Egyptian man by the name of Dr. Mahmood Taher, "why aren't there any women prophets?'

He smiled. "There were," he explained, "great women." His lesson to me wasn't in the words that he spoke, but in the kind and open-minded way in which he received my question. He didn't tell me the question was inappropriate. He didn't rebuke me. He took me seriously. With his honest and gentle effort at an answer, he set me on a path of inquiry that I followed into adulthood. In Allahabad, I was still walking that path, eager to find my spiritual home as a woman born into Islam.

I emerged from my thoughts to the sound of journalists pushing back chairs as they got up at the end of the press conference. I jumped to my feet too and slipped to the front to ask the Dalai Lama another question as he left. He paused in front of me. I started to ask him my question. He didn't seem to understand, but it didn't matter. He giggled and lifted my chin with his right hand. It was a gentle and affectionate touch. It felt like a blessing, like a transmission of spiritual power in the greatest tradition of the masters passing their teachings on to students.

I dashed outside to jump into the back of a truck that was following the Dalai Lama's path. It took us to the Ganges River, where I plunged knee-deep into the water as the Dalai Lama, barefoot and laughing, lit candles in a Hindu ritual. He sprinkled himself with water from the Ganges for a centuries-old ritual that Hindus believe washes away their sins so that they can avoid reincarnation. "I'm very happy to be here," the Dalai Lama said, but when asked if he would join the pilgrims bathing in the icy water, he replied, "I don't think so. It's too cold." This attitude reflected a deeper philosophy of the Dalai Lama that I was starting to appreciate. At the press conference, he said, "I always believe it's safer and better and reasonable to keep one's own tradition or belief." It was dark around me—the day was slipping into night—but at that moment a light went on inside of me. I understood what the Dalai Lama's words meant to me. I had done the Buddhist pilgrimage. I was doing the Hindu pilgrimage. I had never done my own pilgrimage—the pilgrimage to Mecca called the *hajj*. I formed an intention, at that moment, to do my pilgrimage. . . .

The Qur'an says that it is the duty of all able-bodied Muslims to do the pilgrimage to Mecca, but I had never even thought about going. In fact, it's a pilgrimage that most Muslims can never take. The *hajj* is no simple journey. It is an arduous spiritual and physical rite that lasts only five days during a month on the lunar Muslim calendar called Dhul Hijjah, or "the month of the hajj," in Arabic. The *hajj* is meant to be a time to absorb the central messages of Islam: that Islam means having a special relationship with God based on surrendering to divine will and praying to and revering God; that there is a kinship among people that expresses itself through sacrifice for the benefit of others; that life is about struggle—a battle to secure a livelihood and ensure that good triumphs over evil.

For women, the *hajj* is given the value of struggle, or *jihad*. The concept is daunting. *Jihad* is normally associated with military combat, but its deeper meaning is a struggle within our souls to live by the highest spiritual principles we can embrace.

It's said that the prophet Muhammad's wife Aisha asked him, "Do women have to make *jihad*?"

The prophet replied, "Yes, the *hajj* and *umrah*." *Umrah* is an off-season pilgrimage that happens anytime other than the five designated days of hajj.

I knew that this *jihad* beckoned me, and the idea of journey felt familiar to me. My family had been early pilgrims of another sort when my family migrated to America. In Arabic, migrants are called *muhajir*, a word that coincidentally sounds like *hajj*. From my earliest days, I had been a person on a pilgrimage.

Reflections on Life as a Daughter of Islam

Hyderabad, India—I stared at the bare-chested laborer standing on the roof of my childhood home in India, hammering at its final remnants. It made me reflect on my roots and the imprint they left on my identity.

When I left India at the age of four, my grandmother—whom I called Dadi, meaning "paternal grandmother" in my native language of Urdu— dressed my brother and me in matching outfits cut from the same striped cloth (in case we got separated and had to be matched), and she lined my eyes with black kohl, or eyeliner, to protect me from the evil eye. It served me well in a life that, much like most lives, has encountered tests. We lived first in Piscataway, New Jersey, where I spent my girlhood trying to find a place for myself as an immigrant child of America. Watching a children's TV program called *Romper Room*, I waited for the hostess to call out my name when she greeted children in TV land called Mary, Sue, and John, but I never heard her say my name. At home I grew up following the script of a traditional Muslim girl. I stopped wearing dresses when I was nine years old because my father, with his traditional Muslim sensibilities, felt it wasn't proper for me to keep baring my legs.

When I was ten, we moved to Morgantown, West Virginia, where my father got a job as an assistant professor of nutrition at the local univer- sity, West Virginia University. Morgantown is tucked into a north-central corner of the state about seventy-five miles south of Pittsburgh and two hundred miles west of Washington, D.C., along a river called the Monon- gahela. About 90 percent of the population is white. West Virginia Uni- versity is known for its football team, the gold-and-blue Mountaineers, but it has also churned out a record number of Rhodes scholars to Oxford University. West Virginians have a fierce mountain tradition of indepen- dence that I seemed to absorb. I was always proud to be on my side of the boundary line between Virginia and West Virginia. When the war over slavery broke out, our territory had stood on the right side of the issue, breaking off from Virginia to create the free state of West Virginia. In Morgantown, we had a dynamic intellectual community. West Virginia University was the richest academic enclave in the state. Drawn by the university, immigrants from India were one of its largest minority groups, next to immigrants from China. I went to sixth grade at Evansdale Ele- mentary School, across University Avenue from my family's simple three- bedroom apartment in the WVU faculty housing. Unknown to me, feminist scholarship was just starting to take root on campus, where Dr. Judith Stitzel, the mother of one of my classmates, was starting to teach women's studies courses. By no coincidence, her son, David, took my arm and led me across one of the greatest divides between males and females. He was my square-dancing partner. Mrs. Gallagher, our sixth-grade teacher, had sent a note home with all of her students, asking our parents' permission to let us learn to square-dance. My mother invoked what she had been taught in her Muslim family against boys and girls dancing, but I begged and begged for permission to square-dance. Finally, my mother relented.

Some might say that was when my troubles began. But for eight years I lived by most of the *hudud*, or rules of my Muslim culture. I didn't protest when I had to sit with the women in the kitchen while the men sat on the nice Montgomery Ward living room sofas. I could hear the roar of my father's voice as the men engaged in political debate. As I grew up, I cared about the civil war in Lebanon and the Iranian hostage crisis. But I never felt I could enter the men's space, and I didn't—except to whisper messages from my mother to my father to stop talking so loudly.

I knew enough, though, to recognize that women were restrained just because of the gender into which we were born. My junior high journal for Mrs. Wendy Alke's English class is filled with snapshots that reveal that it was in my character to be a free spirit. I chronicled the biking accidents, the kickball games, and the other adventures that filled my free time. Not long after I moved to Morgantown, I shared a seat on my bike with a friend. "The handlebars started shaking. I was tense when all of a sudden the bike went down! We both fell, and I got most of the impact since I was up front! We had to walk the bike all the way back to the Med Center Apts., and on our way we saw a car and thought wow! If that had been two minutes later, we could have been run over!" Another time, I recounted how I broke my arm jumping off a wooden fence in my rush to play baseball with my brother and his friends. "I was going to play baseball. The log twisted, and I lurched forward. I got up and oh! Yelped in pain. My arm had been broken, and I walked home with the help of my friend." These would have been ordinary childhood stories except that in my life they were also symbolic of the freedoms my parents allowed me as a girl. In traditional Muslim cultures around the world, girls aren't allowed to ride bikes in public; they aren't allowed to play baseball with their brothers; and they most certainly aren't allowed to walk home alone. I started earning money before I hit my teen years, babysitting neighborhood children named Bobby and Misty. I chronicled the night I earned $2.50. This was also remarkable because it set me on a path toward economic independence that so many women in more traditional Muslim culture aren't allowed.

It is clear from my childhood expressions that I looked to God for help in my life. As it sleeted outside one November day, I wrote that the Condors won their kickball game during lunch that day. "That means we are tied with them for 1st place and have to play them to see who is No. 1." Invoking a Muslim phrase that means "God willing," I wrote, "*Inshallah*, we are." When my brother fell ill one summer, I took the blame. Earlier I had gotten jealous that he was healthy while I was sick, and I yelled, "I wish you would die!" With my brother sick, "I started crying and crying and everyone else tried to hold it in. We were all praying and praying!" When my brother survived, I prayed in relief and vowed never to curse anyone. "I was afraid we would lose *bhaya* [the Urdu honorific for "older brother"]! Thank you so much God for teaching me not to say such bad things and for saving *bhaya*!" So much is said about Catholic and Jewish guilt, but Muslim culture has its own guilt trips, and I absorbed all the messages that told me my sins could cause damnation. To counter these messages, I looked for inspiration in other sources.

From early on I found strength in the stories of women who challenged tradition. I talked in my journal about Louisa May Alcott's *Little Women*, a tale of strong women, as "my most favorite book."

At many different times in my life, I also felt my culture trying to confine me and define me. From that early age, I could feel the difference between circumstances that were oppressive and those that weren't. I enjoyed a gathering one night celebrating the Hindu holiday of Diwali, or a festival of lights. "Us girls had relay races in the hall and arm wrestling (I beat them all). . . . It was fun all in all." I continued: "The next night . . . there was an Islamic association party. It stunk! The ladies had to go up to a little efficiency apt. (owned by one of the members) because they weren't to sit with men. There were like 15 people in one dinky room! The men carried the food up and oh! it was as if we were in jail!"

As I entered into adulthood I began confronting the boundaries in my life, accepting them at times and daring to challenge them at other times. My father had his own struggles reconciling his culture with his beliefs, but as a scientist he firmly believed in having an open mind and pursuing intellectual inquiry, and he encouraged me to develop these attributes. My father crossed state borders to drive me to New York City so that I could do a summer internship at *Harper's* magazine, but he was also crossing a much more profound kind of line: the cultural tradition that a daughter didn't leave her father's home except to go to her husband's house.

Indeed, to respect these traditions, my parents told me to apply to only my hometown school of West Virginia University, but even there I continued resisting traditional Muslim boundaries. At the age of eighteen, I kissed a man for the first time, and he wasn't my husband. In the study carrels in a building called Colson Hall, our shoes slipped off during an all-night study session, his toes crossed the unspoken physical boundary that my culture and religion had put around me, and he dared to touch my bare feet. The next year I crossed the most sacred boundaries of a woman's body and consummated my love, but it wasn't my wedding night. I wept in confusion over the truths of my physical and emotional urgings and the expectations of my religion and tradition.

I broke my parents' hearts with my social trespasses. I tried to live a double life, but they knew enough to be disappointed. Still, my parents did not remain captive to their cultural traditions, because higher values overrode their fears, and they allowed me to do my graduate work at American University in Washington, D.C. By doing so they helped me find economic opportunity and professional status. I worked for twelve years as a journalist for the *Wall Street Journal* beginning in 1988, flying into new cities, diving into rental cars, and navigating my way to interview CEOs and senators. I spent my young adulthood trying to understand the amalgamation of identities within me.

In 2000 I took a leave from the *Journal* and traveled alone to India to report and write a book. If my Indian world is divided into a "North" that includes the West and a "South" that includes the East, I am a daughter of the South, but a woman of the North. I went to India as an author to research a book on Tantra, an ancient Hindu philosophy in which feminine powers and sexuality are a critical part of worship. I had written a front-page article for the *Wall Street Journal* about the big business of selling Tantric concepts of sacred sexuality at weekend workshops from Santa Cruz, California, to Ottawa, Canada. I had thought I would wander the caves of India studying with Tantric masters, but my itinerary soon became a journey into the corners of my own identity as I tried to traverse the dualities in my life. I thought I was searching for love, but I was in fact searching for the answer to the question of who I was as a woman.

As I traveled in India I embodied the values of self-determination that I had learned in America. To be mobile, I dared what had been unthinkable to me even in America: I learned how to ride a motorcycle. It was a scooter by U.S. standards—a sleek, black, 100-cubic-centimeter machine—but it was my vehicle of empowerment. I rode that Hero Honda Splendor into the Himalayas, having cut my long hair and wearing pants and jackets to resemble a man. Women didn't ride motorcycles there. But no matter how high I went into the Himalayas or how far away from home I traveled, the voices of traditional values echoed within me.

FOUR

Women, Gender, and Sexuality in American Islam

OF all the questions debated in American Islam, none is more hotly contested than the issue of gender and Islam, a subject of great interest to non-Muslim Americans, as well. In fact, the intra-Muslim debate about gender is shaped partly by the assumption among many non-Muslim Americans that "traditional Islam" oppresses women. The ultimate symbol of that oppression for many is the practice of veiling, which is taken by some to be inherently discriminatory. On American television and in the movies, one does not always get to hear the voice of the veiled woman. Instead, one is treated to a silent image of the covered woman and is often expected to see in this image evidence of oppression. Some feminists call this practice "double objectification." That is, not only do women in Islamic societies, like most other societies, face gender prejudice, but they are also silenced by their representation in American society. Many Americans have never actually met a woman who wears a veil or heard them speak about why they wear such a garment.

In American Muslim circles, however, very few Muslim women say that Islam is inherently oppressive of women. To the contrary, many American Muslim women see Islam as a liberating force. But they disagree over what it means to be a liberated Muslim woman. For example, popular South Asian American writer Asma Gull Hasan admits that there is much sexism in the Muslim world, but blames what she identifies as patriarchal culture, rather than Islamic religion, for this phenomenon.

Hasan, who advocates the waging of "gender jihad," praises the United States as a country full of social, economic, and political opportunities for Muslim women. She also believes that the United States provides Muslims a chance to return to the pure Islam of the Qur'an, which she sees as democratic, capitalist, and feminist.

Asma Hasan does not normally wear a *hijab*, or headscarf, and argues that it is modesty of the heart that matters most. In fact, she says, the promotion of the *hijab* is part of a conservative Muslim political agenda. According to her reading of the Qur'an, both men and women need only cover themselves in modest clothing when making their prayers. Many American Muslim women disagree. Some see the *hijab* not as a conservative symbol, but as a sign of their personal and political liberation. While some American Muslim women wear the *hijab* only at the mosque, others wear it both at work and in school. Some see the headscarf as a way of letting others know that they are Muslim; it may even feel like a quiet form of missionary work. For others, the headscarf may be a fashion accessory, a form of adornment that reflects the wearer's sense of beauty. In addition to donning a headscarf, a few American Muslim women wear the face veil—covering all but their eyes. In the United States, those who wear such dress emphasize that it is their choice; their personal freedom comes by submitting fully to the will of God as they understand it.

Some American Muslim women *do* support the notion of polygyny, and there is significant evidence pointing to the presence of extralegal polygynous marriages, especially among African American Muslims. One scholar has estimated that there are thousands of plural marriages among African American Muslims, and argues that there is a good reason for it: so many young African American men are incarcerated or otherwise unavailable that "man-sharing" is one practical and Islamic solution to the dilemma of young African American women who wish to marry. Many women involved in such relationships have reported that they enjoy the sense of extended kinship and community that these arrangements engender; they say their cowives are like sisters. Others complain that their husbands do not treat them equally, as commanded in the Qur'an. It should be stressed that polygyny seems to be the exception among American Muslims. The majority of married American Muslim men, like Muslim men around the world, have only one spouse.

While discussions about the veil and polygamy threaten to monopolize public discourse on gender and Islam, American Muslim women themselves are concerned about a much broader array of issues. In this way, Muslim women in the United States are like other American women of faith. For instance, they insist on the right to read and interpret the meaning of sacred scriptures for themselves. Qur'anic scholar Amina Wadud, an African American convert, sees the Qur'an as a liberating document. Like Asma Hasan, she argues that many Muslim communities are patriarchal and reports that many Muslims have rejected her scholarship as un-Islamic, Westernized, and feminist. Wadud argues that the Qur'an depicts men and women as equal, different, and complementary, and stresses that the Qur'an does not prescribe set gender roles for either. There is no gender hierarchy in the Qur'an, she argues, and women need not always be homemakers, mothers, and wives. Wadud's style of textual interpretation is popular outside the walls of the academy. In formal and informal study groups around the country, American Muslim women read and reread the sacred texts of Islam as a way to understand and renew their relationships to other women, male Muslim leaders, husbands, mosques, non-Muslim workplaces, and neighborhoods. As in Muslim majority countries around the world, feminist interpretations of the Qur'an are not only rendered by Muslim elites but also by Muslims at the grassroots.

American Muslim women, like Jewish, Christian, Buddhist, and other women of faith, also debate the question of what their roles should be as Muslim leaders. Like some ultraorthodox Jewish and socially conservative Christian women, some Muslim women wish to cultivate their roles as homemakers and mothers, not as public figures. Many progressive Muslims, on the other hand, hope to make every leadership position in Islam open to female participation. The controversial issue of women *imams* is a case in point. For the most part, women are prohibited in American mosques from becoming *imams*, or prayer leaders. Progressive Muslims often regard this as a sexist tradition that should be challenged. On March 18, 2005, Amina Wadud led both male and female Muslims in Friday prayers at St. John the Divine Cathedral in New York City—no mosque would offer space due to security concerns—violating what many other Muslims believe to be a strong and clear prohibition against female leadership of mixed-gender congregational prayers. The reactions were many. Some Muslims, especially American Muslims, praised the courage of this group. Others, even liberals, wondered whether supporting female leadership of the prayers was the best way to further a progressive agenda in the Muslim community. Many Muslims, from both the United States and abroad, condemned the participants.

Ingrid Mattson, the female president of the Islamic Society of North America, offered a different solution to the problem of gender discrimination in American mosques. While acknowledging the traditional legal position that women do not generally qualify for the position of *imam*, she argued that American Muslims have given the *imam* too many duties and too much power. Articulating a democratic view of mosque leadership, Mattson called on men and women to divide up the *imam*'s duties and to assert more lay leadership in mosques. Like Mattson, many Muslim women also stress the need for gender equality on mosque executive committees and boards, and women's participation in these bodies continues to increase. In some instances, women have served as chairpersons or mosque presidents—in Toledo, Ohio, for example, where Chereffe Kadri helped to lead the Islamic Center of Greater Toledo through difficult times after September 11, 2001. Some American Muslim women also note that there are few impediments to female leadership in Sufi Islam. Gwendolyn Zoharah Simmons, an American Sufi, argues that American Muslims should look to traditions like Sufism to see a less hierarchical model for gender relations in Islam. Laleh Bakhtiar, another Sufi practitioner, has documented the successes of American women as leaders and participants in various Sufi orders and movements. Many American Muslim women have become leaders in the academic field of Islamic studies, turning the American academy into a training ground for female Muslim scholars and a laboratory for innovative Islamic thought. This phenomenon is reflected in the writings selected for this volume: many of them have been penned by female Muslim professors.

As important as the issue of leadership is, however, American Muslim women have many other concerns, as well. Some are worried about the effects of domestic abuse, poverty, and drug use in the Muslim community. Other American Muslim women work tirelessly to combat homophobia in the community. Like American Muslims more generally, Muslim women in the United States also live under the authority of a government that, in practice, singles out Muslims for government surveillance while also promising to protect their human rights. Every day, Muslim women, like Muslim men, face suspicion from the general public. Just having a Muslim name or wearing a *hijab* immediately puts them at risk. They might be denied a seat on an airplane, they might face employment discrimination, and they might be the subject of stares, fear, and hostility. Muslim women of color, like men of color, may experience further discrimination because of their race. As women, they know gender discrimination—the kind that comes from within the Muslim community as well as that which comes from without. At the same time, Muslim women often laud the ideals, if not always the practice, of the American nation. There is a kind of religious freedom in the United States difficult to find elsewhere. The United States is a wealthy country that offers some degree of economic opportunity to many. And by living in such an ethnically and religiously diverse nation, some say, they have the chance to forge an Islam that is pluralistic, interracial, and socially just.

1. Leila Ahmed, "From Abu Dhabi to America," in *A Border Passage: From Cairo to America—A Woman's Journey* (2000)

Leila Ahmed, professor of women's studies in religion at Harvard Divinity School, was born to upper-class Muslim Egyptian parents in 1940. Ahmed attended an English school in Cairo with Jews, Christians, and Muslims and was raised by her parents to admire European advancements in science, the arts, and democracy. She was also exposed to and shaped by the living Islam of her grandmother and female relatives. Their Islam was women's Islam, forged in the separate social spaces that females inhabited and very different in nature from the "official" and more textual Islam of men. "Islam, as I got it from them," remembered Ahmed, "was gentle, generous, pacifist, inclusive, somewhat mystical." In the wake of the Egyptian Revolution of 1952 and Suez Crisis of 1956, Ahmed left Egypt for England, where she studied at the all-girls Girton College and, eventually, Cambridge University. There she became acutely conscious of European prejudices toward Arabs and Islam, the awareness of which would eventually affect her personal and professional life in important ways. After completing her doctorate at Cambridge, Ahmed took a job in Abu Dhabi to work on issues related to women's education. Then she moved to the United States. Her experiences during the early days of women's studies in America and the challenge of finding room for the discussion of Muslim women within the emerging field are described below. In 1992, Ahmed published Women and Gender in Islam, *the culmination of her thinking about Muslim women's history and Arab feminism, a work that has become a classic in the fields of women's studies and Islamic studies.*

It was no easy transition, the transition to America and to women's studies.

First of all, live American feminism was not anything like what I had imagined. Reading its thoughtful texts in the quiet of the desert, I had, I suppose, formed a notion of feminism as tranquil, lucid, meditative—whereas, of course, the living feminism I encountered once on these shores was anything but a lucid, tranquil, meditative affair. Militant, vital, tempestuous, passionate, visionary, turbulent—any or all of these might be more apt. In the gatherings of feminists—at the various conferences, meetings, and public lectures that I now single-mindedly threw myself into attending—there was a kind of raw, exhilarating energy and a sense, intellectually, of freewheeling anarchy. Almost as if people felt themselves caught up in some holy purifying fire that was burning away the dross and obscurities from their minds, freeing them to dream dreams and see visions and to gather themselves up and prepare to unmake and remake the world, remake it as it had never been made before.

And all this *was* tremendously exhilarating and exciting. But along with exhilaration came shock. For I naturally made a point at these conferences of attending, and often participating in, sessions and panels on Muslim women. Not that these were common. The women's studies conferences I attended when I first came in 1980—I remember one at Barnard, and another in Bloomington, Indiana—focused primarily on white women and were overwhelmingly attended by white women. But such sessions on Muslim women as there were left me nearly speechless and certainly in shock at the combination of hostility and sheer ignorance that the Muslim panelists, myself included, almost invariably encountered. We could not pursue the investigation of our heritage, traditions, religion in the way that white women were investigating and rethinking theirs. Whatever aspect of our history or religion each of us had been trying to reflect on, we would be besieged, at the end of our presentations, with furious questions and declarations openly dismissive of Islam. People quite commonly did not even seem to know that there was some connection between the patriarchal vision to be found in Islam and that in Judaism and Christianity. Regularly we would be asked belligerently, "Well what about the veil" or "What about clitoridectomy?" when none of us had mentioned either subject for the simple reason that it was completely irrelevant to the topics of our papers. The implication was that, in trying to examine and rethink our traditions rather than dismissing them out of hand, we were implicitly defending whatever our audience considered to be indefensible. And the further implication and presumption was that, whereas they—white women, Christian women, Jewish women—could rethink their heritage and religions and traditions, we had to abandon ours because they were just intrinsically, essentially, and irredeemably misogynist and patriarchal in a way that theirs (apparently) were not. In contrast to their situation, our salvation entailed not arguing with and working to change our traditions but giving up our cultures, religions, and traditions and adopting theirs.

And so the first thing I wrote after my arrival and within months of being in America was an article addressing the extraordinary barrage of hostility and ignorance with which I found myself besieged as I moved among this community of women. They were women who were engaged in radically rejecting, contesting, and rethinking their own traditions and heritage and the ingrained prejudices against women that formed part of that heritage but who turned on me a gaze completely structured and hidebound by that heritage; in their attitudes and beliefs about Islam and women in Islam, they plainly revealed their unquestioning faith in and acceptance of the prejudiced, hostile, and often ridiculous notions that their heritage had constructed about Islam and its women. I had come wanting to read and think and write about Muslim women, but it was this that commanded my attention as the subject that I desperately had to address. The first piece I wrote, "Western Ethnocentrism and Perceptions of the Harem," still rings for me with the shocked and furious tones of that initial encounter.

My first year in America, 1979, was also the year of the Iran hostage crisis, and I am sure now that the hostility toward Islam by which I felt myself besieged was more pronounced than usual because of that situation. But as I would learn soon enough, the task of addressing racism for feminists of color in the West is, and has to be, an ongoing and central part of the work and the thinking that we ordinarily do, no less so than the work of addressing male dominance. And so my first experience of American feminism was a kind of initiation and baptism by fire into what has indeed been an ongoing part of my thought and work ever since. Back then, though, it was still early in our understanding of the racist gaze the white feminist movement turned on women of other cultures and races. Audre Lorde, at a conference in 1976 (in a presentation much-anthologized since), was among the first to identify, and speak out against, this strand in white feminist thought, and June Jordan, Bell Hooks, and others followed up with work on the subject.

Also making my initial experience of America a more arduous experience than it might otherwise have been was the fact that I took a job in women's studies. I had come intent on working in this field and had applied for an advertised position as a part-time lecturer at the University of Massachusetts at Amherst. Although the pay was low, I felt that a part-time job was the sensible way into the field, whose scholarly productions I'd been reading about in the desert but about which I had still an enormous amount to learn. A part-time job would give me the time, I thought, to do all the extra reading that I no doubt needed to do.

Of course I found that my part-time job, as is so often the case, was only technically part-time. In fact, preparing classes, teaching, and attending meetings took up every moment of my waking life. I have never worked so hard in my life as in my first couple of years in America. Of course, too, the fact that everything was new to me contributed to making those years so tough. Teaching in a new academic system in a new country must always entail demanding transitions, but I am sure that moment in the history of women's studies in America, rather than, say, taking a job in a more established department, created a whole set of unique hurdles and difficulties.

Women's studies programs in that era, including the program that I joined, had an embattled and precarious relationship with the university. There was sometimes open hostility from faculty members in other departments and, occasionally, condescension and a presumption that the women's studies faculty must be ignorant, undereducated, fanatical women. For me, as someone coming from abroad who had not been part of the American feminist movement, there was one very particular difficulty that I had not anticipated when I imagined that, by working hard and reading widely, I could quickly master the ideas, theories, perspectives that I needed to be familiar with. I could not quickly master them through reading, for the simple reason that a lot of them had not yet found their way into print. The ideas that I heard passionately voiced and argued around me by faculty and also by students were part of a rich, vibrant, diverse, and internally contentious cargo of debates that had been generated by an intellectually vital social movement. This was what I had stepped into in joining women's studies—a living social movement of quite extraordinary but as yet mainly oral intellectual vitality, about to spill over and become a predominantly intellectual, academic, and theoretical force rather than, as it had in part been in its beginnings, an activist social movement, and the continuing evolution of these ideas, that were providing the foundations of women's studies. I stepped, that is to say, too, into the stream of what was as yet a largely unwritten oral culture—the oral, living culture of the feminist movement, a culture to which there were as yet almost no guides, no maps, no books.

There were often passionate debates, both among my colleagues and in the feminist community more widely, between, say, Radical feminists and Marxist feminists, debates that could become quite furious. It was clear that there was a history here, a common, shared evolution, in the course of which particular positions, in relation to this or that issue, had been progressively defined and sometimes had become polarized. But to someone arriving from the Arab Gulf, what these positions and issues were and why they should generate such passion was, at first anyway, profoundly unfathomable. And there was nothing, or very little, in those days, that I could read that would enlighten me and make the issues, debates, and history accessible. Moreover, this culture and history that I had not been part of informed nearly everything in women's studies, not only intellectual issues but also ordinary routines and exchanges and conversations. It was this culture, for instance, that determined that all decisions were to be made by consensus and not by vote. It determined, too, the code of dress—as strict here, in its way, as in Abu Dhabi. For those were the days when whether you shaved your legs or wore a bra signaled where you stood on the internal feminist battle lines and/or your degree of feminist enlightenment. In Abu Dhabi it had been easy to ask about appropriate dress and the meaning of this or that style, but here not only were you supposed to just know, but supposedly there was no dress code and people here—as I was emphatically told when I ventured the question in my early innocent days—simply dressed exactly how they wished. And so there were many ways in which the women's studies culture in which I found myself was an unknown culture to me to which I had no key and maps. But, as with any other culture, after a period of intense immersion, my confusion naturally resolved into comprehension.

Another difficulty arising from my being in women's studies was one I shared with my colleagues. An essentially new field, women's studies as yet had no set syllabi, no texts, no solid, extensive body of scholarship to draw on. And so even devising courses and syllabi and putting them together from photocopies was a demanding task. Even the novels and stories by women that were already being used and that would soon be the staples of feminist courses in literature were not yet in readily accessible form or were just being published and reissued, in large part thanks to the feminist movement and the demand created by women's studies. And the kind of material that a few years later would begin to be available on feminist theory, on women of color in America, on women in Islam, and so on, was also not yet available. In short, women's studies was still in the process of being invented, created, and developed as a field. My colleagues as well as I, a newcomer, were still groping our way forward in this as yet unstudied, uncharted, and indeed uninvented territory, for the most part without textbooks, without established syllabi, without a body of scholarship raising the questions that needed to be raised, setting them out, analyzing them, complicating them.

2. Carol L. Anway, *Daughters of Another Path: Experiences of American Women Choosing Islam* (1996)

When Carol Anway's daughter converted to Islam after marrying an Iranian, Anway was at first surprised and sad. But after a period of adjustment, she came to appreciate her daughter's new religious identity. Anway wanted to learn more about and share the stories of other American women from the United States and Canada who had decided to become Muslims. Distributing a questionnaire to women at various Muslim conventions and through various Muslim social networks, Anway collected fifty-three responses, most of which were from college-educated women in their twenties and thirties. Though Anway did not ask them about their racial identities, she did ask her subjects about their religious orientation. Most of them had been raised as Christians. About 60 percent of them decided to convert after marrying a Muslim man. Most of Anway's respondents were also mothers, and about half of them were full-time homemakers. Almost all considered themselves to be observant Muslims. Their parents' reactions to their conversions were varied—from fully supporting their daughter's choice to breaking off relations with her. In the interview reproduced below, the subject, who remains anonymous, describes her experience in marrying an Iranian man and how becoming a Muslim has changed her life. She shares the regret she feels as a result of her difficult relationship with her parents, but expresses gratitude for the deep sense of peace she has discovered as a practicing Muslim.

My conversion to Islam was a very long and gradual process. I was raised in a culturally Christian household, a place where the major holidays were celebrated but the deeper meanings left unexplored. This was intentional on the part of my parents who felt that much hatred had been done to the world in the name of organized religion. At the insistence of both sets of grandparents, we children were baptized and given some rudimentary Sunday school training. My parents told us that when we were grown we could pick our own religions, if indeed, we wanted a religion.

My religious training left me with a belief in God (how else could one explain all the wondrous interconnections and intricacies of earth and universe?) but no belief in any system of religion. I considered myself a Christian, but in a broad sense: belief in God, belief in Jesus as a prophet, belief in the moral and ethical teachings. However, my upbringing engendered a high degree of skepticism and cynicism, and I questioned every aspect of church dogma. In the end, I decided that I didn't believe in organized religion as it was illogical, internally inconsistent, and hypocritical (having sanctioned many unethical and immoral acts in the name of God).

However, I had a vague, almost unrecognized idea that without religion something essential was missing from life. A life lived without some sense of a higher purpose was just an empty, random chase after perpetually changing desires. So I began a rather half-hearted, disorganized search for my "spiritual" self.

I saw glimpses of the spiritualism that I was looking for in various religions but they all seemed to be missing some essential ingredient. This one had a beautiful sense of peace and tolerance, but had lost its moral and ethical sense in the meantime. That one had a strong element of personal responsibility to others and a high code of personal conduct, but was repressive and suppressed logical inquiry. Another had a strong sense of religious collectiveness and historical context but promoted exclusivism. Still another understood the mystery, beauty, and peace that surrounds God, but was impractical about everyday matters and forgetful of our responsibilities to our fellow human beings. At about this time, I met the man who later became my husband and in trying to understand him and his culture, I came across Islam. Islam's ideas and teachings appealed to me immediately. They were coherent, they were logical, they were moderate, and they promoted a balance of personal responsibility and collective action. They were inclusive and yet outreaching; God was powerful and yet just; God was merciful and yet exacting. I took my *shahada* the day my husband and I were married.

My conversion to Islam at first seemed to require no change in my life. My husband, having lived in the U.S. for some years, and I, having been raised here, followed the cultural norm and separated our "religious life" from our "secular life." The first changes (noticeable to those around us) occurred as we began to raise a family and began to make decisions that affected our child and our life together. If there was one definable turning point in our commitment to God, it came when our oldest child was just three years old. I had a good friend who was a practicing Muslim and with whom I spent a great deal of time. My son was a keen observer and quite articulate for his age. One day around Christmas, he questioned why it was that we called ourselves Muslims if we didn't do any of the (observable) things that Muslims do? He wanted to know why we had a Christmas tree. He wanted to know why I didn't wear a scarf.

I didn't have very good answers for him, and his questions prompted a complete evaluation of the role of religion in our lives. My husband and I debated the merits of raising children with or without a strong religious identity and examined how important we felt religion was for ourselves. In the end, we felt that a sense of religion was important for our child(ren) and, therefore, it was necessary for ourselves as well.

Over the next five years or so we adjusted ourselves and our lifestyle to be within Islamic parameters. Gradually we began to eat only *halal* [permissible] foods and avoided social situations that involved alcohol consumption by others. We began to fast Ramadan, to pray all of our prayers, to study the Qur'an, and became more involved in the Muslim community. Generally, becoming more conscious of Islam meant constantly re-evaluating ourselves and our surroundings. At times the constant evaluation felt constrictive, and we longed for the carefree days of the past where life was lived unthinkingly. However, these times were few, and we would never have seriously considered giving up all that we had gained by living Islam.

Living as a practicing Muslim has brought a sense of purpose to my life. There is a pervasive sense of serenity in the knowledge that life is lived for a purpose. I feel that I have become a much better human being— more compassionate, more moderate, more deep-thinking. There is a richness and a calmness in my life that was not there prior to becoming a practicing Muslim. Life in its broadest sense has become one beautiful, intricate whole.

How I Learned to Live and Practice as a Muslim

I learned to live as a Muslim primarily by reading the Qur'an and by asking questions of knowledgeable Muslims. I also watched and observed Muslims around me.

I learned how to pray by reading a book designed to guide new Muslims through the prayer. Any other questions I had, I asked other Muslims. I also drew upon sources and people in my husband's family. My mother-in-law and father-in-law were particularly helpful as were other relatives abroad who sent books or other resources as I needed them.

The ease or difficulty of taking on any specific Islamic practice has always been directly correlated to how I understood it in connection with what I already knew about Islam. If I didn't understand its significance or see its connection to the intricate "whole" of Islam, I found it difficult to integrate into my life. When I had read enough, asked enough questions, talked enough, and finally understood, I didn't have a problem adding that practice into my life.

My becoming a *practicing* Muslim has had a very profound effect upon my relationship with my parents. My parents regard Islam quite negatively and consider it an oppressive, dogmatic religion. They don't hold religion, in general, in very high esteem and regard Islam, in particular, to be very oppressive of women. However, my only sibling, my sister, is quite supportive of my choice.

I hope that in the future I might be able to sit and talk with my parents about Islam and its role in my life. We have attempted to discuss it many times but have made very little progress. They seem unable to understand that being Muslim brings me peace and joy and has added immeasurable depth to my life. Islam has not taken anything away from who I am, but has only added to it. My parents seem to regard my choice only as a rejection of them and a rejection of my heritage. They believe that I have committed a form of cultural apostasy and blame themselves. They believe that they failed to involve me fully in my own culture. I hope that one day they will accept my choice—perhaps not understand it, but accept it.

There are many points of stress between myself and my parents regarding Islam. They dislike anything that physically marks me (or my children) as "different" (read "Muslim"). They are uncomfortable going out in public with me or my daughters because we wear *hijab* (myself) or modest clothing (my daughters wear pants under their dresses). They were upset when we asked them to stop drinking alcohol in our house when they visited us. They used to bring it with them. They try not to take a picture of me if I have on my scarf. They don't like our children's Muslim names and argued greatly with me about it when our first child was born. My parents are uncomfortable with my husband's and my insistence that family comes first—they feel that I have sold myself short by staying home (although I do work part-time!) and being family-oriented. They wished a "career" for me. They are uncomfortable with our world outlook and find it to be impractical and idealistic. Except for the fact that they believe we are too conservative, they think we are too politically correct. Frankly, most of the time, I am not sure exactly what they think about me because they never *discuss* it openly. I do know from the uncomfortable, explosive, and divisive conversations we have had, that they disapprove of and are disappointed with my choices in life. They can't, however, ever seem to tell me WHY. I believe it is because they are unable to argue against something that is ethical, moral, moderate, and logical—and is something that they taught me to believe in since I was a small child (only they didn't call it "Islam").

In our holiday celebrations, we attempted with our first-born to continue celebrating Christmas with my parents. We changed the emphasis to "helping Grandma and Grandpa celebrate their holiday" and also spoke about the importance of Prophet Jesus (peace be upon him) in Islam. It didn't work for many different reasons. Our child was too young to really be able to make that distinction, and peer pressure to be like all the other Christmas celebrants pushed him toward the popular idea of Christmas. My parents used Christmas to push American culture at him creating an "us versus them" environment and creating confusion and tension in our child. As our next children were born we realized that we didn't want these same scenes replicated with them, and so we gradually stopped going to my parents' house for Christmas. It was a decision that both disappointed and angered my parents. They now celebrate Christmas with my sister and her children and husband.

We do send Christmas cards to my parents, my sister, and my surviving grandparent, wish them a Happy New Year, and call them on Christmas

Day. We also send my family letters or cards on Eid al-Fitr after Ramadan. My family sends us cards at Christmas and my sister also calls several times during Ramadan to see how we are doing. The other Christian holidays (e.g., Easter) were not celebrated in my family as I was growing up and are not a factor now. My mom sends all the grandchildren cards at Halloween (which we do not celebrate but overlook in deference to my parents), Valentine's Day and on their birthdays.

We would love to include my parents in our Islamic celebrations, but they are not comfortable with the idea. They will not accompany us to any gatherings with our Muslim friends if they happen to be visiting us, and in deference to my parents, we usually stay home unless it is impossible to get out of the activity.

We have many difficulties when we visit my parents, most springing from their disapproval of our lifestyle. Our world views are quite different— from politics to the role of "independence" and "materialism" in a person's life. We do have many good times with my parents and want a close and mutually respectful relationship with them.

I met my husband while I was in college, through mutual friends. The characteristics which most attracted me were his generosity of spirit, honesty, compassion, loyalty, intelligence, and his general strength of character. He knew who and what he was and yet he was humble. I greatly admired his strength of character and his generosity to others. He was very accepting and gentle and yet there was strength inside.

My husband had a large role in my conversion to Islam because he was able to answer all my questions, and he spent a great deal of time explaining both Islam and his culture to me. He always included me in all his Islamic or cultural activities and acted as my interpreter, linguistically and culturally. He made Islam available for me and helped me to experience it firsthand. He never, at any point, pressured me to convert. The decision was entirely mine.

My family didn't accept him very well as my "friend" but was fine after we became "engaged." They like him immensely as a human being but blame him for brainwashing me into becoming Muslim. They also blame me for being so gullible. Our relationship with my parents was very good until we became practicing Muslims. We were married in a civil ceremony at the county courthouse and by proxy in Iran (so that relatives who were "clergy" could perform the ceremony for us). Our civil ceremony contained no Islamic elements and our Islamic ceremony was very basic: the marriage contract, the intent (declaration of desire) to be married, the public announcement of our marriage.

The Homeland of My Husband

We try to run our household on an Islamic model and to the extent that Iranian culture is basically an Islamic culture, our household reflects it. We speak Farsi at home and eat mostly Iranian food although tacos, spaghetti, and stir-fry are big favorites (along with roasts and hamburgers). We intend to live in the U.S. for the foreseeable future due to the economic situation in Iran and because we have student loans to repay in this country. We feel that we cannot forsake our debts here, and we could never afford to both live and pay off our loans if we lived in Iran. We have considered moving to another Middle Eastern country. My husband is an Iranian citizen.

My Husband's Family

I have met all the members of my husband's immediate family and some members of the (immense) extended family. I met my mother-in-law and father-in-law before we married, when they visited the United States for a summer. They accepted me very well, although it must have been difficult for them since they are very traditional Muslims and I was your typical twenty-year-old college co-ed. I have been accepted wonderfully by my in-laws, although they have disagreed with the way we have done many things, e.g., getting married as undergrads and having three children while my husband was still in graduate school. However, they have never belabored their concerns. My in-laws lived with us for about a year and then moved down the block for the next year after that. It was a great experience, although it had both its ups and downs! I expect that should we move to Iran, I would fit in fairly well and that I would be graciously accepted by the extended family. I might have a few problems with Iranian culture particularly in those areas which deviate from Islamic norms. Any problems from the extended family might arise from my independence and self-reliance.

I have learned a great deal from my in-laws. They have a wonderful way of relating to their children, a way which engenders respect for others and great amounts of self-esteem. It is interesting to see how a child-oriented and religious-oriented culture operates. My in-laws, by virtue of being a contrast to American culture, have given me a great appreciation for certain elements of my American cultural identity. From all my comparing and contrasting of Iranian and American cultures, I have seen that Islam is truly correct in saying that moderation in all is the right path!

My Position as a Woman

As a Muslim woman I experience the full benefits given to me by God as a member of the human race. I am responsible only to God for how I live my life, and how well I fulfill my duties to Him. The most important right which I enjoy by benefit of being a Muslim woman is the right of equality before God. Among the other rights which are detailed for women in Islam are the right to earn and keep our own money, to retain and/or dispose of our own property, the right to inherit, the right to initiate and contest a divorce, the right to an education, the right to retain our own name after marriage, the right to participate in choosing our own mates, the right to custody of our children.

However, as Islam is a just and fair religion, along with my rights come my obligations. All levels of Islamic society—including the individual and on through the relationship of husband/wife, parent/child, employer/employee, and the society/societal member—are firmly connected by interlocking and mutually reciprocal rights and duties. A right does not exist without a corresponding duty; a duty does not exist without a corresponding right. As an example: it is one of my rights as a wife to be financially supported by my husband—that is his obligation. Among others, my obligation is to try and live within his financial means without complaint, derision, or greed, and to care for his property and assets in his absence. My husband is obligated to treat me with courtesy and respect, and I am obliged to do the same for him. As a member of a society, I am obliged to help my fellow members, and they and the societal bureaucracy at large are obligated to help me in my times of need. There is much misunderstanding on the part of non-Muslims (and some Muslims) regarding the absolute inter-connectedness of rights and obligations—they come as a unit and cannot be separated out to be viewed separately without losing their essential qualities.

I feel no apprehension about my position as a Muslim woman in my marriage. I do not feel that there are any areas of private or public endeavor that are closed to me. I do have concerns regarding the status of some women in those societies and within those marriages where there is ignorance of or misunderstanding of the teachings of Islam. There exist many Muslim societies where deviation from the Islamic norms regarding the status and role of women (as well as other issues) have resulted in a constriction of the role of women. "Cultural Islam" very often is at variance with Islam. Verses from the Qur'an and *hadiths* of the Prophet (peace be upon him) are often taken out of their context of revelation or transmission and used to support patriarchal cultural viewpoints. Both men and women are often uneducated as to the true meanings of Islamic injunctions and, by default, follow the standard cultural practice of their societies.

My child-rearing techniques are directly influenced by being a Muslim. Islam touches all parts of my life and as such I try to raise my children in the most Islamic way possible. My children came into this world as Muslims, innocent and submissive to the will of Allah. It is our great responsibility, indeed both a trust and a test from Allah, that my husband and I raise them to remain Muslim.

The most easily observable Islamic influences on our child-rearing techniques include encouraging the children to follow us in prayer, teaching them Qur'anic verses, using traditional Muslim greetings and everyday phrases, encouraging them to dress modestly and behave with compassion and kindness. We use a lot of modeling and verbal encouragement and reminding, but the children are never forced to join us in any given activity as Islam teaches that there is no compulsion in religion. We do, if necessary, insist that the children remain near our activity (while quietly occupying themselves) so that at least they have exposure to the activity and understand that there are some minimal family standards that they must adhere to. We try to be tactful and discrete when enforcing these standards to avoid provoking outright rebellion.

The major way in which Islam influences my child-rearing techniques is that I try to remember that I am always within Allah's sight. Allah has set high standards of personal behavior for humans, not because He is vengeful, but because He knows that we are capable of rising to meet those standards. I am also always aware that my two recording angels are ever watchful! I try to be patient (this one can be quite difficult!), polite, and respectful; and to act with compassion, sincerity, and understanding towards them. I encourage them to value education and view learning as a life-long endeavor that is not limited to school hours or "school topics." We put great emphasis on doing their personal best at school and elsewhere; to be helpful and kind; not to lie or cheat; to value Allah (and therefore Islam), their family, and their fellow human beings; to stand up for what they believe in, to combine personal piety with outward action; to be sincere and straightforward; and to be generous in thought as well as in action. We also try to view each child as an individual, to view them outside of the influence of birth order, to try not to compare them to their siblings or to ourselves, to try to accept and value those personality traits that are irritating to us but part and parcel of who they are.

Insha'Allah [God willing], our children will grow to be compassionate, productive Muslims. To that end we are always re-evaluating our progress and our child-rearing techniques. We always try to follow the specific Islamic injunctions, but also attempt to follow the "spirit of the law."

My husband is very involved with the care of the children. I work part-time, and while I am at work he is their sole caretaker. He also is with the children when I go to meetings or study groups. He takes the kids to the doctors, takes them out on excursions, takes them on errands, goes to the swimming pool with them, and any number of other activities.

My rights and obligations with my children? When people mention Islam/mothers/mother's rights, they are usually referring to child custody in the event of a divorce. Both my husband and I are of the opinion that the children should go with whichever parent is better able to care for them. Of course, in Islam, divorce is allowed, but exhaustive efforts to keep the family unit intact should be made first. In most cases, it is the mother who is better emotionally equipped to raise the children. Unless circumstances warrant differently, the non-custodial parent has the right to frequent visitation. The custodial parent should be helped financially to raise the children, if it is necessary. All divorces should take place in an Islamic family court with a qualified jurist making the decision.

My obligation to my children is to love them, respect them, and help them grow to be Muslim adults. This is as much an obligation to my children as it is to Allah, who placed these children in my care as a trust from Him. I am obliged to remember that my children belong to Allah, not to me—and I must treat them accordingly.

As specified in the Qur'an, my children's obligations to me are that they should respect me (but I must be worthy of that respect), obey me (as long as I am within the bounds of Islam in my request), and care for me if I attain old age. They have the right to expect love, good physical care, and guidance from me. They have the right to be treated with dignity and respect, as I do.

What I Would Like to Express to Others

I would like the American public to know that I am a Muslim by personal choice. I am a fully mature, intelligent human being, capable of making rational decisions. My decision to embrace Islam is not an effort to fit into my husband's culture or family; it is not the result of too little self-esteem; it is not the result of pressure from my husband. I would also like people to understand that Islam is not repressive of women, it does not condone terrorism, and that it is squarely within the Judeo-Christian tradition. I would like people to realize that Islam stands for moderation and modesty and that there are often great discrepancies between the practices of "cultural Islam" and the directives of Islam.

3. Tarajee Abdur-Rahim, Interview in *American Jihad: Islam After Malcolm X* (1993)

In the interview below, African American Muslim AIDS activist Tarajee Abdur-Rahim describes what life was like as an HIV-positive Muslim woman living in the early days of AIDS awareness. Abdur-Rahim, who published a newsletter about HIV/AIDS for a Muslim audience, captures the unwillingness of some Muslim community leaders in New York to confront the reality of disease while also recording her own equally stubborn commitment to reaching out to and caring for Muslims with AIDS. She also fearlessly shares details about how she contracted the disease and explains how her Islamic faith has been a constant source of comfort and hope. Like other persons of faith who struggle with illness, Sister Tarajee says that AIDS helped her to fashion an even stronger tie to God. Her struggle is one shared by an increasing number of Muslims who have HIV/AIDS or who care for people with the virus or disease. As Abdur-Rahim indicates, there is disagreement among American Muslims about how to deal with HIV. It is characterized by some as a moral disease, by others as social and economic, and by still others as a medical problem. In the last decade, those in the community committed to caring with compassion for HIV-positive persons has noticeably increased, although there is still moral condemnation and/or denial in the community as well.

I took a *shahada* [the declaration of Islamic faith] sixteen years ago. My husband had been Muslim for two years before I took the *shahada*. I thought Islam was cute. For him.

I liked to wear his *thobe* [a long-sleeved robe] and *kufi* [knitted cap]. It looked nice on me. But I just was not interested. I called myself almost proudly an atheist.

I picked up the Qur'an one day and started reading it. It absolutely blew me away. I knew that this was the truth. It made so much sense, I couldn't take *shahada* fast enough. So that meant burning all my micro-miniskirts and my hot pants. And I didn't mind. It didn't faze me in the least. I never wanted to be anything else since.

My oldest daughter must have been about six, and the next was about two. They're twenty-three and eighteen now. Nadine and Hillary. Now they are Latifa and Malika—same children. I've had three more since, all girls.

When I did get married my oldest child was about four or five. We decided we wanted to do it right. We'd already left Harlem to get to Brooklyn. Malik was my friend, my lover, my buddy.

Malik had a drug problem. I used to tease him, tell him he wasn't a good junkie. He was trying so hard, and he just wasn't good at this. He might be clean five or six years, and then go on a binge for a year.

He was quite capable of supporting his own habit. Never took anything from the house. Watching the metamorphosis that he would undergo while he was on drugs—that was the hard part. I'd never see him use. He never did it in front of me or the girls, but I always knew when he'd be using again.

There was no reason to leave this man. He just had a problem that he didn't know how to deal with. And that was the bottom line.

When they started talking about AIDS, I listened and I thought to myself, I don't have anything to worry about: I'm Muslim. I pray five times a day. Malik is Muslim. I told myself, he's doing drugs, not me.

But then I kept hearing about AIDS, and I said, let's go get tested. At first, he didn't want to go, but I needed to know, because by this time I'm hearing that your direct association places you in a high-risk category. He finally agreed and we did go. We were both diagnosed eleven years ago as being HIV-positive.

I was absolutely stunned. I just couldn't believe that I had this virus. But I didn't cry very long. Islam teaches you how to handle anything that occurs in your life. And the way to handle anything is simple: You have faith in Allah. It's that cut and dried. I thought about it and I said to myself, well, at least we have each other. Maybe now he'll leave the drugs alone. And so as quickly as I was afraid, I wasn't afraid anymore.

I said, let's just deal with it. Malik got angry. He got bitter.

There was no support system within the Muslim community that he could turn to. There weren't many support systems available to heterosexuals. This was a gay disease. It was a Haitian disease, it was a white, gay disease, which we now know is absolute foolishness. But at that time, this is what everyone believed. Well, we weren't white, gay, or Haitian. And I knew that this was a bigger thing than what people were realizing. I was very angry at Malik because I wanted him to protect me, not from the virus, but from the elements surrounding the virus. I wanted to sit behind Malik and not worry. I didn't want to worry about the gas bill. I didn't want to worry about what other Muslims thought. And I wanted Malik to make life safe for me. I got angry with Malik behind that, but never about the disease.

I had to venture out. I wanted to see what they were doing in the way of AIDS to use to my advantage. I knew other people had this besides me. Better yet, I knew other Muslims had this besides me. I knew I couldn't be the only one with this virus.

Malik didn't want to attend support groups. He didn't want to know anything. He was just angry: Why would Allah do something like this to him? Why would Allah put him in a position where the strong possibility existed where he would die from something that there was no cure for and leave his children and his wife behind? I'm not a man, and I don't always understand how a man thinks, but I think I understood that.

We fought constantly after that—verbally. I fought his bitterness and his anger, and he fought the way I handled it. I think that as a man maybe it bothered him that his wife was being stronger than him. I wasn't trying to flex muscles. I wanted to protect him too. But I felt like crying sometimes. I wanted to cry but I couldn't. I was too busy being strong to deal with the situation.

Somehow or other as a woman, I found myself slowly leaving my feminine center and approaching things from a masculine center, because I felt that no one was protecting me. So *I* had to protect me. And so I put on my suit of armor, and I had a shield in one hand and a spear in the other. I started going from one support group to another, just to see.

I met everything from little green Martians. But I had fun.

The Gay Men's Health Crisis Center in [Greenwich] village treated me like a queen.

I knew that it was exclusively gay before I went, so I wasn't thrown aback by that. *They* were thrown aback by *my* presence. Forget the fact that I'm female. But I'm a black female, and I'm a Muslim female. I fell into categories all by myself.

When I walked in the door of GMHC and many other AIDS organizations that were exclusively run by gays, the first thing that they did was always the same: They would just sit there looking at me. On some faces I saw [*affected effeminate voice*]: *Oh, she's* clearly *in the wrong place.*

And on some faces, I could see: *I wonder what she's doing here.* And there were some faces that said: *Oooooo, I like that outfit she has.*

It was so amusing to me. They treated me very nice. Of course, they didn't waste any time asking me why I was there. I started talking immediately. I'd go right into introducing myself: "My name is Tarajee. I'm also HIV-positive. I know I'm in the right place."

They had as much fun with me as I had with them. They wanted to know why my hair was covered up and how long it was. They were asking me female questions. That's why it was amusing to me. I could relate. I felt comfortable with them. I was with "the girls." I didn't feel cast aside.

They left the door wide open. I could come and go as I liked. The majority of them found me fascinating. We didn't relate so much on an HIV level as we did on a humanistic level. I went in there not sure what I was looking for, but I came out with a lot. I learned a lot of things about them—their fears, their ways of dealing. More than that, I learned that they bleed when they're cut just like I do. They feel like I feel. They hurt like I hurt. They're no different.

I didn't immediately go into the Muslim community disclosing my HIV status. I would toss a question at a group or an individual, just bring up the subject of AIDS just to watch the reaction. And most Muslims believed that whoever had AIDS had committed a sin and Allah was punishing them.

I saw a lot of fear and anger and denial at the highest level. I suggested to an *imam* that we needed support groups within the Muslim community to deal with Muslims who had the virus. And he said to me, "Sister, you don't need support groups, you got us."

And I said, "That's not being realistic. Suppose I get tired of being single. What measures have you taken to ensure that I find a husband? I can't fornicate, I can't commit adultery. So what measures have you taken to ensure that I stay within the limitations of my *deen* [religion]?"

He said, "Well, we'll cross that bridge when we get to it."

This is typical of the kinds of reactions. He was upset with me because I talked about it too much. I had become too brazen.

He was the first *imam* that I told it to.

I started raising questions: Why isn't the Muslim community dealing with this? Why is everybody so cloak-and-dagger with this issue? What's going on here?

I met a Muslim brother in Manhattan who said to me, "They need to put all Muslims with this AIDS virus in leper colonies. They need to just lock them all away and throw the key away."

So I said to him, "Well, brother, I don't want to be in a leper colony."

He looked at me and said, "I ain't talking about you, I'm talking about all them other people with that virus."

I said, "Brother, I am one of those people with 'that virus.'"

What could he do? He already put his foot all the way down his throat. I just helped him shove it down a little further, that's all. [Laughs.] And I enjoyed myself immensely. I made prayer: *Allah, please forgive me for enjoying myself.*

I asked Allah not to let me be afraid, and that's exactly what I got. You get what you strive for. Allah says man can only get what he strives for. I don't strive for material things. I ask Allah for guidance. I ask Him to protect. I ask Him to show me how to get through this murky water. And He shows me how. And I get other blessings with it to boot.

Malik died three years ago from AIDS. He started back on the drugs again, and he did something that I never saw in twenty-four years of knowing Malik: He turned into a junkie. He finally succeeded, yes he did. When he got finished, Malik wiped out two savings accounts, a checking account; all our insurance policies lapsed. Everything was gone when Malik died. I had to get social services to bury him.

The day he died I was home. I woke up feeling funny, and I knew Malik had died. I knew. And they called me from the hospital and told me. I wasn't surprised. I was glad Malik died. I was glad it was over for him, because he went through sheer hell, and I was always saying to him, get up off your ass and fight this! Don't let this thing take you out of here like that! This is not the way to go. You don't *have* to be miserable. Misery, to me, is optional.

I couldn't make him see what I saw. He was so bitter and so angry he was blinded by it. So I got to a point where I couldn't say much else to Malik on that issue. He just didn't hear what I said. He tore his body down with the drug. I believe that he died from bitterness and anger. It ate him alive.

He had full-blown AIDS about two years before he died. I saw it—before he was diagnosed. We had gone to the Eid prayer, and we were in Prospect Park and I was standing out in the distance talking to a sister, and I just looked up and saw Malik, and I thought to myself, oh my God, he has full-blown AIDS. He wasn't emaciated at that point, but I just knew. I never told him what I saw. The fear bothered me more than anything, because as Muslims we are taught to fear nothing but Allah. I *believed* this.

Malik was afraid of being ostracized. He was afraid of being treated in a condescending manner. He was afraid to let others know that he'd messed up, that he'd made a mistake.

Sometimes Muslims want everyone to believe that they've never done anything wrong, or they're not capable of doing anything wrong. But we're humans. We all mess up from time to time. Allah says this in the Qur'an. This is the way He made us.

This is how many Muslims deal with it. They're more afraid of what people are going to think than they are of having the virus. And I don't understand it. Because I still maintain we are Muslims. If you say, *La il-laha ill Allah* [there is no god but God], you've entered into a covenant with Allah. You have agreed with Allah that He is going to lead you, guide you, take you where you're going. I'm even clearer on that now, since I've had this virus.

The Muslim greeting, male or female, is to hug. Before the virus it was something I used to do automatically. After I contracted the virus and I started to disclose, I stopped doing that.

I stopped for two reasons. Number one: I don't know how afraid people really are. Why subject myself to that kind of pain watching them withdraw? I've seen that happen. Those I know I can do it with, I'm all over them, because they know they can't catch it from me that way. But some people don't know that. I don't want to frighten them and I don't want to hurt their feelings.

I watched that happen to a Muslim brother. He passed two years ago. He contracted AIDS through blood transfusion. He was a hemophiliac. And he was young. He had never been out there in the world.

I remember being at his house when his aunt and her two children came to visit him. He sat on the edge of the bed, and he said to the two little girls, "Come give me a hug." The little girls froze, and right then I understood what was going on.

I thought that maybe he would leave it alone, but he didn't. And he said, "Come; come give me a hug."

Then the oldest little girl, who had to be about eight, said, "My mommy said I can't hug you because you got AIDS."

I was absolutely floored. Not for myself—I understand these things— but for the effect that it had on him. There were several people in the room. I asked them to leave.

He cried and just went to pieces. And I said, "Now listen. You know, even though they love you, everybody is not going to be able to handle this. Some people are very afraid and you have to understand that. They'll be concerned, yes, but they'll still be afraid to touch you. That's just the way it is. Now, you're just going to wipe your face, and you don't put yourself in that position anymore. Ever."

He was twenty-two when he died. He was in the hospital, and I go visit him. I got some oil. I say, "Okay, your surrogate wife is here." I done seen his butt and everything. I'm helping him to the bathroom when he needs it. And I'm giving him a rubdown and making jokes. And a couple of Muslim brothers walk in, and they look at me and [say]: "*Astaghfirlah* [I ask God's forgiveness], sister! That's not your husband, you can't touch him!"

It was just a bunch of foolishness, and they went on so bad with it that I took the bottle of oil and I said, "Well, then, you all do it."

Nobody touched him.

I said to them, "How dare you be so thoughtless. Allah knows my intentions. If breaking my *wudu* [ablution] is all that I did back there, then I'll make another one. If you're not going to offer to help, if you're not going to stick your feet in the murky water, then get out of my way. I got my boots on."

Alcoholism, homelessness, wife abuse, child abuse, homosexuality— it's all the same. These are issues that have to be dealt with. If you sweep them all up under the rug every time you're confronted with them, you're not dealing with anything. And this is the natural tendency.

When Malik was on drugs and I wanted support from the Muslim community, and I'd gone to them with this. I was saying in effect: Help me. Show me what to do. Tell me how to deal with this. I don't want him to be like this. I didn't ask for a divorce. You're a man, he's a man, talk man talk to him. Talk to him the language that you speak better than I can. Maybe he will hear something in what you're saying that I don't know how to convey to him. Malik would not go to the counsel with me, so I was trying to bring the counsel to my house. I want help, and I want it Islamically.

I was told some cute little stuff like: "Who? Abdul Malik on drugs? That brother works every day." In other words: I don't see him doing anything.

AIDS is out there. I want the Muslims who don't have the virus to make AIDS service accessible, and I would like to see the brothers running it Islamically, not based on how you feel.

Brothers get in touch with me, get scared and hang up and not call back ever again. I've had them call, and maybe speak to them for a year, and they won't tell me who they are. And they know I have the virus too.

There's another brother that I've been corresponding with for about three years now. He lives in California. He's married to someone who doesn't have the virus. He found out he had it, and fortunately she doesn't deal with him sexually. My heart goes out to this brother. There's no hugs, there's no kisses, there's no intimate interaction between them. They just deal with the kids. She cooks dinner. That's it. He's miserable to the point where he's talking about how easy it is to commit adultery.

Meanwhile, he's getting ready to have a nervous breakdown, because he has no one to hold his hand. And that's what he's dying from. He's not dying from the virus. I understand her fear. Let him go. Or let him get another wife—someone who's going to take care of his needs. That can't be ignored. That doesn't go away because you have this virus. Touching and holding hands is something profound now. It's not the same anymore. It means something different now.

I remember sitting on a train and this old woman sat next to me, and she went to sleep, and she was leaning on me, and I was just thinking about the beauty of it. The warmth from her. The feeling of her leaning on me, and even when my little girl gets in the bed, I'm so aware of her presence in a way I was never aware before.

So I know what he's talking about.

But I also know what she's talking about.

I had remarried for a hot minute. For about four months to a brother I've known for fifteen years. He knew I had the virus; for four years he asked me to marry him, and I said no because he didn't have the virus.

I finally said yes, but I was uncomfortable the whole time in the marriage. Of course, we used protection. But all I could think about was suppose this thing breaks. My mind was full of supposes. I wanted to kiss. And I wouldn't kiss him. Because I was always worrying about it. I got *nothing* out of that intimately because I couldn't relax, no matter what he said. I don't want the responsibility of hurting somebody that way. So I believe that people with the virus should be with people who have the virus. I just couldn't deal with it anymore. Someone with the virus needs me much more than someone who doesn't have it.

The struggle is not about dealing with the AIDS virus. It's about recognizing the fact that Allah's in charge. It's that simple. People complicate things. People want what they want when they want it. And it's not like that.

I know Who to go to. I took a *shahada*. I entered into a covenant with Allah. I feel like I found that pot of gold at the end of the rainbow. It's almost like I can sense things. AIDS has made me understand who Allah is.

How do I see AIDS at this point? I see it as Allah having presented us with an outrageous opportunity to get our spiritual acts together. But I can't get up there with my spear and my shield and come from an Amazon center and say, "Now look! You all got to get up and do this!" I have to say in a gentler tone, "Protect us. Be there to support us when we run into these brick walls like this. We have work to do, even if it's unpleasant work. We have to protect our interests here."

My children are beautiful. All my girls know except my youngest daughter. She's eight. I'll let her play with her Barbie dolls for now. Why should I traumatize this kid?

The oldest one, I felt she was becoming too curious about the outside world. She wanted to stick her feet in the water and play around a little bit.

Telling her that she was Muslim and she shouldn't do it just wasn't work-ing. I saw her on her way to becoming sexually active, so I said to her, "Now look, if I got this and I'm married, you don't stand a chance, okay? So you got to be real careful."

They cried. And I let them cry for a little while. And then I said, "Okay, you got to come back now. You stay too long, nobody can pull you out. You got to want to pull yourself out, and you won't be able to. C'mon out of that little black hole you're trying to crawl into. We got things to do."

I got them tested. They thought we were going for a routine visit to the pediatrician. Everything came out just fine. None of the kids are HIV-positive. I'm so grateful that my kids don't have the virus, I haven't stopped saying *Allahu akbar*!

4. Asma Gull Hasan, *American Muslims: The New Generation* (2000)

Born in 1974 in Chicago, Illinois, Asma Gull Hasan grew up in Pueblo, Colo-rado. The daughter of a successful Pakistani neurologist and businessman, Hasan attended the Groton School, Wellesley College, and New York Univer-sity Law School. She wrote American Muslims *when she was still in her twen-ties. Hasan, who describes herself as a "Muslim feminist cowgirl," is a popular speaker on college campuses, a frequent guest on various television and radio programs, and a spokesperson for the U.S. Department of State's public-relations program in the Islamic world. She is neither a trained scholar of Islam nor a professional academic, but her lively and accessible writing has garnered positive reviews from a number of critics and pundits. In the excerpt below, Hasan explains why she does not wear a head scarf in everyday life, and she describes her conflicting desires to be a religious Muslim and to date boys. She also chronicles her dispute with her grandfather about the equality of the sexes, and like many other Muslim feminists, identifies culture rather than Islamic religion as the source of patriarchy and discrimination among Muslims.*

Hijab, or the head cover many Muslim women wear, is probably the most enigmatic aspect of Islam in America, for both Americans and American Muslims. Alexander McQueen, British fashion designer for Givenchy and a non-Muslim, created a "couture chador, inspired by a photograph from *National Geographic*." According to a story in *Vogue* (October 1997), he added his own innovation by attaching a cage holding a live bird to the top of the *hijab*. For Americans, the *hijab* looks repressive and may serve as symbolic proof of the stereotype that Muslim women are oppressed. For American Muslims, the *hijab* represents the eye of the storm, with the storm being how American Muslims are interpreting the Qur'an and bringing their modern perspectives to it. To some, wearing *hijab* is a way of showing physically a preservation of traditional Islam, as it was practiced in the country from which the immigrants came, or to show that they are serious about being Muslim. I have no doubt that conservative Muslims' hearts are elated when they see a young woman wearing *hijab*, as if that proves that Islam is surviving in the United States. To others, wearing *hijab* is an act of devotion, a way of serving God.

So where did *hijab* come from? Though there are accounts of head-covering in pre-Islamic Arabia (which would explain why Catholic nuns wear, in essence, *hijab*, not to mention that it is shown in practically every representation of the Virgin Mary), the Islamic basis for *hijab* is a few Qur'anic passages. The first asks that men and women be modest in their appearance and lower their gaze when with the opposite sex. The majority of world Muslims have come to interpret this to mean that women should cover their heads when out in public. The second passage instructs that men and women should cover their heads while praying. Some Muslims read this and come to the conclusion that since everything they do in life is a prayer and/or in service to God they should always cover their heads.

I have a few problems with seeing *hijab* as a Qur'anic requirement, the main one being that, if the above interpretations are true, men are severely, disproportionately, excluded from the *hijab* requirement, particularly in the United States. The modesty passage is directed to both men and women as is the prayer passage. In addition, the modesty passage does not necessarily suggest covering one's head. It actually specifies arms and chest. Furthermore, if everything we do is an expression of prayer, men as well as women should be required to wear *hijab* as there is no exception in the Qur'an. (It does not say "Only womens' actions count as prayer.") Finally, if the whole point of wearing *hijab* is *not to attract attention* to oneself, *hijab* in America certainly does not serve that purpose. Instead it epitomizes the phrase "sticking out like a sore thumb."

The disproportionate application of *hijab* bothers me. I would truly care less about the issue of *hijab* if men wore something similar. I shared this thought with my brother while I was having one of my intellectual rages. "Ali," I said (my family calls my brother by his middle name and not his first name out of respect for the Prophet), "it wouldn't bother me so much that women are going to all this trouble, if men had to do it too." We thought for a moment and realized that Saudi Arabian men cover their heads à la Lawrence of Arabia, an interesting fact considering that Saudi Arabian women are required to cover from head *to toe*, based on Saudi Arabian interpretation of the above Qur'anic passages. My brother and I talked about the matter, and then Ali said, "The Saudi Arabian men must have finally said to the women: 'Fine! We'll wear it too! Now quit complaining!'" Of course, I have no clue why Saudi Arabian men began to cover their heads, but I thought Ali's description was pretty funny.

As you may have gleaned, I don't think the Qur'an and God are asking me to wear *hijab*. I could be wrong, but I believe modesty comes from the inside-out, not the outside-in. I could cover my head but still flirt with my eyes or wear tight clothing. Some young women only wear *hijab* at Islamic gatherings and do not really believe in it. A peer pressure exists at these events. If you looked around and realized you were the only female in the room not wearing a head cover, you would probably feel a little odd. I have experienced that feeling. Usually, when I've noticed it, I've been at an academic Islamic conference, and the women wearing *hijab* there were dressed modestly as well. I attended a much larger, more social gathering of American Muslims and, though I noticed that my sister and I seemed to be the only women not wearing *hijab*, many of the younger women were wearing *hijab* as well as tight pants and blouses, showing off their figures. The hypocrisy stuns me, and I wonder why their parents don't say anything to them. Many women, including the tight-clothing ones, take off their *hijabs* the moment they step outside of such conferences.

This is clearly a contentious issue for American Muslims. It refers directly to the question: how Americanized have Muslims become? A small number of Muslims feel that not wearing *hijab* is tantamount to dating and engaging in premarital sex, a big taboo in American Islam. I don't think my not wearing *hijab* (except when I pray, of course) shows that Islam is losing a battle with American culture, however. What it does show is that being a Muslim in America, and not in an Islamic country with widely-held interpretations that are never questioned, has caused me to read the Qur'an myself and find out what it says and how I interpret it. Even if I don't end up toeing the traditional Islamic line and wearing *hijab*, it's great that I have made an effort to read the Qur'an. Had I grown up in Saudi Arabia, I probably would never have bothered to see what the Qur'an really has to say about *hijab* or anything else. . . .

I was debating with my extended family once during a family gathering whether Muslim women and men should be allowed to pray in the same room. I reasoned that on Judgment Day men and women will stand equally before God with no gender preference. My grandfather piped up, "No, men are superior in Islam!" We were in my uncle's normally quite noisy Suburban, which had now gone silent at my grandfather's words.

My family members waited a moment, and then said things like, "Oh no!" and "You're in for it now, grandfather!" They were saying all this because I am known in my family for responding vehemently to such statements. I stayed levelheaded, however, and asked my grandfather, "You mean in the Qur'an?"

"Yes!" he said.

"I don't think so," I said.

"No, it says it!" he retorted.

After a few minutes of this yes-no business we finally got to the merits of the argument. My grandfather felt that since God's messengers were all male, men must then be superior in God's eyes. I countered that a woman, Khadijah, Muhammad's wife, was the first convert to Islam. Without her faith in Muhammad, *no Muslims would exist.*

I offered other arguments proving gender equality in Islam, but something told me that my points were falling on deaf ears. I joked that my grandfather must have received the Taliban version of the Qur'an. The Taliban are the Islamic revolutionaries who took over the Afghanistan government and banned women from working because they said that was against their interpretations of the Qur'an. The country came to a near stand-still as half the professional population—doctors, teachers—were not allowed to work. Obviously, the Taliban had to modify some of their policies to keep the country functioning. The Taliban validly has pronounced that they put an end to Afghanistani tribal practices which hurt women. They were forced to marry and had no right to property of divorce. So as unenlightened as the Taliban is, they have actually elevated Afghanistan's rural population.

Though I tried to make light of the situation, I was saddened that *my own grandfather* would say such a thing, even if he believed it. Does he really think that I, as a woman, am inferior to my brother, merely because he's male? I see in my grandfather the effects of South Asian culture, which is patriarchal, on his interpretation of the Qur'an. Sure, there are a few passages that taken out of context, interpreted from a patriarchal perspective, or not updated for our times (which the Qur'an instructs us to do) imply women's inferiority. They are by no means passages on which to build tenets of Islam, however. When I asked my grandfather to show me where in the Qur'an it says that women are inferior to men, he replied that it would take him some time to find the passage. As he has still not found it, I presume it doesn't exist or isn't clear in its meaning.

But this is what it came to—my own grandfather, a product of his society and prejudices, saying that women are inferior to men. This despite the fact that women outnumber men in his own family. He has five granddaughters and three grandsons—it's in his interest to see women as equal to men! It hurts, but I understand that we all have to read the Qur'an and make our own interpretation. This is my *jihad* with my grandfather. Who knows—maybe someday my grandkids will disagree with me on a belief, emphasized by my American culture, on something similar.

The debate over the status of women in Islam is probably the best example of how culture affects interpretation. Men like my grandfather have taken a few Qur'anic passages and, coupled with a patriarchal culture have interpreted them in the most literal and self-serving way. It happens in all cultures, not just among Muslims, and such chauvinism existed before Islam, perhaps even before organized religion itself. There is no Islamic basis for demeaning women or oppressing them. Culture is the culprit here, and no one really is immune from that.

American culture often favors men and holds women back. Women are paid less than men for similar jobs. We have yet to elect a female president. We're still arguing over a woman's right to control her body. Sexual harassment and rape are very difficult to prosecute. Office politics, sometimes on a subliminal level, keep women from rising to top positions. However, no one sees the American woman as being as severely oppressed as the Muslim woman. Women *are* oppressed in *some* countries where the majority of the population is Muslim. There, women's literacy rates are often quite low, among many other disadvantages for advancement.

However, such oppression is not mandated by the Qur'an. It is in fact condemned by it. Furthermore, strong Muslim women are all over the place. Benazir Bhutto became the prime minister of Pakistan twice, which is more than we can say for a female politician in the United States. Muhammad's wife, Khadijah, was one of the most successful business people in Mecca. Fatima Mernissi is one of the most intelligent Islamic scholars and a prominent thinker, and she is a woman. My own mother runs the lives of our family as well as being a dynamic volunteer worker and fundraiser. My dad calls her "the boss" and sometimes a tyrant. Here I am writing a book on Islam in America. Do I seem oppressed to you?

The challenge women like my mom and I face is to overcome the cultural baggage that haunts American Muslim women. Though women in Islamic countries are often oppressed, Islam as a philosophy is very pro-woman. However, as with all philosophies, societies, and cultures, contradictions occur in the journey from paper (Qur'an) to practice (my grandfather). Because of these contradictions, Muslim women all over the world are being pulled in two different directions: one is to fulfill the traditional expectations for a Muslim woman, like marriage at a young age and raising a family; the other to explore the new roles for women in the modern world by being career women and community activists.

The problems we face—in trying to express our feminism, become activists, and be independent—are acute versions of what American women in general are going through. As more American women convert to Islam and more young Muslim women like me grow up, it is in our interest, as Americans, not to be like my grandfather and rely on what we have heard through the grapevine, but to encourage all women to explore their identities and their strengths, and instill in them the belief that they can contribute to our society, our economy, our values as much as men can. . . .

I have been part of an e-mail distribution list for the past few years run by the Muslim Public Affairs council (MPAC). . . . On the MPAC distribution list, a debate began with a message from a man who seemed to suggest that American Muslims needed to come up with solutions to the problem of what young Muslims should do who are not being allowed to date because of Islamic traditions, yet are not marrying at a young age. Was there any room for dating in American Islam, he was asking. I believe he was alluding to the fact that young people want companionship, intimate companionship, but aren't really sure they can have that without being condemned by fellow Muslims. It's a valid question because, if we aren't totally arranging marriages of young Muslims, how are they supposed to meet each other? I respected this man's bravery in speaking out in this forum. We all have this issue on our minds, but who wants to bring it up on an e-mail distribution list?

Almost immediately, a few members of the group responded resolutely along the lines of: "There is no premarital sex in Islam, and we shouldn't waste our time talking about this." One woman explained why sex outside of marriage is forbidden in Islam, for very good reasons. It is meant to bring stability to the community. She quoted Dr. Hassan Hathout of the Islamic Center of Southern California as saying that sex outside of marriage is forbidden in Islam because Islam stands for justice between women and men. Sex outside of marriage is an injustice against women, as any negative consequences of such actions are almost totally shouldered by them, specifically pregnancy. In addition, a few offered that the Prophet's solution to carnal desires was to fast, to learn patience and self-control, and to marry, even at a young age. That was about all they said.

Technically, there is no explicit prohibition against premarital sex in the Qur'an, but there are several implicit indicators against it: encouragement of marriage at a young age, modesty in appearance, and so on. Masturbation is also discouraged. One is instructed to fast to control urges. Basically, if you want to have sex and be a good Muslim, you should get married.

This discussion was taking place at the time of the public disclosure of President Clinton's affair with former White House intern Monica Lewinsky. Most on the distribution list seemed to be saying regarding infidelity and sexual misconduct, that we shouldn't talk about sex when there were more important things going in the country and world.

But, I was upset that the issue wasn't taken more seriously. What I mean is that we American Muslims should be talking about how we can solve this issue, not about fasting and marrying at the age of sixteen. So I had what my brother calls a "spaz" and let my feelings known over the Internet.

I wrote in a huff that I thought this topic was really important for a bunch of reasons that I hadn't coherently organized as yet. First of all, it would have been silly for me to get married as soon as I realized I was attracted to men. In the Prophet's time, 1,400 years ago in Arabia, people married around the age of fifteen anyway because they only expected to live to their mid-30s. Second, I want to marry a Muslim and have Muslim kids, yet most of the Muslim boys I met socially and actually had a chance to get to know were "players." I don't think their primary interest was marriage. Third, I wasn't meeting nice Muslim boys who weren't interested in premarital sex because at every event I went to at a mosque, where there might be such boys, we were segregated by gender! So what is a young Muslim girl to do?

Especially when, fourth, I had noticed that many young Muslim women I knew who had dated and had premarital sex with Muslims and non-Muslims were now marrying nice Muslim men. They became acquainted with these boys by dating them, and now they're marrying them. Good girls like me were, as Tom Petty once sang, "sitting home with broken hearts" and had little prospect of a marriage we'd be pleased with. Furthermore, some of the players, who were the children of immigrant Muslims usually, would eventually ask their mothers to find them nice girls from their home country, not girls like me who were already corrupted by American life.

I had a few more thoughts that I didn't add, but my frustration was evident. I'm not yet ready to get married, but why shouldn't I develop relationships, maybe not more than friendship or dating without sex (if that's possible), that could develop into marriage? Why do I have to live like a nun with no companionship until I consent to an arranged marriage? Especially when many Muslim boys are dating and having sex with non-Muslim women because the community doesn't come down as hard on them. Many Muslims have a double standard in disciplining girls versus disciplining boys on such matters. Why should I marry young to fulfill desires but risk my education and career for a family? Furthermore, why is arranged marriage a viable alternative? I'm supposed to marry any boy who charms my parents enough?

Later, I came across a *Minaret* magazine survey of 90 Muslim students in California colleges on premarital sex. My suspicions that barring Muslim youth from each other causes Muslim youth to socialize with non-Muslim youth were somewhat confirmed. Sixty percent had engaged in some sort of physical intimacy without involving sex with non-Muslims; only 6.6 percent had with other Muslims; 28.8 percent had had premarital sex with non-Muslims; 4.4 percent with Muslims. Clearly the goal is not for Muslims to have sex or intimacy only with each other, but to create an environment where Muslims are not turning away from their religion.

Things are different in America. Men and women, boys and girls, meet all the time, in the mall, at work, in school. We can't isolate ourselves from that. Even if we cover a woman from head to toe and tell her to stay in the house all day, at some point, she'll have to call the plumber because the toilet's overflowing, and the plumber could easily be a man. American culture is challenging us as Muslims: how contemporary can we be? How will we solve this problem? The first step, for many, is admitting we have a problem. It's more than condemning premarital sex. As an American and a woman who wants some semblance of a career, I don't really believe in marriage at a young age. As a Muslim, I don't want to become morally lax.

I don't want to have my parents arranging a marriage for me in my thirties. At the same time, many Muslims insist that the Qur'an does not allow for Muslim men and women who are not related to each other to meet. As a young woman who has grown up in America, I'm not willingly going to consent to an "old world" arranged marriage like my mother had. At the same time, I know, as a Muslim and Pakistani, that I'm certainly not free to date, meet (probably have sex with) men. So how do I marry if I don't intend on having an arranged marriage, yet I'm not ready to turn my back on cultural and religious standards against dating? . . .

Some Muslims say that you can meet a member of the opposite sex within Islamic guidelines. You must only be sincere in your interest in marrying this person. You can't just shoot the breeze and hang out with them for the hell of it. As a result, first meetings are loaded with expectation. The man who began the discussion pointed out that we need to move away from this idea of relationships between genders as only leading to marriage and allow men and women to meet accepting in his words, "the possibility that things would not work out." One woman wrote of girls to whom she teaches sex education, who say that young Muslim men are justifying as Islamic all sorts of sexual escapades, especially engaging in premarital intimacy without intercourse, whereas these same men look down on women who engage in similar activities as un-Islamic. She calls this "an abuse of our religion . . . a form of self-including sexuality," and that we should try to be "creative and courageous" in these "challenging times."

5. Azizah al-Hibri, "An Introduction to Muslim Women's Rights,"
in *Windows of Faith: Muslim Women Scholar-Activists
in North America* (2002)

Lebanese-American Azizah al-Hibri (b. 1943), who holds both a JD and a PhD in philosophy, is professor of law at the University of Richmond. An expert in several areas of the law, her writings have appeared in over thirty books and law journals, and she is the founding editor of Hypatia: A Journal of Feminist Philosophy. *Like many Muslim academicians in the United States, al-Hibri is also a social activist and has worked for social change both in the United States and the Islamic world. She is founder and president of Karamah, Muslim Women Lawyers for Human Rights, which "stands committed to research, education, and advocacy work in matters pertaining to Muslim women and human rights in Islam, as well as civil rights and other related rights under the Constitution of the United States." Under her leadership, Karamah has brought together various government officials, community leaders, and academics concerned about a wide array of women's issues. In the excerpt below, al-Hibri outlines her view of traditional women's rights in Islam. While some Muslims in the United States and beyond might find some of her legal interpretations to be too liberal, they would praise her emphasis on the Qur'an and the Sunna of the Prophet as the proper sources from which answers to such questions must be found. Many American Muslims would also agree that in the fight for women's liberation in the Islamic world, non-Muslim feminists should support the efforts of indigenous feminists rather than impose their own sense of what's right on the rest of the world.*

The Islamic Philosophy of Change

With few important exceptions, the Islamic philosophy of change is one of gradualism.

The Islamic philosophy of change does not stand alone. It is an integral part of the Islamic worldview. It is, therefore, no surprise that this philosophy is closely linked to another fundamental Islamic principle, namely, that a society must conduct its affairs on the basis of *shura* (consultation). This latter principle is so basic that it has been viewed as the constitutional cornerstone of any Muslim state. The Qur'anic philosophy of change is also linked to yet another important Qur'anic principle, namely, that there be no compulsion in matters of faith. All these specific principles can be partly subsumed under the overarching principle of freedom of thought. Because abrupt change usually requires coercive action and coercion is the antithesis of freedom, it stands to reason that the Islamic philosophy of change is necessarily one of gradualism.

This divine philosophy of change remains the most suitable for the improvement of the status of Muslim women around the world. Although

gradual change is frustrating, it is, nevertheless, more stable and less de-
structive of society than a radical coercive change. Coercive change, which
reflects a patriarchal preference for the use of force, lasts for only as long
as the source of the coercion continues to exist. It also leaves a great deal
of violence and pain in its aftermath. Furthermore, gradual change need
not be agonizingly slow. If Muslim women (and men) join efforts to dismantle patriarchal society, the objective could be achieved within our
lifetime. To achieve that end we need to develop a clear agenda of our strategic goals and a definite program of action that prioritizes these goals.
Such a program must take into account the differing needs and wishes of
Muslim women in each country. It must demand the proper and equitable
implementation of Islamic laws. It must also stress the Qur'anic foundation for our demands and, simultaneously, actively encourage Muslims to
reengage in the process of *ijtihad* [reasoned interpretation of the Qur'an
and Sunna of the Prophet].

It is from this vantage point of the Qur'anic aversion to coercion and
the need to develop an indigenous Muslim women's movement that I reject all attempts to exercise hegemony over the Muslim world by forcing
upon it, whether through the introduction of international legal instruments or otherwise, a certain model of gender relationships suitable primarily for some other country, belief system, or culture. I also reject all
attempts to use the suffering of Muslim women for the furthering of such
schemes and the fragmentation of Muslim societies. I call for the establishment of an International Muslim Women's Human Rights Commission which reviews human rights violations in Muslim countries and
takes effective steps for their cessation. . . .

Marriage Relations in Islam

Historically, marriage has been an institution that favored men over
women. Through this institution basic women's rights such as the right to
education, financial independence, and freedom of self-fulfillment were
usually denied. A fulfilled woman was, in fact, viewed as one who married, served her husband well, and bore him children. This view, although
less common today, continues to exist both in the West and in Muslim
countries. Yet it is in total contradiction to the Islamic view of women and
marriage.

Islam guarantees for women, among other things, the right to an edu-cation similar to that of the male, the right to financial independence, and even the right to engage in *ijtihad*. Islam also views marriage as an institu-tion in which human beings find tranquility and affection with each other. It is for this reason that some prominent traditional Muslim schol-ars have argued that a woman is not required to serve her husband, pre-pare his food, or clean his house. In fact, the husband is obligated to bring his wife prepared food, for example. This assertion is based on the recog-nition that the Muslim wife is a companion to her husband and not a maid. Many jurists also defined the purpose of the marriage institution in terms of sexual enjoyment (as distinguished from reproduction). They clearly stated that a Muslim woman has a right to sexual enjoyment within the marriage. This view has important consequences in areas such as con-traception and divorce.

It is these rights and views, which are derived from the Qur'an and clas-sical *ijtihad*, that we must actively reclaim. . . . So long as patriarchal (hier-archal/authoritarian) logic prevails, Muslim women will be denied their God-given rights. Qur'anic concepts of family relations must be more ade-quately recognized and enforced in Muslim countries and communities to abolish the authoritarian structure of the marriage institution.

In striving for this result we must recognize the fact that patriarchal logic is deeply entrenched in all societies and is quite resistant to being uprooted. If we, however, follow the Qur'anic approach to change, we will receive the support of many Muslim men and achieve a great measure of success without sacrificing the social cohesion of Muslim communities.

In fostering change the Qur'an resorts to what has been known recently in the West as affirmative action. In a patriarchal society even a general declaration of equal rights is not sufficient to protect women. Conse-quently, divine wisdom gave women further protections. Paramount among these protections is the ability of the Muslim woman to negotiate her marriage contract and place in it any conditions that do not contra-dict its purpose. For example, she could place in her marriage contract a condition forbidding her husband from moving her away from her own city or town. She could also insert a condition requiring him to support her in the pursuit of her education after marriage. She could also use the marriage contract to ensure that her marriage would foster, rather than destroy, her financial independence. This goal is usually achieved by re-quiring a substantial *mahr*.

The Mahr *Requirement*

Despite many patriarchal and Orientalist interpretations that have distorted and even damaged the Muslim woman's rights in this area, the law
of *mahr* was made clear quite early. The *mahr* is a requirement imposed by
God upon men entering marriage as a sign of their serious commitment
and a gesture of goodwill, a matter of great concern to women living in
this patriarchal world. In fact, the giving of *mahr* is not much different
from the Western custom of giving an engagement ring to signal commitment. Islamic law, however, preserved for the prospective wife the right to
specify to her prospective husband the type of *mahr* she prefers. One
woman may prefer cash, another property, depending on her relative
needs or even taste. A third woman may choose something intangible
(nonmaterial) as her *mahr*, such as education. That is acceptable also. A
woman of meager means may prefer to ask for capital that she could immediately invest in a business. In fact, she could even use that capital to
start her own business. Her husband would have no access to either the
capital or income from that business even if he were in need because legally, her *mahr* belongs to her alone. . . .

Mahr, therefore, is not a "bride price" as some have erroneously described it. It is not money the woman pays to obtain a husband nor money
the husband pays to obtain a wife. It is part of a civil contract that specifies
the conditions under which a woman is willing to abandon her status as a
single woman and its related opportunities in order to marry a prospective
husband and start a family. Consequently, as in Western prenuptial and
nuptial agreements, the contract addresses matters of concern to the prospective wife and provides her with financial and other assurances. In
short, it is a vehicle for ensuring the continued well-being of women entering matrimonial life in a world of patriarchal injustice and inequality. . . .

Family Planning

Another measure for guarding the interests of women in particular and
the Muslim community in general is provided in the area of family planning. Islam values the family structure and, like Judaism and Christianity, encourages procreation. Islamic law, nevertheless, differs from both
traditions in its liberal approach to family planning. It shares with some

Judeo-Christian traditions the view that contraception is permissible. Coitus interruptus (al-'azl) was practiced by members of the Muslim community during the time of Prophet Muhammad. Indeed, the Prophet knew that some of his companions, including his cousin Ali, practiced it, yet he did not prohibit it.

Al-Ghazali, a prominent twelfth-century jurist, argues that contraception is always permitted. He makes an analogy between intercourse and a contract. A contract consists of an offer and acceptance. So long as the offer has not been accepted, he notes, it can be withdrawn. He even suggests that a woman can engage in contraception to preserve her beauty but adds that it is disliked (makrouh) if used to avoid female offspring. Jurists have, however, conditioned the practice of al-'azl upon the consent of the wife. Some even argue that if the husband practices al-'azl without the wife's permission, he has to pay her a fine because he has detracted from her sexual enjoyment, her established right.

Until recently, the majority of traditional jurists have taken a relatively liberal view toward abortion that properly balances the rights of the mother and the rights of the child. They recognized a period of early pregnancy that could be terminated at will and a subsequent period in which the embryo became ensouled. The jurists argued that when the embryo became ensouled, increasingly stringent criteria should be used to justify abortion (such as the health of the mother). More recently, relying on medical data, jurists have adopted the view that the embryo is ensouled soon after conception. It is desirable that Muslim women physicians and jurists reexamine this recent conclusion to determine its validity.

Maintenance

Classical Islamic jurisprudence entitles the woman to maintenance by her husband. Even if fully financially independent, she is not required to spend any of her money except as she wishes. Furthermore, the wife is under no duty to do any housework although she may engage in such work on a volunteer basis. Some traditional jurists suggested that the wife was entitled to monetary compensation for her volunteer housework activity.

The law of maintenance is based on the Qur'an, but unfortunately it has been used to assert the general superiority of men over women. The relevant Qur'anic verse simply states that men may gain qiwamah (advisory, caretaking status) vis-à-vis women if only they satisfy two preconditions.

First, the male must be the (financial) maintainer of the woman. In other words, if he is not carrying her financial responsibility, then he has no standing to interfere in her affairs by providing unsolicited advice. Second, the male must also possess qualities (such as financial acumen, real estate expertise, etc.) that the advised woman needs to reach a particular decision but lacks (at that point). Without these two qualifications (which, incidentally, may change from time to time and from one decision to another), men may not even presume to provide advice or be caretakers (*qawwamun*).

Because the Qur'an was revealed in a world that was and continues to be highly patriarchal, it engaged in affirmative action to protect women. The revelation about maintenance provided women against poverty. It also made clear that maintenance alone does not suffice for a man to claim *qiwamah* over a woman. . . .

Despite all the rights and guarantees offered by Islam to women, most men still use women as uncompensated laborers in their households. Furthermore, they not only expect them to produce heirs but also to nurse these heirs. . . . Yet most Muslim jurists do not require Muslim women to nurse their children except to save the life of the child. Instead, the husband is required to hire a wet nurse (or buy milk formula) if the mother does not want to nurse. If the husband divorces the wife, and she nurses the child after the divorce, jurists agree that she is entitled to monetary compensation for that nursing. Hence, while masquerading as Islamic family law, a significant amount of the present family law in Muslim countries is influenced by local custom and patriarchal tradition.

Polygyny

Western writers have treated polygyny as one of the most controversial Islamic practices. Thus, it may be surprising to discover that Qur'anic reasoning clearly favors monogamy. The major Qur'anic verses at issue are two. One *ayah* states: "If you fear that you shall not be able to deal justly with the orphans, marry women of your choice, two, or three, or four; But if you fear that you shall not be able to deal justly [with them], then only one or that which your right hand possesses. That will be more suitable to prevent you from doing injustice." The other *ayah* states that men cannot deal justly with their wives when they marry more than one woman [4:129].

Some Muslim jurists have interpreted the first *ayah* to mean that a man has the right to marry up to four wives as long as he is equally just with each of them. In providing this interpretation, these jurists ignored the first part of the *ayah* which conditions the permission upon a certain context that obtained at the time of its revelation, namely, one of justice and fairness concerning the treatment of orphaned wives. Secondly, these jurists ignored that last part of the *ayah*, which states that (even in that context) justice considerations make it preferable to marry only one wife. Consequently, this highly conditional and fact-specific verse was interpreted as if it articulated a general rule. Of the two conditions, the first was ignored altogether, whereas the second was reduced to the duty of exercising fairness in treatment and maintenance among the wives. These same jurists also ignored the second *ayah*, which flatly states that men are incapable of satisfying the condition precedent for engaging in polygyny, namely, justice and fairness.

Other traditional jurists, however, concluded that the Qur'an is clear in advocating monogamy as the general rule. They also added that insofar as polygyny causes the first wife harm, it is forbidden altogether (*haram*). Several traditional jurists also recognized the right of the woman to place in the marriage contract a condition barring the prospective husband from additional (polygynous) marriages.

Yet practices of polygyny continue in some Muslim societies as a sign of economic or sexual power. As such, they are similar to the Western practice of having concubines or extramarital lovers. It is part of patriarchal custom and not religion. But religious scholars who attempt to criticize the practice or change the law are criticized for succumbing to Western influences.

Western neoorientalist critiques of Islam, thinly disguised as "feminist" critiques, have managed only to complicate the task of Muslim women. These critiques tend to be motivated more by a feeling of superiority and a desire for cultural hegemony than by a desire to help the female "Other" (in this case, the Muslim woman). The neoorientalist attitude is evidenced by the fact that only negative and distorted stereotypes of Muslim women are propagated in international fora. Furthermore, these Western "liberators" have taken it upon themselves to "explain" Islam, criticize the Qur'an, and redefine and prioritize the demands of Muslim women over these women's objections. This attack on Islam by unqualified biased commentators offends the religious sensibilities of all Muslims, male and female, regardless of their points of view.

Significantly, while Muslim women struggled repeatedly in international fora to raise basic issues of survival and development, such as hunger, water, war, and disease, patriarchal Western women have insisted on making the veil, clitoridectomy, and polygyny their primary preoccupations instead. They have even selected and funded some secular "Muslim" women to act as spokeswomen for the rest of the Muslim women. Needless to say, this neoorientalist attack on Islam has adversely impacted the civil rights of Muslims in Western countries and has poisoned the well for Muslim women seeking to regain their God-given Islamic rights in their own societies. Unfortunately, this state of affairs has alienated many Muslim women from the Western feminist movement.

6. Amina Wadud, *Qur'an and Woman: Rereading the Sacred Text from a Woman's Perspective* (1999)

Originally named Mary Teasley, Amina Wadud (b. 1952) grew up as the daughter of a Methodist minister in Washington, D.C. She converted to Islam in the early 1970s, and like many African American converts then and now, adopted an Islamic name. Wadud, a professor of religious studies at Virginia Commonwealth University, studied Arabic at the American University of Cairo and holds a PhD in Islamic studies from the University of Michigan. First published in 1992, her academic research on gender in the Qur'an has been read by Muslim feminists around the world. She argues that while the Qur'an establishes both spiritual and temporal equality between men and women, many of its male interpreters, expressing the chauvinism of their various cultures, have misread the holy word and used it to support gender hierarchies. In the excerpts below, Wadud explains how, in her view, the Qur'an does not discriminate on the basis of gender but on the basis of piety. She also argues that female figures discussed in the Qur'an provide excellent examples of how women are the equals of men.

Wadud has put her academic arguments into practice. In 1994, she first made waves across the English-speaking Muslim world by offering a lecture (technically right before the regular khutba, *or sermon) during Friday prayers at the Claremont Main Road Mosque in Capetown, South Africa. Women have not traditionally served as sermonizers, and her appearance caused some controversy among South African and other English-speaking Muslims. But that was nothing compared to the criticism she received for leading a mixed-gender congregational prayer a decade later. After Wadud led the 2005 mixed-gender prayers in New York, some believers even threatened her life, and she was forced by her university administrators to offer her courses one semester via videolink from her home. Undaunted, Wadud has continued her work—her most recent book is titled* Inside the Gender Jihad.

For the most part, the Qur'anic consideration of woman on earth centers on her relationship to the group, i.e. as a member of a social system. However, it is also important to understand how the Qur'an focuses on woman as an individual because the Qur'an treats the individual, whether male or female, in exactly the same manner: that is, whatever the Qur'an says about the relationship between Allah and the individual is not in gender terms. With regard to spirituality, there are no rights of woman distinct from rights of man.

With reference to the individual, the Qur'an most often uses the term *nafs*. On earth, the individual is given responsibility and capacity. Both determine the recompense of the individual in the Hereafter.

Individual capacity is expressed as follows: "Allah does not tax a *nafs* beyond its scope. For it (is only) that which it has earned, and against it (is only) that which it has deserved" (2:286). There is no distinction between the male and the female with regard to individual capacity. With regard to their potential relationship with Allah, they are the same. With regard to personal aspirations, they are also the same. . . .

When various social systems determine differences between men and women, they conclude these differences a[re] indications of different values as well. There is no indication that the Qur'an intends for us to understand that there is a primordial distinction between males and females with regard to spiritual potential. Therefore, whatever differences existing between males and females could not indicate an inherent value, or else free will would be meaningless. The problem arises in trying to determine when and how these differences come into being.

Sayyid Qutb says that "the *fitrah* [primordial nature] makes the man a man, and the woman a woman," but he goes on to emphasize that this distinction has no inherent value. Al-Zamakhshari, on the other hand, says that men are "preferred" by Allah over women in terms of "intelligence, physical constitution, determination and physical strength," although he cites no place in the text which states this. Such an assertion cannot be erased by saying that "men have no right to overcome women by coercion, or display arrogant behaviour towards them." Al-'Aqqad says that men deserve preference over women.

I hope to demonstrate the negative effects of interpretations which place an inherent distinction between males and females and then give values to those distinctions. Such interpretations assume that men represent the norm and are therefore fully human. Women, by implication, are less human than men. They are limited and therefore of less value. Such interpretations encourage the stereotypes about women and men which severely hamper the potential of each. In addition, these interpretations justify the restrictions placed on the woman's right to pursue personal happiness within the context of Islam. Most troubling is the tendency to attribute these interpretations to the Qur'an itself rather than to the authors who hold them.

I do not hold such views, nor do I find support for them in the Qur'an. It is interesting to note that even those Muslim authors who issue these interpretations accept that the Qur'an aims to establish social justice. However, it is obvious that their interpretation of social justice does not extend fully to women. It is like Thomas Jefferson and the writers of the American Constitution saying that "All men are created equal" without intending in the least to include equality between black men and white men.

I propose that the Qur'an depicts human individuals as having inherently equal value by looking at three stages in human existence. First, in the creation of humans, the Qur'an emphasizes the single origin of all humankind: "He created you (all) from a single *nafs*" (4:1). Second, with regard to development here on earth, the Qur'an emphasizes that the potential for change, growth and development lies within the *nafs* of the individual (or the group) as well: "Allah does not change the condition of a folk until they (first) change what is in their *anfus* [selves]" (13:11). Finally, all human activity is given recompense on the basis of what the individual earns (4:124).

This leaves me to ask the following questions: Is there any way to understand the distinction between individuals? Do these distinctions reflect a particular value system? Do they follow delineated lines between the two sexes?

Distinctions Between Individuals: Taqwa

The Qur'an does make distinctions between things and between people. It establishes that the Hereafter is of greater value than this world. It also distinguishes within the Hereafter and on this earth. The value of the distinctions between humankind on earth can be clearly summed up by the Qur'anic statement in *surat Al-Hujarat* (49:13): "We created you male and female and have made you nations and tribes that you may know one another. *Inna akramakum 'inda Allah atqa-kum* [Indeed the most noble of you from Allah's perspective is whoever (he or she) has the most *taqwa*]."

This term *taqwa*, one of the most essential in the Qur'anic Weltan-schauung [or Qur'anic worldview], has various translations and definitions. For this research I will consider it to mean "piety," that is, a pious manner of behaviour which observes constraints appropriate to a social-moral system; and "consciousness of Allah," that is, observing that manner of behaviour because of one's reverence towards Allah. In the Qur'anic Weltanschauung, this term always reflects both the action and the attitude. I do wish to reiterate that this multidimensional term is essential in the Qur'an.

The Qur'anic passage above reconstructs all the dimensions of human existence. It begins with creation. Then, it acknowledges the pair: male and female. These are then incorporated into larger and smaller groups, here translated as "nation" and "tribe" respectively. "That you may know one another," or simply that being distinguishable allows identification. If we were all alike, with nothing to distinguish us, we would have no way of knowing each other or being known.

The culmination of this verse and its central aspect for this discussion is: "the most noble of you from Allah's perspective is whoever (he or she) has the most *taqwa*." The distinguishing value from Allah's perspective is *taqwa*. Provided that *taqwa* is understood in both its action and attitude dimensions, this verse is self-explanatory. Allah does not distinguish on the basis of wealth, nationality, sex, or historical context, but on the basis of *taqwa*. It is from this perspective then that all distinctions between woman and woman, man and man, and between woman and man, must be analysed.

It is worth noting here that this verse follows verses which reprimand the individuals of both genders for mocking, defaming and backbiting one another (49:11–12). One might attribute greater or lesser value to another on the basis of gender, wealth, nationality, religion or race, but from Allah's perspective, these do not form a valuable basis for distinction between individuals (or groups)—and His is the true perspective.

Finally, I wish to point out that the three commentators whose exegetical works were consulted for this research all state that the apparent and worldly things which humans use to judge between one and another are not the true criteria for judgment. They do not agree, however, on what is included in these apparent things. In analyzing this verse, only Sayyid Qutb acknowledges that gender is used as a basis for mockery and defamation, which then must be denounced as a false, worldly aspect of superiority. He states that the verses are inclusive of all the variations among humankind: gender, colour, etc., "because all will return to a single scale, that of *taqwa*."

Al-Zamakhshari mentions that the references to both males and females, with regard to mockery, is more emphatic than the omission of both would be, but does not go to conclude explicitly that gender could be used erroneously for distinction or superiority.

Maududi says that in these verses "The whole of mankind is addressed" in order to prevent a great evil which is universally disruptive, and that is prejudice due to "race, colour, language, country and nationality." He does not include gender. He quotes Ibn-al-Majah as saying. "Allah does not see your outward appearances and your possessions, but He sees your heart and your deeds." I believe that the heart and deeds are genderless on the basis of this verse: "Whoever does good from male or female, and is a believer, all such will enter Paradise" (4:124).

Distinctive Female Characters in the Qur'an

I will discuss only three Qur'anic female characters: the mother of Moses, Mary, and Bilqis, the Queen of Sheba. The details in the lives of these women are very different but their stories have been retold by exegetes without the female vision and without focusing on that which transcends their femaleness.

Moses was born at a time when Pharaoh was slaughtering all male Jewish infants. Allah decrees that this child will fill the office of prophecy.

> And We inspired the mother of Moses, saying: Suckle him and, when you fear for him, then cast him into the river and do not fear nor grieve. Lo! We shall bring him back to you and shall make him (one) of Our messengers.
>
> (28:7)

The first pronouncement in this verse speaks soft words to the mother of Moses. It promises to return the suckling child to her. Then it announces that Allah will make him a messenger. Note the tenderness the Qur'an demonstrates towards this woman's desire to nurture her child. Although the child is living under the threat of Pharaoh's orders to slaughter such children, the child is saved to fulfill the decree of Allah. The desire of his mother towards the child is not directly part of that decree. Yet, the Qur'an details that aspect—in fact, mentions it first.

Not to be underestimated in its significance is that the Qur'an states that Umm-Musa received *wahy* [revelation], thus demonstrating that women as well as men have been recipients of *wahy*. Thus Umm-Musa demonstrates the point that women are distinct with regard to some aspects, but universal with regard to others.

As I mentioned before, Mary is the only woman referred to by name in the Qur'an. This is because in the Qur'an, Jesus was created in the womb of Mary by special decree and not by normal biology. He is called "the son of Mary" to demonstrate the significance of his birth. Family relations in the Qur'an are labeled in terms of the father or a male ancestor, but since no father is mentioned for Jesus, he cannot be called in this manner. Most important, from the perspective of the Qur'an, he was not the son of God. Although Mary is called by name in the Qur'an, she is also given one of the honorific titles common at that time in Arabia and employed in the Qur'an when specific women are mentioned: she is called "sister of Aaron."

In her story, a messenger appears before her carrying Allah's message that she is to bear a child. She responds, "How can I have a child and no mortal has touched me, neither have I been unchaste?" (19:20). Once she has accepted the decree, the Divine *ruh* [spirit] is blown into her, and she bears the child.

When the time for delivery comes, the Qur'an describes her pains of labour and her statement: "Would that I had died before this time and been long forgotten (rather than to feel such pains)" (19:23). She is like every other woman who bears a child. Then the Qur'an demonstrates Allah's sympathy for her predicament: "Grieve not!" (19:24) and she is asked to eat, drink, and be comforted (19:26).

Despite the centrality of Jesus to Christianity, no similar affirmation of the unique experience of childbirth is given such detailed consideration in any Christian theological work—not even in the Bible. That special function is elevated to the status worthy of detailed mention to attest to its significance in the Qur'anic worldview. We are not left to just take it for granted.

Again, in this instance, as with Umm-Musa cited above, it is generally considered necessary only that a certain child be delivered to birth or to safety. Yet, the Qur'an includes these details to highlight the fact that the priority of saving the child, in each case, is also viewed in the light of the concern for the respective mothers.

Finally, one simple grammatical consideration with regard to the significance of Mary to all believers. The Qur'an classifies her as "one of the *qanitin*" (66:12), using the masculine plural form of the word that indicates one devout before Allah. There is no reason not to use the feminine plural form—except to emphasize that the significance of Mary's example is for all who believe—whether male or female. Her virtue was not confined by gender.

Finally, I will discuss Bilqis, the Queen of Sheba. Despite the fact that she ruled over a nation, most Muslims hold leadership as improper for a woman. The Qur'an uses no terms that imply that the position of ruler is inappropriate for a woman. On the contrary, the Qur'anic story of Bilqis celebrates both her political and religious practices.

Although the verse does point out (perhaps as peculiar) that she was "a woman" ruling (27:23), this is nothing more than a statement quoted from one who had observed her. Beyond this identification of her as a woman, no distinction, restriction, addition, limitation, or specification of her as a woman who leads is ever mentioned.

The Qur'anic story continues: she was powerful, well provided for, and "has a magnificent throne" (27:23). However, she and "her people [worshipped] the sun instead of Allah" (27:24).

Solomon sends a letter to the Queen of Sheba "In the name of Allah" and invites her and her people to submit to worship of only Allah (27:29–31).

When she reads the letter, she says to her advisors: "Lo! There has been thrown to me—a noble [*karim*] letter" (27:29). She then asks them to advise her in this affair of hers for "I decide no case until you [advise me (on it)]" (27:32).

Although she operates within the normal protocol and asks her advisers for consultation on this matter, she has already given an indication of her perspective by describing the letter as *karim*. Thus, her postponement of the decision on this case is not for lack of decisive ability, but for protocol and diplomacy.

> They said: we are lords of might and lords of great prowess, but it is for you to command; so consider what you will command. She said "Lo! Kings, when they enter a township, ruin it and make the honour of its people shame. Thus will they do. But lo! I am going to send a present to them, and see with what (answer) my messengers return."
>
> (27:33–5)

Solomon rejects the gift, stating that he has no need because Allah has given him a good position in both worldly and spiritual terms (27:36–7).

In verse 42, the story resumes after she has decided to pay him a personal visit. As she is a ruler, such a decision carries importance. It means that she has determined that there is something special and unusual about this particular circumstance which warrants her personal attention and not just that of ambassadors. Perhaps it is his first letter which is written "in the name of Allah" or because he rejects her material gift.

While she is en route to him, Solomon has her throne (the same one mentioned above) miraculously transported to him and uses it to test her wisdom. She is led to it and asked, "Is your throne like this?" She answers, "(It is) as though it were the very one." (27:42). The existence of a throne so like hers, or of her throne itself, indicates something of the beyond-worldly power which Solomon commands. She goes on to say, "Knowledge was bestowed on us in advance of this, and we have submitted to Allah (in Islam)" (27:42).

Some interpret her decision to send a gift rather than to show brute strength as "feminine" politics. I place both her worldly knowledge of peaceful politics and her spiritual knowledge of the unique message of Solomon together on the same footing to indicate her independent ability to govern wisely and to be governed wisely in spiritual matters. Thus, I connect her independent political decision—despite the norms of the existing (male) rulers—with her independent acceptance of the true faith (Islam), despite the norms of her people.

In both instances, the Qur'an shows that her judgment was better than the norm, and that she independently demonstrated that better judgment. If her politics were feminine, then her faith was feminine, which, by implication would indicate that masculinity is a disadvantage. Her faith and her politics may be specific to females, but they both were better. They indicate one who has knowledge, acts on it, and can therefore accept the truth. This demonstration of pure wisdom exhibited in the Qur'an by a woman can hopefully be exhibited by a man as well.

7. Khalida Saed, "On the Edge of Belonging," in *Living Islam Outloud: American Muslim Women Speak* (2005)

"Khalida Saed" is a pseudonym used by this lesbian Muslim to protect her identity. While many socially conservative Muslims have joined conservative American Jews and Christians in opposing homosexuality as an evil and immoral practice, lesbian, gay, bisexual, transgendered, and queer (LGBTQ) Muslims— and their straight allies—have formed organizations, many of which exist in cyberspace, to offer support to the increasing number of Muslims who have come out of the closet. One such group, al-Fatiha, has held conventions in which LGBTQ Muslims pray together, socialize, discuss Islamic topics, and exchange opinions freely. Some LGBTQ American Muslims have written queer fiction that gives voice to the trials and joys of the being queer and Muslim. Others are revisiting some of the sources of Islamic tradition, especially the Qur'an, to reread the text from a queer perspective. In this article, the writer, an Iranian American woman, describes the pain of coming out to her mother and the hope that one day she will find full acceptance in the Muslim community.

> *This is also one of those things girls get hospitalized for, like masturbating.*

As long as I can remember I have teetered on the edge of *something*. I have not always been an American. Sometimes I wasn't a Muslim. I never wanted to be a lesbian. But I have never had any doubt that I didn't belong fully in any of these identities. I teetered on the edge of belonging to the lesbian community and being invincible within it, on the edges of being American and Iranian, and on the edge of Islam. I have been juggling several identities all of my life, and it never occurred to me to complain at first. It seemed that the less I complained, the less people would notice that I wasn't fully part of their community—and community is the reason for everything I do.

When I was fourteen, I came out as a lesbian to my mother. Her response was typical. She was distressed. She wove God/Allah into her arguments and ended the whole thing with "It's a phase." She also hit me, and cried, and locked me up in my room. I missed two days of school. The most compelling argument she came up with was that I was far too Americanized and that my sexuality was an offspring of the American values I had internalized. This last argument may or may not have a ring of truth to it. I'm not sure I would have had the balls to discuss my sexuality at all, or even consider it, if my American side hadn't told me I had the right. Discussing matters of the vagina certainly isn't very Muslim-lady-like. My mother and I have never spoken about it since. I was horrified at having hurt my mother. Honestly, it never occurred to me that my personal sexual orientation would hurt her. I was THAT naïve. Our relationship today is as close as it can be when two people refuse to bring up the pink elephant in the middle of the room.

We are not unlike many American immigrant Muslim families. Sexuality of any kind is not discussed. She would have been more supportive of me if I had never come out to her at all and we had left it unsaid all of these years. Sex has been the one issue we cannot get over as a family. Sex has been the one "condition" in the unconditional love parents are supposed to offer their children. A woman's virginity is the most valuable bargaining chip she can bring to marriage. And she will get married one day, or else it reflects badly on her entire family and ruins the chances of marriage for her younger siblings. Bringing up lesbianism was the ultimate form of discussing sexuality. Not only was I talking about sex, but I was refusing to participate in the biggest institution religion ever created: Heterosexual Marriage.

"They don't have jobs, they live on the street,
and they want to be men, for God's sake!"

My mother holds some of the biggest stereotypes of what a lesbian is supposed to be, but I don't blame her, because her notion that queerness is a strictly white Western construct is not that far removed from what my own ideas had been growing up—I believed that if I were to live success-fully as a lesbian in America, I had to cut my hair, listen to Melissa Ether-idge, despite my own musical tastes, and put aside my political priorities in favor of gay civil rights issues. There were no lesbian-Middle-Eastern-Muslim-immigrant-female role models in mainstream America. There were barely any female role models at all. I could hardly leave my own house without interrogation from both of my parents and my older brother, so I didn't have access to the Lesbian, Gay, Bisexual, Transgendered, and Queer (LGBTQ) youth community where I might have found a need for my voice and my unique experiences. There was very little for queer youth to do in New York City if they had a 4:30 p.m. curfew on weekdays and needed special permission to go out on weekends.

The dominant feeling I remember from those days is extreme loneli-ness and isolation. I deeply regretted my sexuality. It was a death sentence on my family relations. I knew that when I grew up, I would have to choose between my family and my own life. In my culture, choosing any-thing other than family is considered the epitome of selfishness. No com-promise can be struck. I remember my mother saying that people "loved themselves too much." I began to equate self-love with anti-Islamic prin-ciples. People who loved themselves too much could not live within the confines of Islam and family. So I did the only thing I thought would make my family happy. I began wearing a *hijab* and started a Muslim Stu-dent Association in my high school.

I collected all the signatures, organized all the meetings, and when it came time to hold elections, I dutifully let all of the men run for president and vice president even though they hadn't done the work. A good Muslim woman never expects glory or credit, or so I thought. I was extremely proud of my ability not to dwell on not having been nominated for office or cred-ited as the founder. I thought I was on my way to becoming fully Muslim and belonging to that community. But I never managed to stop being queer.

Every time I get a new girlfriend, I have to introduce her
as my best friend to my parents. They think I'm very social.

I met "Jane" while I was active in the Muslim Student Association, and she became my first girlfriend. She was a junior in my high school; I was a freshman. She was my first kiss. We held hands and kissed for about a month before we broke up. We pretended to be devastated, but since we hadn't told anyone we were together, it was a nonevent, like all of my other relationships with women would be until I left home. Jane and I also did something much more important to me at the time than kissing; we went to some meetings for youth at the local Gay and Lesbian Community Center. I barely remember Jane, but I remember the meetings. When I first walked into the room, my heart stopped. There were about forty kids sitting in a huge circle. It took about twenty minutes to go around the room and state our names and ages because kids kept taking up too much time and giving out all of this information about themselves. There were a lot of boys with names like "Tanshelique" and "Diamond." I loved every one of them. As my turn to state my name approached I remember being very nervous and not knowing what to say. Should I give my real name? Should I state my real age? And when it was finally my turn, I blurted out everything about myself that I could possibly remember. I think I even included my middle name and place of birth. We all had a need to find someone with whom I could share all of myself.

> *If you wear lots of makeup it will make you look sixteen,*
> *then the truant cops won't pick you up, but the lesbians*
> *won't know you're a dyke . . .*

School time was the only part of the day where my family couldn't dictate what I did, whom I spoke to, or whom I loved. I began cutting school to seek out places with other queer youth. This meant going into the East Village and maneuvering around the drug addicts, the cops, the truancy police, and the drug pushers. My grades began to slip. I had prided myself on being a straight A student, but suddenly none of that mattered. All that mattered was belonging, and I felt that on Christopher Street. I hated nights because when the streetlights came on I had to go home. I became extremely depressed as my life became increasingly volatile and abusive. The stress of being poor and minority and of having a family to raise took a huge toll on my parents. They were scared of losing their children, and they had every right to be. By all definitions we were becoming less and less Iranian and more and more New Yorkers every year. Our grasp of our own language was dwindling, and we had lost our accents completely. I equated all things Iranian and Muslim with being anti-gay, and therefore anti-me, and those messages were reinforced by the mainstream LGBTQ movement. My sister regarded all things Muslim as completely foreign to anything she was interested in.

My parents tried to control us through fear and anger. There was no attempt to bridge the gap between religious and cultural identity and sexual orientation when I was growing up. No one was doing that work for youth. I did not realize it *could* be done. Thus I rejected Islam in all of its forms because I could not find a place for myself in Islam. I left the Muslim Student Association. They wouldn't allow female leadership anyway, and I had started the whole damn thing! I felt completely isolated in the world. I was extremely depressed and desperately wanted to find a way to be all of myself somewhere. I felt that I embodied the word "foreigner" everywhere I went. So when it came time for college, I left home.

Being gay and Muslim? That's like sinning
automatically, for no reason, all the time!

While I relished the freedom, it came at a hefty price. My entire extended family was shocked because going away to college when you're female and Muslim is a contradiction no one ever gets over. It's simply not done. I was the first in my family to do it, and I felt as if I had fought my way there and through college alone. It was the first time I lived and interacted with people with whom I had nothing in common. My first taste of the dorms away from my beloved city and away from my family was horrible. I faced racism, homophobia and worst of all, defeat. Out of my loneliness came independence, which was the best thing that ever happened to me. I learned how to survive.

When I was twenty years old, I found a website on the Internet for the Al-Fatiha foundation. I was horrified. The website featured a rainbow flag with a star and crescent. It was the symbol of Islam against a *very* gay backdrop. It was a national group for LGBTQ Muslims, and it was unapologetic. I immediately shut the computer down and walked away. I revisited the website every day for an entire year, and I pretended to be horrified each time. In 2001, my girlfriend dragged me to my first Al-Fatiha conference in Washington, D.C. I was petrified, but I felt like I was finally being honest with myself.

One of the first people I saw was a huge man who looked like he just stepped out of the pages of a *hadith*. He had a huge presence and reminded me of all the *imams* from my past. I would later find out that he was the first openly gay *imam*. This didn't comfort me at all. I wanted to turn and run. I don't know what I expected from a Muslim LGBTQ conference, but I had not expected an *imam*. My girlfriend held my hand, but we didn't actually join the conference until the next day. I needed that entire night to build up my confidence. Mostly, I was terrified that it would not live up to my expectations. This was my last hope of finding someone to tell me that it was OK for me to be who I was. I didn't know how to reinterpret the Qur'an so that I was included. There were so few mentions of women and even fewer positive ones. I had no patience for the religion anymore. I didn't understand why I was a sinner when I obviously came wired this way. I don't remember a time when I didn't love women. I didn't make the choice, but I was supposed to be punished for it. I didn't want to hear it again. I didn't want that message validated for me. But I was equally not ready to hear that it was OK to be a lesbian and be a Muslim woman. I didn't know how to do that even more than I didn't know how to stop being guilty.

When I finally joined the conference, it was a wonderful and soothing and spiritual experience. I don't think I lied about who I was once the entire time I was there. I even prayed more regularly than I have ever prayed before in my life. At the time, I found it hilarious that the one time I found myself totally holy and totally Muslim was when I was at a conference for Lesbian, Gay, Bisexual, Transgendered, and Queer people. I stood side by side with men and women and prayed. Leaving that carpeted hotel room that served as the mosque for the conference was like leaving Mecca. I felt shocked that I could be that affected by religion when I wasn't really looking for it. I never found that feeling when I was looking for it in mainstream Islam. I felt cleansed.

I joined the board of Al-Fatiha immediately because I wanted to give that same feeling of belonging to other people. It wasn't enough that I had reconciled my sexuality and spirituality; I had to demand it for other people as well. I had heard that people in Al-Fatiha received death threats and harassing e-mails and phone calls. I had heard that it was dangerous, and I certainly felt a sense of danger even being at the conference. I was not scared of other people in the LGBTQ community; I was terrified of other

Muslims. Being a member of Al-Fatiha includes speaking publicly, creating community for people all over the United States, finding funding for all of the conferences, and making sure that women and youth are heard. Al-Fatiha restored my faith in Islam because it included women in its leadership and insisted on inclusive prayer spaces where women were not relegated to the basement and forced to wear *hijab* even if they did not wear them normally. Women were even encouraged to lead prayer.

This was the Islam every woman dreams about. It is also the Islam that made the most sense to me. Progressive Islam operates under the belief that anything that sanctions discrimination against anyone is anti-Islamic. It is the belief that working toward social justice is an integral part of religion. It is the branch of Islam that is distinctly American and definitely a better fit into my life. I realize that a lot of what I had been attributing to Islam is really a byproduct of my own culture. Patriarchy and sexism are not necessarily Islamic traits but are actually cultural traits. Realizing this has allowed me to give religion another chance. I have also been empowered to begin reinterpreting the text outside the confines of sexism and homophobia. This sense of renewed life and spirituality is the biggest gift given to me from Lesbian, Gay, Bisexual, Transgendered, and Queer Muslims.

So you don't want to get married? What did you waste all that time going to college for, if not to be more appealing to a husband?

My family has come to terms with my decision not to enter an arranged marriage. I am in my midtwenties, which is ancient in my culture. I am in a wonderful relationship with a woman I met during college. I never saw myself in a long-term healthy relationship with another woman. She comes from a very supportive and loving family that has embraced me over the last three years. She challenges me to be more expressive and more of myself. She encouraged me to attend the Al-Fatiha conference, and I joined Al-Fatiha's board of directors with her support. When I was voted co-chair of the organization she celebrated it with me, and when I received my first death threat she crawled under the covers of our bed with me and we told each other stories until it was safe to come out. She had gone out of her way to study Islam, Farsi, and Iranian culture so that she can understand my struggles and the choices in life. I have studied African American culture and history to understand her experiences. We have a love that matured gradually. I take her with me whenever I travel, and she takes me with her whenever she travels. When we are apart, we call each other three or four times a day. And like all good lesbian couples, we intended to stay together.

Last year we decided to get married (that gay *imam* would actually come in handy), and I wonder what I'll tell my family. I have no real hope of ever having them support me the way that they have supported my brothers and sisters. I want to marry my partner. I really do. But I'm not sure how joyous that day will be without any of my family. If I invite all two hundred of them, I might get one percent to attend, but I would risk my safety on the wedding day and the safety of my partner and her family as well. I'm not sure what the point of a public ceremony is without the public acknowledgment of family. Who would speak my native language at my wedding? Who would bring the bad traditional music? Who would cry for my lost childhood? So I delay my wedding year after year. It is hard enough to be in an interracial relationship, and then being lesbians, and being young, and being a Muslim immigrant in the post-9/11 era, and being so decidedly American in Muslim society . . . it's all so complicated and difficult to negotiate.

I would be really excited if I could have just one community to belong to in my everyday life. The LGBTQ community has a lot of racism work to do before we can be fully accepted as a couple and as individuals in it, and the Muslim community has tremendous homophobia work to do. I have decided to work on the Muslims. They are the group most important to me and most precious in my life. Al-Fatiha is the vehicle that I am using to accomplish this at the moment.

In my heart I secretly wait for the day when I will gather up my courage, walk into my mother's house with my head held high, and ask her to sew me a wedding dress, just like her mother sewed hers. And while we're on the subject of fantasy scenarios, I imagine her wiping tears of joy from her eyes as she leads me to the sewing machine to take my measurements. She will then do the customary passing down of jewelry. She'll take out my grandmother's pearl set that her mother gave her on her wedding day and extend it to me, saying, "You know, I always liked that girlfriend of yours. Tell me more about her mother and her family."

8. Imam Zaid Shakir, "An Examination of the Issue of Female Prayer Leadership" (2005)

Raised in California's public-housing projects, African American Zaid Shakir (b. 1956) converted to Islam in 1977, the year after he joined the U.S. Air Force. The 1983 recipient of a BA in international relations from American University in Washington, D.C., Shakir went on for his master's in political science from Rutgers University in 1986, and then taught for several years at Southern Connecticut State University. During this time, he also served as imam of Masjid al-Islam in New Haven. Imam Zaid left the United States in 1994 to study Arabic, the Qur'an, and Islam for nearly seven years at Abu Nur University in Syria. Upon his return, he became a well-known writer and thinker among various American Muslims, and took a post as a scholar-in-residence at the Zaytuna Institute, a Muslim educational academy and think tank in Hayward, California.

Written on March 25, 2005, the article below is Zaid Shakir's reaction to Amina Wadud's leading of males and females in public congregational prayer in New York on March 18, 2005. Imam Zaid, who is steeped in the classical religious science of fiqh, *or Islamic jurisprudence, quotes several authoritative scholars from the classical period of Islam, and uses logic, analogy, source criticism, legal precedent, and his knowledge of the Arabic language to support his opposition to woman-led, mixed-gender congregational prayers. In the first section of his article, which constitutes most of the excerpt reproduced here, Imam Zaid questions the use by some of a certain hadith—a report of the Prophet Muhammad's words and deeds—to support the female-led, mixed-gender public prayer. He begins and ends his discussion of this issue with an appeal for humility, patience, and unity among Muslims, and he expresses his view that true liberation is to be found less in social upheaval and more in personal piety and human beings' personal relationships with God.*

Imam al-Jurjani mentions that *fitnah* is "that which clarifies the state of a person, be that good or evil." It is also defined as "strife breaking out among various peoples." In both of these meanings the controversy surrounding the "historic" female-led *jumu'ah* [Friday congregational] prayer is a *fitnah* for many Muslims in this country. This is undeniable when we see the deep divisions, bitter contestation, and outright enmity it is creating in the ranks of the believers. This is so when we see some people's very faith shaken. This is so when we see spiteful accusations hurled by some Muslims at others. This is so when we see non-Muslims of nefarious intent seeking to exploit the situation to create confusion among the general public and the Muslims as to what Islam is, and who are its authoritative voices.

As I consider this a *fitnah*, the first thing I wish to say about this matter is that we should all stop for a moment and take time to ask God to protect us. We should ask God that He protects the fledgling Muslim community of this land. We should ask that He bless us to have wisdom equal to the challenges He has placed before. We should ask Him that He grants us all the strength to continue working for Islam in our various capacities. We should ask Him to help us to resist the many and increasingly sophisticated efforts to divide us.

Having said that, I wish to clarify my position concerning this matter. What I write below is based on the Sunni legal and linguistic tradition, as it has been historically understood. This is the tradition of the Islamic orthodoxy, which remains to this day, the only religious orthodoxy, which has not been marginalized to the fringes of the faith community it represents. . . .

The Hadith of Umm Waraqa

The Prophet (peace be upon him) commanded Umm Waraqah, a woman who had collected the Qur'an, to lead the people of her area in prayer. She had her own *mu'adhdhin* [person who performs the call to prayers].

This narration, found in the compilations of Abu Dawud, ad-Daraqutni, al-Bayhaqi, al-Hakim, the *Tabaqat* of Ibn Sa'd, and other sources, is questioned by some scholars of *hadith* (prophetic tradition) because of two narrators in its chain of transmission. The first is al-Walid b. 'Abdullah b. Jumay'. Imam adh-Dhahabi mentions in *al-Mizan* that although ibn Ma'in, Imam Ahmad, and Abu Hatim considered him an acceptable narrator, others refused to accept his narrations, among them Ibn Hibban. Imam al-Hakim also questioned his probity. Ibn Hajar al-'Asqalani mentions that al-Aqili said there was inconsistency in his narrations.

Although a case can be made for accepting the narrations of al-Walid, based on those who do affirm his probity, the state of another narrator in the chain of this *hadith*, 'Abd ar-Rahman b. Khallad, is *majhul al-hal* (unknown). Al-Walid also relates this tradition from his grandmother. Imam ad-Daraqutni mentions that her state is also unknown. In the opinion of the overwhelming majority of scholars, the existence of a narrator whose state is unknown would make the transmission conveyed by that chain weak. This combination of two potentially weak narrators makes it questionable to use the tradition of Umm Waraqa as the basis for establishing any rulings in the Divine law.

While the questionable nature of this *hadith* does not undermine the widespread acceptance it has received from the earlier scholars, it does make it difficult to use as the primary evidence for a major precept of the religion, which is the case in this discussion.

Were we to assume that the tradition is sound, it would still be difficult to use it as the basis for establishing the permissibility of a woman leading a public, mixed-gender congregational prayer, for reasons we shall now mention, if God so wills. First of all, the Prophet, peace and blessings of God upon him, advised Umm Waraqa to stay in her house—"*qarri fi baytiki.*" This command is of import, as it creates two possible scenarios for the prayer she led. Either she remained in her house to lead the congregation, or she left her house to lead it in a mosque at an outside location. If she left her house to lead the prayer, she would have been acting contrary to the order of the Prophet, peace and blessings of God upon him. There is no transmitted evidence that the prayer took place outside of her home. Hence, we can conclude that her mosque was in her house.

Her establishing the prayer in a mosque located in her home would be consistent with numerous narrations where the Prophet, peace and blessings of God upon him, permitted various companions to establish mosques in their homes. Imam al-Bukhari mentions that al-Bara' b. 'Azib led congregational prayers in the mosque in his house—"*salla al-bara' ibn 'azib fi masjidihi fi darihi jama'atan.*" Imam al-Bukhari also mentions a *hadith* where the Prophet, peace and blessings of God upon him, went to the house of a blind companion, 'Itban b. Malik, to establish a mosque there. Ibn Majah produces several narrations of this event. In fact, the Prophet, peace and blessings of God upon him, ordered the generality of believers to establish mosques in their homes. 'Aisha relates, "The Messenger of God ordered that mosques be established in the homes [*dur*, plural of *dar*], and that they be cleaned and perfumed."

Based on these and other relevant narrations, we can safely conclude that

Umm Waraqa had a mosque in her house, and that the prayer she led was not in a public place outside of her home. A more controversial point is who was being led in the prayer? Here there are three possibilities: her *mu'adhdhin* (prayer caller) and two servants; the women from the neighborhood surrounding her home; the women of her house. As for the first possibility, the wording of the *hadith*, along with the narrations we quoted above, would lead one to believe that the residents of her house were being led in the prayer. All of those narrations use *dar* to refer to house. This would support the interpretation of *dar* as "house" as opposed to "area." This interpretation is also consistent with the literal meaning of the term *dar*. Al-Fayruzabadi, Ibn Mandhur, and Raghib al-Isfahani all define *dar* as a walled structure encompassing a building and a courtyard. An interpretative principle relates that "the origin in expressions is their literal meaning, there is no resorting to derived meanings without a decisive proof." Hence, the term *ahla dariha* would be best translated "the people of her house."

Based on what has been narrated that would apparently include a male and female servant, along with the old man who was appointed by the Prophet, peace and blessings of God upon him, to serve as her *mu'adhdhin* (caller to prayer). [Some supporters of female-led prayer have rejected] this interpretation, arguing that three people would not need a *mu'adhdhin*. This is not the case. Those scholars who consider the *adhan* (prayer call) a right associated with the obligatory prayer, or a right associated with the congregation, hold it to be Sunna (highly desirable in deference to the prophetic practice) to issue the call for any congregation assembled to undertake the five obligatory prayers. The size of the congregation in this regard is irrelevant. According to a *hadith* mentioned by al-Bukhari and others, even a person who is praying alone in an isolated area should make the call to prayer. . . .

On the basis of this interpretation, it is related that Imams al-Muzani, at-Tabari, Abu Thawr, and Dawud Adh-Dhahiri allowed for females to lead men in prayer. Some modern scholars use this interpretation to allow for females to lead men in prayer in the confines of their homes, if the males lack the qualifications to lead the prayer. The relevant point here is that the prayer was a private matter, conducted in the confines of Umm Waraqa's home, limited to the inhabitants of her house.

Were one to reject this first line of reasoning, a second possibility is that the people being led in prayer came from the area surrounding Umm Waraqa's home. This is the interpretation preferred by [at least one supporter of the female-led congregational prayer]. It has a basis in narrations from the Prophet, peace and blessings of God upon him. In the *hadith* of 'Itban b. Malik, it is related that *"ahli'd-dar"* [people of the house] used to gather there—*"fathaba fi'l-bayt rijalun min ahli'd-dar."* Ibn Hajar mentions in his commentary on this *hadith* that *ahli'd-dar* refers to the people of the neighborhood—*"al-mahallah."*

Based on this understanding, it is not unreasonable to interpret [the term] *"ahla dariha"* in the *hadith* of Umm Waraqa, as the people of her "area". . . . However, we are not left to guess as to who those people are. Imam ad-Daraqutni's narration of this *hadith* mentions that Umm Waraqa was ordered to lead her women in prayer—*"wa ta'umma nisa'aha."* Hence, if the people praying with Umm Waraqa were from the surrounding area, they were all women, as Imam ad-Daraqutni's version of the *hadith* makes clear. Here the text specifically states, "her women." Ad-Daraqtuni's version would clarify a potentially vague expression in the other versions.

A third possibility, also based on joining between the majority narration and ad-Daraqutni's version of the *hadith*, would lead us to understand that the people of Umm Waraqa's house were all women. Hence, *"ahla dariha"* (the people of her house) being led in prayer were women. There is no transmitted evidence to the contrary, as the opinion that *ahla dariha* were the two servants and the *mu'adhdhin*, mentioned above, is an assumption. In al-Mughni, Ibn Qudama al-Maqdisi mentions the incumbency of accepting this third interpretation. God knows best.

This latter understanding that Umm Waraqa only led women in prayer is strengthened by two ancillary evidences: (1) The numerous narrations mentioning that 'Aisha, Umm Salama, and other female Companions led all-women congregations; (2) and the fact that when the Prophet, peace and blessings of God upon him, established a mosque in the house of 'Itban b. Malik, the congregation was all male—*"rijalun (men) min ahli'd-dar."* It would therefore make perfect sense for the Prophet to establish an all-female congregation elsewhere.

Summary and Rulings

Based on the *hadith* of Umm Waraqa, its possible interpretations, and the other *ahadith* [pl. of *hadith*, meaning a report of the saying and deeds of the Prophet Muhammad and his companions] that mention women leading the prayer during the prophetic epoch, the Sunni jurists have deduced the following rulings:

1. The Shafi'i and Hanbali schools [two of the four major Sunni Islamic schools of legal thought] allow for a woman to lead other women in prayer without any restrictions. She can lead such prayers in the mosque or other places. The Hanafis [another school] permit a woman to lead other women in prayer. However, they hold it to be disliked. All three of these schools stipulate that the woman leading the prayer should stand in the middle of the front row, without being in front of the women praying along with her. This is based on the description of the prayer led by 'Aisha and Umm Salama. The Malikis [another school] hold that a woman cannot lead other women in the prayer.

2. Of the three Sunni schools that hold it permissible for a woman to lead other women in prayer, none of them hold it permissible to lead men. Although there is a minority opinion in the Hanbali school which permits a woman to lead men in *tarawih* [the special night prayers recommended during the month of Ramadan] if certain conditions prevail, providing she stands behind them.

3. Imam an-Nawawi mentions the following ruling in the *majmu'*, "If a woman leads a man or men in prayer, the prayer of the men is invalid. As for her prayer, and the prayer of the women praying with her, it is sound." As for *jumu'ah* [Friday congregational prayers], he mentions the following, "if a woman leads men in the *jumu'ah* prayer, there are two rulings [concerning her prayer]. They have been mentioned by al-Qadi Abu Tayyib . . . the preponderant opinion is that her prayer is invalid, the second is that it is lawfully begun as the noon prayer."

4. Some modern scholars hold it permissible for a woman to lead men in prayer within the confines of her house, if there are no men qualified to lead the prayer. . . .

Conclusion

From what we have presented above, it should be clear that a woman leading a mixed gender, public congregational prayer is not something sanctioned by Islamic law in the Sunni tradition. Her leading the Friday congregational prayer is even more unfounded, as she would be required to do things that are forbidden or disliked in other prayers. Saying this, we should not lose sight of the fact that there are many issues in our community involving the neglect, oppression, and in some instances, the degradation of our women. Until we address those issues, as a community, in an enlightened manner, we are open to criticism, and will likely encourage various forms of protest.

In addition to gender issues, we are faced by many other nagging concerns. These problems defy simplistic solutions. Only through the attainment of the prophetic virtues that Islam seeks to cultivate in its adherents will we have a chance to even begin dealing with them. One of the greatest of these virtues is humility. Perhaps, if the men of our community had more humility, we would behave in ways that do not alienate, frustrate, or outright oppress our women. Greater humility will help immensely in improving our condition. Our Prophet, peace and blessings of God upon him, has said in that regard, "No one humbles himself/herself for the sake of God except God elevates him/her." In addition to this elevation, one interpretation of this *hadith* is that the esteem of the humble person will be magnified in the hearts of others. Certainly, a healthier appreciation of each other would go a long way towards relieving the growing tension between the sexes in some quarters of our community.

We must also understand that Islam has never advocated a liberationist philosophy. Our fulfillment in this life will never come as the result of breaking real or perceived chains of oppression. That does not mean that we should not struggle against oppressive practices and institutions. However, when we understand that success in such worldly struggles has nothing to do with our fulfillment as human beings, we will be able to keep those struggles in perspective, and not be moved to frustration or despair when their outcomes are counter to our plans.

Our fulfillment does not lie in our liberation, rather it lies in the conquest of our soul and its base desires. That conquest only occurs through our enslavement to God. Our enslavement to God in turn means that we have to suppress many of our souls' desires and inclinations. Therein lies one of the greatest secrets to unleashing our real human potential. This is so because it is our spiritual potential that separates us from the rest of this creation, and it is to the extent that we are able to conquer our physical nature that we realize that spiritual potential.

We must all realize that we will never achieve any meaningful change in our situation relying on our own meager resources. The great sage Ibn

'Ata Allah as-Sakandari has said, "Nothing you seek through your Lord will ever be difficult; and nothing you seek through yourself will ever be easy." Now is the time to give ourselves to our Lord, totally. The trials and tribulations we are currently witnessing will only intensify as we move closer to the end of time. If we are not living for our Lord, relying on His guidance and help, and trusting in His wisdom, we will find it very difficult to negotiate our way through this world.

When we live for our Lord it becomes easy to live with each other. If in our personal relations we can come to embody the spirit of mutual love, mercy and affection, encouraged by our Prophet, peace and blessings of God be upon him, we will be able to live together in harmony, and make a beautiful and lasting contribution towards the uplift of men and women alike. The times we live in cry out for such a contribution. The question is, "Who will respond?"

9. Laury Silvers, "Islamic Jurisprudence, 'Civil' Disobedience, and Woman-Led Prayer" (2005)

Laury Silvers (b. 1964) is not what many Americans picture when they think of a Muslim woman. The daughter of American comedian Phil Silvers—best known for his role as "Sergeant Bilko"—Silvers describes herself as "culturally Jewish, Southern, and LA-old school Punk." She also holds a PhD in Islamic studies from the State University of New York, Stony Brook, and is an expert on Sufism, or Islamic mysticism. She teaches courses on Islam at Skidmore College in upstate New York. A frequent participant in the American Islamic blogosphere, Silvers shares personal reflections and philosophical insights on everything from the joys of professional wrestling to the theological implications of Hurricane Katrina. She has also become an advocate for marginalized Muslims in the United States and a voice for female empowerment. Here she challenges the opposition of Imam Zaid Shakir to woman-led, mixed-gender congregational prayers. Silvers wants to work within the traditions of fiqh, or Islamic jurisprudence—and calls for jurists to make a better case in support of female-led prayer—but she questions Imam Zaid's methodology and his application of the law in this case. Invoking the memory of Rosa Parks and the civil rights movement in the United States, she argues that the Muslim community's conscience must be applied in any ruling concerning the question of whether women should lead the prayers.

Professor Hina Azam and Imam Zaid Shakir have presented well-argued pieces upholding the prohibition against woman-led prayer. Although it may seem to some of their readers that the matter has been settled, the question of woman-led prayer is still open to debate. In fact, Prof. Azam challenges the progressive movement to locate a new approach to the question of woman-led prayer since she finds it cannot be resolved through the currently accepted principles of interpretation. This essay is not an answer to that challenge, but a two-part call. First, it is a call for that challenge to be taken up by scholars of Islamic jurisprudence. Second, it is a call for Muslims to stand behind women in prayer as a matter of "civil" disobedience in the face of a clear injustice, even in the face of the discomfort of both men and women in the community at large. Through the Qur'an, the Sunna, and the principles of Islamic jurisprudence, we will, God willing, find a broadly accepted path that will permit woman-led mixed-gender public congregational prayer.

The progressive movement argues that there is a clear social injustice arising from the prohibition of woman-led congregational prayer. Prof. Azam herself has admitted the desirability of having women lead the Friday prayers. She says, "Heaven knows I have wished for women to be able to lead *salat al-jumu'a*." The prohibition of female imams is part of the larger problem of women's marginalization in the Muslim community. Prof. Azam says that women are considered good Muslims when they are most invisible: "Women in the Muslim community generally, and in the mosque in particular, are seen as being 'good Muslims' when they are most silent, most unobtrusive, most compliant with male-driven policies. Walls and curtains, crowded and substandard prayer areas, prohibitions from entering the 'main' area or going through the 'main' door, lack of comfortable and direct access to *imams*/scholars, gender separation of couples and families upon entrance into the mosque—all of these contribute to a feeling of alienation among Muslim women."

Imam Zaid Shakir likewise comments: "Saying [that women are not permitted to lead the prayer], we should not lose sight of the fact that there are many issues in our community involving the neglect, oppression, and in some instances, the degradation of our women. Until we address those issues, as a community, in an enlightened manner, we are open to criticism, and will likely encourage various forms of protest."

The marginalization of women is so deep-rooted that even Imam Zaid, whom I know to be a long-time supporter of women's rights in Islam, demonstrates a habituated paternalism when he uses the phrase "our women" in the passage above. The alienation of women explains in part why so many Muslim women and sympathetic Muslim men do not attend the mosque, nor participate actively in the Muslim community. If one of the goals of the congregational prayer is to bring about social cohesion—our shoulders meeting to bar against the divisive influence of Iblis [the Devil]—then the present order of the mosque works against an important purpose of the congregational prayer.

The social benefits of woman-led congregational prayers are likewise clear. As women assume positions of religious authority, they will join working women and homemakers as role models in the community. Disrespect of women in our community is related to the high value that is placed on their invisibility in the public sphere and in the mosque. Women are best when not noticed, even working women and homemakers, and so it follows that women and their needs end up being forgotten in the community. With women religious leaders in our community, women's concerns will be directly represented by other women, rather than second-hand (if at all) by men. Simply put, women *imams* are not invisible. The presence of female religious leaders will habituate members of the community to accept the worth of women in all arenas of Muslim life. Young women and men who grow up in Muslim communities in which women of authority are visible and treated with respect as a matter of course will be less likely to disrespect themselves and other women. Young people will grow up knowing that a person's knowledge and love of God are what is most valued in the community, rather than one's gender.

Prof. Hina Azam and Imam Zaid Shakir's essays demonstrate that the prohibition is in part based on the lack of a clear, specific permission for a woman-led public mixed-gender congregational prayer. Prof. Azam argues that there is a lack of clear permission for a woman-led Friday prayer specifically, but not a woman-led mixed-gender congregational prayer in some other cases. Imam Zaid Shakir argues that there is a lack of clear permission for a woman-led public congregational prayer in general. He also indicates that while there is no clear prohibition against woman-led prayer in the Qur'an or in the Sunna, there is sufficient legal reasoning on different aspects of the issue to indicate with certainty that woman-led mixed-gender prayer is prohibited. According to the interpretive principle that "certainty cannot be cancelled by doubt," the doubt that is raised by the lack of both a clear permission and a clear prohibition does not allow us to argue that the prayer can be permitted. I do not dispute this legal principle, nor the legal reasoning that leads Prof. Azam and Imam Zaid to uphold the prohibition. But several scholars of jurisprudence have considered the matter in a different way. They state quite simply that since there is no clear prohibition in the Sources, woman-led mixed-gender prayer is permissible if a particular Muslim community agrees to it. I hope that these will be the first of many voices supporting the validity of woman-led prayer.

I would argue that the presence of doubt articulated by Prof. Azam and Imam Zaid, as well as the approval of the prayer by several scholars, allow us to keep pressing the issue in the face of continuing injustice. Islamic jurisprudence is a human system developed out of a human struggle to interpret the Divine intent from our sacred sources, the Qur'an and the Sunna. But there is nothing sacred in the scholars themselves. Prof. Azam asks us, "Is it possible that all of those jurists over hundreds of years were wrong and you are right?" There is a tendency in Prof. Azam's and Imam Zaid's pieces to honor the legal tradition by refusing to question it even in the face of social wrongs that they themselves admit. I share their love of the Islamic legal tradition, but I cannot sanctify human interpretation by imputing infallibility to the process. Neither it seems could many scholars of Islamic jurisprudence over the years. There are examples past and present demonstrating that jurists have understood their obligation to use their minds and their consciences to work in creative ways to counter injustice that had been supported previously by clear legal permissions. For instance, consider the long-standing Qur'anically established practice of slavery. Objections of conscience to the practice of slavery over time led scholars to restrict the conditions of its practice so as to make it prohibited in all but name only. The scholars never found a clear ground for the prohibition of slavery from within the logic of Islamic jurisprudence, but in following their conscience they found an alternative mode to restrict the practice to the point of prohibition. A student of Islamic legal theory would argue that slavery is an example from *mu'amala* [rules governing humans' obligations to one another] not *'ibada* [rules governing human's obligations to God], so the situations are not comparable. I argue that we should think beyond these divisions, as important as they are, to remember that scholars were willing to finesse a "prohibition" from a clear legal permission derived from the Qur'an itself in order bring practice in line with their consciences. Prof. Azam has challenged the progressive movement to find an alternative mode of interpretation so that she might one day attend a mosque with a woman *imam*. I in turn challenge scholars on the basis of their consciences to work within the system to find a way to permit woman-led mixed-gender congregational prayers.

One does not need to leave the tradition to find this legal possibility. There are innovative modes of legal interpretation well-established in the history of Islamic jurisprudence. For instance, the notion of *maslaha* may end up being of some use in correcting matters of clear injustice in our community. *Maslaha* can be summarized, from one perspective, as a principle of legal interpretation resting on the notion that God is Just, He has commanded His servants to enact His justice in the world, and that He has not disclosed every possible legal cause from which we may derive rulings in the Qur'an or through the Prophet's practice (even those causes that can be induced through analogical reasoning from these Sources). While legal theorists differ on whether *maslaha* stands as an alternative to the already established *usul a-fiqh* [the roots of Islamic jurisprudence] or as a necessary component of it, it nevertheless provides a theoretical tool to approach critical issues affecting the Muslim community as a whole.

Lastly, I would like to address the matter of *fitna* raised by Imam Zaid. He argues that the community is in disarray, indeed some Muslims' faith has been challenged, because a woman led a congregational prayer. I would like to draw a parallel with the Civil Rights movement in order better explain why supporters of woman-led prayer are willing to challenge the comfort of the community at large. Seen in the light of the courageous Rosa Parks, women who have led mixed-gender congregational prayers have dared to come forward from their place in the back of the mosque to stand in front of men. Just like whites, Muslim men have not been eager to give up their legislated privilege to stand in front of women in prayer and to lead women in other matters. Like the supporters of the Civil Rights movement, all of us would say that the fight is worth it. With the greatest respect to Imam Zaid, I would like to recast his closing words in the context of the Civil Rights movement only to elucidate how supporters of woman-led prayer understand the situation. Please read the following passage as if he had written it in response to Rosa Parks' courageous act.

We must also understand that Islam has never advocated a liberationist philosophy. Our fulfillment in this life will never come as the result of breaking real or perceived chains of oppression. That does not mean that we should not struggle against oppressive practices and institutions. However, when we understand that success in such worldly struggles has nothing to do with our fulfillment as human beings, we will be able to keep those struggles in perspective, and not be moved to frustration or despair when their outcomes are counter to our plans. Our fulfillment does not lie in our liberation, rather it lies in the conquest of our soul and its base desires. That conquest only occurs through our enslavement to God. Our enslavement to God in turn means that we have to suppress many of our souls' desires and inclinations. Therein lies one of the greatest secrets to unleashing our real human potential. This is so because it is our spiritual potential that separates us from the rest of this creation, and it is to the extent that we are able to conquer our physical nature that we realize that spiritual potential.

Read in this light, the passage should give a better sense of how women and their allies experience women's relegation to the invisible in our community and our dismay at Imam Zaid's call for quietism and maintenance of the status quo.

Opinions against woman-led prayer typically argue that a woman bending over in front of men will promote fornication and adultery. Though I decline to discuss the absurdity of this argument, at least in the contemporary North American context, as well as the grave insult it constitutes to the character of men, I suggest several formations of the prayer the last two of which would nullify this concern. Particular communities can organize the prayer in any number of ways according to their sensibilities. A woman imam could stand in front of mixed-gender lines, in the center of men and women in separate but side by side sections, in front of the woman's section side by side, or in front of the women in a woman's section entirely separate from the men—in which case, the prayer could be delivered over loudspeaker and television to the men's section as it is now for women.

Serious social upheaval is not likely to occur as our community confronts the question of woman-led prayer. Several scholars have approved woman-led prayer if the congregation agrees to it. I argue that this stipulation will lead to a greater discussion of women's role in the community in general, not just the desirability of women leading the congregational prayer in particular. Even if a specific community of Muslims ultimately decides against woman-led prayer for themselves, the discussion will benefit all Muslims since it will encourage communication about women's concerns. It will moreover ensure that a particular community will come to terms with the issue before woman-led prayer takes root among them.

In the meantime, I argue that Muslims should gather to pray behind women as a matter of "civil" disobedience whether or not they understand the prayer to be permissible at this point. One can simply perform the "valid" prayer later if one is concerned about it.

We can challenge this and other injustices in our community on two fronts, (1) by working within the tradition of Islamic jurisprudence—and here I would like to echo Omid Safi's call in the Progressive Muslim Union statement for women to be educated in the *madrasa* system—and (2) by acting as conscientious objectors to rulings that are destroying the fabric of our community and hampering the growth of faith and practice among Muslims.

10. Ingrid Mattson, "Can a Woman Be an Imam? Debating Form and Function in Muslim Women's Leadership" (2005)

A white, Roman Catholic Canadian by birth, Ingrid Mattson (b. 1963) began her journey to Islam after coming to know some Senegalese and Mauritian Muslims in Paris. "They were poor and humble, but carried a light within them," she has said. "I was drawn to them and wanted to understand what made them essentially different from anyone I had ever met. They were not particularly observant Muslims in the legal sense, but they carried the spirit of Islam within them. I decided to research their culture and religion more when I returned to Canada. As I did this, I found myself drawn more and more towards Islam. Finally, I realized that, despite myself, I had become a Muslim." After converting to Islam, Mattson went on to take a PhD from the University of Chicago, specializing in Islamic law and ethics and early Islamic history. She has since become a well-known leader in North American Muslim circles. Elected president of the Islamic Society of North America in 2006, she is also director of the Islamic chaplaincy program at the Hartford Seminary.

Refusing to focus only on the debate over whether the shari'a *(or Islamic law and ethics) does or does not permit a woman to lead mixed-gender public prayers, in the passages below Mattson instead offers a critique of the American mosque, calling for greater participation on the part of both men and women in the life of the mosque. She affirms the need for the empowerment of women in American mosques. But she also cautions American Muslims against giving any one individual, whether male or female, too much power and responsibility in overseeing the life of the community. Instead, she advocates a more egalitarian model that would invest in a number of leaders the responsibility for meeting the needs of mosque-goers.*

Before we discuss the variety of approaches that can be taken to advance the religious leadership of Muslim women, we should state why we consider this to be a valid and important goal. In other words, why does women's religious leadership matter?

In our experience, the main reason this is an issue of concern for many Muslim women is that they feel that religious authority has too often been used to suppress them. It is the rare Muslim woman who has not had some experience of being excluded from the mosque, having had to listen to demeaning sermons, or having been subjected to patronizing marriage counseling by religious leaders. This does not mean that this is the dominant experience of all Muslim women. There are, of course, many competent male religious leaders who are sensitive to women's experiences and listen to their counsel and their concerns. When few or no women in a community have recognized spiritual authority or positions of leadership, however, there is a good chance that the women of that community will experience religious authority negatively. This is a serious matter, because it defeats the very purpose of religious institutions, whose primary purpose is to bring people closer to God. We need to be conscious of the unfortunate reality that institutions—including religious institutions—often develop in ways that lead them to defeat the very purposes they were created to serve.

In many cases, Muslim women feel that restrictions placed upon them in the name of Islam are unjust, but they have neither fluency in the Islamic legal discourse nor the religious authority to convincingly argue their objections. As a result, some simply suppress their inner voice that calls for justice; others cannot do that. . . .

It is my observation that when this religious leadership does not include women, their experiences, concerns and priorities will not be well represented. I am aware that there are those who would argue that this is not inevitable. There are those who are convinced that men are capable of guiding and leading the Muslim community in a just manner without female peers. I would argue that common sense tells us that even the most compassionate and insightful group of men will overlook some of the needs and concerns of the women of their community. More compellingly, experience teaches us that when women are not in leadership positions in their communities, they are often assigned inadequate prayer spaces (if any), they are cut off from much vital religious education, and they have few means to access the rights they possess in theory. There are many reasons why women's leadership is important; the most important one for Muslim women is so they will not be prevented—by being blocked from sacred texts or houses of worship and study—from accessing the liberating message of obedience to God alone. . . . The main challenge for Muslim women, in earlier times and today, is not only to increase their knowledge, but also to increase their authority by attaining a position in society that enables them to effectively help others. . . .

If religious office is an important consideration in women's religious leadership, is it therefore necessary for women to be "imams"? In my experience, this is the question most frequently posed by observers of the American Muslim community when religious leadership and gender is discussed. No doubt this is because the leader of a local congregation—the priest, minister or rabbi—appears to be the most familiar and influential religious authority in the lives of Americans who attend religious services. The *imam*—the leader of Islamic congregational prayers—is the closest Muslim counterpart to the clergy of American Christianity and Judaism.

The problem I have with this question is that if we assume that the center of religious power and authority lies with the *imam* (and we are not assuming this about ministers and rabbis either), not only might we be misunderstanding the past and present reality of the dynamics of Islamic religious leadership, we may be narrowing the possibilities for a relevant, more gender inclusive religious leadership for Muslims in the future. It is my view that it may be more helpful to begin with a functional approach to identifying religious leadership in the Muslim community than to assume that certain positions are the norm and then try to squeeze women into those positions.

Form and Function in Islamic Worship

In making this proposal, I am keenly aware of the possibility of eliciting suspicious or negative responses from some Muslims because of the conservative principles I have identified as so important in Islamic thought. This is particularly true when it comes to worship, where adherence to the prophetic Sunna is essential. Of course, Muslims look to the Prophet as their normative model in all areas of life, but in acts of worship (*'ibadah*), it is obligatory, especially because although the Qur'an exhorts believers to pray, fast, etc., most of the details of these rituals are derived from the Sunna. Deviations from established prophetic practices are considered odious by Muslim scholars who make frequent reference to the statement the Prophet made during one of his Friday sermons, "The best of speech is the book of God, the best guidance is the guidance of Muhammad, the most evil matters are the most recent ones, every innovation [*bid'a*] is an error." It is a widespread tradition that the person delivering the Friday sermon (the *khatib*—the preacher) quotes this statement before he begins his own sermon.

This conservative approach to forms of worship, this revulsion at innovation (*bid'a*) is responsible for preserving a remarkable unity among Muslims as they have established communities across the globe over the last fourteen centuries. The core of Islamic worship, despite some slight differences among schools of law and regional communities, remains remarkably uniform. Across the world, Muslims fast during the month of Ramadan, pray five times a day, reciting the revelation in the original Arabic, and travel to Mecca to make the pilgrimage together. This uniformity in ritual practices is perhaps the most important factor in preserving a sense of unity and community among Muslims, despite their great diversity of cultures, political structures and even theological orientations.

I have a personal anecdote to illustrate this point. A few years ago I was praying in a mosque in China with a group of American Muslims. None of us shared a common language, but we wanted to communicate to the Chinese Muslims that we would be combining our prayers according to the prophetic Sunna because we were traveling. We said the Arabic word *musafir*, "traveler," and immediately the women understood our purpose and made sure that the late afternoon prayer (*'asr*) did not begin in the mosque until we had time to catch up on our delayed noon prayers (*dhuhr*). None of these women, and few from our group, could use the Arabic language for communication. However, we all shared common core rituals, identified by the Arabic terms used in the Qur'an and the Sunna, and thus were able to both communicate basic information about our worship and were able to pray together.

But there is the catch to this story: if Muslims are so conservative and uniform in their worship, why is it that this exchange I had with Chinese Muslims took place in a "women's mosque," a phenomenon I had never experienced, nor heard of, before traveling to China? A greater paradox was to be found in the fact that, although these women followed the minority Hanafi [one of the four major schools of Sunni law] legal position that women should not pray together in congregation, the woman's mosque was headed by a *nu ahong*, literally, a "woman imam." I had never heard of such a thing—how could I understand this phenomenon within the context of the paradigms of religious leadership I had learned?

To begin to understand this apparent paradox, we might want to consider the relationship between the function and form of the imam. The term "imam" literally means "leader" in the Arabic language and is normally used to signify a person who is a leader in some religious field or practice. For example, a person can be a leader in scholarship; in this sense, the eponyms of the Sunni schools of law are called "Imam" (Ahmed, Malik, al-Shafi'i and Abu Hanifa). The term "imam" also applies to the person who performs the function of leading a congregational prayer. Many statements attributed to the Prophet Muhammad indicate the primary importance of the five daily prayers (*salawat*) as opportunities for forgiveness, spiritual refreshment and dialogue with God. That these prayers are primarily intended to strengthen the relationship between each individual and his or her Merciful Creator is demonstrated by the fact that they must be attended to whether one is alone or in the company of others. It is not obligatory that these prayers be made in congregation, unless one is in a setting that provides the necessary conditions for congregation. If we examine these conditions set by traditional Islamic scholarship, we see that maintaining a communal unity is an implicit goal. Thus, if one enters a setting where a congregational prayer is being held, one should join the group, and not establish another prayer group or pray by oneself. According to the Sunna of the Prophet, all congregational prayers, even if the congregation is only a few people, need to be led by one person.

Given the importance of congregational prayer in Islam, we expect Islamic tradition to pay significant attention to the requirements for leadership of the prayer. What I find fascinating and significant is that the requirements are almost always relational and contextual. The most important criteria are the ability to recite the Qur'an since this is the primary liturgical element of the prayer, and knowledge of the rules for performing the prayer. Other relative considerations that the various legal schools emphasize somewhat differently include age and piety. Some of the contextual considerations include the place in which the prayer is being held. Thus, no man can lead prayer in another man's house without his permission, just as no one can lead prayers in the mosque if the appointed *imam* is present without his permission.

The majority of legal schools consider it "recommended" (*mandub*—a technical term indicating a religiously meritorious act) for women to pray together in congregation with one of them leading as *imam*, if they are not praying with the general (i.e., male inclusive) congregation. These schools base their position on a number of reports that the wives of the Prophet Muhammad led women in congregational prayer. Many of the Hanafi scholars who reject the practice of women praying in congregation do not mention the example of the wives of the Prophet. It seems in this matter, as with a number of other issues, the Hanafi school retains a position that was formulated on the basis of reasoning early in Islamic history when they did not have access to all the *hadith* that were later compiled for easy reference.

Many Sunni scholars claim that there is a consensus that women should not lead men in prayer, although they acknowledge that a few scholars have made exceptions for family congregations and the optional night prayers in Ramadan (*tarawih*) if the only qualified person available to lead in those situations is a woman. There are many indications from the Sunna that when men and women prayed together, the Prophet explicitly ordered that women should pray behind the men. The primary purpose of this arrangement seems to be to keep women from having to undergo scrutiny by men as they are praying, but there may be other reasons. The Sunna, not the Qur'an, is the main source of legislation for prayer. It is only because of *hadith* that we know the timings of the five daily prayers, how many *rak'at* [units of prayer] there are in each prayer, whether the prayers should be recited loudly or silently, etc. Similarly, we only know the timing and forms of Friday congregational prayer from the *hadith*, not the Qur'an. The arrangements for congregational prayer established by the Prophet must therefore be followed—necessarily in order to be faithful to the Sunna—and then to maintain unity among Muslims in this fundamental part of ritual life.

In light of this discussion of the imamate of prayer, how are we to make sense of the phenomenon of women's mosques in China? What does it mean to be an imam of a (women's) mosque, if the *imam* does not lead others in congregational prayer? Are Chinese women's mosques strange deviations, or are they useful models for building relevant Islamic institutions?

In an excellent study of the women's mosques of China, Maria Jaschok and Shui Jingjun show that some Muslims are now concerned that these women's mosques, which have existed in China for hundreds of years, may be considered the kind of reprehensible innovations we have mentioned. There is no doubt that this concern is due to the influence of the "salafi" discourse in modernist Islam that is hostile to many of the institutions of traditional Islam. However, in the context of traditional Islam, women's mosques do not seem particularly strange. In fact, like many of the religious institutions of traditional Islam, their establishment was a relatively simple case of form following function. To understand what I mean by this, we need to return to the "innovation" *hadith* we discussed earlier. In his commentary on the "innovation" *hadith*, the great medieval scholar Imam al-Nawawi said:

> What is meant by (innovation in) this (*hadith*) is most innovations. . . . Scholars say that there are five classes of innovation: obligatory, laudable, prohibited, reprehensible and permitted. Among the obligatory (innovations) are: organizing the proofs of the theologians against the heretics and innovators and things like that. Among the laudable (innovations) are writing books of (religious) knowledge, building *madrasas* (religious schools) and *ribat* (religious retreats) and other things.

Thus, even the ubiquitous *madrasas* in the Muslim world can be considered innovations, albeit, laudable innovations.

Alongside the establishment of religious schools and other institutions across the Muslim world, form following function also led to the specialization of religious professionals in all fields. Islamic courts, for example, developed multiple specialized offices to ensure that the aims of the court were met. In any court of significance, the judge (*qadi*) may have been assisted by a number of the following professionals, among others: clerk (*katib*), official character witness (*muzakki*), advisors (*mashura*), mufti (*jurisconsult*) and various expert witnesses (*shuhud*), including female expert witnesses. A similar tendency towards specialization is seen in the area of ritual law. Even at the beginning of the twentieth century, the Umayyad Mosque of Damascus employed a number of individuals to perform only one of each of the following functions: give the call to prayer, lead the daily prayers, repeat certain utterances of the imam for those who were too far away to hear them (*tabligh*), preach the Friday sermon, recite certain parts of the Qur'an on particular days, recite special litanies (*dhikr*) at certain times of the day, scent the mosque with incense, supplicate for particular causes, recite devotional poetry during various seasons and teach all different religious disciplines.

Some scholars might not use the discourse of innovation with respect to these developments at all. Rather, these scholars may refer to new practices and institutions as "means" (*wasa'il*) to an end (*ghayah* or *maqsid*). I once heard a lecture by a strict Saudi scholar, famous for his dislike of innovation, who was asked by his (even stricter) student if the lines drawn on the floor of the mosque should be considered an "innovation." Even this scholar felt this was taking things too far and he replied along these lines, "You are confusing means with ends. The lines are simply a way to achieve straight prayer rows; they have no meaning in themselves." Then he referred to the legal maxim, "What is necessary in order to fulfill an obligation is itself an obligation. . . ."

It is in this context that we can consider the establishment of women's mosques in China as a means to a vital end without abandoning the Prophetic Sunna: Muslims in China wanted to transmit their faith to their children; Chinese Muslim leaders believed that women needed to be educated in their faith in order to teach their children; in accordance with Islamic (and Confucian) norms of gender segregation, women needed their own space to learn their faith; it was not suitable for men to staff women's mosques; communities appointed female leaders—"imams"— for the women's mosques. All of this was done without violating the traditional rules of ritual law: female *imams* do not conduct Friday congregational prayer and, in accordance with their Hanafi legal tradition, they do not even lead other women in daily congregational prayer. Rather, these women teach other women how to pray, how to read Qur'an, they visit the sick, they wash the bodies of deceased women and they live in the women's mosque, available to give spiritual support, advice and assistance to women in need. . . .

What Kind of Religious Leadership Do We Want?

The reality is that many American Muslims are unhappy with their religious leadership, but they have not taken the responsibility to reshape their institutions and do what is needed to cultivate better leadership. According to the Qur'an, this is not a responsibility we can avoid.

In recent years, the tendency in American Muslim communities has been to concentrate religious authority in the office of the *imam*, who is also expected to perform multiple, distinct functions for the community. In addition to leading the daily prayers and giving the Friday sermon, the *imam* is expected to represent the community to the public, draft marriage contracts, issue judicial divorces, teach children, teach adults and counsel people with all kinds of problems, among other things. In addition, the *imam* may, whether he is explicitly authorized to do this or not, make policy decisions for the community, such as what kind of educational gatherings and spiritual practices will be permitted in the building, how the prayer space will be divided between men and women, and how charitable contributions will be spent. It is no wonder that so many American Muslims are dissatisfied with their local religious leadership. No one person could perform all these functions well. Even if he could, given that the *imam* for the general congregation has to be male, placing all religious authority with the *imam* means that women will necessarily be excluded from this field. How, then, should we structure the leadership of our communities?

A few years ago, I conducted a workshop with a Muslim women's organization in North Carolina. I divided the women into groups and asked each group to come up with a list of the functions they felt needed to be performed in a competent manner by someone in their local mosque. Then I asked them to create positions that would allow different people to perform those functions. In the end, I asked each group to share their ideal slate of leaders and officials for their community. When they shared their results, it turned out that everyone felt that it was most important to have an *imam* who could recite the Qur'an well. This indicated to me that the charisma of the office of *imam* really derives from the blessing manifest in the Qur'an. At the same time, the women agreed that they did not want the person who was charged with carrying that blessed recitation to do anything disgraceful or dishonorable. The *imam* should act in an ethical and dignified manner in order to be worthy of reciting the Qur'an. Many of the women did agree that their communities needed women in leadership positions. Some felt that a female scholar or spiritual leader would be most helpful, others felt that their communities needed a female counselor or social worker, in particular, to help the *imam* understand the dynamics of family conflict. Some of the women said that if their mosque could afford to pay for only one professional, they would like to hire a youth director, and the community members could take turns leading the prayers.

It is my hope that all American Muslim communities will undertake this kind of creative, visionary and thoughtful dialogue about their priorities and needs. Unfortunately, because the present leadership of many local communities is so poor, it is difficult to even begin a process of renewal. Many Muslim communities do not have clear governance procedures and there is often confusion over who is authorized to make important decisions. Muslim communities must establish better procedures for decision making. At the same time, the urgency of a sound decision-making process does not mean that Muslims will arrive at a clear and easy method of determining religious authority. It is my opinion that this should not necessarily be viewed negatively. Rather, I believe it is only proper that religious authority should continually be negotiated (informally and formally) among fellow believers in the Muslim community. I realize that this fluidity makes many people anxious, so they flee to the comfort of a rigidly hierarchical model (usually some form of *bay'ah*—an oath of obedience to a religious leader). In this, I am reminded of the words of the Canadian philosopher John Ralston Saul when he argues that the genius of humanity lies in our attempt to keep a number of different qualities in balance. We cannot let just one of the essential qualities, like reason or memory, dominate the others. "We are uncomfortable," Saul states, "with our genius being tied to attempting an equilibrium we will never achieve." Likewise, I would argue that the genius of religious authority in traditional Islam is that it is always relational, and that every member of the community must take part in creating and sustaining authority; otherwise, it is oppression.

Let us take the common problem of the way the prayer space is divided between men and women in mosques. In some North American mosques, only men are in leadership positions, both as *imams* and as trustees of the institution. Many of these men, if they are interested in justifying their authority at all, consider that it derives from their knowledge and their (self-perceived) religiosity. Many of the women and youth of the community believe these self-appointed leaders to have no real religious authority—only power. They experience unauthorized power as oppression when they find themselves being forced out of the main prayer hall and generally treated like nuisances in the mosque. What justification is offered for this treatment? The response these men may give is that according to the Sunna, women are not obligated to attend the mosque and further, according to some *hadith*, it is better for women to pray at home.

It is at this point that we recognize the need for women who are both knowledgeable about Islamic law and authorized to participate in community decision making. A hypothetical female scholar might respond to this justification saying, "The sources you cite may be authentic, however, you fail to mention that during the time of the Prophet, women not only came regularly to the mosque for prayers, there were also women living in the mosque. All the men of that time were not pious. The Qur'an itself mentions 'hypocrites' (*munafiqun*) who tried to create problems among believers. Yet women still came day and night to the mosque. Further, the Prophet Muhammad explicitly stated, 'Do not forbid the maidservants of God from the mosques of God.' If you cannot forbid them, do you really think it is permissible to harass and discourage them? Where do you think you get the authority to do such a thing?" Female board members might put forth the following argument, "It is true that in some contexts it is better for women to pray at home. But we have women in our community who live by themselves; they need to come to the mosque to learn about their religion and to strengthen their faith. Other women have recently immigrated to this country, they are lonely and depressed at home, they need to get out and be with other Muslims. They could go to the mall, but wouldn't it be better to come to the mosque?"

Of course, there is no guarantee that every woman present on a mosque board would represent the concerns of other women well. Inclusive representation is a necessary, but not sufficient condition for good governance. Muslim communities must have accountable leadership as well as inclusive decision-making bodies. Such a community will, in turn, help develop informed and responsible individuals who can represent their values and concerns to the larger society. In contemporary North American society, there are many opportunities for religious leadership that are not directly related to traditional Islamic models. In many American faith traditions, "lay" leaders can serve in public and private institutions on ethics boards, as chaplains and as student leaders. In Islam, there should be no distinction between lay and clergy and these new opportunities for religious leadership should not be neglected or marginalized by the Muslim community. The best way American Muslims can ensure responsible religious leadership is to allow the functions we want performed to determine the positions and institutions we create, and to support the men and women best able to perform these functions.

FIVE

American Muslim Politics
and Civic Engagement After 9/11

OST American Muslims are loyal and law-abiding citizens or
permanent residents of the United States. The overwhelming
majority of American Muslims believe that Muslims should be
active participants in American political life and public affairs. Most
proudly and publicly proclaim their patriotism and celebrate America as
a land of freedom and opportunity where they can freely practice their religion. Most also believe that American Muslims should donate to non-
Muslim American social-service agencies, participate in interfaith
activities, and support worthy non-Muslim political candidates. American Muslims have condemned, absolutely and unequivocally, the use of
terror to accomplish political ends.

One might say that American Muslims hold these views in common
despite their diversity. Like Americans as a whole, they disagree about a
whole host of other social, economic, and cultural issues. They are Demo-
crats, Republicans, and Independents. How Muslims vote depends on
who they are—their race, gender, age, religious views, sexual orientation,
national origin, class, and more. Some are social conservatives who oppose gay rights and want to ban abortion, like some orthodox Jews and
evangelical Christians. Other American Muslims are far more concerned
with poverty at home and abroad, a lack of equal opportunity, and the
state of public schools. Generally speaking, African American Muslims
want their representatives to focus on domestic issues, while first- and
second-generation immigrants are often more vocal about U.S. foreign

policy in the Muslim world. But even this generalization does not always hold true.

While there is no widespread American Muslim conspiracy to harm the United States or its citizens, there are some American Muslims who see the U.S. government and even American society as a malevolent force in the world. Some view America as immoral. As a result, these Muslims might eschew participation in elections, discourage their children from serving in the military, and avoid American popular culture. For example, the Tabligh Jama'at, a relatively nonpolitical organization with South Asian roots, fears that integration into popular American Muslim culture will threaten Muslim piety and identity. Hizb Tahrir, or the Liberation Party, sees the United States as *dar al-kufr*, the abode of disbelief, and has been known to hope for the country's mass conversion to Islam. There are also some American Muslims who have sworn allegiance to militant organizations and political ideas that most American Muslims would consider repugnant. American Taliban John Walker Lindh is a famous example.

But when examining the influence and impact of "radical" American Muslims, it is important to make a distinction between violent anti-American activists and conservative Muslims in general. Just because one is a socially conservative critic of American culture does not mean that one is anti-American. As mentioned in previous chapters, a long-running theme in American Islam, as in American religion more generally, is the notion that society is corrupt and in need of religious revival. Many socially and theologically conservative Muslims who are critical of American society stress the need for a return to personal piety in the face of what they saw as the immoral behavior of modern Western society—like other American practitioners of old-time religion, they denounce greed, sexual impropriety, and cling to what they call a literal reading of their religious scriptures. Some have even said that in order to be saved from a decline in values, the United States should become an Islamic state. But few of these persons have advocated the violent overthrow of the U.S. government. Like many of their Christian missionary brothers and sisters in U.S. history, they have said that they hoped to convert Americans to Islam using only peaceful means.

Most American Muslims, however, have no strategy or hope to turn the United States into an Islamic state. Instead, they want to be fully Muslim and fully American, and they argue for the compatibility and complementary nature of American and Islamic values. They may wish to change certain elements of U.S. foreign and domestic policies, but they intend to do so using the same means that every other mainstream group uses. Like other Americans, American Muslims attempt to make their voices heard in American politics and the public sphere by supporting a variety of national public interest groups. One of them, the Islamic Society of North America (ISNA), attempts to address a wide variety of issues, from politics to prayer, important to Muslim American life. ISNA, which was born out of the Muslim Students Association in 1982, has also focused on Muslim community development. Organizations operating under its umbrella include the Muslim Students Association, the Islamic Medical Association, the American Muslim Engineers and Scientists, and the American Muslim Social Scientists. ISNA also distributes a popular magazine called *Islamic Horizons*. Its national headquarters is located in Plainfield, Indiana, a suburb of Indianapolis.

Some Muslim political organizations are more narrowly focused on political activism and lobbying in Washington, D.C. Among them is the Council for American-Islamic Relations (CAIR), founded in 1994. CAIR often leads the fight against anti-Muslim prejudice in the United States. Its representatives, for example, regularly appear on cantankerous "shock-talk" shows, where they are generally hit with a barrage of questions equating American Muslims with terrorists. CAIR also lobbies government officials on foreign policy issues like the "war on terror" and the Israeli-Palestinian conflict, and it represents the civil rights of American Muslims. Some of the organization's critics, in an effort to delegitimize it, have deemed it "radical" and "extremist," although such claims have not stopped many "moderate" Muslims from supporting its efforts. CAIR has played an important role in bringing to light the many hate crimes against Muslims in the United States.

ISNA and CAIR are only two of the many groups that attempt to organize Muslims into viable public interest groups. Others are the Muslim American Society, the Islamic Circle of North America, the Muslim Public Affairs Council, and the various progressive Muslim groups. There are important ideological splits in the American Muslim community that can be observed in their diverse platforms. For example, after 9/11, the Progressive Muslim Union and Muslim WakeUp! began to articulate loudly and publicly, partly through their deft use of the Internet, an interpretation of Islam that was critical of war, gender discrimination, jingoism, unequal distribution of resources, and intolerance. Many Muslims, especially those associated with the ISNA and other old-line immigrant organizations, argued that the progressives went too far. Some Muslims rejected them as heretics beyond the pale of Islam, especially when progressive Muslims questioned time-honored traditions of Islamic religious practice. All of this intra-Muslim disagreement shows the richness of American Muslim engagement in American public life.

The proliferation of different national organizations with differing agendas also reflects religious divisions within American Muslim communities. Some Muslims, especially Sufi Muslims, Ahmadi Muslims, and Isma'ili Muslims, have complained that they feel marginalized in many of the national groups, especially those with a more conservative, "fundamentalist" bent. Even some Twelver Shi'a have reported that they are made to feel "lesser" in groups that stress Sunni identity or groups led by Sunni Muslims. As a result, they have supported organizations that they consider to be more inclusive. Or they have created their own national organizations. Ahmadi Muslims in the United States, for example, sustain their own national organization, and have continued to publish an American Muslim magazine, the *Muslim Sunrise*, since the 1920s. Their goals are to "rejuvenate Islamic morals and spiritual values, . . . encourage interfaith dialogue, . . . defend Islam, . . . correct misunderstandings about Islam in the West, [and] advocate peace, tolerance, love and understanding among followers of different faiths."

Another key dividing line in the life of American Muslim advocacy groups is racial and ethnic identity. ISNA and CAIR, for example, are generally dominated by immigrant Muslims. African American Muslims, on the other hand, *tend* to follow the leadership of African American leaders like W. D. Mohammed or Louis Farrakhan. W. D. Mohammed's national community of mosques and Louis Farrakhan's Nation of Islam are, arguably, the best organized African American Muslim associations. W. D. Mohammed publishes the *Muslim Journal*, a newspaper dedicated to covering international, national, and local issues of concern to black Muslims. Similarly, Farrakhan is responsible for the *Final Call*, a newspaper that is distributed in part by a network of usually young, bow-tied men who sell the paper on the streets of urban black America. Thousands come from long distances to see both men speak during their public appearances.

No matter what their race or ideology, most American Muslims have attempted to articulate a view of Islam and politics that is thoroughly democratic. Some American Muslim scholars, echoing the efforts of

Muslim reformers in the 1800s, have applied readings of the Qur'an, Sunna, and Islamic jurisprudence to argue that democracy is the most Islamic form of governance currently available. An increasing number of Muslims has argued that their faith can be a powerful tool in the reconciliation of Jews, Christians, and Muslims; they refuse to relegate Islam to a private role, insisting that any public form of Islamic activism be pluralistic. In the face of what most Muslims view as unfair discrimination against them, American Muslims have also seized the vocabulary of the U.S. Constitution and especially the Bill of Rights to argue for their civil liberties and to ask for government protection against anti-Muslim violence. While nearly all Muslims have condemned terror, many have joined other critics of the Bush administration and American foreign policy to argue that U.S. policies in the Middle East and around the world have fueled anti-Americanism and terrorism.

In one way or another, American Muslims after 9/11 refused to be marginal or marginalized in American public life.

1. Council of American-Islamic Relations,
"The Status of Muslim Civil Rights in the United States" (2005)

After 9/11, despite the appeals of American leaders, there was a violent backlash against some American Muslims. Unfortunately, this violence was part of a larger pattern: during the hostage crisis in Iran from 1979 to 1981, the Gulf War of 1991, and other crises involving the Middle East, some Americans who merely "looked" Muslim have been the victims of various forms of discrimination. Such violence inspires fear and anxiety among American Muslims, and civil rights organizations like CAIR have attempted to document anti-Muslim discrimination, ask for help from government officials, and use the courts when necessary to seek relief. After 9/11, in reaction to the war on terror, increased domestic surveillance, and the Patriot Act, many American Muslims also began to view their own government as discriminatory. Many American Muslim individuals and organizations joined the American Civil Liberties Union and other public interest groups in attempting to protest and change what they see as violations of their rights to privacy, due process, and habeas corpus. In so doing, one might argue, these persons show just how much they have become part of an old American tradition—fighting for individual rights in the face of the state's encroaching power.

Nearly four years removed from the 9/11 terror attacks, the greatest tragedy to befall our nation in modern history, our country has learned certain lessons that will hopefully lead us to a stronger, safer and more
vibrant society for people of all races, faiths and cultures.

Since the 9/11 attacks, the most disturbing legal trend is the growing
disparity in how American Muslims are being treated under the law on
many different levels.

In order to fully understand the status of civil rights in the post-9/11
era, it is essential that this report offer a documented historical overview
of major federal law enforcement initiatives, high-profile national cases
and statistical evidence of anti-Muslim discrimination in the United
States, particularly those incidents that occurred during the last calendar
year of 2004.

In 2004, CAIR processed a total of 1,522 incident reports of civil rights
cases compared to 1,019 cases reported to CAIR in 2003. This constitutes a
49 percent increase in the reported cases of harassment, violence and discriminatory treatment from 2003 and marks the highest number of Muslim civil rights cases ever reported to CAIR in our eleven year history.

In addition, CAIR received 141 reports of actual and potential violent
anti-Muslim hate crimes, a 52 percent increase from the 93 reports received in 2003.

Overall, 10 states alone accounted for almost 79 percent of all reported
incidents to CAIR in 2004. These ten states include: California (20.17%),
New York (10.11%), Arizona (9.26%), Virginia (7.16%), Texas (6.83%),
Florida (6.77%), Ohio (5.32%), Maryland (5.26%), New Jersey (4.53%) and
Illinois (2.96%).

There have also been decreases, both in real and proportional terms, in
certain categories from the previous year as well. For example, workplace
discrimination complaints to CAIR constituted nearly 23 percent of complaints in 2003. In 2004, the number of workplace discrimination complaints decreased to almost 18 percent of the total complaints.

In addition, complaints involving governmental agencies decreased
from 29 percent in 2003 to 19 percent in 2004. Internet harassment of
American Muslims also decreased from 7 percent of total complaints in
2003 to less than 1 percent of total reported complaints in 2004.

By far the greatest increase from last year, in both real and proportional terms, occurred in the area of unreasonable arrests, detentions,
searches/seizures and interrogations.

In 2003, complaints concerning law enforcement techniques accounted for only 7 percent of all reported incidents. In 2004, however, these reports rose to almost 26 percent of all reported cases to CAIR.

Although not a scientific study, there are several factors which may have contributed to the increase in total number of reports to CAIR over the past year. These include, but are not limited to, the following:

1. An ongoing and lingering atmosphere of fear since the September 11 attacks against American Muslims, Arabs and South Asians;
2. The growing use of anti-Muslim rhetoric by some local and national opinion leaders;
3. Local Muslim communities, through the opening of new CAIR chapters and regional offices, now have more mechanisms to monitor and report incidents to CAIR at the grassroots level;
4. Following the infamous legacy of the USA PATRIOT Act, other federal legislation and policies which severely infringe on the civil and constitutional rights of all Americans continue to be passed;
5. Increased public awareness about civil liberties and the impact of federal law enforcement initiatives on constitutional and civil rights.

In our conclusion, CAIR recommends that further congressional inquiries, inspector general reports from federal agencies and impact litigation continue to be used to ensure that the civil and legal rights of all Americans are never placed in jeopardy again.

Background and Findings

In the months directly following 9/11, Attorney General John Ashcroft, using his powers under section 412 of the now infamous USA PATRIOT Act, rounded up and imprisoned well over 1,200 Muslim and Arab men based solely on pretextual immigration violations. The most disconcerting fact about these mass round-ups was the fact that the Justice Department refused to disclose the detainees' identities, give them access to lawyers or allow them to have contact with their families.

In April 2003, Inspector General Glenn A. Fine reported that at least 1,200 men from predominantly Muslim and Arab countries were detained by law enforcement officials nationwide. An August 2002 Human Rights

Watch report documents cases of prolonged detention without any charge, denial of access to bond release, interference with detainees' right to legal counsel and unduly harsh conditions of confinement for the over 1,200 detainees. Georgetown University law professor David Cole said that, "Thousands were detained in this blind search for terrorists without any real evidence of terrorism, and ultimately without netting virtually any terrorists of any kind."

In addition to the indiscriminate immigrant dragnet after September 11, several high profile cases against American Muslims further stigmatized the American Muslim community.

For example, after spending seventy-six days in solitary confinement and being labeled a "spy" in most media circles, where can Army chaplain and West Point graduate Captain James Yee go to regain his respectability after being falsely accused of treasonous crimes that could have resulted in the death penalty? Where might Oregon attorney Brandon Mayfield reclaim his good name after being falsely linked by the FBI to the Madrid train bombings of March 11, 2004? How does Sami Al-Hussayen resume a normal life with his family after being found not guilty of "aiding terrorists" while serving as a webmaster and exercising his First Amendment right to free speech?

The American Muslim community has always categorically condemned acts of terrorism and believes that those who break the law should be prosecuted to the fullest extent of the law. However, in order to remain consistent with the constitutional hallmarks of due process and "equal protection" under the law, it is essential that our law enforcement agencies enforce and apply the law in a consistent manner to all people rather than selectively target people based on their religious or ethnic affiliation.

It is time once again for American society to reclaim its true legal tradition and judge a person on the criminality of their acts, not on the color of his skin or the religion to which she adheres.

The Dragnets of John Ashcroft

Under United States immigration law, an "absconder" is defined as an "alien who, though subject to . . . [deportation], has failed to surrender for removal or to otherwise comply with the order." According to a January 2002 memorandum sent to federal immigration and law enforcement officials, the Deputy Attorney General of the United States estimated that there are approximately 314,000 absconders, or deportable illegal aliens, living in the United States today. Of these 314,000, only about 6,000, less than 2 percent, originate from Muslim or Arab nations. Although over 90 percent of absconders are from Latin American countries, the Justice Department began selectively targeting absconders only from predominantly Muslim and Arab countries in the past few years. However, their selective targeting of Muslims and Arabs after September 11 bore almost no criminal fruits. By the end of May 2002, the Justice Department admitted that out of 314,000 absconders, only 585 had been located. More embarrassingly, not a single terrorist had been apprehended.

Whereas all Americans have been greatly affected by 9/11 and its aftermath, young males from Arab and Muslim countries have been most profoundly affected by the dragnet conducted by the Department of Justice in our ongoing "war on terror." In addition to the law enforcement dragnets conducted by the Justice Department after 9/11, certain congressional legislation has also been passed which has stirred great debate in all American circles as to how to best balance national security interests whilst still safeguarding the civil liberties guaranteed to every American by our Constitution.

The Secret Roundup

Glenn A. Fine, Inspector General for the Department of Justice, officially reported that at least 1,200 men from predominantly Muslim and Arab countries were detained by law enforcement officials nationwide within two months of 9/11. The Inspector General conceded in his official report that a senior officer in the Office of Public Affairs stopped reporting the cumulative count of detainees after 1,200 because the "statistics became too confusing."

In August 2002, Human Rights Watch (HRW) released a 95-page report, entitled *Presumption of Guilt*, which documented cases of prolonged detention without any charge, denial of access to bond release, interference with detainees' right to legal counsel, and unduly harsh conditions of confinement for the over 1,200 detainees. HRW's findings were later confirmed by Inspector General Fine's report, which also identified a pattern of "physical and verbal abuse" by correctional staff at the Metropolitan Detention Center (MDC) in Brooklyn, New York.

The September 11 detainees comprised citizens from more than 20 countries. The largest number, 254 (or 33 percent), were from Pakistan, more than double the number of any other country. The second largest number (111) was from Egypt and there were also substantial numbers of detainees from Jordan, Turkey, Yemen and India. The ages of the detainees varied, but by far the greatest number, 479 (or 63 percent), were between the ages of 26 and 40.

Sample Cases [of Civil Rights Abuses]

March 21, 2003—A Muslim American family of Palestinian descent became victim of property damage when their van was bombed outside their home in the Chicago suburb of Burbank, Illinois. The individual responsible for the crime had been convicted earlier of criminal damage to property in 2001 for vandalizing an Arab-owned furniture store two days after the 9/11 attacks.

December 12, 2003—A Muslim woman was shopping in a New York toy store when a man followed her, verbally accosted and assaulted her. She reported the incident to the police and the attacker was arrested.

March 2, 2004—In San Diego, a man of Portuguese descent was beaten by a group of four white men who mistook him for being Middle Eastern. They yelled racial slurs at him and told him to go back to Iraq.

March 3, 2004—A San Antonio, Texas, man was sentenced to 30 years in prison for setting a series of fires at Muslim-owned convenience stores and other businesses in the city. The County District Attorney referred to the man as a "terrorist" for his connection with another attack against a Muslim-owned business when the arsons began in 2003.

April 24, 2004—A Muslim woman and her son were harassed, threatened and attacked by another woman while shopping in Pennsylvania. The woman yelled that American troops were fighting in Iraq and Afghanistan so that women did not have to dress like her and also hit her with her cart repeatedly. Employees of the store refused to call security when she requested that they do so and did not assist her in finding a phone to call the police.

May 27, 2004—A Muslim man and his family were verbally harassed by a patron while eating at a restaurant in Florida. The offender called them "terrorists." When the Muslim man complained, the manager elected to remove him from the premises instead of the offender.

June 21, 2004—A Muslim man reported that while riding on a van that runs from New York to his home in Paterson, New Jersey, a group of Latino males harassed him. They hit him on his arm and made comments like, "take the bombs off before I kill you." The driver did not say anything until they began cursing him in Spanish at which point she asked them to stop.

June 26, 2004—While driving home in Illinois, a Muslim woman was harassed and physically assaulted. Three individuals asked her for a lighter. When she replied that she did not have one, they became angry and said, "Stupid Muslims, F-cking Muslims" as they surrounded her car and repeatedly kicked it. When the victim stepped out of her car to confront them, one of the individuals punched her in the face and tore her *hijab* from her head.

July 14, 2004—A Muslim-owned grocery store was torched and completely destroyed. Anti-Arab slurs that read, "F-ck you Arab" were found spray-painted on the scene.

July 30, 2004—A Muslim woman from New York was soliciting donations on behalf of a charitable organization when she was verbally and physically attacked.

August 13, 2004—A cabbie in New York was punched in the face while driving a cab near Ground Zero after the offender said to him, "You are Muslim." The offender was drunk and later charged with third degree assault and harassment.

August 23, 2004—In Tucson, Arizona, a Muslim family of Jordanian origin reported that their car was vandalized in the parking lot of their apartment building. Allegedly the car's tires were slashed and the windshield was smashed. A note taped to the vehicle read, "You are not welcome here. Go back home you stupid f-ckers."

September 12, 2004—In California, a Muslim man and his children placed an order at a drive through Burger King, when he overheard an employee say to his co-workers, "Look, Osama Bin Laden" is here.

October 27, 2004—A community member filed a report of graffiti on a ME-TRA stop in Illinois that read, "Kill all Muslims B4 they kill U."

October 29, 2004—Two Staten Island men were arrested and charged with hate crimes for allegedly hitting a Muslim student at Stony Brook University while shouting anti-Muslim slurs. Suffolk County police charged the 19 and 20-year old with criminal trespass in the second degree and aggravated harassment in the second degree as a hate crime. The two men allegedly knocked on a student's door and awoke him at about 4 a.m. The victim said he opened the door and the two men went into his room and began throwing items at him, hitting him and overturning furniture, all the while calling him anti-Muslim names.

December 1, 2004—In Chesterfield, Virginia, a Sikh-owned gas station was destroyed by fire and anti-Muslim graffiti was found on a nearby trash container and shed. The fire is being investigated as an arson and possible hate crime.

December 21, 2004—A fire that took place at a used car lot in Nebraska is being investigated as arson and a hate crime. Swastikas were spray-painted on the walls. Most of the graffiti involves derogatory references to Latinos and Arabs.

2. Laila Al-Marayati, "American Muslim Charities: Easy Targets in the War on Terror," in Pace Law Review (2005)

Laila al-Marayati is an American woman of Palestinian descent. A board-certified obstetrician-gynecologist, she has served as a director of women's health at the Northeast Valley Health Corporation in Southern California and as a clinical professor at the University of Southern California School of Medicine. Like so many of the Muslim professionals described in this book, she is also a social and political activist. Past president of the Muslim Women's League, a Los Angeles–based organization, al-Marayati lectures frequently on women's rights in Islam, reproductive health, and violence against women. From 1999 to 2001, she worked as one of President Bill Clinton's appointees on the U.S. Commission on International Religious Freedom. Marayati has also played a key role in establishing and directing KinderUSA, a charity focused on providing health care, food, recreation opportunities, and transportation for Palestinian children in the West Bank and Gaza Strip. In this article, published in a law review, Marayati criticizes the Bush administration's largely unsuccessful prosecutions of Muslim charities who allegedly aid terrorist

*organizations, arguing that the administration is motivated mainly by politi-
cal rather than security issues. She predicts that due to the suspicion with
which all Muslim charities are treated, more and more American Muslims
will stop donating to Muslim agencies focused on relieving the suffering of
Muslims abroad.*

Within three months of the terrorist attacks on September 11, 2001, President Bush announced the designation of the Holy Land Foundation
based in Dallas, Texas, as a terrorist organization. He made this announcement at a press conference in the Rose Garden four days after a
request from Israeli Prime Minister Ariel Sharon. Since then, three other
Muslim charities based in the U.S. were similarly designated, their assets
frozen and their operations completely disrupted. The U.S. government
has not obtained a single terrorist conviction of any of the principals of
these organizations nor has the government proven conclusively that any
of the funds were used to finance activities at all related to the events of
9/11 or to al-Qaeda. Yet, the government continues to display its closures
of Muslim charities as evidence of progress being made in the War on
Terror. . . .

Under the International Emergency Economic Powers Act (IEEPA), the
government can block the assets of entities suspected of providing material and other support for terrorism (other than medicine or religious materials such as Bibles). Executive Order 13224, issued by President Bush on
September 23, 2001, "prohibits U.S. persons from transacting or dealing
with individuals and entities owned or controlled by, acting for or on behalf of, assisting or supporting, or otherwise associated with, persons
listed in the Executive Order." Those designated and listed under the Executive Order are known as "Specially Designated Global Terrorists"
(SDGTs). . . .

Closures of Muslim American Charities

HOLY LAND FOUNDATION

Based in Dallas, Texas, the Holy Land Foundation (HLF) was the largest
Muslim American humanitarian organization providing assistance overseas with a budget of close to $12 million per year. HLF provided services

in the West Bank and Gaza Strip, Kosovo, Chechnya and elsewhere. To the average Muslim living in the U.S., HLF was a trusted name. On December 4, 2001, HLF was designated under IEEPA as a terrorist organization because, the government alleged, they were providing assistance to Hamas [the Palestinian Islamic political party, militia, and social service organization] in the Occupied Territories. The case of HLF continues with the recent arrests and indictments of several board members and employees of the organization, all of whom were not required to post bail and who currently are awaiting their trial to begin in the fall of 2005.

The case against HLF is mainly built around allegations related to financing charitable works that had supposed links to members of Hamas. The current indictments primarily revolve around donations to various *zakat* [alms] committees throughout the West Bank and Gaza which are comprised of members of the local Palestinian community and include individuals of various sociopolitical affiliations. Other non-Muslim organizations in the U.S. and elsewhere also fund projects through the Zakat committees because they provide an efficient means of disbursing assistance to the local groups most suited for the humanitarian projects at hand. Yet, no other organization has been targeted for working with the *zakat* committees besides HLF. None of the court cases to date appears to document an actual money trail of funds going from HLF to individuals or organizations resulting in actual terrorist activity.

Once HLF was so designated and its assets were frozen, the organization challenged the designation, lost and then appealed to the D.C. Circuit Court of Appeals where they lost again. Finally, the Supreme Court refused to hear their case. Based on these cases, the judge who is adjudicating the [civil] suit filed . . . against HLF, feels there is ample evidence to support the allegation that HLF funded terrorism which will result in a substantial financial award to the plaintiffs who are citizens of Israel as well as the U.S. (see below).

GLOBAL RELIEF FOUNDATION (GRF)

Based in Illinois, GRF was the second largest American Muslim charity doing international work in Bosnia, Afghanistan, Kashmir, Chechnya and Lebanon. On December 14, 2001, GRF was designated by the Treasury department as a terrorist organization and its operations were shut down due to the freezing of its assets. While the government's actions were upheld in court, no charges of terrorism were filed against any individuals. The main fund-raiser for GRF, Rabih Haddad, underwent closed deportation hearings due to supposed immigration violations. He was deported to Lebanon the following year where he lives as a free citizen of that country and all charges against him related to terrorism were dropped.

BENEVOLENCE INTERNATIONAL FOUNDATION (BIF)

Also based in Illinois, BIF was designated on December 14, 2001, along with GRF. The efforts of BIF were concentrated in Bosnia and elsewhere. Eighteen months prior to the designation, BIF had begun to work in the Occupied Territories. The government's case was enhanced when they obtained documents in Bosnia linking leaders of BIF to Osama bin Laden during the late 1980s when the U.S. government and military were actively supporting bin Laden and the *mujahideen* against the Soviets in Afghanistan. During the criminal case, the government never provided evidence that BIF funded al-Qaeda. The case was built around previous associations that occurred ten years prior to the designation. Ultimately, Enam Arnaout, the executive director, entered into a plea bargain whereby he admitted to using some funds to provide boots and blankets to Chechen and Bosnian fighters. In this case, the government did reveal that the funds were not being used according to the donors' wishes, which is fortunate, but again, no links to terrorism were ever proven. In fact, "the court held that the offense to which Arnaout pled guilty, racketeering conspiracy, was not a crime of terrorism defined by law," and that the government was unable to prove that the Bosnian and Chechen beneficiaries were involved in any acts that could be considered terrorism.

Despite this fact, officials of the Treasury Department refer to BIF as having links to bin Laden in direct contradiction to the final judgment issued by the court. For example, in March 2003, Juan Zarate, Deputy Assistant Secretary in the Office of Terrorist Financing and Financial Crime, claimed that the designation of BIF, "a Chicago-based charity that was supporting al-Qaida" was an "example of the international community taking common action to cut off the flow of funds to al-Qaida." His testimony referred to BIF as a supporter of terrorism despite the fact that the case to prove such allegations was still pending in court. Ultimately, the government dismissed all charges that BIF and Arnaout provided material support to any terrorist individuals or organizations. . . .

Consequences on Muslim Charitable Giving

Through the Treasury Department, the U.S. government is able to freeze the assets of any organization before actually charging any individuals with engaging in terrorism or the support thereof. In addition, the Treasury Department is not obliged to prove its case in a court of law unless the targeted organization challenges the designation with the Treasury Department itself. Once the assets are frozen and the community becomes aware that an organization is under investigation, even if the accusation has no merit, the damage is irreversible resulting in the demise of the enterprise. Despite the fact that the government has not been able to show in any of the cases to date that funds were used to directly finance and support terrorism, all of the groups now are completely defunct.

Few have ventured to fill the void, meaning that only a small number of Muslim American groups remain that provide humanitarian assistance abroad. Prior to these closures, there were fewer than a dozen Islamic organizations based in the U.S. doing charitable work abroad that were known to the community. Only two new organizations have emerged since 9/11. All groups function with the awareness that they can be closed down at any time regardless of any actions they take to remain transparent and function within the law. Despite attempts by the Administration, the Treasury Department and others to reassure American Muslims that neither they nor their institutions are being targeted unfairly, the facts suggest the opposite.

In addition, the government's actions against Muslim American charities have little, if any, impact on making the rest of the American public more secure. Instead, these high profile cases result in the more dangerous consequence of leading people to believe that things are safer when they have made no difference whatsoever despite massive expenditures of taxpayer money.

For many years, Muslims in the United States felt they were fulfilling their religious obligation by giving to groups that provided and those that continue to provide humanitarian assistance overseas in places like Lebanon, Kosovo, Palestine, Africa, South Asia, Chechnya and Afghanistan to name a few. Local and national groups engaging in grassroots issues such as civil liberties protection had to sell the idea that donating to those efforts also qualified as *zakat*. Now that the community's choice of groups providing humanitarian assistance internationally continues to dry up, many have diverted their giving to focus on community-based activities in the United States. In addition, fear of being placed on a "government list" for donating to a charity that is suspect, negatively affects giving patterns as well. As a result, the yet-to-be-documented trends in giving among American Muslims are likely undergoing tremendous shifts.

The Treasury Department and the American Muslim Community

At the start of Ramadan in 2004, the Secretary of the Treasury issued a "Ramadan" statement, cautioning Muslims against giving to questionable groups: "When you open your hearts to charity during Ramadan, we encourage you to educate yourself on the activities of the charities to which you donate, to help ensure that your generosity is not exploited for nefarious purposes." He included the list of twenty-seven groups that have been so designated by the U.S. government for supporting terrorism and noted that it is a crime to support them in any fashion.

The government appears to function under the basic assumption that charitable donations on behalf of Muslims have been and will be corrupted intentionally or unintentionally and therefore, all acts of Muslim giving overseas are suspect. To date, the government has not been able to demonstrate a "money trail" that would confirm unequivocally the allegation that American Muslim charitable funds have been used to finance terrorism. However, the cloud of suspicion continues to grow despite modest efforts on the part of the Treasury Department and other branches of government to convince the community otherwise.

The Treasury Department has engaged with the Muslim community on a variety of levels since they began their efforts to interdict funds directed at terrorist groups.

In 2002, the Treasury Department issued "Anti-Terrorist Financing Guidelines: Voluntary Best Practices for US-Based Charities" as a response to demands from the American Muslim community, according to Juan Zarate, during a speech at the Convention of the Muslim Public Affairs Council (MPAC) in December, 2002. The guidelines mainly provide recommendations that mirror most due diligence practices of charitable organizations with a few additions, some of which are cumbersome, impractical and unrealistic. For example, the Guidelines advise charities to determine if the financial institution with which the foreign recipient maintains accounts is a shell bank, operating an offshore license, licensed in a jurisdiction that is non-cooperative in the fight against money-laundering, licensed in a jurisdiction where there are inadequate money-laundering controls and oversight, etc. Section 4 of the Guidelines outlines these and other measures that would require a great expenditure of resources on the part of the charities, something that would be very difficult, especially for smaller organizations. In addition, the areas in greatest need are often the areas that have the least amount of government control and oversight, making it difficult to comply completely with the Guidelines in all circumstances.

At various meetings with the Muslim community, Treasury officials confirmed that complete compliance with the Guidelines does not protect against seizure of assets, closure, government investigations and ultimate designation as an entity supporting terrorism if the government so wills. In other words, full compliance with the Treasury Guidelines does not offer "safe haven" from government action against any group.

Shortly after the Guidelines were issued, the Treasury Department began to meet with Muslim groups, such as the Islamic Society of North America (ISNA) and MPAC, for what Treasury considered to be the "next step" in providing guidance with respect to charitable giving. Treasury sponsored a gathering that included individuals from the Better Business Bureau's Wise Giving Alliance and the Evangelical Council on Financial Accountability to encourage Muslims to follow their models in forming an umbrella group under the auspices of an organization like ISNA which ultimately would provide some sort of "seal of approval" for member groups. At ISNA's annual convention in Chicago in the fall of 2004, the representatives of Muslim charities doing work in the U.S. and abroad raised concerns about which groups could best lead this effort and questioned whether Muslims needed to organize separately in the first place.

The major question raised was, what could a separate Muslim umbrella organization offer that was not already being provided by more experienced, well-established groups, such as InterAction? At the meeting, the representative from the Treasury Department replied that "you have some things on your radar screen that we don't." Such a statement is open to various interpretations but, at a minimum, was not reassuring. When pressed about the role of Treasury in facilitating a process that would enable Muslims to give without worry, he acknowledged that the Treasury Department emphasizes investigation and enforcement, not facilitation.

Most importantly, however, is the fact that an umbrella organization that vets groups and issues a "seal of approval" does not give American Muslims what they want: a guarantee that the group is doing legitimate work from the *American government's* point of view, that the group is not under investigation by any branch of law enforcement, and that they, as donors, will not be targeted by law enforcement under any future investigation.

After the closure of IARA at the start of Ramadan in 2004, Muslims in New Jersey called upon the government to issue a "white list" of acceptable charities to which they could donate without fear of donating to groups with terrorist ties. The Justice Department rejected the request stating that it was impossible to fulfill. According to Juan Zarate, Assistant Secretary for Terrorist Financing and Financial Crimes at the Treasury Department, "You can't have the U.S. government picking favorites in a multi-billion dollar industry." He also cited market and First Amendment concerns as limitations.

After the assets of HLF were frozen in 2001, Muslim donors expressed a desire to have their money returned or at least be transferred to another group providing similar humanitarian assistance. Once the HLF case was denied a hearing by the Supreme Court, the leaders of the organization agreed to file an application with OFAC for a license to release the funds to another group, namely, the Palestine Children's Relief Fund, a U.S.-based organization providing medical and surgical services to Palestinians. The request was denied due to two lawsuits pending against HLF. The government's refusal to honor the wishes of the donors to have their funds transferred to groups whose record is unscathed again belies the government's claim that it is not interested in obstructing legitimate Muslim giving.

Soon after its assets were frozen, BIF applied for a license from OFAC to release over $700,000 to fund a Tuberculosis hospital in Tajikistan and a Women's Hospital in Daghestan. Despite evidence of the valid, humanitarian nature of this work, OFAC refused to grant the license because it was concerned that "even funds sent to seemingly legitimate charities can be at least partially diverted to terrorist activities overseas" that OFAC is unable to monitor adequately.

In November 2004, a federal judge ruled that HLF, along with several others, as alleged supporters of Hamas, were liable for damages (around $600 million) as filed by the Boims, an American Israeli family whose son was killed in a terrorist attack in Israel in 1996. Now that one of the pending cases has been decided in favor of the plaintiff, the community's worst fears have been realized. Not only is their money not reaching the intended recipients, it is being diverted to individuals who actively oppose efforts to help vulnerable Muslim groups, especially among Palestinians. There is no doubt that the families of any victims of murder should be adequately compensated. However, the funds of law-abiding, unwitting donors should not be used for such purposes since they themselves are not part of the lawsuit.

Indeed, attorneys in these cases want even more. In November 2002, a friend and advisor to the Boims, attorney Nathan Lewin, testified before the Senate Judiciary Committee that the seized funds of the designated groups should be made available to the plaintiffs' attorneys in these types of cases if the groups are unsuccessful in their motion to dismiss. Similarly, the funds should go to the plaintiffs' attorneys if the plaintiffs prevail at the pretrial stage. He argues that the government should share secret evidence with the plaintiffs' (but not defendants') attorneys. Finally, he advocates specifically going after donors to charities named in these lawsuits.

While the Boim case goes to appeal, a victory on behalf of the plaintiffs would set a worrisome precedent, especially since the government, so far, has not shown how funds raised by HLF actually got into the hands of a terrorist individual or organization. Without such proof, similar cases can be filed against any organization that some day may be designated as "terrorist" under the vagueness of IEEPA and any subsequent statutes that could emerge in the wake of the Patriot Act.

Political Considerations

The cases against the Muslim charities are based on allegations related to activities that took place years before the current War on Terror began. Yet, the timing of their closure as well as that of high-profile arrests over the past three years clearly demonstrate a pattern on the part of the government designed to give the impression at regular intervals that they are making progress against terrorism, as if each case is a new development. It is true that the removal of the "wall" between law enforcement and intelligence (that is, to enable law enforcement to use surveillance information in criminal cases) and other provisions of the Patriot Act have facilitated the actions of the government post 9/11. It doesn't make sense to go after groups or individuals simultaneously if the timing itself can be used to the government's advantage. Also, several of the closures have coincided with the Muslim holy month of Ramadan, when giving is at its peak and therefore the government has the best chance to seize a larger amount of money. Of course, these considerations are denied by government officials, but the average observer cannot be faulted for drawing such conclusions.

Despite government allegations at the time of the terrorist designations of American Muslim charities, not a single court case has resulted in a conviction that is related to the events of 9/11 or to al-Qaeda. Nevertheless, during testimony on Capitol Hill, the Treasury Department repeatedly cites the cases of GRF, BIF and HLF as models of success in their efforts to disrupt terrorist financing. They refer to the loss of appeals by HLF as evidence that the courts uphold and defend the government's position, thus justifying their actions to date. At the same time, they consistently fail to acknowledge in their testimony that there are no terrorist convictions among these cases. At times, Treasury officials contradict the actual rulings in the cases. For example, in his testimony in March 2003, Juan Zarate stated that BIF was closed for ties to al-Qaeda. However, the indictment itself issued against Arnaout in October 2002 "contained almost no specific allegations that BIF funded al-Qaeda."

During the 1990s HLF was under surveillance by Israeli intelligence resulting in the closure of its offices and the arrests of employees in the West Bank and Gaza who were subjected to torture and forced confession. Ultimately, President Bush's decision to designate HLF upon the request of Ariel Sharon reinforced the perception that the assault on one of the major Muslim American charities was carried out as a favor to the government of Israel and not necessarily as a means of making Americans living in the U.S. safer. Since then, there is a growing perception among American Muslims that Muslim charities that continue to provide aid to Palestinians will be singled out and targeted for investigation and closure, not because of any wrongdoing, but simply because they assist Palestinians. The alleged link of IARA to Hamas and the fact that GRF was targeted months after beginning work in the Occupied Territories contribute to this perception. . . .

All of the Specially Designated Global Terrorists listed by the Treasury Department are Muslim. Despite the fact that numerous other groups provide assistance in high-risk areas throughout the Middle East, Africa and Asia, no non-Muslim charitable organization has been designated as a supporter of terrorism. In view of the fact that no terrorism convictions have resulted from the closures, it appears to many that Muslim groups are singled out because they are Muslim, first and foremost. And, since the government is not obliged to prove its case justifying a designation, mere suspicion of wrongdoing will suffice. The absence of terrorist convictions does not inhibit the government from claiming victory, as long as the "terrorist designations" are upheld in the courts, even if they are based on faulty evidence and lack of due process. As a result of the perceived inequities and injustices, Muslims feel they are singled out based on their religion and that other religious groups, such as Christian organizations, receive preferential treatment, further perpetuating the idea that the government is attacking Islam in general and seeking ways to open up the Muslim world to Christian missionaries. While there may not be any truth to such thinking, the perception in the community is real and has negative repercussions both here and abroad.

The Future

One positive consequence of the increased scrutiny of Muslim charitable organizations is a better understanding on their part of the need for transparency and accountability. In the past, Muslim groups did not publish annual reports, conduct audits or engage in the same kind of oversight that is commonplace among other charitable institutions. This was a result of inexperience as opposed to any devious intentions. But now there is a growing awareness of basic expectations, not only to protect an organization from attack by law enforcement, but mainly to provide assurances to donors that their money is being spent according to their wishes. In addition, this better serves the beneficiaries. In the end, Muslim groups know that being transparent and open might help in mounting an effective legal defense if they are ever targeted by the U.S. government, even though it won't guarantee anything.

Despite concerns about the constitutionality of the use of government "lists" of suspected terrorists, Muslim groups are using them to screen donors, employees and beneficiaries as they are now prone to being more conservative in their efforts to minimize any likelihood that they could be investigated or shut down. Yet the sense of uncertainty remains and is likely to increase in the near future. In addition, only a few new Muslim American humanitarian organizations have emerged since 9/11, meaning that, in this country, fewer than a dozen groups exist that provide assistance abroad on behalf of the American Muslim community.

Muslims are committed to following through with their religious obligations, but not if it means sacrificing their legal status in this country, losing their jobs or their hard-earned money, or becoming the subject of an FBI investigation. The government's efforts have had an effect that impacts the already small contribution of American Muslim giving internationally. Based on the evidence offered to the public to date, one can hardly conclude that the seizure of assets, intimidation of the community, and dwindling opportunities for Muslims to give to Muslim charities that work overseas has had any meaningful effect on the War on Terror.

In fact, these actions may actually make things worse. Muslims around the world pay attention to the treatment of their brethren here in the U.S. Others see how democracy works when American Muslims are able to engage in the full expression of their religious faith, including almsgiving. When American Muslims, through their own institutions, help provide humanitarian assistance to Muslims in need, they help convey a positive image of what it means to be American. While we may be winning by a show of force at this point, the long-term success of U.S. efforts to promote values of freedom, democracy and equality will be thwarted when we target the wrong groups at home simply because of political expediency.

The ever present threat of the "terrorist designation" issued by the Treasury Department functions based on the principle of "guilty until proven innocent." The use of secret evidence, hearsay, erroneous translations, guilt by association and press reports in recent court cases further erodes the ability of charities to rely on basic assumptions regarding their constitutional rights, especially when the courts ultimately favor the government when "national security" allegedly is at stake. Over-zealous surveillance tactics of the intelligence community such as wiretapping, infiltrating organizations by bribing employees to work as spies (thereby disrupting normal and lawful humanitarian activities), and engaging in other forms of harassment—when added to the above bleak picture—will not only chill, but will freeze completely American Muslim charitable giving overseas. Perhaps this is the goal of the U.S. government. However, no one should be fooled into thinking that America or the American people will be much safer as a result.

3. *United States of America v. Earnest James Ujaama* (2002)

Once given the keys to the city of Seattle, community activist Earnest James Ujaama (b. 1966) pled guilty in 2003 to a charge of conspiring to aid the Taliban government of Afghanistan. An African American convert to Islam, Ujaama became an entrepreneur and well-known community leader in Seattle. He penned three books, including the Young People's Guide to Starting a Business Without Selling Drugs. *He was also a harsh critic of U.S. foreign policy. When he was initially detained as a material witness in another prosecution, some said he was a political prisoner. Ujaama maintained his innocence. In exchange for his 2003 guilty plea, the government dropped the terrorism and gun charges against him. Ujaama admitted that he traveled to Afghanistan in 2000 to deliver money and computer equipment to Taliban officials—an act that was against the law. Ujaama also agreed to cooperate with U.S. officials in further investigations and prosecutions of terrorists. He was sentenced to two years in prison. Some critics said that the sentence was too light. The government defended the plea bargain on the grounds that Ujaama's cooperation would protect America against much larger threats. It might have been, as well, that the government's case against Ujaama was weak and that prosecutors feared an acquittal if the case had gone to trial. The original indictment reproduced below is a significant—and some would say sad—document in the history of Muslims in the United States. It is important to emphasize that the indictment outlines the charges against Ujaama—most of which were never proven in a court of law. Some readers may regard the original indictment as evidence of the threat posed by Islamic terror; for others, it may be proof that the government is using or abusing the war on terror to prosecute its larger foreign policy objectives and domestic agendas.*

United States District Court
Western District of Washington at Seattle

United States of America, Plaintiff v. Earnest James Ujaama, . . . Defendant
   The Grand Jury charges that:

COUNT ONE

(Conspiracy to Provide Material Support and Resources)

A. Introduction

1. As used in this Indictment, "Al Qaida" is the foreign terrorist organiza-
tion that was designated as such, effective October 8, 1999, pursuant to Sec-
tion 219 of the Immigration and Nationality Act, and is also known as "the
Base," the Islamic Army, the World Islamic Front for Jihad against Jews and
Crusaders, the Islamic Army for the Liberation of the Holy Places, the
Usama Bin Laden Network, the Usama Bin Laden Organization, the Is-
lamic Salvation Foundation, and the Group for the Preservation of the Holy
Sites.

2. As used in this Indictment, "jihad" is an Arabic word meaning "holy
war," in this context, the taking of actions against persons or governments that are deemed to be enemies of a fundamentalist version of Islam,
including destruction of property and loss of life.

3. As used in this Indictment, "bayaat" is an Arabic word meaning an
"oath of loyalty" that one person pledges to another.

4. During the times relevant in this Indictment, unindicted coconspirator #1 resided in London, England.

5. During various times relevant in this Indictment, Earnest James
Ujaama, (hereinafter, "Ujaama"), whose birth name was James Earnest
Thompson, and who also has used and adopted the names Bilal Ahmed,
Abu Samayya, and Abdul Qaadir, visited and resided in London, England;
and visited and resided in Seattle, Washington.

B. Object of the Conspiracy

6. Beginning at a time uncertain, but no later than the fall of 1999
and continuing through the present, in the Western District of Wash-

ington and elsewhere, Earnest James Ujaama . . . did knowingly conspire, combine, confederate, and agree together with other persons known and unknown to the Grand Jury, within the jurisdiction of the United States, to

(a) provide material support and resources, that is, training, facilities, computer services, safehouses, and personnel, to Al Qaida, a designated foreign terrorist organization, in violation of Title 18, United States Code, Section 2339B; and

(b) provide material support and resources, that is, training, facilities, computer services, safehouses, and personnel, knowing and intending that they were to be used in preparation for and in carrying out a conspiracy to destroy property and murder and maim persons located outside the United States, in violation of Title 18, United States Code, Sections 2339A and 956.

C. Purpose of the Conspiracy

7. The purpose of the conspiracy was to offer and provide facilities in the United States of America for training of persons interested in violent jihad; to provide safehouses in the United States of America for the conspirators; to recruit persons interested in violent jihad and jihad training; to provide actual training of such persons in firearms, military and guerilla tactics, and related activities; and to sponsor partially trained personnel for further violent jihad training and operations coordinated by Al Qaida, in order to assist such persons and groups to promote violent jihad activities around the world.

D. Manner and Means of Conspiracy

8. It was a part of the conspiracy that Ujaama pledged and maintained bayaat to unindicted coconspirator #1.

9. It was further a part of the conspiracy that Ujaama expounded and advocated the statements, writings, and beliefs of unindicted coconspirator #1 concerning the need to engage in violent jihad through armed acts of aggression against Western governments and other governments not adhering to fundamentalist Islamic principles as interpreted by unindicted coconspirator #1, in an effort to persuade persons to meet unindicted coconspirator #1, to recruit persons to pledge bayaat

to unindicted coconspirator #1, and to assist in conducting global violent jihad.

10. It was further a part of the conspiracy that Ujaama, unindicted coconspirator #1, unindicted coconspirator #2, unindicted coconspirator #3, and other persons planned to arrange and conduct training in firearms, military and guerilla tactics, and related activities in the United States of America for persons desiring to engage in global violent jihad.

11. It was further a part of the conspiracy that the conspirators searched for and identified one or more potential sites in the United States to conduct such training.

12. It was further a part of the conspiracy that Ujaama established one or more World Wide Web sites for unindicted coconspirator #1, through which unindicted coconspirator #1 espoused his beliefs concerning the need to conduct global violent jihad against the United States of America and other Western nations.

13. It was further a part of the conspiracy that the conspirators planned to provide training in the United States of America to persons desiring to engage in violent jihad so that such persons would be bona fide candidates for further violent jihad training in training camps operated by Al Qaida abroad, including in Afghanistan.

14. It was further a part of the conspiracy that unindicted coconspirator #1 would and could provide requisite letters of introduction or sponsorship for such persons for entry into Al Qaida training camps.

E. Overt Acts

15. In furtherance of the conspiracy, the following overt acts were committed within the Western District of Washington and elsewhere by one or more conspirators:

a. During the Fall of 1999, and at other times throughout the conspiracy period, Ujaama advised others that he was sponsored by unindicted coconspirator #1 and had attended violent jihad training camps, which were operated by Al Qaida.

b. In or about early October 1999, Ujaama and other persons, known and unknown to the Grand Jury, traveled from the Seattle, Washington, metropolitan area to a parcel of property in Bly, Oregon, where Ujaama and other persons engaged in firearms practice.

c. During October 1999 and November 1999, at Bly, Oregon, and at Seattle, Washington, Ujaama led discussions with other coconspirators concerning the need for further training in order to be able to attend violent jihad training camps in Afghanistan, the commission of armed robberies, the building of underground bunkers to hide ammunition and weapons, the creation of poisonous materials for public consumption, and the firebombing of vehicles.

d. In or about October 1999, after visiting the property in Bly, Oregon, Ujaama proposed to unindicted coconspirator #1 the establishment of a jihad training camp on the Bly property by faxing a proposal from a commercial copy center to unindicted coconspirator #1, which fax, among other things:

i. compared the terrain of the Bly property to that in Afghanistan;

ii. stated the Bly property could store and conceal guns, bunkers, and ammunition; and

iii. invited unindicted coconspirator #1 to stay at the Bly property as a safehouse.

e. On or about November 26, 1999, unindicted coconspirators #2 and #3, as emissaries of unindicted coconspirator #1, arrived in New York, New York, on an Air India flight, and then traveled to Bly, Oregon, via Seattle, Washington, for the purpose of evaluating the Bly property as a jihad training camp.

f. In or about late November 1999 and December 1999, unindicted coconspirators #2 and #3 inspected the proposed jihad training camp at the Bly property, they met potential candidates for jihad training, they established security for the Bly property through the use of guard patrols and passwords, and they and others participated in firearms training and viewed a video recording on the subject of improvised poisons.

g. While at the Bly property, unindicted coconspirator #2 identified himself as a "hit man" for Usama Bin Laden.

h. In or about December 1999 or January 2000, Ujaama returned to London, England, where he worked for unindicted coconspirator #1.

i. In or about February 2000, unindicted coconspirators #2 and #3 resided in Seattle, Washington, where they expounded the writings and teachings of unindicted coconspirator #1, and where unindicted conspirator #2 provided urban tactical training.

j. Beginning in or about 2000, and continuing through 2001, Ujaama, using the name Abu Samayya, designed and otherwise participated in the operation of the Supporters of Shariah (SOS) website, which unindicted coconspirator #1 used throughout this time period to advocate violent jihad against the United States of America and other Western nations.

k. During May 2002 and June 2002, unindicted coconspirator #2, the self-described "hit man" for Bin Laden, contacted a cooperating witness and discussed the government investigation and whether he should travel to Seattle to assess the situation.

l. During May 2002 and June 2002, Ujaama contacted a cooperating witness in an attempt to determine whether another individual who participated in the activities at Bly was cooperating with the government's investigation. Ujaama told the cooperating witness that he would discuss the matter with others.

All in violation of Title 18, United States Code, Sections 2339B, 2339A, and 956(a)(1) and (b).

COUNT TWO

(Using, Carrying, Possessing, and Discharging Firearms During a Crime of Violence)

1. The Grand Jury realleges and incorporates by reference paragraphs 1 through 15 of Count 1 of this Indictment.
2. During the fall of 1999, within the Western District of Washington and elsewhere, Earnest James Ujaama did knowingly use, carry, possess, and discharge firearms, during, in relation to, and in furtherance of a crime of violence for which he may be prosecuted in a court of the United States, namely, Conspiracy to Provide Material Support and Resources, as charged in Count 1 of this Indictment.

All in violation of Title 18, United States Code, Sections 924(c)(1)(A)(iii) and 2. . . .

> John McKay, United States Attorney
> Andrew H. Hamilton, Assistant United States Attorney
> Floyd G. Short, Assistant United States Attorney
> Todd L. Greenberg, Assistant United States Attorney

4. Fiqh Council of North America,
"Fatwa Against Terrorism" (2005)

After 9/11, the position of most national and international Muslim reli-
gious leaders was unambiguous. They condemned, in the clearest terms
possible, al-Qa'ida's attacks on 9/11 as un-Islamic acts. But for various rea-
sons, many non-Muslims in the United States did not receive that message,
and in the years after 9/11, American Muslims continued to reassure non-
Muslim Americans that they repudiated Usama bin Ladin and terrorism
more generally. In 2005, the Fiqh Council of North America, a body of reli-
gious scholars who are trained in Islamic law and ethics, issued a fatwa, an
authoritative interpretation of Islamic law and ethics, condemning terror-
ism. Quoting the Qur'an and the hadith, the Council denied that terrorists
were martyrs and required Muslims to cooperate with authorities in help-
ing to find and arrest any would-be terrorists. Though not every fatwa is-
sued by the Fiqh Council is universally recognized as legitimate or binding
by American Muslims, this particular ruling almost was. Every major
American Muslim organization joined to express its support of the state-
ment as did over three hundred mosques and local Islamic centers across
the United States.

In the Name of God, the Compassionate, the Merciful.

The Fiqh Council of North America wishes to reaffirm Islam's absolute condemnation of terrorism and religious extremism.

Islam strictly condemns religious extremism and the use of violence against innocent lives.

There is no justification in Islam for extremism or terrorism. Targeting civilians' life and property through suicide bombings or any other method of attack is *haram*—or forbidden—and those who commit these barbaric acts are criminals, not "martyrs."

The Qur'an, Islam's revealed text, states: "Whoever kills a person [unjustly] . . . it is as though he has killed all mankind. And whoever saves a life, it is as though he had saved all mankind" (5:32).

Prophet Muhammad said there is no excuse for committing unjust acts: "Do not be people without minds of your own, saying that if others treat you well you will treat them well, and that if they do wrong you will do wrong to them. Instead, accustom yourselves to do good if people do good and not to do wrong (even) if they do evil" (Al-Tirmidhi).

God mandates moderation in faith and in all aspects of life when He states in the Qur'an: "We made you to be a community of the middle way, so that (with the example of your lives) you might bear witness to the truth before all mankind" (2:143).

In another verse, God explains our duties as human beings when He says: "Let there arise from among you a band of people who invite to righteousness, and enjoin good and forbid evil" (3:104).

Islam teaches us to act in a caring manner to all of God's creation. The Prophet Muhammad, who is described in the Qur'an as "a mercy to the worlds" said: "All creation is the family of God, and the person most beloved by God (is the one) who is kind and caring toward His family."

In the light of the teachings of the Qur'an and Sunna we clearly and strongly state:

1. All acts of terrorism targeting civilians are *haram* (forbidden) in Islam.
2. It is *haram* for a Muslim to cooperate with any individual or group that is involved in any act of terrorism or violence.
3. It is the civic and religious duty of Muslims to cooperate with law enforcement authorities to protect the lives of all civilians.

We issue this fatwa following the guidance of our scripture, the Qur'an, and the teachings of our Prophet Muhammad—peace be upon him. We urge all people to resolve all conflicts in just and peaceful manners.

We pray for the defeat of extremism and terrorism. We pray for the safety and security of our country, the United States, and its people. We pray for the safety and security of all inhabitants of our planet. We pray that interfaith harmony and cooperation prevail both in the United States and all around the globe.

Members of the Fiqh Council of North America

Dr. Muzammil H. Siddiqi, Chairman
Dr. Deina Abdulkadir
Shaikh Muhammad Nur Abdallah
Dr. Taha Jabir Alalwani
Shaikh Muhammad Al-Hanooti

Shaikhah Zainab Alwani
Dr. Jamal Badawi
Dr. Ihsan Bagby
Dr. Nazih Hammad
Shaikh Yahya Hindi
Dr. Abdul Hakim Jackson
Dr. Mukhtar Maghraoui
Dr. Akbar Muhammad
Shaikh Hassan Qazwini
Dr. Zulfiqar Ali Shah
Dr. Muhammad Adam Sheikh
Dr. Ahmad Shleibak
Dr. Salah Soltan

Endorsed by the Following National Organizations:

Council on American-Islamic Relations (CAIR)
Islamic Society of North America (ISNA)
Muslim American Society (MAS)
Muslim Public Affairs Council (MPAC)
Islamic Circle of North America (ICNA)
Mosque Cares, Imam W. D. Muhammad
Muslim Student Association of the U.S. & Canada (MSA)
Association of Muslim Social Scientists
American Federation of Muslims of Indian Origin
American Muslim Alliance
Association of Muslim Scientists and Engineers
Canadian Council on American-Islamic Relations
Council of Shia Muslim Scholars of North America
Islamic Networks Group & Affiliates
Islamic Resource Group
Islamic Schools League of America
Islamic Sharia Advisory Institute of North America
Kashmiri American Council
Latino American Dawah Organization
Minaret of Freedom Institute

Muslim Ummah of North America
Project Islamic HOPE
United Muslims of America
USA Halal Chamber of Commerce, Inc. & The Islamic
    Center for Halal Certification

5. Omid Safi, "Being Muslim, Being American After 9/11," in *Taking Back Islam: American Muslims Reclaim Their Faith* (2002)

Omid Safi (b. 1970) is an Iranian American. An expert in the social and intellectual history of Islam, he is the translator of Islamic texts and author of several articles and books about premodern Muslim mystics. He has held professorships at Colgate University and the University of North Carolina at Chapel Hill. Safi is also a public intellectual who has given over four hundred lectures and interviews about everything from U.S. foreign policy in the Muslim world to Sufi music. He is a founding figure of the North American progressive Islam movement, which is simultaneously critical of the U.S. government and Muslim extremism. In the article below, Safi calls on Muslims to reject intolerance in their communities, and he asks Americans to insist on a more just foreign policy toward Muslim-majority countries. In doing so, he combines the ideals of his faith with his commitments as an American patriot.

Terror, terror, terror. Terrorist, terrorist, terrorist. War on terror. War on terrorism. This barrage of phrases comes at us with mind-numbing frequency. Russia, Israel, and China have now hijacked the language of "war on terrorism" to combat their own oppressed citizens and neighbors.

Beyond its undeniable emotional appeal in light of September 11, the war on terrorism remains ill defined. What are its aims, apart from the vague promise to "root out terrorists"? Who determines what groups constitute terrorists, beyond those responsible directly for the crimes against humanity of September 11? How will it move from a unilateral United States show of force to a truly global quest for justice? When, if ever, will this war on terrorism end?

In the post–September 11 era, the space for public dissent and discussion of this "war on terrorism" continues to shrink. The minute one stands up to question its logic, its target, its victims, its methods, one is accused of treason: "You are being unpatriotic." Yet it is critical for American Muslims to insist on precisely such a space. For us, it is a "space in the middle" because it means critiquing both U.S. foreign policy and the actions of some groups marked by Muslim identity, such as al-Qaeda.

We speak for the dignity of human life, all human life, no matter what race, religion, or nationality. We speak for the inalienable right of all of God's children to live in peace and security. We criticize both the hideous actions committed by Muslim extremists and the hypocrisy of our own American government in putting profit before freedom, foreign policy interests before human rights.

This "space in the middle" is not a popular or easy place to be. Many Muslims will not be pleased to hear my criticism of some Muslim communities. Some may even go so far as to accuse progressive Muslims of having "sold out." Some non-Muslim Americans will object to my criticism of United States foreign and domestic policy. Many will see this as being unpatriotic in a time that the nation still needs healing and unity.

Since September 11, I have been told repeatedly, "We must stand by our president." I politely, firmly, passionately, and compassionately disagree. I love my children very much, much more than I love our president, and yet I criticize some of their actions. I criticize them not because I wish to abandon them, but precisely because I love them.

I see a difference between nationalism and patriotism. If nationalism implies that I somehow identify more with the citizens inside a national border than with those outside of it, I will not abide by this "ism." My identification is with all of God's children, the American and the Russian, the South African and the Indian, the Israeli and the Iranian, the Palestinian and the Chinese. As complicated as identities are, I aim to identify with the "children of Adam" (Bani Adam), as the Qur'an calls the universal community of humanity. Patriotism, on the other hand, is different. To me, patriotism is about upholding the ideals upon which this great nation was founded, even if those ideals have not always been perfectly adhered to. I write this essay as an American Muslim, committed to pursuing social justice and peace for all of God's creatures. I write this as a patriotic American Muslim who calls on both Muslims and Americans to strive for the highest ideals of our traditions, while adopting self-critical perspectives. I call on us to rise up and be counted.

A Plea to Muslims

Let me start with my Muslim brothers and sisters. It has been difficult to be a Muslim in America since September 11, with the constant bombardment of images about "terrorists" and "suicide bombers" associated with us. Yet, I call on my Muslim friends—whom I love so dearly—to rise above this and take responsibility for ourselves and for our communities.

Far too long, we have sat silently—I have sat silently—when someone gets up in our Islamic centers, our mosques, and vents poison. How many foaming-at-the-mouth, hate-filled speeches about "the Jews" and the "corruption of women" and the immorality of "the West" have I heard in our sacred spaces? Enough is enough. No more shall we divert attention from abusive situations, class warfare, and institutional injustice by directing our wrath at various other enemies. It is time for Muslims to be true to our destiny, bringing justice, peace, and compassion to that one race to which we all belong: humanity.

I am tired of being always spoken for, but never speaking. I am tired of hearing people like Osama bin Laden telling us that being Muslim means killing Americans, and I am tired of President Bush telling us that Islam is peace. While the second is more pleasing to my ears, I know—I suspect all honest Americans know—that Muslims have their saintly souls and their zealots, just as every other tradition. I will not settle for the simplicity of either perspective but push ahead for something more complex and real, something that approaches the subtlety and complexity of the lives of more than one billion Muslims.

I am tired of turning on CNN and MSNBC (and, worse, Fox "News") and seeing every quack and charlatan all of a sudden becoming an "expert." I am tired of seeing policy makers who pontificate on affairs that have life-and-death consequences for the citizens of these regions, yet they have never stopped to look into the eyes of the human beings whose lives they are impacting. I am tired of hearing the disciples of Samuel Huntington and his vile "Clash of Civilization" theory fill posts in the State Department and attempt to turn Islam into the new anathema after the fall of Communism. I am tired of seeing book after book of the historian Bernard Lewis, repeating his rant that dismisses all Arab encounters with modernity as failed and weak. I am tired of all this nonsense.

I want to hear 1,001 Muslim voices, agreeing, arguing, covering every point on the spectrum. I want us to figure out what Islam is, what it can be. To speak is to have power; to be silent is deadly. I do not expect all of us to agree on everything, but I do expect us to talk intelligently and compassionately, and to listen, and to be heard.

A Plea to Americans

Let me now address my fellow American citizens. I have less and less faith in a political system that seems to have been hijacked by an assortment of special interest groups. I do have faith, however, in the basic decency of most Americans. I call on Americans to demand that our government lives up to the great ideals upon which it was founded. Our nation has strived for freedom and human rights. We have at times fallen short of these ideals, with the horror of slavery, the treatment of Native Americans, among other sins. At other times, we have nobly dared to dream the loftiest, particularly with our humanitarian work after World War II and during the Civil Rights Movement. Yet most Americans are unaware of the way our government's foreign policy has so frequently departed from the pursuit of the very ideals that our nation is built upon. Far too often, we have put the pursuit of the dollar before the pursuit of dignity. While this hypocrisy—let's call it what it is—has been the case in so many regions of the world, it has particularly characterized our interaction with the Muslim world.

Yes, it is true that no other nation has committed so much to humanitarian causes. Yes, it is true that American soldiers time and again stand up as peacekeeping forces in many regions. It is also true, sadly, that our own government time and again has supported corrupt tyrannical dictators in many parts of the world. One can point to many examples in the Muslim world. For example, in 1953, the CIA sponsored a coup in Iran to remove the democratically elected prime minister, Mohammed Mossadegh. What was his crime? He wanted to claim Iranian oil for Iranians. So our own government tramples over the principles of democracy in order to once again make a buck in oil. In place of Mossadegh, the United States reestablished the monarchical rule of Shah of Iran, who ruled as a dictator. Is this what a democratic nation like the United States should be supporting?

And this is not an isolated case. In the beginning stages of the "War on Terrorism," our government secured the support of Pervez Musharraf, the military dictator who took over Pakistan in a coup. In order to secure his compliance, we promised Pakistan billions of dollars in military aid. Is this what a democracy like the United States should be doing? Is this wisdom, arming both the Pakistanis and the Indians with billions of dollars of military equipment when twice in the past few years they have gone to the verge of nuclear war? Why is it unpatriotic of me to ask my government to apply the standards of democracy, freedom, and human rights in its dealing with foreign countries?

The hypocrisy of U.S. foreign policy goes on and on. Since the 1930s, the government that I pay my taxes to has supported the Saudi Arabian monarchy, the same regime that uses its petro-dollars to export its brand of Wahhabi Islam around the world. This is the same Wahhabism that is a literalist, extremist interpretation that has attempted to exile all soul and spirit from Islam. The same Wahhabism that is responsible for the oppression of so many of my Muslim sisters. Why on Earth would our own government be supporting the Wahhabis and their regime? One word: oil. Saudi Arabia is the third-largest producer of oil consumed in the United States, and so long as there is a drop of cheap oil under the sands of Saudi Arabia, our government will turn a blind eye to the human rights violations in Saudi Arabia and in other countries that import Wahhabi ideology. As long as the financial interests of the United States oil companies count for more than justice and human dignity, we will hypocritically support the Saudis.

Let's be more specific. We engaged in a massive bombardment of Afghanistan, an already poor country utterly devastated by our assault. We used the most powerful types of nonnuclear bombs. In doing so, we killed thousands of innocent Afghani civilians who had nothing to do with September 11, nor did they have anything to do with harboring terrorist groups like al-Qaeda. In attacking the Taliban, we have pointed out how they have imposed the worst type of gender segregation on its citizens and made life a living hell for Afghani women and children when they were in power. But here is my point: If we object to the Taliban's inhumane version of Islam, why do we not object to the root source of the Taliban's interpretation of Islam? Taliban ideology is nothing but Saudi Wahhabism, mixed in with Pakistani Secret Police and a dash of CIA military training. Why do we blast the bastard child of Wahhabism to the

Stone Age while continuing to turn a blind eye to the source of fanaticism, the Wahhabis in Saudi Arabia? Again, one word: oil.

Reclaiming Islam

We American Muslims want our faith back, as a spiritually powerful means of transforming ourselves and our world. We want our democracy and our civil rights back. In the months after September 11, perhaps one thousand Arabs and Muslims were detained without being formally charged with crimes. And then there is the racial profiling of Arab-American communities in Michigan and elsewhere, so benignly called voluntary interviews by the FBI. Is this how we treat other religious and ethnic minorities? After Michael Bray attacked abortion clinics, did we round up all evangelical Christians who follow the Army of God movement? When Timothy McVeigh blew up the federal building in Oklahoma City, did we round up all members of the Christian Identity movement? Or is it somehow more acceptable to do this to American citizens who are Muslim because they are not "really American"?

I will not sit silently and accept the absurd detention of Afghani prisoners in Guantánamo Bay in Cuba. Surely there are some real terrorists among them, some al-Qaeda soldiers who must be brought to justice. The international community has a legal process for this: the International War Tribunals at The Hague. Why do a mass of Arab and Afghani suspects continue to be held without representation in Cuba? Among the hundreds held there are many Afghani tribesmen who were caught up in political games more complicated than they realized but who in no way, shape, or form supported the atrocious terrorist actions of September 11. Why are they not classified as "prisoners of war"? And if they are prisoners of war, they must be entitled to Geneva Convention rights. Yes, I realize the irony of insisting on civil rights even for those who set out to destroy the symbols of American life. But I will not accept trampling over internationally agreed-upon rights in order to save those very rights. The ends do not justify the means.

Time and again I have heard people argue that "these are desperate times, and they call for desperate measures." The absurd and painful truth about the above is that I have never seen a person say, "These are desperate times, so please take away my civil rights. Please come and search my home. Please hold me for month after month without charging me with a crime. Please single me out in airport security." Of course not. They mean that it is okay to take away Arab or Muslim civil rights.

Staying Put in the U.S.

From time to time, I hear from people who say, "If you disagree with U.S. foreign policy, get the hell out." I am not leaving. I was born here, and my children were born here. I love the promise of America, the goal of what it can be, too much to leave it. I hold this as the responsibility of a patriotic citizen. I am a social critic not because I hate America but because I am committed to seeing us live up to our lofty ideals. I will abandon neither my faith nor my commitment to the patriotic ideals of America.

My parents migrated to America not because they were ashamed of their own homeland of Iran and not even because they were looking for financial reward. Our family has deep roots in Iran that go back centuries, and we were quite well-off there. We moved to this country because of the promise of freedom and human rights. My family still believes that this is one country where human beings are born with the possibility of pursuing human dignity without oppressive and draconian measures imposed by the government.

I will work with my fellow progressive Muslim brothers and sisters to reform Islam in this complicated world. Let us as progressive Americans also insist on an America that we can be proud of. We will insist on this "space in the middle," from which we can find inspiration in the highest ideals of Islam and America while painfully and honestly offering our critique when we act contrary to those ideals. The Qur'an calls the community of Muslims "a spiritual community of the middle, to be witnesses for humanity" (2:143). Today, during the "war on terrorism," being a Muslim of the "middle community" means being a witness, calling both Muslims and Americans to the highest good of which we are capable.

Caught in the middle we are, alone and frightened, but silent we will not be. Let us speak with conviction and compassion, concern and courage, and pray that other like-hearted progressive souls will join this middle community.

6. "Yaphett El-Amin for [Missouri] Senate District 4" (2006)

While some speak theoretically about Muslim involvement in American politics, Yaphett El-Amin has been doing it. The daughter of St. Louis Argus publisher Eddie Hasan, El-Amin (b. 1971) was first elected to the Missouri State House in 2001. Offering support at her swearing-in ceremony in Jefferson City, the Missouri capital, were Muhammad Nur Abdullah, the former Sudanese American president of the Islamic Society of North America and a past leader of a large suburban mosque in St. Louis; Nation of Islam minister Donald Muhammad; and Imam Samuel Ansari, head of a Sunni African American mosque in St. Louis that follows the teachings of Imam W. D. Mohammed. El-Amin attended the University of Arkansas at Pine Bluff, where she received a BS in political science in 1994. In 1997, she became a Democratic committeewoman and eventually secured the nomination for a seat in the Missouri House. In 2006, she launched a bid for the State Senate and came in second in the Democratic Party primary. Some of her State Senate campaign literature, reproduced below, indicates how one American Muslim politician sounds a lot like other American politicians. Though El-Amin lost her primary election for the Missouri Senate, her husband, Talibdin El-Amin, won the Democratic nomination to replace his wife in the Missouri House, and in an adjoining district, Jamilah Nasheed, another African American Muslim woman, won a four-way race for the party's nomination to represent District 60. In North St. Louis, a predominately African American section of the Gateway City, African American Muslim politicians are making their mark on American political history.

Representative Yaphett El-Amin has devoted her life to public service and the people of North St. Louis. Born and bred in the community she now represents, Rep. El-Amin understands the concerns of her constituents and fights hard everyday to build a stronger, safer, more promising future for the people of Missouri.

Throughout Rep. El-Amin's life, she has developed a special understanding of the people she now represents in the State House. They have been her friends, neighbors, students, teachers, employers and employees.

She has served her community as an activist, youth counselor, teacher, and a two term state representative. Now she's taking the fight to the State

Senate, because a strong community deserves a strong voice in Jefferson City.

Becoming the first person in her family to graduate college was a life-changing experience for Yaphett, and upon graduation she returned to the neighborhood to counsel troubled children for the state Department of Youth Services. As a youth specialist, Yaphett taught math classes and served as a guidance counselor, helping kids to get back on the right path.

Working to improve her community awakened a sense of leadership and civic duty in Yaphett that propelled her into a life of public service. In 2001, voters chose Yaphett to represent the 57th district in the Missouri State House. She was elected unopposed to a second term in 2003. Yaphett has been an energetic legislator and a tireless advocate for her constituents, serving on the Job Creation and Economic Development Committee, the Appropriations Committee, the Special Committee on Education Funding, and the Medicaid Reform Commission.

She worked with the Missouri Attorney General to ensure the fair allocation of state contracts through the Minority and Women owned business program, which generated over $900 million worth of contracts for women & minority-owned businesses. And she successfully advocated for local workers to build Highway 70 & Highway 40, securing an additional $2.5 million in job training funds for low income and minority workers.

Through her experiences, Yaphett has developed a deep commitment to education. Working with troubled teens taught her that improving public education must always be government's number one priority. Keeping kids in school is the first step, which is why she introduced and passed an innovative truancy bill in the State House that aims at putting students back into the classroom.

But she's not stopping there. Yaphett knows there is a direct relationship between education and economic success, and she has fought tirelessly to secure more funding for school repair, teacher pay raises, and reentry programs. Public education is the key to a greater Missouri, and it will always be Yaphett El-Amin's number one priority in the State Senate.

Yaphett and her husband Talibdin have two children, Hasan, 5, and Ruqaiyah, 18 months. She serves on the board of directors for Universal Services Federation, a nonprofit philanthropic organization. Rep. El-Amin works with various civic and community organizations, advocating for issues impacting seniors, children, and the working poor. Rep. El-Amin received a lifetime achievement award from the St. Louis Teachers and

School Related Personnel Union Local 420, in recognition of exceptional leadership and dedication in support of public education, labor and working families. She also received "A Heart for Children" award from Support-A-Child International in recognition of her efforts to bring about positive change to at-risk youth and children.

Education

"Education has always been my top priority. I believe our schools can compete and succeed. That's why I've spent the last four years working hard to see that our children and our educators get the resources they deserve."

When Representative El-Amin says education is her first priority, she means it. Her career in the State House has been marked by big ideas backed up by hard work in the service of Missouri's children. She has sponsored and passed numerous education bills that take an innovative approach to help more students get the tools they need to succeed.

Seniors

"Seniors have spent a lifetime making sacrifices for their communities. I'll make sure Missouri government is responsive to the unique challenges that seniors face, and I'll never burden seniors by cutting their health insurance or taking away their right to vote."

Rep. El-Amin believes that seniors should be treated with kindness and respect. She secured funding for a home-repair program, helping seniors care for their homes and live with dignity.

Medicare

"Healthcare is a fundamental human right. I'll stand up for affordable and accessible health insurance for every Missourian."

Rep. El-Amin thinks everyone has a right to basic healthcare. That's why she has fought tirelessly to restore the Republican cuts to Medicaid funding for nearly 100,000 poor, elderly, and disabled Missourians.

Small Business

"I believe that small businesses, not big corporations, are the anchors of our community."

Rep. El-Amin has worked with the Attorney General to ensure the fair allocation of state contracts. As a result, over $900 million worth of contracts went to women and minority-owned businesses.

Economic Opportunity

"A strong economy creates a strong community. Working families and small businesses are the heart of our economy, and I've spent the last four years creating nearly 50,000 new jobs for Missourians on the Job Creation and Economic Development Committee."

Rep. El-Amin has always been an advocate for employment opportunity and workers' rights. She successfully advocated for local workers to build Highway 40 & Highway 70, and brought an additional 2.5 million dollars in job training funds for low income and minority workers.

7. Khaled Abou El Fadl, "Islam and the Challenge of Democracy" (2003)

Since the beginning of the modern era, Muslims committed to Islamic reform and renewal have argued that Islam and democracy are fully compatible, or even better, that democracy is the best means to achieve the ideals of the Qur'an and the Sunna of the Prophet. Some Muslims, particularly in the era of decolonization, rejected that view, trying to discredit it as a "Westernization" of traditional Islam. Many argued that Islam was a total way of life and that society should be governed by the divine law and ethics, called shari'a. In this rebuttal, American Muslim scholar Khaled Abou El Fadl (b. 1963) counters that any law, even one said to be based on the Qur'an and the Sunna, is only ever an attempt to understand the divine will. The making and prosecution of law is an inevitably human and thus imperfect process. Democracy, Abou El Fadl asserts, provides the most Islamic means for the making of just laws in human societies. Abou El Fadl, the Omar and Azmeralda Alfi professor of Islamic law at the University of California–Los Angeles,

was educated in Egypt, Kuwait, and the United States. He holds a J.D. from
the University of Pennsylvania and a Ph.D. from Princeton University.

Although Muslim jurists debated political systems, the Qur'an itself did
not specify a particular form of government. But it did identify a set of social and political values that are central to a Muslim polity. Three values
are of particular importance: pursuing justice through social cooperation
and mutual assistance (49:13, 11:119); establishing a non-autocratic, con-
sultative method of governance; and institutionalizing mercy and compassion in social interactions (6:12, 54; 21:107, 27:77, 29:51, 45:20). So, all
else being equal, Muslims today ought to endorse the form of government
that is most effective in helping them promote these values.

The Case for Democracy

Several considerations suggest that democracy—and especially a constitutional democracy that protects basic individual rights—is that form.
My central argument . . . is that democracy—by assigning equal rights of
speech, association, and suffrage to all—offers the greatest potential for
promoting justice and protecting human dignity, without making God
responsible for injustice or the degradation of human beings. A fundamental Qur'anic idea is that God vested all of humanity with a kind of divinity by making every person the viceroy of God on this earth:
"Remember, when your Lord said to the angels: 'I have to place a vicegerent on earth,' they said: 'Will you place one there who will create disorder and shed blood, while we intone Your litanies and sanctify Your
name?' And God said: 'I know what you do not know'" (2:30). In particular, human beings, as God's vicegerents, are responsible for making the
world more just. By assigning equal political rights to all adults, democracy expresses that special status of human beings in God's creation and
enables them to discharge that responsibility.

Of course, God's vicegerent does not share God's perfection of judgment and will. A constitutional democracy, then, acknowledges the errors
of judgment, temptations, and vices associated with human fallibility by
enshrining some basic moral standards in a constitutional document—
moral standards that express the dignity of individuals. To be sure, democracy does not ensure justice. But it does establish a basis for pursuing

justice and thus for fulfilling a fundamental responsibility assigned by God to each one of us.

In a representative democracy some individuals have greater authority than others. But a democratic system makes those authorities accountable to all and thus resists the tendency of the powerful to render themselves immune from judgment. This requirement of accountability is consistent with the imperative of justice in Islam. If a political system has no institutional mechanisms to call the unjust to account, then the system itself is unjust, regardless of whether injustice has actually been committed. If criminal law does not assign punishment for rape, then it is unjust, quite apart from whether that crime was ever committed. It is a moral good in and of itself that a democracy, through the institutions of the vote, the separation and division of power, and the guarantee of pluralism at least offers the possibility of redress.

We have a provisional case for democracy, then, founded on a fundamental Islamic idea about the special status of human beings in God's creation. It is provisional because we have not yet considered the great challenge to that case: how can the higher law of *shari'a* [the body of Islamic law and ethics], founded on God's sovereignty, be reconciled with the democratic idea that the people, as the sovereign, can be free to flout *shari'a* law?

God as the Sovereign

Early in Islamic history the issue of God's political dominion (*hakimiyyat Allah*) was raised by a group known as the Haruriyya (later known as the Khawarij) when they rebelled against the fourth Rightly Guided Caliph 'Ali Ibn Abi Talib. Initially the supporters of 'Ali, the Haruriyya turned against him when he agreed to arbitrate his political dispute with a competing political faction, which was led by a man named Mu'awiya.

'Ali himself had agreed to the arbitration on the condition that the arbitrators be bound by the Qur'an and give full consideration to the supremacy of the *shari'a*. But the Khawarij—pious, puritanical, and fanatical—believed that God's law clearly supported 'Ali. So they rejected arbitration as inherently unlawful and, in effect, a challenge to God's sovereignty. According to the Khawarij, 'Ali's behavior showed that he was willing to compromise God's supremacy by transferring decision making to human agency. They declared 'Ali a traitor to God, and after efforts to reach a peaceful resolution failed, they assassinated him. After 'Ali's death, Mu'awiya seized power and established himself as the first caliph of the Umayyad Dynasty.

Anecdotal reports about the debates between 'Ali and the Khawarij reflect unmistakable tension about the meaning of legality and the implications of the rule of law. In one such report members of the Khawarij accused 'Ali of accepting the judgment and dominion (*hakimiyya*) of human beings instead of abiding by the dominion of God's law. Upon hearing of this accusation, 'Ali called on the people to gather around him and brought out a large copy of the Qur'an. 'Ali touched the Qur'an while instructing it to speak to the people who had gathered around 'Ali. Surprised, the people gathered around 'Ali exclaimed, "What are you doing? The Qur'an cannot speak, for it is not a human being!" Upon hearing this, 'Ali exclaimed that this was exactly his point. The Qur'an, 'Ali explained, is but ink and paper, and it does not speak for itself. Instead, it is human beings who give effect to it according to their limited personal judgments and opinions.

Such stories are subject to multiple interpretations, but this one points most importantly to the dogmatic superficiality of proclamations of God's sovereignty that sanctify human determinations. Notably, the Khawarij's rallying cry of "Dominion belongs to God" or "The Qur'an is the judge" (*la hukma illa li'llah* or *al-hukmu li'l-Qur'an*) is nearly identical to the slogans invoked by contemporary fundamentalist groups. But considering the historical context, the Khawarij's sloganeering was initially a call for the symbolism of legality and the supremacy of law that later descended into an unequivocal radicalized demand for fixed lines of demarcation between what is lawful and unlawful.

To a believer, God is all-powerful and the ultimate owner of the heavens and earth. But when it comes to the laws in a political system, arguments claiming that God is the sole legislator endorse a fatal fiction that is indefensible from the point of view of Islamic theology. Such arguments pretend that some human agents have perfect access to God's will, and that human beings could become the perfect executors of the divine will without inserting their own human judgments and inclinations in the process.

Moreover, claims about God's sovereignty assume that the divine legislative will seeks to regulate all human interactions, that *shari'a* is a complete moral code that prescribes for every eventuality. But perhaps God does not seek to regulate all human affairs, and instead leaves human beings considerable latitude in regulating their own affairs as long as they observe certain minimal standards of moral conduct, including the preservation and promotion of human dignity and well-being. In the Qur'anic discourse, God commanded creation to honor human beings because of the miracle of the human intellect—an expression of the abilities of the divine. Arguably, the fact that God honored the miracle of the human intellect and the human being as a symbol of divinity is sufficient to justify a moral commitment to protecting and preserving the integrity and dignity of that symbol of divinity. But—and this is 'Ali's central point—God's sovereignty provides no escape from the burdens of human agency.

When human beings search for ways to approximate God's beauty and justice, then they do not deny God's sovereignty; they honor it. It is honored as well in the attempt to safeguard the moral values that reflect the attributes of the divine. If we say that the only legitimate source of law is the divine text and that human experience and intellect are irrelevant to the pursuit of the divine will, then divine sovereignty will always stand as an instrument of authoritarianism and an obstacle to democracy. But that authoritarian view denigrates God's sovereignty. . . .

Shari'a *and the Democratic State*

A case for democracy presented from within Islam must accept the idea of God's sovereignty; it cannot substitute popular sovereignty for divine sovereignty but must instead show how popular sovereignty—with its idea that citizens have rights and a correlative responsibility to pursue justice with mercy—expresses God's authority, properly understood. Similarly, it cannot reject the idea that God's law is given prior to human action but must show how democratic lawmaking respects that priority. . . .

It is important to appreciate the centrality of *shari'a* to Muslim life. *Shari'a* is God's way; it is represented by a set of normative principles, methodologies for the production of legal injunctions, and a set of positive legal rules. As is well known, *shari'a* encompasses a variety of schools of thought and approaches, all of which are equally valid and equally orthodox. Nevertheless, *shari'a* as a whole, with all its schools and variant points of view, remains the Way and Law of God.

The *shari'a*, for the most part, is not explicitly dictated by God. Rather, *shari'a* relies on the interpretive act of a human agent for its production and execution. Paradoxically, however, *shari'a* is the core value that society must serve. The paradox here is exemplified in the tension between the obligation to live by God's law and the fact that this law is manifested only through subjective interpretive determinations. Even if there is a unified realization that a particular positive command does express the divine law, there is still a vast array of possible subjective executions and applications. This dilemma was resolved to some extent in Islamic discourses by distinguishing between *shari'a* and *fiqh*. *Shari'a*, it was argued, is the divine ideal, standing as if suspended in midair, unaffected and uncorrupted by life's vagaries. The *fiqh* is the human attempt to understand and apply that ideal. Therefore, *shari'a* is immutable, immaculate, and flawless; *fiqh* is not.

As part of the doctrinal foundations for this discourse, Sunni jurists focused on the tradition attributed to the Prophet, stating: "Every *mujtahid* (jurist who strives to find the correct answer) is correct," or "Every *mujtahid* will be [justly] rewarded." This implied that there could be more than a single correct answer to the same question. For Sunni jurists, this raised the issue of the purpose of or motivation behind the search for the divine will. What is the divine purpose of setting out indicators to the divine law and then requiring that human beings engage in a search? If the divine wants human beings to reach the correct understanding, then how could every interpreter or jurist be correct? Put differently, is there a correct legal response to all legal problems, and are Muslims charged with the legal obligation of finding that response?

The overwhelming majority of Sunni jurists agreed that good faith diligence in searching for the divine will is sufficient to protect a researcher from liability before God. Beyond this, the jurists were divided into two main camps. The first school, known as the *mukhatti'ah*, argued that every legal problem ultimately has a correct answer; however, only God knows the correct response, and the truth will not be revealed until the Final Day. Human beings for the most part cannot conclusively know whether they have found the correct response. In this sense, every *mujtahid* is correct in trying to find the answer; however, one reader might reach the truth while the rest might mistake it. God, on the Final Day, will inform all readers of who was right and who was wrong. Correctness here means that the *mujtahid* is to be commended for making the effort, but it does not mean that all responses are equally valid.

The second school, known as the *musawwibah*, argued that there is no specific and correct answer (*hukm mu'ayyan*) that God wants human beings to discover: after all, if there were a correct answer, God would have made the evidence indicating a divine rule conclusive and clear. God cannot charge human beings with the duty to find the correct answer when there is no objective means of discovering the correctness of a textual or legal problem. If there were an objective truth to everything, God would have made such a truth ascertainable in this life. Legal truth, or correctness, in most circumstances depends on belief and evidence, and the validity of a legal rule or act is often contingent on the rules of recognition that provide for its existence. Human beings are not charged with the obligation of finding some abstract or inaccessible, legally correct result. Rather, they are charged with the duty to diligently investigate a problem and then follow the results of their own *ijtihad* [reasoned judgment]. According to al-Juwayni, for example, what God wants or intends is for human beings to search—to live a life fully and thoroughly engaged with the divine. . . . In summary, if a person honestly and sincerely believes that such and such is the law of God, then for that person it is in fact God's law.

The position of the second school in particular raises difficult questions about the application of the *shari'a* in society. This position implies that God's law is to search for God's law; otherwise the legal charge (*taklif*) is entirely dependent on the subjectivity and sincerity of belief. Under the first school of thought, whatever law the state applies is only potentially the law of God, and we will not find out until the Final Day. Under the second school of thought, any law applied by the state is not the law of God unless the person to which it applies believes it to be God's will and command. The first school suspends knowledge until we are done living and the second school hinges knowledge on the validity of the process and ultimate sincerity of belief.

Building upon this intellectual heritage, I would suggest that *shari'a* ought to stand in an Islamic polity as a symbolic construct for the divine perfection that is unreachable by human effort. As Ibn Qayyim stated, this is the epitome of justice, goodness, and beauty as conceived and retained by God. Its perfection is preserved, so to speak, in the Mind of God, but anything that is channeled through human agency is necessarily marred by human imperfection. Put differently, *shari'a* as conceived by

God is flawless, but as understood by human beings is imperfect and contingent. Jurists ought to continue to explore the ideal of *shari'a* and to expound their imperfect attempts at understanding God's perfection. As long as the argument constructed is normative, it is unfulfilled potential to reach the divine will. Significantly, any law applied is necessarily an unrealized potentiality. *Shari'a* is not simply a collection of *ahkam* (a set of positive rules) but also a set of principles, a methodology, and a discursive process that searches for divine ideals. As such, *shari'a* is a work in progress that is never complete.

To put it more concretely: if a legal opinion is adopted and enforced by the state, it cannot be said to be God's law. By passing through the determinative and enforcement processes of the state, the legal opinion is no longer simply a potential—it has become an actual law, applied and enforced. But what has been applied and enforced is not God's law; it is the state's law. Effectively, a religious state law is a contradiction in terms. Either the law belongs to the state or it belongs to God, and as long as the law relies on the subjective agency of the state for its articulation and enforcement, any law enforced by the state is necessarily not God's law. Otherwise, we must be willing to admit that the failure of the law of the state is in fact the failure of God's law and ultimately of God Himself. In Islamic theology, this possibility cannot be entertained.

Of course, the most formidable challenge to this position is the argument that God and His Prophet have set out clear legal injunctions that cannot be ignored. Arguably, God provided unambiguous laws precisely because God wished to limit the role of human agency and foreclose the possibility of innovations. But . . . regardless of how clear and precise the statements of the Qur'an and Sunna are, the meaning derived from these sources is negotiated through human agency. For example, the Qur'an states: "As to the thief, male or female, cut off (*faqta'u*) their hands as a recompense for that which they committed, a punishment from God, and God is all-powerful and all-wise" (5:38). Although the legal import of the verse seems clear, it requires at a minimum that human agents struggle with the meaning of "thief," "cut off," "hands," and "recompense." The Qur'an uses the expression *iqta'u*, from the root word *qata'a*, which could mean to sever or cut off but could also mean to deal firmly, to bring to an end, to restrain, or to distance oneself. Whatever the meaning derived from the text, can the human interpreter claim with certainty that the determination reached is identical to God's? And even when the issue of meaning is resolved, can the law be enforced in such a fashion that one can claim that the result belongs to God? God's knowledge and justice are perfect, but it is impossible for human beings to determine or enforce the law in such a fashion that the possibility of a wrongful result is entirely excluded. This does not mean that the exploration of God's law is pointless; it means only that the interpretations of jurists are potential fulfillments of the divine will, but the laws as codified and implemented by the state cannot be considered the actual fulfillment of these potentialities.

Institutionally, it is consistent with the Islamic experience that the *'ulama* can and do act as the interpreters of the divine word, the custodians of the moral conscience of the community, and the curators who point the nation toward the ideal that is God. But the law of the state, regardless of its origins or basis, belongs to the state. Under this conception, no religious laws can or may be enforced by the state. All laws articulated and applied in a state are thoroughly human and should be treated as such. These laws are a part of *shari'a* law only to the extent that any set of human legal opinions can be said to be a part of *shari'a*. A code, even if inspired by *shari'a*, is not *shari'a*. Put differently, creation with all its textual and nontextual richness, can and should produce foundational rights and organizational laws that honor and promote these rights. But these rights and laws do not mirror the perfection of divine creation.

According to this paradigm, democracy is an appropriate system for Islam because it both expresses the special worth of human beings—the status of vicegerency—and at the same time deprives the state of any pretense of divinity by locating ultimate authority in the hands of the people rather than the *'ulama*. Moral educators have a serious role to play because they must be vigilant in urging society to approximate God. But not even the will of the majority—no matter how well educated morally—can embody the full majesty of God. And in the worst case—if the majority is not persuaded by the *'ulama*, if the majority insists on turning away from God but still respects the fundamental rights of individuals, including the right to ponder creation and call to the way of God—those individuals who constituted the majority will still have to answer, in the Hereafter, to God.

8. Shamim A. Siddiqui, "Islamic Movement in America—Why?" in *Muslims and Islamization in North America: Problems and Prospects* (1999)

Islam, like Christianity and Buddhism, is a missionary religion, meaning that historically speaking, Muslims have actively sought converts to their faith. While some non-Muslim Americans have expressed anger and fear over Muslim missionary efforts in America, others have replied that it is their First Amendment right as Americans: Muslim missionaries, like Christian missionaries, can try to convert as many persons as they wish. South Asian American Shamim Siddiqui (b. 1928) is one such Muslim missionary. A former member of the Pakistani Jamaat-i Islami, he immigrated to the United States in 1976. Like other missionary-minded Americans, he believes that bringing America to the true religion will cleanse the country of its sins. Islam, Siddiqui has argued for over two decades, will cure America of its social ills and will strengthen its economy. By supporting an Islamic movement in America, he asserts, Muslims will fulfill their duty to establish the authority of God in all of God's creation. Siddiqui would like to see the United States become an Islamic society or state. As one observer has pointed out, he advocates an evolutionary rather than a revolutionary program of Islamization. Siddiqui directs Muslims to work within the boundaries of the U.S. Constitution, using persuasion, service to others, and voting, to establish the United States as a Muslim country.

The world has reached the stage where international communism is dead. The demise of the Soviet Union has rewarded the United States of America with the claim to be the only superpower of the world. America is championing the cause of freedom, and free market economy, mixed with liberalism, in every sphere, to establish a "New World Order." But her pursuit is half-hearted, full of compromises and double standards— strong against weaker nations, like Iran, Iraq, Haiti, Cuba, and Sudan, but timid against the giants with huge foreign markets like China, India, or where other Western interests take precedence. America has thus become hypocritical in the manifestations of her ideals, which are for symbolic gestures only. As such, there is a big gap in improvement both on the ideological side and in the exercise of her political will to carry out her goal and vision to a successful end around the world.

On the other hand, Islam, which stands for justice, equality, and peace, possesses a superb ideology (a profound, benevolent, and all encompassing concept of life), advocates a comprehensive guidance for the human society, both in individual and collective spheres, presents the perfect model of Prophet Mohammed for mankind to follow in every walk of life, is being ignored by the Muslim countries themselves. The Muslim countries so far failed to produce a practical model of Islam and teachings in the present context of the world anywhere on the surface of the earth.

Humanity is, thus, standing today in gloom and total frustration. Neither could the lone superpower and its European allies deliver the good to mankind nor could the Muslims present a model of a modern Islamic state in accordance to Allah's *din* [religious obligations] anywhere in the world.

In the present global state of affairs, when both the superpower and the Islamic movements around the world are trying to produce and present a model of their respective ideologies, and when none could succeed so far, it is desirable to find out what is the best place where both ideologies could be implemented in a homogeneous way.

What America professes to advocate is security of life, liberty, pursuit of happiness, democratic process, human rights, family values and a free-market economy. Islam emphasizes these and many more values of its own concept of life in a very refined way, with all its checks and balances, so that only the good of each remains and flourishes and the evil is eliminated. To attain the values, which Islam advocates, an Islamic society creates an environment of God-consciousness (*taqwa*), a sense of accountability after death and the concept of *amanah* or trust. These are the dominating concepts of the Islamic way of life. They go a long way in producing the character, which can guarantee the implementation of values that are only cherished by America, but refined, implemented and accomplished by Islam. Islam provides the loving model of Prophet Mohammed to follow and get inspiration from his life-pattern. Islam, if embraced and followed properly, will produce that responsible character in American men and women that may transform America into a model society for mankind to aspire. In other words, America provides the appropriate place where its values can be welded into predominant Islamic values to produce the best model of Islam through democratic or a true representative process. America may turn out to be the laboratory of Islam for the twenty-first century.

It is, therefore, in a positive response to an urgent call of the time that a genuine effort should be made to introduce Islam to the people of America, interwoven with the values, which are equally cherished in this country, in a palatable manner. It requires long-term planning, a devoted and dedicated team of workers, and an organized effort.

But here is the great tragedy. There are Muslims who live in America. They are a part of the socio-cultural-educational and economic process of this country. They have their homes and hearth on this land. They are enjoying the luxuries and benefits of the system, but at the same time do not want to improve America's growing sickness. They dream of bringing revolution to some distant lands of Asia, the Middle East, or Africa. They do nothing except condemn America as a society of the *"kuffar"* (infidels), but enjoy its material benefits. They are indeed accountable to Allah and to their progenies for the inactivity to do good to the land, which provides them the bread, butter, and all other luxuries day in and day out.

It is therefore incumbent that the issue of building the Islamic Movement in America is discussed in detail. I will pinpoint the inherent logic behind this urgency and bring forward the reasons for its essentiality.

Obligations of Muslims

Qur'an ordains in verse 33 of *sura* [chapter] 41 and verse 67 of *Surah al-Maidah*: Every Muslim has to fulfill the responsibility of *shahadah alan-nas* (witness to mankind). This directive is for all times to come. If a Muslim does not call the people of the land to the fold of Islam through organized *da'wa* efforts, he or she is actually supporting the *batil* [false] structure.

Obligations as Citizens

As citizens of America, Muslims are sailing in the same boat in which America is sailing. If the boat sinks, Muslims will sink with it. If the boat survives, Muslims will keep floating along with it. But the tragedy is that the boat is sinking slowly—morally, economically, and politically, and the Muslims are unmindful of the forthcoming tragedy. As America is beset with innumerable problems, it is the Muslim's moral and religious obligation to come forward with Islamic solutions for America's problems. As citizens of America, Muslims have the right to disseminate and launch upon a campaign for the propagation of Islam as an alternate way of life to the people of the land, and not exercising this right and duty is concealment of the truth (*kitmanul-haq*).

Better Da'wa Opportunities

Efforts toward the establishment of Allah's *din* or *khilafah ala minhaje-nabuwah* [establishing authority, viceregency, in accordance with traditions of the Prophet Muhammad] are going on in different Muslim countries under different names and styles. But the environment is not congenial for the rule of Islam as a power anywhere in the Muslim world. In every Muslim country, the power bases are not the masses but vested interests who are bent upon perpetuating the power in their hands by all means. Also, the interference of the Western powers in the internal affairs of the Muslim countries is rampant, with devastating effects on the social, economic, and political aspects of life. Human rights are violated everywhere. In short, most of the Muslim countries today stand socially Westernized, morally corrupt, politically exploited and economically ruined with no will or vision of their own. Muslim masses have no say in the affairs of their own countries. They stand as silent spectators. They are no longer the decisive factor in deciding their own future and fate in terms of the ideology they love most.

Thus the possibilities for the emergence of an Islamic state anywhere in the Muslim world are remote in the near future. Current Islamic movements around the world are lacking in *hikmah*, well-formulated approaches, solutions to problems, inspiring models, resources, smooth sailing at home, political will and a "team" of dedicated brothers and sisters which is prepared to give all that they possess for the *din* of Allah. The Islamic movement from Jakarta to Casablanca is the same, more or less.

However, the circumstances in America are better and more conducive for building an Islamic movement to establish and prosper than in other parts of the world. America is a government of law. Democratic processes are deep-rooted in the body-politic of the country. Human rights are guaranteed through its Constitution. The judiciary is independent and strongly defends and protects human rights against all kinds of encroachments and violations. Freedom of speech is perhaps limitless and unfettered. Rights of movements, mobilization of faith and conviction are all guaranteed and protected. America, thus, provides the right environment for the spread of Islam here, which the Muslim world has failed to offer so far to its adherents.

Muslims of America can plan and implement *da'wa* at least until the vested interests of the land create impediments. . . . That is the well-defined process ordained by Allah in the Qur'an (*surah al-ankabut*: Verses 2–3 and *surah al-baqarah*: Verses 155–56). The stages of trial and tribulations come to polish the commitments of a Muslim *da'i* [missionary] and strengthen his or her character. It is now incumbent upon the Muslims of America to concentrate whole-heartedly in building a solid Islamic Movement in America starting, of course, from their own houses.

The Islamic Movement in America will be another front besides the Islamic Movements in the other countries, to pave the way for a success of the movements in the Muslim world. The success of the Muslim world now depends on how soon the Muslims of America are able to build up their own indigenous movement for the spread and introduction in the body-politic of this country.

America: A Heterogeneous Country

America has a unique position in the community of nations. It is a heterogeneous county. People from almost all nations of the world now comprise the nation of America. It depicts a rainbow of nationalities and different cultures. America is a country of immigrants and its doors are still open. Every year, more than a million people migrate to this land of opportunities. Everyone contributes to its diversity wherein lies its strength. They contribute to its economy, enjoy the benefits of Constitutional guarantees and materialistic bounties along with the curses of liberalism in every walk of life. Here the Muslims can carry out the mission of their life to a great extent unhindered, through its democratic process and constitutional safeties, available under the law, to each and every citizen, irrespective of race, color, faith, or ethnic background. America is thus, better set to build the Islamic Movement in comparison to the rest of the world.

Muslims of America are generally well off—many are financially affluent, and highly educated. They realize their unique position where Allah
in His infinite mercy has placed them. They must also realize their responsibility as a *da'i* in a foreign land.

America: Matured for Change

America is the citadel of capitalism, which has reached its zenith and is
now slowly drifting down the hill. The material progress in America is
due not necessarily to capitalism but the extraordinary research and development programs carried out in the public and private sectors. Capitalism and liberalism have actually created gigantic problems for this
country, which need to be resolved. Some of the major problems are: the
growth of a lopsided economy, unbalanced budgeting, frequent cycles of
recession and fear of inflation, ever-increasing gaps in the economy of the
haves and the have-nots, dismantling the family system and corroding
family values, general moral decadence, increasing tolerance of the gay
culture, sexual anarchy, etc. The list of problems is endless.

In the midst of these growing problems the echo of the 1992 presidential election was "change." Bill Clinton came to power uniquely through
raising the slogan of change. But none of the political parties has a program to change the character of the people. Though the moral decay is
eating away the vitals of this supra-nation, the leaders are beating about
the bush, crying to protect the family values and bring "change" simply
as slogans. Amidst this promise of change, it makes no difference who
comes to power. The social, economic, and political condition of America has gone beyond repair. No Band-Aid treatment is going to work.
The main cause of this deterioration lies somewhere else! It lies in deny-
ing the authority of the Creator while living on His earth and enjoying
His bounties and believing or behaving as if this is the only life and
there is no accountability after death. This has made humans irrespon-
sible, reckless and unreliable in both their individual and collective life.
The denial of the Supreme authority and the negligence of the concept
of accountability in the Hereafter have resulted in unbalanced society
and an economy which is uncertain and bereft of *baraka* (blessings).
The verdict of the Qur'an is very clearly: "But he who turns away from
remembrance of Me, he/she will face a narrow (tight or depressed)

economy, and I will bring him/her blind to the assembly on the Day of Resurrection" (20:124).

America today stands at the crossroads. Its economy is uncertain. Its political institutions have gone corrupt. Its moral values are withering away. Its resources are thinning out. Both home and foreign fronts are staggering. America needs a change. These moments offer immense opportunities to the Muslims of America to come forward and present Islam to the inhabitants of this great country as an alternate way of life in an eloquent but organized and disciplined manner. It will be possible only when this responsibility will be undertaken, not by individuals, but by an organized, disciplined, and indigenous Islamic Movement of America.

Socialism never made any headway in America. It was never akin to the taste of the American people. Capitalism and its evil effects are being harvested by the American society as a whole. At this juncture, if an Islamic movement is built up in America which pinpoints the shortcomings of capitalism, elaborates the fallacies of democracy with vivid illustrations from its own system, exposes the devastating consequences of the liberal life-style, there is every possibility that the American people may think of changing over to a better system, a better ideology. Here, it may be observed that the Christian Church has been and is condemning the system too, but it could not and cannot produce an alternate to capitalism. Hence, it could not succeed. Islam presents an alternative to the prevailing system. There is thus every possibility that the people of the land will be attracted to the Islamic system of life.

It is, therefore, essential that it is brought to the attention of the American intelligentsia as well as the masses, as an alternate way of life.

A Game of Rebound from the Muslim Perspective

War strategies in the present context of the world have changed and been given new dimensions. It is now mostly fought on enemy land by propaganda campaign and attracts propaganda literature. Muslims have to take the issue of restoration of *khilafah* [caliphate] with the wisdom of a *mu'min* [believer]. This is the *hikma* [wisdom] of the *din* [religion] and the Muslims have to resolve how to get the campaign expedited on all fronts.

The Muslim leadership of the Islamic Movements in the world must also support the Muslims of America in this worthy cause. This, in fact, is the strategy of rebound; playing the game in America and reaping the harvest in the Muslim world. The *umma* [global community of Muslims] as a whole has to play this game of rebound as the only way to check and eliminate the interference of the Anglo-American-French-Zionist hege-monies in the affairs of the Muslim world.

The *umma* failed to provide and present to the Russian people Islam as an alternative way of life or an Islamic society as an alternative to com-munism and capitalism anywhere in the world to attract them and serve as model for humanity to follow. As such, they fall back on capitalism and liberal democracy. There was no other choice before them. In its wake, Muslims lost a great opportunity to guide the destiny of mankind. We have missed the bus. Let us not do it again!

Future Prospects

A successful Islamic movement in America will muster public opinion against her interference in the internal affairs of the Muslim world and the political leadership will then have no choice but to refrain and give up the game of interference. This is possible only when Muslims of all backgrounds take a united step. A successful Islamic movement in America will herald an era of introducing and spreading Islam in the Caribbean, South America and elsewhere in the Northern Hemisphere. An organized *da'wa* effort can bring this change anywhere. However, the blatant interference of America in the affairs of the Muslims must be accepted as a challenge by the Mus-lims who must work toward "*iqamatudeen*" or rule of God in America.

9. American Islamic Congress, "A New Guide to Muslim Interfaith Dialogue" (2006)

In contrast to Shamim Siddiqui, many Americans do not wish to convert others to Islam so much as they wish to learn more about their non-Muslim neighbors and their faith traditions. Most American Muslims, approximately 90 percent in one poll, support interfaith dialogues and cooperation with persons of other faiths on issues of mutual concern. After 9/11, nearly every major American Muslim organization boosted its interfaith efforts, includ-ing the Islamic Society of North America, the Muslim American Society, the

*Council of Islamic-American Relations, and the American Islamic Congress
(AIC). The AIC was established after 9/11 by American Muslims who said
that they "had been silent for too long in the face of extremism." Muslims
from Hartford, Connecticut, founded the organization, and they were soon
joined by brothers and sisters from across the United States. Today, its board
members include Zainab al-Suwaij, Harvard professor Ali Asani, and Bar-
onness Emma Nicholson. Al-Suwaij, its executive director, was generally supportive of the American-led campaign against Saddam Hussein in Iraq and
the AIC has devoted much effort toward the rebuilding of the country. The
AIC has also participated in several interfaith initiatives, including a memorial vigil for slain* Wall Street Journal *reporter Daniel Pearl, interfaith tours
and panels, and the writing of a guide to interfaith activities.*

Religious pluralism—as exemplified by interfaith events—is one of our
society's greatest assets. Americans embrace pluralism because of our
overriding faith in the dignity of individuals and the groups that they
form, whether that dignity rests on religious or non-religious foundations. As individuals and groups, we comprise a variety of perspectives,
personalities, ideas, and emotions.

Interfaith dialogue—in its American context—is in many ways a new
phenomenon for Islam. In the United States, civil society has matured to
the extent that people of different religions can meet and discuss each
other's faith on equal, respectful terms that reach mutual understanding.
This occurs despite the fact that the central narratives and tenets of different religions often directly contradict one another. At the same time, interfaith dialogue with Islam is also new for America, as religious leaders
struggle to engage the country's new fastest-growing religion.

We want to help American Muslims celebrate diversity and difference,
driven by a commitment to respect and receptiveness. This guide is designed to be both reflective and practical, to help Muslims and non-
Muslims come together to strengthen what is best about America and our
respective traditions.

The Problems So Far

In many communities across the country, there has been a critical breakdown in dialogue between Muslim and non-Muslim communities. Part of

this is due to strong undercurrents of hate speech in segments of the community, stemming from interpretations of religious traditions, political conflicts, and general ignorance. Moreover, since September 11, 2001, many Muslim Americans are confused about how to engage the American public.

• *Interfaith dialogue is not about conversion.* Some peoples' conception of interfaith dialogue is focused on conversion, rather than mutual understanding. There are many books on how to convert others to Islam and on refutations of Christianity and Judaism. These publications reflect an attachment to the debates of an earlier era, not a contemporary respect for religious diversity. Conversion of non-Muslims should not be the aim of Muslim outreach programs. A dogmatic approach to interfaith encounters encourages suspicion and competition not coexistence, parochialism not pluralism.

• *Interfaith dialogue is not about politics.* Interfaith exchanges sometimes also become an excuse for advancing political agendas. Muslim spokesmen sometimes use events to push foreign policy positions on Iraq, Israel, Kashmir, and US influence abroad. When this happens, Islam is not engaged on its own terms, but rather becomes a platform for politics—as if all 1.2 billion Muslims share the same political views.

• *Non-Muslims should not see Muslims as exotic.* On the flip side, many Americans see Muslims as exotic "others," and interfaith discussions often remain stunted at the superficial level: "Oh, you make *hummus* at home! And what is the cloth on your head called?" The religious discussion rarely goes beyond basic theological differences and simple cultural trappings.

• *Religions should not be reduced to simple generalizations.* Often, dialogue begins and ends with the point that Islam, Christianity, and Judaism are all monotheistic faiths. There is little exploration of how these religions developed historically and culturally in distinct ways over centuries. Nor is there much exploration of how people of different faiths can learn from one another in the present. Non-Muslims approach these exchanges either with hostility to a "jihad religion" or with a tendency to gloss over points of controversy. As a result, religions are boiled down to simplistic ideas, without consideration of the diversity of interpretation within each religious tradition. Presenters often make statements such as "X is true Islam, but Y is not." These simplifications suppress the vital but muted debate that has taken place historically and is currently taking place beneath the surface in Muslim communities. Understanding of one's religion and place in the world can only take place in a context of open discussion, within one's own community and in dialogue with other communities.

• *Interfaith dialogue is an opportunity.* In our free and open society, religious groups can share their solutions not only for reconciling tradition and modernity, but also for the pressing problems of the day. As newcomers to America, Muslim immigrants, through interfaith dialogue, can take the opportunity to learn about how other religious communities have come to terms with their traditions within the American experience. But if Muslims and non-Muslims engage in circuitous interfaith encounters, then they cheat themselves, and miss out on the wonderfully diverse experience of engaging peoples of all faiths in twenty-first-century America.

The Five Pillars of Interfaith Dialogue

Our approach to interfaith dialogue rests on five pillars:

I. *Islam is a dynamic civilization with a rich history.* Islam is not a collection of religious tenets that exist in a vacuum. The development of Islam occurs in historical context. Islam, like all religions, has faced challenges in adjusting to modernity and encountering other religions. Islam is a dynamic civilization that is today in the process of reconciling itself with the challenges of modernity in communities throughout the world.

II. *Islam is not monolithic.* Muslims have a wide diversity of religious and political views. Just as Christians and Jews are not monolithic in their practices and politics, so too are Muslims diverse. For instance, there is the massive ethnic and religious diversity within Islam, ranging from the skeptics to fundamentalists, Sunnis to Shi'is, Arabs to Indonesians—all of whom represent and participate in . . . the diversity that is Islam.

III. *Break the silence.* We should feel comfortable discussing hot-button cultural and political matters. Muslims can achieve genuine dialogue with others if we generate open dialogue amongst ourselves. We should empower everyone in our community to not feel discouraged or intimated about speaking their minds. This involves encouraging people to ask difficult questions in a friendly manner and to get to the heart of each other's concerns.

IV. *Self-criticism is a sign of strength.* American Muslims can take the lead in working for a brighter future for the Muslim world. Rather than shy away from shortcomings, we should feel free to address the massive problems facing the Muslim world: the threat posed by radicals who advocate violence and religious supremacy based upon their interpretation of religious texts; the social status of women; the treatment of minorities; and the lack of civil society, democracy, and economic development.

V. *Reach out beyond Jews and Christians.* We should be careful not to limit dialogue to Christianity and Judaism. Given Islam's troubled history with polytheistic and post-Muhammad faiths, we must begin to engage the many other religions that are blossoming in America alongside us: Hindu, Buddhist, Shinto, Baha'i, etc. If we can establish constructive dialogue with these groups, we will be opening up a new chapter in Muslim interfaith dialogue.

Getting Started

There are several steps that you can take to begin organizing and participating in interfaith dialogue events.

• *Find a dialogue partner.* Contact leaders or active members of your local churches, synagogues, Hindu temples, or other religious or interfaith organizations and simply ask if they would be interested in participating in an interfaith dialogue. It could also be helpful to speak with other members of your local Muslim community beforehand to get a sense of how many people might be interested in attending an interfaith dialogue event.

• *Start small.* Large-scale events, though desirable, are extremely difficult to organize. It takes experience with planning and attending small-scale events (e.g., holiday celebration, interfaith meal, joint community service activity) to successfully organize an event that includes hundreds of participants. Smaller-scale events that involve no more than a couple dozen participants offer the advantage of intimacy, which can better create an atmosphere of sharing and openness.

• *Forge a bond at the leadership level.* Even if you do not plan to organize an interfaith event for a while, it is very important to establish and maintain a dialogue with leaders of the communities that you hope to engage. If leaders develop a relationship, then it is much easier for community members to follow suit.

• *Talk ahead of time.* Before participating in an event, meet in advance with non-Muslim leaders to discuss concerns your community members may have with interfaith dialogue. Openness ahead of time will resolve tensions that may exist amongst participants.

• *Seek ways to continue to build dialogue.* Relationships often fade if they are not maintained. Once an event is planned, you should try to quickly plan future events with the same group and extend the dialogue to other related groups.

Suggested Activities

Working within the framework of our five pillars of Muslim interfaith dialogue, we propose a set of activities and suggested readings that can be used for conducting interfaith events.

ISLAM IS A DYNAMIC CIVILIZATION WITH A RICH HISTORY:

To demonstrate the historical evolution of Islam to event participants, you should craft short lessons, powerpoint presentations, or handouts on specific periods and centers of Islam:

- Mecca and Medina during the life of the Prophet Muhammad
- Umayyad Damascus
- Abbasid Baghdad
- Fatimid Cairo
- Umayyad Spain
- Suleiman the Great in Istanbul
- Ottoman Empire

When discussing Muslim life today, it is important to emphasize the recent historical and political context of extremism within Islam in contrast to the long history of Muslim thought and culture. Muslim history is filled with episodes of cultural flowering, geographical and demographic expansions, ups and downs.

To illustrate: Trace a Muslim concept through its history of interpretations and understandings; e.g., *jihad* (spiritual struggle, defensive war, holy war), *amr bi-l-maʿruf wa-l-nahi ʿan al-munkar* (commanding the right and forbidding the wrong).

ISLAM IS NOT MONOLITHIC:

Prepare slide shows or powerpoint presentation that exhibit the many "faces of Islam" with its multiple ethnicities and nationalities. These presentations should also include current demographic statistics.

Read excerpts from different strands of Muslim thought (e.g., Sunni, Shiʿi, Sufi). These readings should serve as a starting point for discussing similarities and differences between groups such as Sufis, Sunnis, Shiʿis, and Ismaʿilis.

Ask each event participant to write down and share five examples of ways "you think you are different from everyone else in the room"—in other words, "What makes your experience unique?" As participants describe their uniqueness, discussion leaders should also encourage people to discuss how others can relate to these unique qualities. Discuss the effects of national identity and local culture on the way Islam is understood and practiced. Compare and contrast the experiences of American, Saudi, Iraqi, Egyptian, Indonesian, Pakistani, and/or Nigerian Muslims.

BREAKING THE SILENCE:

Ask each event participant to list ten questions that "you want to know the answers to about your own religion and the religions of your fellow participants." Moderators will then present and discuss these questions with the group.

Ask each event participant to list five issues that "you feel get too much attention in your religious community and five issues that get too little attention." Moderators will then present and discuss these questions with the group.

SELF-CRITICISM IS A SIGN OF STRENGTH:

Distribute handouts that profile courageous social activists who are taking the lead in the Muslim world to speak out on issues of human rights, minority rights, civil liberties, and/or women's rights.

Ask each event participants to write down five things that "you are most proud of in Islam and five things that you are least proud of regarding Muslim practice." Moderators will then present and discuss participant responses. Ask members of other religious groups present to do the same with their religion.

REACHING OUT BEYOND JEWS AND CHRISTIANS:

Invite local Hindus and Baha'is to talk about their faiths and attend their cultural/religious events.

Ask to be included on the mailing list of these communities to get a better feel for their programs and for opportunities to join together.

Consider having interfaith panel discussions on issues that are not so religiously charged, e.g.: city council elections, faith-based funding, affirmative action, social service funding, local environmental concerns, recycling.

10. Patricia S. Maloof and Fariyal Ross-Sherriff, "Challenges of Resettlement and Adaptation of Muslim Refugees," in *Muslim Refugees in the United States: A Guide for Service Providers* (2003)

While many Muslims in the United States are busy organizing themselves into viable public interest groups, it is important to keep in mind that some recent Muslim immigrants, especially refugees, are just trying to survive in the United States. Their stories constitute another important part of American Muslim interaction with the U.S. government and American society. From 1988 through 2003, Muslims accounted for approximately 15 percent of the 1.4 million refugees who sought asylum in the United States. These Muslims came from seventy-seven different countries, though most refugees hailed from Bosnia, Afghanistan, Iraq, Serbia, and Somalia. They are largely men and women forced by the devastations of war to seek refuge. Because they have been dislocated by force, they sometimes face particular difficulty in adjusting to life in the United States. Health-care workers, educators, social workers, and other service providers have struggled to address the needs of these Muslims, and experts like authors Maloof and Ross-Sherriff have been called on to help these professionals meet the refugees' needs. The challenge of doing so is great, since they speak different languages, practice different forms of Islam, come from different kinds of families, and subscribe to different ethnic and national identities. What applies to one refugee from Sarajevo in the former Yugoslavia may have little to do with a Somali refugee from East Africa. In the excerpts below, Maloof and Ross-Sherriff offer several different case studies for service providers and provide discussion questions meant to spur conversations among them. These case studies are, arguably, relevant to a much broader audience of Americans. The experiences of Muslim refugees in the United States raise important questions about what it means to be American for Muslims and non-Muslims alike.

Case Study

An extended family of twelve persons from Kosovo arrived in Phoenix, Arizona. The grandmother, one son with his wife, and their three children composed one core family. A second son with his wife and four children composed the second core family. Of the seven children, four were school-aged, two were toddlers, and one was an infant. The resettlement agency had arranged for each core family to have its own apartment, but the apartments were in two different buildings within the same apartment complex. The management promised the resettlement office that, as soon as an apartment opened in either building, one of the core families could move into the same building with the others. Nevertheless, the refugees in both core families insisted on living together. In the evening, all twelve people would come to one apartment for dinner and then spend the night together. During the day, all family members who were not in school or looking for a job would be in one apartment.

The family was also dissatisfied with this living arrangement because they were too far from the mosque and the *halal* market. They did not mind taking public transportation, but it was expensive and the ride took one and a half hours each way.

After several months of warnings, the management office lost patience with the family for being out of compliance with the lease, since one core family had essentially moved in with the other. The occupancy rules did not allow for this many people in one apartment of the size that they had. There were repeated warnings and discussions with the resettlement office and the refugees. Eventually, eviction was threatened.

The resettlement agency staff had explained the situation several times to the refugees. The case manager even had them sign a statement for their file indicating that they knew they were in violation of their lease and that this could cause them to face eviction. The refugees had signed the statement willingly. They were very clear on what they wanted—they wanted to live together. They told the caseworker that, regardless of the consequences, they would not comply.

Finally, with the help of the mosque, the family's caseworker was able to find a large apartment closer to the mosque and the *halal* market for the family.

POSSIBLE QUESTIONS FOR DISCUSSION:

1. What happened in this scenario from the perspective of the refugee family?
2. What happened from the perspective of the landlord?
3. Why do you think the family continued to share the apartment, in spite of being warned of the possible consequences?
4. What are some possible approaches that the caseworkers might take to this problem?

Case Study

Two single sisters from the Sudan were resettled in Seattle, Washington. During employment orientation, the job developer at their resettlement agency discussed the issue of wearing *hijab* in the workplace, explaining that, for safety reasons, the women might need to make some accommodations in their attire while at work.

A few weeks later, the job developer took one of the sisters to an interview at a hotel. She was surprised to see her client come to the interview without the *hijab*. The employer was very pleased with the interview, and the Sudanese woman was hired to work as a housekeeper at the hotel.

The following day, however, the job developer got a call from the employer. The employer said that the Sudanese woman had arrived for her orientation at the hotel that morning with her head covered, and had explained to the employer that her religion required her to cover her head and to wear long sleeves under her uniform. The employer wanted to know why the woman and the job developer had not addressed this need during the interview.

In the meantime, the other sister had found a job at a fast food restaurant with the help of her job developer. During the interview, the refugee woman and the job developer explained to the employer that the woman was planning to wear a *hijab* and long sleeves at work, and inquired whether this would be a problem. The employer was hesitant at first, but the job developer suggested that the woman could wear the *hijab* under her cap and a long-sleeved shirt as a part of her uniform. The employer seemed pleased with this suggestion, and the woman was hired to work as a cashier.

POSSIBLE QUESTIONS FOR DISCUSSION:

1. Compare the two scenarios in this case study. How are they different? How are they similar?
2. Why was the first employer upset with the new employee and the job developer?
3. Why do you think the first sister came to the job interview without her *hijab*?
4. How do you explain the second employer being more accommodating than the first one?
5. What successful orientation strategies on the part of the job developer can you identify? What less successful ones?

Case Study

The Tahir family arrived in Manchester, New Hampshire, as refugees from northern (Kurdish) Iraq. Although the parents had not attended school, their two daughters had both had some schooling. The daughters, Elham and Mahassin, began attending high school immediately after their arrival. The father, whose English proficiency was limited, worked two jobs to support his family; the mother, who did not speak any English, was a homemaker.

The Tahir family came from a religious and conservative culture whose traditions they maintained in their new home. The girls were not allowed to appear in public without wearing *hijab*, and they were not allowed to have male friends.

At school, the social worker observed that the two girls were not socializing with American students. Most of their friends were other refugee girls. The social worker was also aware that the girls were a target of mockery from some of their classmates because of their accent, their demeanor, and their conservative dress. Although the girls were making strides academically, socially they tended to be isolated and act shy around others.

In an effort to help Elham and Mahassin, the social worker decided to invite their parents to come in for a talk. She sent an invitation letter home with the daughters, who translated it for their father. After he had heard the contents of the letter, the father asked his daughters if they were having problems in school. In the Tahir family's culture of origin, the purpose of school is understood to be academic learning, and socialization is an intra-family matter. Problems in school in this context would mean problems with academic achievement. The girls replied that they were not having any problems in school, and their father decided that he did not need to meet with the social worker. Although the social worker sent the father similar requests later, the parents did not acknowledge her requests at all.

Finally, the social worker contacted the Tahir family case manager at the resettlement agency, and the caseworker arranged for an *imam* from the community to visit the family. The *imam* described the differences between the functions of school in the United States and its functions in the family's culture of origin, and described how observant Muslim parents could meet the expectations of a school system in the U.S. in ways that were consistent with the Qur'an and the teachings of the Prophet Muhammad. He explained that local law required the daughters to be in school, and showed how the basic tenets of Islam supported the father's involvement in his daughters' education.

Following this conversation with the *imam*, the parents agreed to meet with the school social worker. Before they did so, they visited again with the caseworker, who helped them understand more about the school system, especially the importance of non-academic aspects, so that they felt prepared to talk with the social worker. The caseworker also visited with the social worker before the Tahirs' appointment to discuss the family's culture and religion.

POSSIBLE QUESTIONS FOR DISCUSSION:

1. How would you explain the behavior of the classmates, the Tahir girls, and the father?
2. What are the cultural issues in this story?
3. If you were the social worker, would you deal with this matter differently? How?
4. Why do you think the parents did not respond to the social worker's requests at all?
5. In your opinion, how can service providers prevent situations similar to this one from taking place?

Case Study

A family of nine, mother, father, and seven children aged three months to twelve years, arrived in Louisville, Kentucky, from a refugee camp in Kenya. The four school-aged children were soon enrolled in school and seemed to be adjusting well.

A month after the start of the school year, the parents received a phone call from a school administrator, asking them to come to school immediately. The father, who spoke some English, was concerned and called the family case manager at the resettlement agency, but could not reach her.

When the parents arrived at the school, they were led to the nurse's office, where they were met by the school counselor. She informed them that their eight-year-old son Ali had slipped on the playground and scraped his arm. When the nurse examined him prior to dressing his injury, she noticed burn marks on his stomach. The counselor explained that the school was required to report any signs of suspected child abuse to Child Protective Services, and that the parents could not take their son home until a social worker had had a chance to talk to them.

The concerned parents saw their son talking to a social worker in the next room. They did not understand what kind of "abuse" the counselor was talking about. Soon the social worker came in to interview the parents. He asked about burn marks on Ali's stomach and forehead. The parents explained that the traditional healer in their village had burned small holes in Ali's skin in order to cure ailments he had had as a baby and toddler. The father insisted on taking his son home, but the social worker explained that he would have to take Ali to the hospital for further tests, and that the child could not be returned home until it had been determined that he would be safe there.

POSSIBLE QUESTIONS FOR DISCUSSION:

1. Why are Ali's parents suspected of abusing their son?
2. What is the social worker from Child Protective Services likely to do next?
3. What are the cultural communication issues in this story?
4. In your opinion, how could service providers prevent this kind of scenario from happening?

American Muslim Spirituality and Religious Life

RELIGION is not merely a set of beliefs or doctrines about the supernatural; it is even more than a feeling of closeness to God. Religion certainly includes beliefs in the supernatural, doctrines about God's nature, and feelings about God, but religion is also about practices, rituals, ethics, and aesthetics. Taking a broad view of Muslim religious life and spirituality necessarily renders a diverse and multilayered picture that cannot possibly be limited to the "five pillars of Islam." Often, in what might be called the "boilerplate" introduction to Islam, the five pillars, including the declaration of faith, daily prayers, alms, fasting, and the pilgrimage, are asserted to be "the foundation of Muslim life," the heart of Muslim practice. Some American Muslims would agree, at least theoretically. But one must be careful in interpreting the meaning of these practices; their importance often changes depending on who is performing them and when and where they are doing so. Performing the pilgrimage to Mecca in a wheelchair, for example, may be different than doing it on foot. Or keeping the Ramadan fast while in prison may serve a different function than fasting in one's home.

A truly broad and inclusive view of American Muslim spirituality reveals more than the five pillars. In addition to prayer and fasting, there are hip-hop songs about Allah, Islamic poetry, and advice columns about how to raise teenage Muslims in America. In real life, the crystal-clear dividing line between Islamic "religion" and Muslim "culture" disappears. Even if Muslims, like all other persons of faith, strive to eliminate cultural aspects from the practice of what they see as "pure" Islamic religion, it seems impossible to do so. Living Islam is inevitably affected by the everyday dilemmas and the historical contexts in which American Muslims find themselves. Different histories, economic circumstances, ethnic and linguistic backgrounds, and gendered experiences shape what it means for American Muslims to have faith in God. In my view—and this goes for all religions—there is no religious tradition that stands outside of human history. Because we are human beings, no matter what we do, our encounter with the supernatural, however conceived, is shaped by our own limited understanding. Our limitations define, quite literally, what it means to be human. We do not have a God's-eye view of the world; because our feet are firmly planted on the earth—at least most of the time—we see only what is in our line of sight. Like the character in the Jim Carrey movie *Bruce Almighty*, in which the protagonist is given the powers of God and goes crazy listening to everyone's prayers, some of us consider our own limited nature to be a blessing.

How we relate to one another is another sign of our limitations as human beings. Even when we do not wish to do so, we create boundaries between others and ourselves. The American Muslim community, like other communities, is full of social boundaries that affect the shape and color of American Muslim religious practice and spirituality. American Muslims, as we have seen, have been divided by race, ethnicity, and class, but even so, they have still affected one another's religious practices, political platforms, and cultural orientations. For example, while there was a chasm between indigenous African American Muslims and immigrant Muslims in 1930s, we know from the history of Islam in Detroit that African American Muslim practices were influenced by the presence of immigrants from the Middle East. Or more recently, some African American Muslims have helped to awaken a larger concern for racism among some non-black American Muslims, and progressive Muslims from a variety of racial backgrounds have incorporated antiracism into the heart of their Islamic reform agendas. Sometimes, crossing boundaries leads to the creation of new ones. When some American Muslims moved across lines of race and class to join Salafi groups in the 1970s, they also separated themselves from the rest of the Muslim community. They broke some social barriers only to create others.

American Muslim religious practices have also been influenced by larger trends in American religious culture. Take the American mosque. Well over 1,200 mosques are now located in American inner cities, towns, and suburbs; the buildings themselves express a wide variety of architectural styles, and include converted city storefronts, grand Middle Eastern–style structures, and small houses. Like many American churches, synagogues, and other religious centers, mosques often house schools and recreational areas, in addition to the *masjid* proper (place of prostration, or prayer). The *imam* (or prayer leader) of the mosque may also act as its administrative and spiritual leader, especially in many African American mosques. In these contexts, the *imam* performs duties similar to those of a minister, priest, and rabbi. In other mosques, however, *imams* are relegated to the role of teaching about Islam, delivering the Friday sermon, and leading the Friday prayers. An elected president or chairperson often leads these mosques. These elected leaders generally maintain employment outside the mosque, and in the case of predominately immigrant mosques, are generally professionals of one sort or another. Many leaders, whether *imams* or committee members, work on a volunteer basis, receiving little or no compensation for their services. Whether the *imam* or a board of directors runs the mosque, these arrangements parallel American styles of religious leadership more generally. Like other religious practitioners in the United States, members of one mosque are also free to split off to form another mosque, thereby contributing to the diversity of Islamic thought and practice. The relative lack of state interference in the governance of religious institutions facilitates such creative fragmentation.

While larger trends in American religions have influenced American Muslims, it is also clear that American Muslim spirituality and religious life is not and never has been purely "American." The story of Islam in the United States is global and transnational. From the time of the West African slaves who were forced into slavery until today, Muslim persons, ideas, institutions, symbols, and texts have traveled back and forth from North America to wherever else Muslims have been. Since 1965, the pace of such globalization has increased. As air travel, migration, business links, and communications quicken and become more frequent, ideas, events, and trends in Muslim-majority countries have a more immediate influence on Muslims in the United States. More American Muslims also travel abroad, taking Arabic in Damascus, studying with Sufi masters in West Africa and Turkey, going on pilgrimage to Mecca, and teaching in Indonesia. When they return, they disseminate their knowledge in variety of ways; some, for example, have helped to translate more and more

Islamic texts into English—not just the Qur'an and the words of the Prophet Muhammad, but also poetry, philosophy, psychology, and spiritual advice. American Muslims in general also increasingly participate in a global, English-language virtual *umma*, a cybercommunity of Muslims. By using the resources available on the Internet, American Muslims can also forge their own understandings of Islamic law and ethics. One need not be a trained *'alim*, a religious scholar, or hold a prestigious position at an Islamic university to publish one's opinions; one only needs access to the World Wide Web.

There is no way that one chapter can capture the full breadth of contemporary American Muslim spirituality and religious practice. The documents below are examples of religious phenomena that may or may not represent the views of other American Muslims. Some are prescriptive, meaning that they advise other Muslims on how to lead a religious life. Many Muslims, like other persons of faith, do not necessarily follow such guidelines, though they may recognize them as ideals. Other documents are descriptive; they describe the feelings of practitioners toward aspects of their religious and spiritual lives. There are also a number of genres sampled: autobiography, song lyrics, Internet chat, academic prose, interviews, and position papers. Taken as a whole, this group of readings gives a sense of how Islamic religion is being taught, imagined, and performed in the United States. But by no means does it exhaust the catalogue of activities that encompasses American Muslim religious life and spirituality.

1. Betty Hasan Amin, "*Hajj* in a Wheelchair," *Azizah Magazine* (2002)

Atlanta resident Betty Hasan Amin was determined to make the hajj, *or annual pilgrimage to Mecca. But her journey would be more difficult than most. Betty Hasan Amin can't walk. An African American Muslim, Amin is an advocate for all persons, both Muslim and non-Muslim, with disabilities. She has worked with the Atlanta Alliance on Developmental Disabilities, the Interfaith Disabilities Network, Atlanta's Al-Islam Mosque, and even sued the Metropolitan Rapid Transit Authority (MARTA) to increase accessibility and opportunities for the disabled. When a local Clara Muhammad School was renovated in 1991, she helped the project's architects to make sure that the new building was wheelchair-user friendly. Because of her activism and the work of other American Muslims, more American Muslim buildings and events are becoming friendlier to persons with disabilities. Signing for the deaf sometimes occurs at Friday prayers and Braille Qur'ans are provided for the visually impaired. While there are hopeful signs, many American Muslims still report serious problems. Without rethinking accommodation, it can be dangerous for disabled persons to perform certain rituals, especially the pilgrimage to Mecca. Some Muslims might argue that a serious disability exempts one from religious obligations impossible to perform in a safe manner. But in the piece below, Betty Hasan Amin argues that her disability should not prevent her from expressing her devotion to God and praises the Almighty for the strength to perform this important practice.*

Locking my electric wheelchair into place behind the steering wheel of my specially-equipped van, I took a deep breath. I was beginning the journey of a lifetime—*hajj*! I knew that *hajj* would be a life-altering event. I also knew that, while *hajj* can be a struggle for an able-bodied person, it would be even more of a challenge for me, a paraplegic in a wheelchair with complex medical needs.

Paralyzed by a fall as a seventeen-year-old high school senior, through determination I managed to earn two college degrees during a time when curb cuts were unheard of and schools and colleges were fraught with architectural barriers. Now a divorced single mother, I was raising two sons, teaching at an Islamic school and feeling blessed with the Islamic faith that gave me the strength to strive toward realizing my human potential to its fullest.

Driven by love of Allah and a burning desire to fulfill the fifth pillar of Islam, I placed my trust in Allah. I also tied my camel! I made numerous and careful preparations for my journey. I attended *hajj* classes at the mosque, where I heard reports from numerous *hajjis* [people who had already gone on *hajj*]. I spoke at length to a brother who had recently performed *hajj* in a wheelchair himself. I secured the services of a sister and of a married couple who would accompany me on my trip; Sister Rasheedah Id-Deen, with years of nursing experience behind her, would assist me with personal care and needs, along with Sister Binta Kareem. Sister Binta's husband, Ocei Kareem, would take charge of the logistics of transporting me. Although I would be gone only four weeks, I painstakingly packed enough medical supplies, herbal remedies and energy foods to last me three months. Wary of the availability of electrical supply on the plains of Mina and Arafat, I opted for a manual wheelchair. As I euphorically drove off with three other sisters that May morning in 1992 to join a group of forty other Muslims bound for Mecca, I felt amply prepared.

Hand-carried by Brother Ocei and another brother on and off the Dulles Airport bus, I experienced humbling feelings of dependence that I had not felt in years. Fortunately, Saudi Airlines had been apprised of my situation, and had a small chair ready for me that was especially designed to maneuver through the narrow airplane aisles. I was lifted onto the chair, and braced myself for the ride and transfer to my seat at the rear of the plane filled with Muslim pilgrims. Before I could get there, however, a non-Muslim couple who anticipated my difficulty stopped me. Out of the graciousness of their hearts, they offered me their seats at the front of the plane. Their kindness helped to calm me, and with the pilot's recitation of *surah al-fatiha* [the opening chapter of the Qur'an], we took off on our flight to Jeddah.

When we landed eleven hours later, I was loaded onto an elevette lift and lowered onto the tarmac by airport workers. I felt apprehensive during this procedure, wondering about the workers' procedure, wondering about the workers' abilities to deal with the disabled. I reminded myself to be patient, though, realizing that things would be different here in Saudi Arabia; there would be many cultural distinctions.

As we worked our way through customs, we waited while our tour group's leaders went to the aid of a stranded sister from Wisconsin. This woman, Sister Zainab, was being refused entry into the country because she was a single woman traveling alone. The brothers from our groups assured the officials that she could join our group. Although I did not realize it at the time, Allah had sent me another helper. Sister Zainab was a registered operating room nurse, and days later, she began to assist Rasheedah with my medical care, exhibiting great skill and concern.

At the crowded airport, the sisters helped me to don my *ihram* [the special garb worn by Muslims on the pilgrimage]. Then we moved onto a shuttle that took us to the staging area where we waited for a bus to take us to Mecca. The wait was long and hot, but certainly not dull! I watched, astonished and fascinated, the flow of arrivals of different groups of people from all over the world. When our bus finally arrived, though, I was greatly disappointed and saddened at its appearance—it was terribly old, without a wheelchair lift and with doors so narrow the brothers had to turn me sideways to lift me onto the bus.

My wheelchair, medical supplies, baggage and specially designed wheelchair cushion were packed on top of the bus with the rest of the luggage. As the bus took off, so did my cushion; I spent the remainder of my trip sitting on make-shift pillows, diligently trying to avoid dangerous pressure sores.

Upon our arrival at our apartment, I saw that it was at the top of three flights of stairs. For the duration of our stay, I would have to be carried up and down those stairs sometimes two and three times a day as we went back and forth from prayers. The part of Mecca in which we stayed had a large African population, and the neighboring men often willingly came to the assistance of the group's brothers to carry me. As at the beginning of this journey, I again felt humbled by my dependence.

When our group finally made our way to Masjid Al-Haram [the Great Mosque in Mecca] . . . reverence and awe overwhelmed all of us. Tears flowed. A small voice inside me, however, told me to dry those tears, and soon I realized why—I would need all my strength and clarity. As I approached the *masjid* door in my wheelchair, a custodian jumped up and blocked my way. He shouted a torrent of angry words in Arabic, and then gestured brusquely. A look of great disdain on his face, he began to make shooing motions and sounds. Hurtfully, I saw that I was being shooed away from the Haram door the way a fly would be shooed away from a banquet!

The brothers in our group stepped forward and attempted to explain the particulars of my situation, but to no avail. We were being refused entry because I was in a wheelchair! I could not believe this was happening. I thought to myself, "He's kidding! I didn't travel thousands of miles to be prevented from performing my rites." But he was not kidding, and adamantly continued to refuse us entry.

I was shocked and angry. Here I was, a woman in a wheelchair, receiving the least possible compassion in Mecca, the place where I had expected the most sensitivity. I summoned the strength and determination I had learned during my twenty-six years of life as a disabled person, and decided to try another door.

The guard at the next door refused us in a similar situation. Undaunted and unbowed, we tried a third door. Again, our entry was barred. We tried a fourth and a fifth door, but were shooed away again. After being turned away from seven doors, and now a great distance from where we had begun, I began to feel disheartened. My inner voice, however, told me to hold on, pray and trust in Allah.

We decided to try one more time, this time at the doors of Safa and Marwa [the hills between which Hagar ran, looking to find water for Ishmael]. At this door sat a quiet elderly man, who looked like he was eighty years old. Not only did he allow us in, but he wrote a note in Arabic and told us, surprisingly in English, to show this note if we should have any more problems. *Alhamdulillah* [Praise be to God], that note was a great blessing, and did make things much easier. (Years later, I had it translated and learned that it said that the bearer was affiliated with the Atlanta Masjid, and should she expire while making hajj, to please contact the American Embassy.)

Once admitted, the brothers with me went off . . . , and I remained in the care of two hired Nigerian men. They lifted me into a large basket, and hoisted me onto their heads, and trotted toward the Ka'ba for *tawaf* [the ritual circumambulation of the Ka'ba]. My exhilaration at finally performing my rites was tempered by a great fear of toppling out of this unsteady device and being trampled by the swirling crowd below! There I sat, so far away from home, and completely dependent on people I did not know, whose language I could not speak nor understand, in an unfamiliar land. At that point, I realized the interdependence of humanity. During *sa'i* [the devotional act of walking between Safa and Marwa to commemorate Hagar's search for water], relieved to be on the ground in my familiar wheelchair, I repeated my *du'a* [supplicatory prayer] in a stronger voice.

When I was lifted into a bus headed for Arafat, I sat in great anticipation with my two attendants and two older sisters from our group. Unfortunately, as we sat in a three-hour traffic jam, fumes from the other buses exacerbated my respiratory problems, and my seat became increasingly uncomfortable. Then, when we finally reached Arafat, I could not get off the bus. The buses were parked so close together that the brothers could not carry me between them. I sat there on the bus all day, and made my prayers and *du'a* in my seat. At first I felt annoyed, thinking that I should be making a greater sacrifice, enduring the Saudi desert heat, but eventually I realized that being allowed to remain on the air conditioned bus was a mercy from Allah.

As we prepared to depart from Arafat, my attendant and his wife left for a quick trip to the bathroom. Meanwhile, the bus driver decided it was time to leave! I was nearly in a frenzy as I begged him not to go just yet, and tried to explain that I could not walk and was waiting on my attendants to come back. Neither the bus driver nor any of the other passengers could understand me, and off we drove. All I could do was whisper desperately, "Lord, I am at Your mercy, here in the dark, driving somewhere I don't know, with people who can't understand me and don't know me. The only two people on this bus I know can't lift me. Please help me, Allah."

At Muzdalifa [where pilgrims gather stones for the ritual stoning of the devil], everyone got off the bus. The driver shouted and gestured to me to get off, too. I tried to make him understand that I could not walk, and would need to be carried. He could not understand, and kept shouting. I knew that the two elderly sisters with me had neither the strength nor the expertise to lift me, so the sisters did the best they could and volunteered to pick up my pebbles for me. The bus driver finally gave up and left, and I slept on the bus alone.

We arrived back in Mina the next morning. When the bus had emptied, the driver again shouted and motioned for me to exit the bus. After some time an African man seemed to understand the problem, and lifted me out of the bus and into my chair. We did not know where we were, and this man kindly pushed me around and around for some time with the two elderly sisters wandering along with us. I began to despair, feeling that we would never find our camp. I told myself, "Allah knows every grain of sand, every leaf that falls. Out of all these million of people, I know Allah sees me." I felt a great surge of faith, a great spiritual assurance. I mentioned to our helper that we were Americans. He turned in another direction and pushed me along for some time more, but now with direction. Finally, we rounded a corner and I saw our tent!

What an emotional reunion that was! The sisters cried and hugged us. The brothers hugged and thanked the African brother who had brought us back. Brother Ocei had been completely distraught, and was overwhelmed at my appearance. *Alhamdulillah*, Allah is most great.

The next three days were wonderful. The stoning was performed by proxy for me by the brothers. We met many other pilgrims, and shared ethnic foods. During those times, my disability was a non-issue.

Back in Mecca, however, I began to suffer severe chills. Sitting on the hard bus seat for hours without medical attention had taken its toll. Someone suggested that I go to a nearby medical trailer set up for pilgrims, but when we got there, it was completely inaccessible. We decided to go to the hospital, but were greeted, again, by non-negotiable steps. The brothers decided to carry me into the hospital. There, I was examined by a congenial doctor who was thrilled to meet an American Muslim. He told me that I had a large, advanced necrosis decubitus, and that they could not treat it there as it required surgery. My condition was serious.

Our group still had four more days before we were to return home. Leaving the group and arranging a flight out was an impossibility. I realized that I would have to exert mind over matter—I could not die. I had two small sons to whom I must return to raise as Muslims. Sister Rasheedah and Sister Zainab cleaned and packed the decubitus with gauze. I prayed to Allah and begged Him to spare my life and to return me safely home.

Sheer faith and determination kept me going. I accompanied the group to Medina, endured the long bus ride, and felt elated to feel the warm peacefulness of the Prophet's city. We prayed in the Prophet's Mosque with a great sense of tranquility. But when we left, I made the terrible discovery that the bag contained all of my medical supplies was missing! All of the bags had been left on a security dolly outside the mosque. My bag was the only one missing. Everyone is the group searched high and low for that bag, on other dollies, inside other bags, even in the trash. There was no sign of it; it was gone!

I returned to Mecca ill, having chills and without any medical supplies, but still filled with determination to complete the remaining rituals of *hajj*. This time, I learned that I could circumambulate on the top floor of the Haram. The brothers took turns pushing me, and I managed to complete my farewell *tawaf*.

On the shuttle to Jeddah Airport, I endured one last difficulty. When the bus attendant placed me in a space beside the door, I quietly wheeled myself to a safer spot. The attendant came back to roughly and rudely fling me back to where he thought I should be. That area by the door was unsafe for even an able-bodied person, and certainly no place for a person in a wheelchair! With defiance born of my human dignity, I moved back into the safer position, locked my chair into position and stared the bus attendant straight in the eyes. There I stayed.

Alhamdulillah, I made it safely back to Atlanta where I underwent two surgeries and remained in the hospital for eight weeks. My trip to Mecca had increased my gratitude to Allah for his loving kindness and mercy.

I realized how difficult it is for disabled people who live in countries without legislation in favor of the disabled in areas of education, employment or housing. With a new appreciation for American technology and medical advances, too, I sense an obligation to share our knowledge with the rest of humanity. *In sha' Allah* [God willing], I pray that I might be instrumental in helping the Muslim community, both inside and outside of America, to be inclusive of everyone in the Islamic community.

2. Abdul Rauf, "Who Is God?" in *Qur'an for Children* (1995)

Many American Muslim children are encouraged by parents and community members alike to study the Qur'an. Sometimes, children attend weekend sessions at an Islamic center. Parents also read the Qur'an to their children at home and ask them to memorize certain key verses. Some children are trained in the age-old tradition of Qur'anic recitation, while many others are simply encouraged to become familiar with the holy book and its meanings. Many Muslim adults around the world do not read the Qur'an so much as they listen to it being recited. As most non-Muslims note when they first pick up the Qur'an, it is not an easy book to read from beginning to end. In fact, most Muslims, especially children, do not read it that way. They often start with the shorter chapters of the Qur'an at the end. Or in the case of Qur'an for Children, *they are given a thematic guide. In each chapter, a theme is introduced, and the author and editor select what they consider to be the verses in the Qur'an that address that theme. Each relevant verse is reproduced in Arabic, transliterated into English letters, and then translated into English. The author and editor provide review questions at the beginning and end of each section of their guide. In the chapter excerpted below, the author and editor present verses that contain answers to an all-important question: "Who is God?" After each verse, in parentheses, the author and editor provide the chapter and verse from which the Qur'anic text is selected.*

Section 2: God Is One

1. Your God is One God (2:163).
2. He is the One God (112:1).

3. God is All-powerful (2:109).

4. Truly God is Gentle and Compassionate to mankind (2:143).

5. God is the Lord of mighty Grace (2:105).

6. He is the Acceptor of Repentance; Compassionate (9:104).

7. He befriends the righteous (7:196).

Section 3: God's Bounties and Blessings

1. Whatever blessing you have, it is from God (16:53).

2. Truly in the creation of the heavens and the earth and the alternation of night and day and the ship that runs in the sea with profit for people and the water that God sends down from the heaven thereby reviving life with it to the earth after it is dead and His scattering in it all kinds of animals, and the alteration of the winds and the clouds spread between heaven and earth, there are the signs for a people who understand (2:164).

3. Of His signs is the creation of the heavens and the earth and the diversity of your languages and your colors (30:22).

4. If the sea were ink for the words of my Lord, the sea would surely be exhausted before the words of my Lord are exhausted (18:109).

5. If all the trees on earth were pens and the sea (were ink) with seven seas more to help it the words of God would not be exhausted (31:27).

6. He gave you hearing, sight and heart that you might thank Him (16:78).

Section 4: God Is Aware of Our Deeds

1. God is aware of whatever you do (2:234).

2. God is not unmindful of what you do (2:85).

3. Truly God knows what you do (16:91).

4. He is with you wherever you may be (57:4).

5. Truly nothing is hidden from God on earth or in the heavens (3:5).

6. Whatever good you do, God knows it (2:197).

7. God knows what you conceal and what you reveal (16:19).

8. God knows all that you reveal and that you conceal (7:99).

9. He knows what you do secretly or openly. He knows what you earn (by your deeds) (6:3).

10. Whether you hide your word or say it openly, He truly has knowledge of the secrets in the hearts (67:13).
11. Whether you reveal anything or conceal it, truly God has knowledge of all things (33:54).
12. Whether you show what is in your minds or conceal it, God shall call you to account for it (2:284).

Section 5: God Helps Us

1. God intends ease for you. He does not intend to put you to difficulties (2:185).
2. He who fears God, (God) makes for him his path easy (65:4).
3. I listen to the prayer of the petitioner when he calls on Me (2:186).

Section 6: Seek God's Help Alone

1. Whoever holds firmly to God will be guided to a right path (3:101).
2. Thee do we worship and from Thee we seek help (1:4).
3. When you have taken a decision, then trust in God. Truly God loves those who put their trust (in Him) (3:159).
4. If God helps you, none shall overpower you. If He forsakes you, who is there, after that, who can help you (3:160).

3. Shakina Reinhertz, *Women Called to the Path of Rumi: The Way of the Whirling Dervish* (2001)

Among the many Sufi orders to have flourished after 1965 is the Mevlevi, known to some as the whirling dervishes. The Mevlevi order traces its roots to the thirteenth-century poet known in America simply as Rumi. Rumi wrote in Persian but lived in modern-day Turkey, where a Sufi order was established by those influenced by and devoted to his mystical understandings of God's love. They referred to the poet as Mevlana, or "our master." In order to experience God's love more deeply, to know God more closely, disciples of the order developed an elaborate set of rituals that combined music, dance, and the recitation of both poetry and Qur'an. Called the sema, literally meaning "audition," the ceremony begins with an opening procession of the semazens, or participants, who wear long robes and tall, cylindrical hats. Prayers, hymns, and music may be performed. There is a long series of salutations between the participants and their leader, the shaykh, who eventually sits, facing in the direction of Mecca. Then comes the heart of the ritual: Extending one's arms with the right palm facing up and left facing down, the participant turns counterclockwise, pivoting on the left foot. Each movement, each turn, is a form of meditation and prayer.

Early Turkish immigrants to the United States may have indeed practiced "the turn" on American soil over a hundred years ago, but the ritual remained largely unnoticed until after 1965. In the 1970s, Suleyman Hayati Dede, the Mevlevi shaykh from Konya, Turkey, visited North America and commissioned his son, Jelaluddin Loras, to teach the turn in the West. Loras became president of the Mevlevi Order of America (MOA) and attracted followers around the country through his lectures, workshops, and personal example. Unlike traditional orders, the MOA invited women to turn alongside men, and many women felt called, as author Shakina Reinhertz puts it, to the path of Rumi. Below, Reinhertz interviews two women about their experiences as Sufi practitioners. These interviews show the important role played by the teacher in the practice of Sufism and they reveal what this mystical practice means to two American women.

[Testimony of] Melike

I had always heard of whirling dervishes. Actually my mother used to associate whirling dervishes with crazy people. Maybe she started the whole thing! When I was a child, she used to say, "Oh, you're acting like a whirling dervish!" So I grew up thinking it meant crazy. Little did I know.

I had seen Suleyman Dede with the whirling dervishes sometime in the 1970s. Then, in 1980, when the Sufi community invited Jelaluddin Loras to San Francisco, he dressed in *tennure* [the dervish's costume] and turned for us. Some time later, after he was invited to live here, I kept asking, "When is he going to start a class? I want to learn it." As soon as he did, I was there. I knew I was going to take the class even before he decided to give it.

MEETING SULEYMAN DEDE

In 1984 I went to Turkey on my own to meet Jelaluddin's family and to visit Mevlana's tomb. The hospitality of the Turkish people overwhelmed me. It began with someone on the plane who took me to the bus station in Ankara to help me get on the right bus and insisted on paying my way. The day after I arrived, I decided to go to Dede's, but I wasn't sure where he lived. I walked up to a taxi cab driver and said, "Suleyman Dede's" and he took me to a little house. It seemed that everyone in Konya knew Dede, which was interesting, as it is not a small town.

The family had no idea that I was coming. Jelaluddin had sent them a letter about my visit, but they hadn't received it. All they knew was that somehow I was acquainted with their son in California. They made me feel very welcome and were so happy to hear news of Jelaluddin. I brought a Turkish translator, because I knew I couldn't speak to them without one.

People were coming to see Dede, staying for a few minutes and then leaving. I remember being filled with light, filled with love. His whole being was love, he loved everybody—it made no difference who they were or what they were. Immediately, he insisted that I move in. For various reasons I wanted to stay in the hotel, at least for that night. I wasn't feeling well and I wanted a little bit of space on my own, but Feriste Hanum, his wife, also insisted that I stay. "Dede told you to stay, you must stay!" she said. So I moved in.

After that first brief meeting I went back to the rug shop that was a base for me because several of the people there spoke English, including an English girl who had come to visit Mevlana [Rumi]. She was connected with the Sufis in Spain and with Idries Shah. I walked into the rug store after being at Dede's and she said, "My God, what has happened to you, you're totally filled with light! Light is just pouring out of you!" It was from being in Dede's presence. It was a blessing to be around him and his love.

THE POWER OF RUMI'S LOVE

The girl from the rug shop had brought her mother with her from England. The older woman had been in a difficult relationship and wanted to get away, so she went on this trip with her daughter. At Rumi's tomb she walked in the door and started crying without understanding why. Later, she came to me thinking I could explain it. I certainly couldn't, but I loved that she had that experience, especially since she had no previous connection with Mevlana at all. Every day that she was in Konya she went back to the tomb and cried. That was my experience too—going to his tomb and being filled with love and the tears of my heart opening.

THE SHAIKH AND MY FEET

When I stayed with Dede and Feriste it was the middle of winter and very cold. In the house they only heated the one room where we slept. There were two beds raised off the floor, and a mattress on the floor. The previous year, Dede had a stroke, so he would mostly stay in that room, and was always happy to see people. He sat up cross-legged all the time on his bed and she slept on the floor on the mattress.

In my training, I had been taught not to put my feet toward the head of the sheikh—it is considered very rude, an insult. The way my bed was situated, however, my feet were pointed straight at Dede's head. I couldn't go to sleep the first night, because I kept trying to curve my feet away from his head. He realized what I was thinking and he sat up in bed, gently reaching over to tuck my feet in, like I was this little child that he was taking care of.

FERISTE HANUM

Feriste was a strong, fiery woman, unafraid to speak up. She also was very aware of culture. For her, Dede was the final word—like when she said to me, "Dede asked you to stay, you must stay!" While I was staying with them, I wanted to go to town. I was an experienced traveler and wanted to go sightseeing in Konya. Feriste didn't think it was such a great idea for me to go off by myself every day. I had my headscarf tied behind my neck, which is the way I was comfortable in wearing a scarf. As I was leaving, she'd stop me at the door, untie the scarf from behind my neck and tie it real tight under my chin.

Feriste was very devoted to her children. They came first, and she wanted to know that everyone was happy and taken care of.

INSPIRATION FROM A SAINT

While I was in Konya in 1984, I visited different places connected with Mevlana. One day I took a bus to a place with very beautiful rolling hills that I thought was the gravesite of Mevlana's cook, Atesh Bas. No one was there. For a long time I looked at the landscape on the outskirts of Konya and then I just started turning. I turned and turned in this incredibly inspirational place. That was the end of the experience, so I thought.

On the next trip to Konya, in 1994, we all went to the cook's grave and it wasn't the same place! I described to Jelaluddin where I had been previously and found out it was the home of a woman musician who had lived at the time of Mevlana. She was a hermit and she would play music that Mevlana could hear from a distance. When she died unexpectedly, he was very sad. At her home, I had felt so inspired, although at the time I didn't know her story or who she was.

There was also another woman dear to Rumi buried in Konya, one of his *murids* [students], a saint known as Fakhru-'n-nisa. When Dede was alive they had to exhume this woman's body to relocate her grave. When they opened her original casket, she had not decomposed. She was exactly like she had been when she died, except for one tiny spot on her foot.

THE SPIRIT OF GUIDANCE AT WORK

Before that trip to Konya in 1994, I was living in Virginia and hadn't been connected to the whirling dervish scene for probably five or six years. I had an old invalid cat that had just died and I was feeling very sad. A friend of mine told me that the whirling dervishes were coming to Washington, D.C., so I went to the performance. One of the singers began singing the *na'at* [poem sung in praise of the Prophet Muhammad]—it was Kani Karaca, a world-renowned singer whom I had always wanted to meet. I had heard his voice on tapes previously. He is a blind man with an exquisite voice. Tears started pouring down my face as I watched the ceremony. I realized how much this tradition really moved me; that it was such a deep part of me.

That night I wound up staying in a couple's house in a room they had originally been prepared for Celaleddin Chelebi, the head of the Mevlevi Order. At the last minute, Celaleddin Chelebi had decided to stay at the hotel with the dervishes. On the wall of this room was a drum—a *tar*—painted with a Mevlevi symbol. The moment I saw it, I knew that Jelaluddin had painted it. "Where did you get this?" I asked my host. "Jelaluddin Loras gave it to me," he said. We looked at each other and realized, simultaneously, that he had stayed at my house many years before, for several weeks, and here he had anonymously invited me to stay at his home! We were both totally amazed.

"We've got to call Jelaluddin," he said. Jelal was in Turkey at the time, so I called some friends who had his phone number. "We are going to Turkey in a few weeks, Melike, you really should go," my friends suggested. The next week I was on the plane to Konya! That journey was such a blessing. With the Grace of God we were allowed to do the turning ceremony at Mevlana's tomb and at the Galata Turbe in Istanbul.

I had dropped out of the whole scene for years, but when I was in Konya during that last trip I saw the words of Mevlana, "You cannot escape this circle of lovers!" It's true, you cannot escape! Once you've been touched, you are a part of this circle. The heart yearns for more of that feeling of unity and love and joy!

THE MEVLEVI PATH

I studied turning not knowing what it was going to be. Previously, I'd read Rumi's poetry, which I love. In the years since, I have gotten deeply connected to him. His path is love and that has always been my path—to love everyone and everything.

When I was studying with Jelaluddin Loras, participating in *zikrs* at least once a week, and turn classes, my life became filled with understanding the Mevlevis. I began to understand the practice of honoring the guest—cooking for others, putting their needs before one's own, really practicing love—seeing that the practice of love is the greatest teaching, and seeing people transformed. At the same time, I realized that we have our human ways and there are ways to refine our humanness and to work on ourselves. What better way than to try to treat anyone who comes into your midst as the honored guest?

THE NATURE OF TURNING

I've been thinking about why I do the turn—something I've never asked myself before. Through my involvement in Tai Chi and trying to understand the way energy moves in a body, I have come to know that there is a force, a strength and an openness of spirals that is infinite in nature. A friend of mine was explaining the mathematics of infinity: numbers spiral, shells spiral, flowers spiral and the internal martial arts spiral. Energy is much stronger and alive in that type of movement because the form itself creates movement. The spiral energy creates vortexes.

Without blockage, energy flows through unimpeded. It happens in turning too. If there are blockages, like when your mind is busy, the energy doesn't move, it doesn't flow. It flows only if the mind is empty, so it is a fabulous practice in emptying oneself. Physically, you need to have your spine open, because that is the axis you turn around. Your arms are your wings, and they are flying. They are wide open.

It is not always possible to be empty, and that is part of life too. When you can let go and become empty, you become full, but not filled. As it pours through, it is like a cleansing. The energy is pouring down and through, in and out, no stopping, no grabbing. Let it go. Bless the world!

At the same time you are grounded and you're centered because you have to be. If you are not, you lose it. Turning encompasses many ideals of being; of relaxing and emptying, opening and meditating, grounding and centering. Breath is really the key to all of it. If your breath is not in harmony you lose your rhythm.

When you are turning with others, in *zikr* or *sema*, you need to have a consciousness of more than yourself. You have to flow with the group, feel where the whole circle is, feel the turners on both sides of you. You need to be in harmony and balance with everyone in the circle. Where does it need energy? Where does it need to get a little clearer so that the circle is more harmonious? You are always looking for that harmony while you are turning around the center of yourself; looking to know where the center of the circle is, as well as your own center. The more *semazens* [participants] there are turning, the more blending one needs to do. This is what people feel when they watch the *sema*. Something happens in the energy and atmosphere that keeps them coming back, because they feel the transformation in the space. I also agree with Murshid Sam [Lewis of the Sufi Ruhaniat International] when he says, "The watcher is the prayerful devotee; the dancer is Divine."

As I turn I just pray that I do God's will. It is a time to remember, a time to just let go of everything else and pray, a time to be open, to be centered, to be focused and to be loving. Something happens. I don't know what else to say. It is a sacred journey as all of life is. I don't really see any beginning. It is beyond the beyond. The cause behind the cause.

ADAB

Adab is common sense with respect. Rumi said, "There are hundreds of ways to kneel and kiss the ground." It is the respect that matters, not the way you do it. If you respect a plant, if you respect a dog, if you respect another human life, you treat it correctly. *Adab* can be translated as "manners," but manners can be such a superficial thing. You can be really good in your manners and a real creep. You can try to charm people all you want, but what comes through is who you really are.

Adab is kindness and respect for a person. Kindness in how one treats another, awareness of the other and what they are needing, and that they are the most important. Learning can come with it too—how to make others feel special, to have them become the honored guest.

God is everything, *La ilaha illa Allah hu* [there is no god except God only]. This is a huge realization, that everything is God. So where do you start? Hazrat Inayat Khan says, "If you have no God, create one." If you start respecting one, it grows to two; soon it can be all, if you really work in that direction.

[Testimony of] Kera

There were about twenty-two of us in the first class, and many of those people are still turning today. The class was not what I had thought it would be in terms of learning how to actually do the turn. It was hard. We had these boards with pegs in them, and salt, since Jelaluddin wanted us to learn the way that it was taught originally.

Jelal told us a story about Shems Friedlander, author of the popular classic *The Whirling Dervishes*, who had studied the turn with Jelal's father, Suleyman Dede, in Turkey. They had this especially grueling practice with the boards and the salt. Shem's toe had gotten cracked or cut, and it hurt. It was raw, and here he was putting salt on it. It was painful and bleeding, but Shems was really into the turn, so he was still practicing. Dede came over to him and said, "What are you doing?" Shems said, "Oh, I'm doing the practice!" Dede said, "No, you're not, you're making stew!" That story stuck with me and reminded me that it wasn't about the form, it wasn't about getting it right or standing up straight, it wasn't about all the things that Jelal always used to correct us for. The practice is about intention.

WHY I TURN

The first time that I was ever in *sema* was like nothing I'd ever felt before. It was a lift-off. I was a bird in flight. In those days I practiced a lot and was competent with the form, so I didn't have to worry about being dizzy or falling down and I was freed from the concern of doing it right, which gave me the opportunity to be involved in what it really was. In the first *sema* there were moments of true connectedness to the tradition and the power of the practice, incredible joyfulness and freedom of spirit! I was hooked! I said to myself, "This will always be important to me; this will always be part of me, and will always be my path, my journey."

Before a recent *sema* I hadn't practiced and I knew I was going to wobble. I said to Jelaluddin, "You know, I'm really kind of worried because I haven't practiced. What happens if I fall down?" He looked me square in the eye, and said "Just get up!" and I said "Oh, okay." I got it again, that this practice is not about doing it right. I'm here because I am grateful to be invited to turn, and that I'm part of the tradition. Jelaluddin, as guardian of this sacred ceremony, has given me permission to turn, and the opportunity to participate. I want to be part of *sema* because it has such power and beauty. It's like coming to the well and taking a cup of light out of it and having a drink. That is why I turn.

MY SPIRITUAL JOURNEY

As I got older I felt there was something really missing from my life. I was fortunate enough to go to Boston College, which in and of itself was kind of a strange thing. A nice Jewish girl from New York, going to a school where all the professors were Jesuit brothers! I thought they were fascinating. I remember having this one teacher who, I believe now, was truly an enlightened man. I remember watching him and thinking that I was hallucinating—he was so animated in his speech that I saw sparks flying off his fingertips. I had never experienced anybody with that much life or that much energy. He taught a comparative religion class, and I loved it. "Here's what I've been looking for!" I thought, "a pallet of religions."

The class went into Buddhism, Hinduism, Judaism, Catholicism and more. Among the videos that were shown was a clip of Sufi Sam and the Dances of Universal Peace. I was captivated. When I spoke to my teacher he was extremely encouraging, telling me to pursue my interest in religion. I took many, many classes and got a degree in Philosophy. In Boston I also became aware of Sufi dancing, and started going.

When I moved to San Francisco I wanted to meet people and be part of something. I knew that Sufi Sam had been in San Francisco and when I looked in the *Bay Guardian* I found a little ad announcing a group. I went. That first night I walked in, Andalieb, who also joined the first class, was at the door. Immediately I felt welcome, drawn in, so I started going once a week. I began other classes too, going to the *khanqa* [a Sufi lodge], participating in activities and becoming part of the community.

Eventually, I moved into the *khanqa*. When I started to get involved in the Mevlevi order and the turn, I felt like I had found what I was looking for. I knew this was really the point where it all came together for me. I think this may apply to any spiritual path: there is the time spent getting there, time for figuring out where you are, and then you just need to keep going. Everything just funnels down to this point of understanding. Once you understand, then you are free.

THE PRACTICAL APPLICATION OF SPIRITUAL LIFE

My spiritual practice helps me in my daily life. I know that when I'm frightened or worried or angry I can start doing a practice in my mind. I can be in the middle of my office, with all these people around, and I can bring what I know to the situation. That remembrance changes how I feel, right then and there, and nobody knows about it. It always is a challenge. How do you live the inner journey and the outer journey at the same time? How do you integrate your spiritual path into your daily life?

Washing the dishes or mopping the floor, or rocking your baby, or driving to work; whatever it is, you have the opportunity to bring your spiritual self into that situation. What is really challenging is to not lose sight of who you are or what you are connected to, and still be in this world and bring heart to what you do. At times I forget. I'm not around other people who remind me, so I have to remind myself, which is hard with all the distractions in my daily life. I'm distracted by my children, by my job, by the people I'm with. But this is all the more opportunity to think about what I need to do, so that I can bring harmony to my life and not feel frustrated or abandoned.

SEMAZENBASHI

When Jelaluddin told me he wanted me to be the *semazenbashi* [the dance master], I was honored and also scared. I thought, "I'd rather turn. I don't want to do that." I thought that it shouldn't have been me, and I questioned if I could fulfill the trust he was giving me—to pull everybody together during the *sema*. I had never even led a dance class.

Once again I realized it wasn't about the form. The importance of the feeling became even clearer, since in this role all communication would be in silence. What happened that night was very special—I really grew into myself as the person that Jelal believed I was. I was able to facilitate as opposed to leading. It was about inner guidance, and being in the moment. There is really nothing that you can do if someone gets off center while they are turning. You can simply stand there with them and just breathe, and see if they get it. A great experience for me!

REFLECTIONS ON OUR FIRST CLASS

In the first class with Jelaluddin we grew as people as much as we grew as *semazens*, as Mevlevis, and as seekers on a spiritual path. In the process of training, we all tried to be so precise, to have the form right. I think we all wanted to be perfect. Until the first *sema* all we knew was the form. But that first *sema* was so different from the practices, so alive! It has always felt like a special gift to me that I was there, and I was part of it, and that I'm still part of it. As long as I'm alive, I will always be part of the *sema*. Whenever I can, I will be there, and if I'm not there in presence, I'll be there in spirit.

4. Tazim R. Kassam, "The Daily Prayer (*Du'a*) of Shi'a Isma'ili Muslims" (2001)

Though the Twelver Shi'a, or Ithna 'asharis, account for the largest group of Shi'a in the United States, another Shi'i group with a strong presence is the

Sevener Shi'a, or Isma'ilis. The Isma'ilis trace their origins to a disagreement over the successor to the sixth Imam in 765 AD. They are divided into subgroups. Among them are the Nizaris, followers of the Aga Khan, who is recognized as the living Imam. These Muslims, who live in various places around the world, often call their meeting places jamatkhanas *and deemphasize various aspects of Sunni Islamic ritual. The current Aga Khan, Prince Karim Shah, receives monetary donations from his followers and in turn helps fund a number of different public institutions, including health clinics and schools often known for academic excellence. Thousands of Nizaris, who trace their roots to East Africa and South Asia, came to the United States in the 1970s as refugees; today, several of them are prominent and successful college professors.*

Tazim Kassam, a professor of religious studies at Syracuse University, is one of them. Born and raised in Kenya, the East African country that was home for many years to a large Indian immigrant community, she studied at McGill University in Montreal, Canada, where she took her BA and PhD in the history of religions. She also studied Hindustani music at the University of Bombay and eventually applied her aesthetic sensibility to a book about the song traditions of Isma'ili Muslims in South Asia. Kassam has also served as leader of the Study of Islam section of the American Academy of Religion, the "trade organization" for religious studies scholars in North America and beyond. In this excerpt from a book about religious practice in the United States, Kassam explains the theological, scriptural, and spiritual meanings of Isma'ili daily prayer and offers a translation of the text. Kassam's interpretations reveal the similarities and differences between the Isma'ili prayer and other Islamic prayer traditions, shedding light on the spirituality of a relatively unknown Muslim group while also highlighting themes at the core of Islamic spiritualities in the United States.

Every day before sunrise and around sunset a familiar scene occurs in many cities across Canada and the United States: Shi'a Isma'ili Muslims assemble in their *Jamatkhanas* (places of assembly) to pray in fellowship. . . . Following the Qur'anic injunction to be in a state of ritual purity (*ghusl* or *wudu*) during prayer, they bathe and dress in fresh and formal attire before they set out to "establish worship at the two ends of the day" (11:14). They enter the *jamatkhana*, remove their coats and shoes in an anteroom while greeting each other *ya ali madad* (Ali help us!), and walk into a modest prayer hall for a worship service that takes about half an hour. The focal point of this service is called the *du'a*, a ritual supplication that is recited in Arabic. Isma'ilis are required to recite the *du'a* thrice daily in the *jamatkhana*. Those unable to attend a *jamatkhana* to pray in congregation must recite the obligatory *du'a* in a timely fashion at dawn and dusk wherever they find themselves.

The *du'a* embodies, expresses, and confirms the religious life and identity of the Isma'ili Muslims. . . . The Isma'ili *du'a* is best understood within the context of the highly cultivated inner devotional life in Islam. God says in the Qur'an: "Remember Me and I shall remember thee" (2:152). With respect to prayer and worship, Prophet Muhammad said: "For everything there is a polish to clear away rust and the polish of the heart is remembrance of God." In response to the commandment to worship and in the personal quest for God, Muslim societies over the centuries have evolved a rich, expressive tradition of prayers and devotions.

In Islam, prayer is associated with several Arabic terms including *salat*, *du'a dhikr*, and *'ibadah*. These four terms are mentioned often in the Qur'an. *Salat* refers to the obligatory, canonical prayer performed five times daily by Sunni Muslims. The *salat* is a set prayer rite consisting of a series of bodily movement, such as bowing and prostrating, done in conjunction with a fixed recitation in Arabic that includes verses from the Qur'an. The form and content of this ritual prayer was established centuries ago on the basis of the Prophet's example (*sunna*) and consensus (*ijma'*) of Sunni schools of law. *Salat* (pl. *salawat*) also refers to the formulaic prayer of calling down blessings on the Prophet and his descendants enjoined in the Qur'an on all Muslims: "May God bestow peace and blessings upon (Prophet) Muhammad and upon the family of Muhammad!"

Du'a (call, plea) is generally regarded by Muslims to be a spontaneous, individual prayer consisting of personal supplications and petitions to God. *Du'a* (pl. *ad'iyah*) both incorporates and imitates the plentiful invocations and prayers present in the Qur'an, which is itself the matrix of Muslim devotions. Unlike the ritual *salat*, which is an established communal liturgy offered at specific times, *du'a* is offered individually at any time and is usually voiced silently, inwardly, with hands upraised, the palms held open to receive blessings. It is customary for Muslims to remain seated in the *masjid* (place of prostration, mosque) after performing the *salat* to invoke God's name (*dhikr*) thirty-three times and then to offer a *du'a*. Completing the supplication with words of gratitude (*al-hamdulilla*), the palms are drawn over the face and down, crossing the shoulders, as if one were anointing oneself with divine blessings (*baraka*).

Although spontaneous and informal in origin, many individual prayers have been composed for special needs and compiled into prayer handbooks. *Du'a* is a distinctive feature of the Shi'a tradition that lovingly rehearses and transmits from one generation to the next the supplications of its Imams. The first Imam, Hazrat 'Ali, was much given to *du'a* and urged his followers to recite them. Because the Imams were oppressed by those who rejected their divine right to leadership, they adopted *du'a* as a medium for teaching the meaning of the Qur'an, the principles of Islam, and the message of the Prophet's household. Through their own example, they taught *du'a* as a means to instill piety, devotion, and righteous conduct. Hundreds of prayer books have been preserved by the Shi'a containing these supplications. . . .

Regardless of the type of prayer, the primary aim of all Muslim devotions is to seek spiritual and worldly peace (*salam*) through surrender and submission (*islam*) to God's will: hence, the word *muslim* literally means one who submits or surrenders oneself to God. This sentiment is echoed in numerous ways in the ordinary conduct of Muslim life including the customary Muslim greeting "May peace be upon you and God's mercy and blessings!" (*as salamu 'alaykum wa rahmatulahi wa barakatahu*). The most comprehensive term for worship in Islam is *'ibadah*. Derived from the verb "to serve," it emphasizes that the ideal response of humanity toward God is veneration and obedience, adoration, and servitude. God's servant (*'abd*) follows God's will out of a profound love and awe of God as Creator, Sustainer, and Lord of all worlds (*rabb al-'alamin*). The simple acts of lifting up the hands with palms open, bowing (*ruku*), and prostrating the body (*sujud*) manifest these feelings of penitence, reverence, humility, and adoration.

The term *du'a* is used in a special way by present-day Isma'ili Muslims to denote a prescribed obligatory ritual prayer in Arabic that is recited thrice daily in a congregational service held in the *jamatkhana*. The services held in the *jamatkhana* at the two ends of the day also include other devotional activities such as singing hymns, reading sermons, and making food offerings. However, the recitation of the fixed Arabic *du'a* is the key ritual prayer without which the service remains incomplete. An Isma'ili who arrives at a service after the *du'a* has been recited must quietly recite it alone to fulfill this obligation. Thus, the *du'a* occupies a functional status similar to that of the obligatory ritual *salat* observed by Muslims generally.

The Isma'ili *du'a* is in Arabic, the universal language of Islam, and is composed of six cycles or parts. Parallel structures within the *du'a* create an internal rhythm and balance. Each of the six parts opens with the Qur'anic formula *basmala* (In the Name of God, the Compassionate, the Merciful) and closes with *sujud* or prostration (O God, to Thee is my prostration and prayer). The first half of each part contains select verses from the Qur'an that convey fundamental Islamic and Isma'ili principles. The second half of each part consists of a supplication followed by a *salat* or *tasliyah*, namely, calling down blessings upon the Prophet and his household. In parts II, IV, and VI the hands are raised up with open palms before making supplications for forgiveness, sustenance, and divine aid. During the fifth part, a few moments of silence are observed for repetition (*dhikr*) of *ya ali, ya muhammad*. The whole *du'a* itself is tied together elegantly with the formula of gratitude, *al-hamdullila* or "Praise be to God!" . . .

The importance of expressing gratitude and singing God's praise is indicated in the Isma'ili *du'a* by its occurrences at the beginning and end of the six parts. Except for human beings, who possess free will, all creation instinctively bears witness to and praises God: "The seven heavens and the earth and all that is therein praise Him, and there is not a thing but hymns His praise; but ye understand not their praise!" (17:44). Gratitude goes hand-in-hand with submission to God's will since God is also "Master of Judgment Day" (*malik yaum al-din*). Creation is not a frivolous diversion but a momentous and purposeful act of God. Like Jews and Christians, Muslims believe that at the end of time (*qiyama*) all creatures will be weighed for their deeds and misdeeds. Death does not mean extinction. The body may perish but the soul, which is eternal, must face the consequence of its deeds in the hereafter. Hence, life in this material world (*al-dunya*) is believed to be a preparation for divine felicity in the next world (*al-akhirah*). The Qur'an states that an abode of peace (*dar al salam*) awaits the righteous in the hereafter: "For them will be an abode of peace in the presence of their Lord. He will be their protective friend because they acted (righteously)" (6:128). Part II of the *du'a* contains the prayer, "Give us, O Sustainer, a life of peace and usher us in to the abode of peace." Peace is a state of integrity and harmony that may apply to many dimensions of everyday life, but the ultimate destiny of the soul is to attain everlasting peace. . . .

All six parts of the Isma'ili *du'a* end with *salat*, or calling down blessings on the Prophet, 'Ali and the Prophet's family, and the Imam of the time. No Muslim prayer is complete without the *salat* or *tasliyah* in keeping with the command; "Verily, God and his Angels send blessings upon the Prophet. O ye who believe! Call down blessings upon him and peace" (33:56). Most blessings on the Prophet are variations on a single sentence, "May God call down blessings on our lord Muhammad and on the family of our lord Muhammad and greet them with peace." This prayer extends to all prophets; whenever the name of Muhammad or a biblical prophet such as Abraham is mentioned, Muslims utter *sallalahu 'alayhi wa al-salam*: "May God bless him and give him peace!"

This brings us to the core of the Isma'ili *du'a*, which is the recognition of the authority and leadership of 'Ali and the Isma'ili Nizari line of imams. Before the *sujud*, every part of *du'a* ends with the testimony, "Our lord Shah Karim al-Husayni is the present living Imam." Several Qur'anic verses in the *du'a* pertain to the Shi'a understanding of 'Ali and the Imams as trustees of the Prophet's teachings and God's revelation. In Part II, verse 4:59 commands the believers to obey God, the Messenger, and *ulu al-amr* are 'Ali and the divinely appointed Imams. Their authority refers to their office as interpreters par excellence of the Qur'an. Isma'ilis, a subsect of the Shi'a, believe that Revelation has two aspects: the formal, literal, external text of the Qur'an (*tanzil*) and its spiritual, symbolic, hidden meanings (*ta'wil*). God entrusted the Prophet with both the exoteric and esoteric aspects of the Qur'an. Following God's command, the Prophet, in turn, entrusted the *ta'wil* or esoteric wisdom of the Qur'an to 'Ali. This divine inheritance is passed on from one imam to the next through explicit designation (*nass*). After the Prophet, the imams alone were endowed with the capacity to mine the Qur'an for its divine secrets because God had bestowed upon them knowledge (*'ilm*) of all things.

Without the divinely sanctioned appointment of 'Ali, the Prophet's mission would have remained incomplete because, although the exoteric aspect of divine revelation and law ceased with the Prophet's death, the esoteric aspect of divine guidance continues through symbolic and contextual interpretation. For the Shi'a, the Qur'anic verse "O Messenger! Proclaim what has been sent down to thee from thy Lord, for if thou did not do so, thou hast not delivered His Message" (5:67) indicates that the Prophet was divinely commanded to proclaim 'Ali as his vicegerent and as the *amir al-mu'minin*, Commander of the Believers.

God thus ensured that the message of the Qur'an and the teachings of Islam would remain alive and relevant for all time through 'Ali and successive imams. In gratitude and recognition of their Imams' timely guidance, in Part VI of the *du'a*, the Isma'ilis recite the names of forty-nine Imams including that of the present, living Imam, Shah Karim al-Husayni (b. 1936). . . .

God's Light cannot be contemplated directly by the human mind, which is too imperfect an organ of knowledge. As long as it is confined by the limits of the material world, God can speak to humankind only through symbols and parables. According to Imam Ja'far as-Sadiq, "The light descends upon the most noble men; it shone through our Imams, so that we are the lights of the heavens and the earth. To us is heaven committed and from us are the secrets of science derived, for we are the destination that all strive to reach . . . we are the Proofs of the Lord of the Worlds." For the Shi'a the Imams are thus illuminated and irradiated with divine light (*nur*).

At the end of reciting the *du'a*, each member of the Isma'ili Muslim congregation turns to the person on the right and on the left to shake hands while saying *shah jo didar*, which means: "May you glimpse His divine countenance!" While it may not be possible to see God with physical eyes, God may be witnessed spiritually through single-minded devotion and prayer. This is the ultimate goal of the Isma'ili devotee (*murid*)—to be blessed with a glimpse of the Divine countenance. The Qur'an describes the shining faces of those who have had that beatific vision as follows: "Some faces on that day will be bright, looking upon their Lord" (75:22).

In conclusion, the ritual prayer of the Isma'ilis is at once a daily act of devotion and submission as well as a clear affirmation of their Shi'a Muslim identity. As an obligatory prayer for all Isma'ilis, the recitation of the *du'a* unites this diverse and scattered community in a frontierless faith of fellowship. By testifying to the Oneness of God, the authority of God's divine revelation in the Qur'an and the example and teachings of the Prophet Muhammad as God's last Messenger, the Isma'ilis affirm their participation in the Muslim *umma* [global community of believers]. Their recognition of 'Ali and the Imams as commander of the Believers who are divinely appointed and inspired to interpret the Qur'an identify them as Shi'a. And finally, their declaration of allegiance to the forty-ninth Imam Shah Karim al-Husayni, His Highness Prince Aga Khan IV, as the present living Imam anchors their historical lineage as Nizari Isma'ilis. . . .

Isma'ili Du'a

PART I

In the name of God, the Compassionate, the Merciful.

All praise is due to God, the Sustainer of all beings, the Compassionate, the Merciful, the Lord of the Day of Judgment. Thee alone we worship and Thee alone we seek for help. Guide us to the straight path, the path of those whom Thou hast blessed, not of those who earned Thine anger nor of those who have gone astray. (Surah al-Fatiha 1:1–7)

I prostrate before Thee and I rely upon Thee; from Thee is my strength and Thou art my protection, O Sustainer of all beings!

O God! Let Thy peace be upon Muhammad—the chosen, and upon 'Ali—the favorite, and upon the Imams—the pure, and upon the evidence of Thy authority—the lord of the age and the time, the present living Imam, our lord Shah Karim al-Husayni.

O God! To thee is my prostration and prayer.

PART II

In the name of God, the Compassionate, the Merciful.

O ye who believe! Obey God and obey the Messenger and (obey) the holders of authority from amongst you. (Surah an-Nisah 4:59)

And We have vested (the knowledge of) everything in the manifest Imam. (Surah Ya-Sin 36:12)

(Raise hands) O God! O our Lord! Thou art the peace, from Thee is the peace, and to Thee returneth the peace. Give us, O our Sustainer, a life of peace, and usher us into the abode of peace. Blessed art Thou, our Lord, the most High, O the Lord of Majesty and Reverence.

O God! O our Lord! From thee is my support and upon Thee is my reliance. Thee alone we worship and from Thee alone we seek for help. O 'Ali! Help me with thy kindness.

There is no god except God. Muhammad is the Messenger of God. 'Ali—the master of believers—is from God.

Our lord shah Karim al-Husayni is the present living Imam.

O God! To Thee is my prostration and prayer.

PART III

In the name of God, the Compassionate, the Merciful.

O Messenger! Proclaim what has been sent down to thee from thy Lord, for if thou did not do so, than thou hast not delivered His Message; and God will protect thee from the people. (Surah al-Ma'ida 5:67)

There is no god except God, the Ever-Living, the Eternal. There is no god except God, the Sovereign, the Truth, the Evident. There is no god except God, the Lord of the Day of Judgment.

There is no hero except 'Ali, there is no sword except (his sword) Dhu'lfiqar. Seek in times of difficulty the help of your lord, the present living (Imam) Shah Karim al-Husayni.

O God! To thee is my prostration and prayer.

PART IV

In the name of God, the Compassionate, the Merciful.

Lo! Those who swear allegiance unto thee (Muhammad), in truth they swear allegiance unto God; God's hand is upon their hands. Then he who breaks his oath breaks it hurting his own soul. And he who fulfills what he has pledged with God, God will grant him a mighty reward. (Surah al-Fatah 48:10)

(Raise hands) O God! Forgive us our sins, give us our bread, have mercy upon us in the name of Thy closest Messengers and Thy pure Imams, and in the name of our lord and our Imam, Shah Karim al-Husayni.

O God! To Thee is my prostration and prayer.

PART V

In the name of God, the Compassionate, the Merciful.

O ye who believe! Betray not God nor the Messenger, and betray not your trusts while you know. (Surah al-Anfal 8:27)

O our Lord! Forgive us our sins, make our tasks easy, give us our bread, and have mercy upon us. Verily, Thou art powerful over all things.

(Repeat silently) O 'Ali, O Muhammad! O Muhammad, O 'Ali!

(Raise hand) O Imam of the time! O our Lord! Thou art my strength and thou art my support and upon thee I rely. O present living Imam Shah Karim al-Husayni, thou art the true manifest Imam.

O God! To Thee is my prostration and prayer.

PART VI

In the name of God, the Compassionate, the Merciful.

Say: He is God, One! God is Absolute, Everlasting. He did not beget nor was He begotten and there is none like unto Him. (Surah al-Ikhlas 112:1–4)

O God! In the name of Muhammad—the chosen, and 'Ali—the favorite, and Fatima—the radiant, and Hasan and Husayn.

O God! In the name of our lord 'Ali; our lord Husayn; our lord Zayn al-'Abidin; our lord Muhammad al-Baqir; our lord Ja'far al-Sadiq; our lord Isma'il; our lord Muhammad bin Isma'il; our lord Wafi Ahmed; our lord Taqi Muhammad; our lord Razi al-Din 'Abd Allah; our lord Muhammad al-Mahdi; our lord al-Qa'im; our lord al-Mansur; our lord al-Mu'izz; our lord al-'Aziz; our lord Hakim al-Amr Allah; our lord al-Zahir; our lord al-Mustansir bi'llah; our lord al-Nizar; our lord al-Hadi; our lord al-Muhtadi; our lord al-Qahir; our lord 'Ala Dhikri al-Salam; our lord 'Ala al-Din Muhammad; our lord Jalal al-Din Hasan; our lord 'Ala al-Din Muhammad; our lord Rukn al-Din Khurshah; our lord Shams al-din Muhammad; our lord Qasim Shah; our lord Islam Shah; our lord Muhammad bin Islam Shah; our lord Mustansir bi'llah; our lord Abd al-Salam; our lord Gharib Mirza; our lord Abu Dharr 'Ali; our lord Murad Mirza; our lord Dhu'l Fiqar 'Ali; our lord Nur al-din 'Ali; our lord Khalil Allah 'Ali; our lord Nizar; our lord Sayyid 'Ali; our lord Hasan 'Ali; our lord Qasim 'Ali; our lord Abu al-Hasan 'Ali; our lord Khalil Allah 'Ali; our lord Shah Hasan 'Ali; our lord Shah 'Ali Shah; our lord Sultan Muhammad Shah.

(Raise hands) And in the name of our lord and our present living Imam Shah Karim al-Husayni, have mercy upon us and forgive us.

Verily Thou art powerful over all things. And all praise is due to God, the Sustainer of all beings.

May you glimpse the Lord's divine countenance! (handshake)
O God! To Thee is my prostration and prayer.

5. Aminah McCloud and Frederick Thaufeer al-Deen,
A Question of Faith for Muslim Inmates (1999)

Malcolm X is perhaps the most famous American who converted to Islam while in prison. But he is only one of thousands who have become Muslim in federal and state prisons and local jails. Most incarcerated Muslims are African Americans, though black Muslims subscribe to a number of different Muslim groups—Sunni Islam of various sorts, the Nation of Islam, the Five Percenters, the Moorish Science Temple, and others. Wardens and chaplains, who are required to recognize the religious freedom of inmates, struggle with such religious diversity, and sometimes hire religious experts to help them distinguish between legitimate and illegitimate Islamic practice. Whatever one thinks of such interventions, they clearly represent an assertion of the state's power to define and shape religious behavior. And in many cases, Sunni Islamic norms are sometimes held up as the criteria by which all other Islamic groups are measured.

In answering questions about the practice of Islam in prison, officials may consult local imams, religious scholars, and publications like the manual excerpted below. Authored by Islamic studies professor Aminah McCloud and long-time prison chaplain Frederick Thaufeer al-Din, this manual utilizes several classical Islamic legal sources in answering questions that practicing Sunni Muslims may face in prison. After the authors pose frequently asked questions, they essay answers first by reproducing relevant passages from the Qur'an and the hadiths, the reports of the sayings and deeds of the Prophet Muhammad and his companions. Then, they turn to three additional sources. One is Al-Muwatta, or "The Well-Trodden Path," a book compiled and edited by religious scholar Malik ibn Anas (d. 796), traditionally regarded by Sunni Muslims to be a reliable description of the rites, customs, and traditions that the early Muslims of Medina agreed were proper. The second is Reliance of the Traveler, *a manual of fiqh, or Islamic jurisprudence, largely associated with the Shafi'i school of Islamic law and ethics. The third is the* Encyclopedia of Islamic Law, *a modern English-language compendium of the views of the Ja'fari Shi'a school and the four Sunni schools of Islamic law and ethics, including the Maliki, Shafi'i, Hanbali, and*

Hanafi schools. Finally, the authors offer their own views based on their interpretations of these sources.

Prescribed Fasting

Q. Under whose sighting of the new moon (*hilal*) should Muslims in North American prisons begin to:

> A. Observe the start of a month?
> B. Fast in the month of Ramadan?
> C. Celebrate the two festivals (*'id*)?

QUR'AN

They ask you concerning the new moons. Say: They are but signs to mark fixed periods of time in (the affairs of) men, and for pilgrimage (2:189).

HADITH: SILENT

MUWATTA

Abd Allah ibn Umar reported that when talking about Ramadan, the Messenger of Allah declared, "do not begin the prescribed fast until you see the new moon (crescent) of Ramadan and do not end the prescribed fast until you see it (the new moon of Shawwal [the tenth month of the Islamic calendar]). But if it should be hidden under clouds, count the days of Ramadan (as thirty and break your fast).

RELIANCE OF THE TRAVELER

Prescribed fasting in Ramadan is only obligatory when the new moon of Ramadan has been sighted (i.e. in respect to the person who sees it, though for those who do not see it, it only becomes obligatory when the sighting is established by the testimony of an upright witness).

If it is too overcast to be seen, then (the preceding lunar month of) Shaban is presumed to last for thirty days, after which people begin the prescribed fast of the month of Ramadan. If the new moon is sighted during the day (before noon on the last of the thirty days) it is considered as belonging to the following night (and the ruling for that day does not change).

If the new moon is seen in one city but not another, then if the two are close (i.e. in the same region), the ruling (that the new month has come) holds for both. But if the two are not close, then not (the people far from the place where it was seen are not obligated to fast), not close meaning in different regions, such as the Hijaz, Iraq and Egypt.

If a person knows by calculations of lunar movements or the position of the stars that the next day is Ramadan, the prescribed fast is nevertheless not obligatory (for him or the public), though it is permissible for him alone.

If it is difficult to learn which month it is, for someone imprisoned or the like (such as someone being held in a dark place who cannot tell night from day, or someone who does not know when the Ramadan has come because of being in a land without habitations or people who know when it is), then such a person is obligated to reckon Ramadan as best he can and perform the prescribed fast. Such a fast remains valid if it remains unknown as to whether the month fasted actually coincided with Ramadan, or if it did coincide with it, though if the month fasted was before Ramadan, it is not valid.

ENCYCLOPEDIA OF ISLAMIC LAW

The Hanbalis, Malikis, and Hanafis state that if the sighting of the new moon has been confirmed in a particular region, the people of all other regions are bound by it, regardless of the distance between them. . . . The Ja'faris and the Shafi'is observe that if the people of a particular place see the new moon while those at another place do not, in the event of these two places being close by with respect to the horizon, the latter's duty will be the same; but not if their horizons differ.

DISCUSSION

As a matter of course, there is a crescent moon (*hilal*) at the beginning of each lunar month and each individual Muslim should practice sighting the moon in preparation for sighting to begin the month of Ramadan.

Whether one should attempt to use a human sighting of the moon rather than various technologies to predict the presence of the new moon is a different issue, but is indeed the focus of the current debate.

Allah has provided a portion of His guidance in signs (*ayat*) for humankind to seek out and understand. In addition, Allah has provided means for believers to constantly remind themselves that their dependence must be on Him only. The exercise of physically sighting the moon for months of Ramadan is one such reminder. Surely God knows about weather conditions since they are also under His control but that does not absolve one from the exercise itself. Issues surrounding the use of technology for predicting the presence of the *hilal* are rooted in the same discussion. Reliance on technology without an understanding of at least one purpose of this sign could be described as one of the things believers are warned against. Believers are to place their priorities in the guidance, not in themselves. Straying from the path is easy for the unwary.

For an inmate Muslim community, where for various reasons the capacity to go out and attempt to sight the *hilal* for the month of Ramadan may not be possible, there are several possibilities. Inmate communities may also not have access to the findings of other external communities. The community can take the word of a sighting from the nearest Muslim community or the announcement of the sighting from overseas.

This can be simply accomplished by asking the chaplain to call the *imam* of the local community. In the event that even this is impossible, a calendar may be obtained from one of the national associations [like ISNA]. The order of procedure, however, should be maintained. First, attempt to sight the *hilal*, but if unable, contact the nearest community or set up communication such that someone from that community contacts the chaplain and, as a last resort, have on hand a calendar. There is little in the struggle of Islam that is designed to promote personal whim or convenience as a basis for acting, or as a source of truth.

We recognize that in the United States there are Muslims of all schools present. Their interpretations follow the dictates of their schools and may differ in even one community thus providing the current chaos. We do not intend to extend the chaos but to provide a clear understanding of what the classical interpretations are and the possibilities for the inmate community. Additionally, there is an effort to standardize the beginning and ending of Ramadan in the United States.

Q. What is a fasting Muslim to do when directed by correctional officers to drink water during the period of fasting in order to provide a urine sample (used to see if the inmate is using drugs in the penal setting) in the month of Ramadan, or else face a write-up and possible penalties?

QUR'AN

The month of Ramadan is the month in which we sent down the Qur'an to mankind for guidance, also clear signs for guidance and judgment, so every one of you who is at home during that month should spend it in self-restraint (2:184–185).

HADITH

Narrated Abu Hurairah: The Prophet said, "Whoever does not give up forged speech and evil actions, Allah is not in need of his food and drink (i.e., Allah will not accept his fasting)."

Narrated Abu Hurairah: The Prophet said, "If somebody eats or drinks forgetfully then he should complete his fast, for what he has eaten or drunk has been given to him by Allah."

Narrated Umar bin al-Khattab: Allah's Messenger said, "When night falls from this side and the day vanishes from this side and the sun sets, then the fasting person should end his fast."

RELIANCE OF THE TRAVELER

Once begun, it is unlawful to interrupt either an obligatory fast-day or an obligatory prescribed prayer, whether it is current, a make-up or vowed.

ENCYCLOPEDIA OF ISLAMIC LAW

Those things from which it is obligatory to refrain during the prescribed fast (*mufitirat*) from dawn to sunset are: eating and drinking which deliberately invalidates the prescribed fast and necessitates making up for the fasting days missed in the opinion of all the schools; sexual intercourse; seminal emission; vomiting (deliberate); cupping (Hanbalis); injection (all schools); inhaling a dense cloud of suspended dust (Ja'faris);

application of collyrium (Malikis); the intention to discontinue the prescribed prayer (Ja'fari and Hanbali).

DISCUSSION

The average correctional officer, especially in a new facility, has little understanding of the Islamic worldview/philosophy, although Ramadan and
its requirements are listed in the procedure books of nearly every prison.
Therefore, occasionally, officers will require a urine sample. These samples are required of prisoners unannounced and at any time of the day to
make sure that prisoners are not using drugs. Failure to comply with this
directive (i.e., failure to provide a urine sample) for whatever reason, can
be cause for incurring a "shot," a disciplinary report against the inmate.

It is incumbent upon the consultant *imam* to prepare a training program, by means of lecturing at annual training, videos, or the printed
page. This program should be designed to inform correctional staff and
workers about Muslim inmate living. The information should address the
issue of Ramadan and of drug testing during that time. Both are mandatory and the disobedience of both results in penalties. Fortunately, both
can be accommodated. In the Operations Memorandum of the Federal
Bureau of Prisons dealing with Urine Surveillance, the provision exists
for a delay in securing urine samples from Muslim prisoners during the
month of Ramadan. State and local jails and prisons should be encouraged to adopt that memorandum's provisos as their own.

It should be noted, however, that the drinking of water under these circumstances does not break the fast. There are grounds for holding that
the drinking water is against the prisoner's will and that the fast is not
broken because of a compulsion. This is similar to the situation of a
woman whose husband insists that she have sex during the day during
Ramadan. He nullifies his fast, but she does not. . . .

Food

Q. May Muslims eat kosher meats normally procured for Jewish prisoners
or the meat generally provided for the general population of inmates,
where, for financial and other reasons, ritually slaughtered (*zabihah*)
meats are unavailable?

QUR'AN

O you who believe! Fulfill all obligations. Lawful unto you are all four-footed animals with the exceptions named. Forbidden to you are: dead meat, blood, the flesh of swine, and that on which has been invoked the name of other than Allah; that which has been killed by strangling, or by a violent blow, or by a wild animal, unless you are able to slaughter it; that which is sacrificed on stone . . . The food of the People of the Book is lawful to you and yours is lawful to them (5:1–5).

Eat of that on which Allah's name has been pronounced, if you have faith in His signs. Why should you not eat of (meats) on which Allah's name has been pronounced, when He has explained to you in detail what is forbidden to you—except under compulsion of necessity? Eat not of that on which Allah's name has not been pronounced: That would be impiety (6:118–121).

O you who believe! Eat of the good things that We have provided for you, and be grateful to Allah, if it is Him you worship. He has only forbidden to dead meat, blood, and the flesh of swine (2:172–173).

HADITH: SILENT

RELIANCE OF THE TRAVELER

The *hadith* shows that when a person doubts that something is permissible, he should not do it. The question arises, is refraining from it in such a case obligatory or recommended?—to which our *imams* explicitly reply that it is the latter, because a thing is assumed to be permissible and fundamentally not blameworthy, as long as some prior reason for considering it unlawful is not known. For example, when one doubts that one of the conditions for valid slaughtering has been met, conditions which make it lawful, the assumption is that it remains unlawful (since initially the animal was alive, a state in which it is unlawful to eat, while it only becomes lawful by a specific procedure, i.e., by Islamic slaughtering), so that the meat does not become lawful except through certainty (that it has been slaughtered). The case of meat is exceptional in this, since most other foods are initially permissible, and one assumes they remain so unless one is certain something has occurred which has made them unlawful.

DISCUSSION

First, it is important to distinguish between *halal* and *zabihah*. *Halal* refers to the legal category of lawful (in this instance food). *Zabihah* refers to the added condition (slaughter of meat according to Islamic law) that must be fulfilled before meat falling under the *halal* category can be eaten.

All schools agree that all fish are *halal*. Some scholars in the Hanafi school, however, hold that some of the creatures that come out of the water are not fish, such as shellfish and thus the eating of them is reprehensible (*makruh*) but not forbidden (*haram*). Some of the scholars consulted for this work considered chicken in the regular market *halal* because industry standard practice is that their throats are cut prior to death. These same scholars noted that the general industry standard in some states also required cutting the throats of sheep and cows prior to death and considered this meat *halal*. Since the state requirements vary and a good deal of research remains to be done on industry standards, prisoners in state facilities are encouraged to eat *halal* meat and recommended to investigate the standards for their state. The federal prisoners have already litigated this issue and won the right to eat *halal* meat.

When prisoners are in solitary confinement or other kinds of segregation units and cannot know what it is that they are being given to eat, because meats and vegetables have been mixed together in a "loaf" or "stew," they are to eat it to prevent starvation. This is the exceptional condition. The exceptional condition is to prevent starvation when there is no alternative; the believer must eat what is available.

At least one of the presumptions of the intentions behind requiring a certain diet for Muslims is God's promise to protect both the nature of the way of life and the believers. Throughout Islam this protection is manifested in a number of ways—the protected recitation of the Qur'an, the models of the prophets, modesty, exemplary behavior, special dietary laws, and others.

The issue of eating what is permissible is extremely important because it is one of the specified commandments in the Qur'an. This commandment comes in the context of an exhortation to "eat of what is good (*tayyibun*)." A Muslim must be God-conscious and follow what He commands.

In situations where there is a claim that the food served by the prison does not meet religious standards (i.e., pork or pork by-products, and foods cooked in lard), prisoners may find themselves having to put forth a grievance. Prisoners should be aware, however, that special treatment to accommodate a need for a special diet may be initially rebuffed with recourse to "common fare."

We must now turn our attention to a discussion of *zabihah* meat. There are four major concerns—whether the animal in question is lawful for Muslims to eat, whether or not the lawful animals were raised for human consumption (which many times determines what is fed to the animal), whether or not the name of God was pronounced over the animal as it was being killed, and how the killing was carried out.

Of the meat Muslims may eat, some scholars have asserted that killing in the prescribed manner is crucial because it quickly rids the animal's body of toxins that are released into the bloodstream at the time of death and because it prevents potential prolonged agony to the animal.

When the concern is whether or not the animal is lawful, the Qur'an is clear on what foods are unlawful and which are lawful. On the subject of raising animals, some scholars have speculated that when animals are raised for some other purpose such as sporting, fighting or work, they are not lawful as food (unless there is necessity such as starvation). When the concern is "whose name is pronounced on it," the issue is slightly more complicated. The Qur'an asserts that "only forbidden you is dead meat, and blood, and the flesh of swine, and that on which another name has been invoked besides that of Allah," such as another person or the name of a prophet.

The manner of killing is also very important. The Qur'an asserts that forbidden are "that which has been killed by strangling, or by a violent blow (as used to be the case in most U.S. slaughter houses), or by a headlong fall, or by being gored to death; that which has been (partly) eaten by a wild animal." This implies that the persons charged with slaughtering animals must adhere to the prescribed manner.

There are many more elaborations on making meat *halal* that will not be covered here. Prior requirements in current acts assert the rights of prisoners who have religiously mandated dietary laws. In those instances where the administration has had no requests for special diets, Muslims surely can bring this information to their attention.

Q. Under what conditions may a Muslim inmate work in an area of the prison wherein he/she may have contact with swine flesh and/or its by-products, given the often, nearly universal mandatory initial assignment of all new prisoners to the prison's food service area?

QUR'AN

He has only forbidden you not eat dead meat, and blood, and the flesh of swine, and that on which any other name has been invoked other than God. But if one is forced by necessity, without willful disobedience, not transgressing due limits, then he is guiltless for God is oft-forgiving and Most merciful (2:173).

HADITH: SILENT

RELIANCE OF THE TRAVELER

Impurity means . . . dogs and pigs, or their offspring. . . .

DISCUSSION

An important issue here, as with many things in Islam, is "intention." The Muslim is forbidden pork meat or flesh as food. Contact with swine flesh or bodily fluids is considered contact with *najasa* or "impurity," as is human urine and feces. Non-consumptive contact with pork is not disobedience, but it is an impure thing requiring washing which is to be avoided where possible. Contact with pork flesh does not soil a Muslim forever. Muslims may readily clean themselves after such contact and perform the prescribed prayer (*salat*) or resume normal Muslim life.

The fact that the Muslim is in prison reduces some of her/his freedoms to decide which jobs they will work. In some instances a particular detail (job) may be assigned for that prisoner's personal protection from other inmates. Many, if not most prisoners want to work in the kitchen although few want to do dishes. As a desirable job, the Muslim must consider how to best accommodate him/herself. Kitchen jobs have equipment such as rubber gloves that enable the Muslim (e.g., a dishwasher) to have contact with pork food items without touching them directly.

Inmates who are Muslim should inform prison officials at the point at which they are initially received into the prison that they are Muslim. When they are confronted with the possibility of working in areas wherein they are more than likely to come into contact with pork products, they should seek to resolve the dilemma by using gloves. Where the option does not exist for an alternative job assignment, or the inmate wants to work in this desired job, the Muslim inmate may work for the prescribed period in a job wherein he/she comes into regular non-consumptive contact with pork flesh, and so forth, non-halal meat, etc.

6. Suhail Mulla, Online Advice About
Muslim Youth (2004 and 2005)

The World Wide Web has emerged as a place where the everyday practice of Islam in the United States is discussed and debated. In addition to the burgeoning number of Muslim chat rooms and informational Web sites, some national and international Muslim organizations sponsor online dialogues in which Muslims may direct questions or concerns to religious experts and community leaders. The Muslim American Society, for example, has offered users the chance to ask social worker Suhail Hasan Mulla's opinion about rearing Muslim children in America. Mulla, who holds a BA in African American Studies and a master's degree in social work, brings his considerable experience as counselor for troubled youth to the task. He has served as a program director of the West Valley Boys and Girls Club and has worked for the Los Angeles Unified School District's Sylmar Juvenile Hall, one of the largest juvenile detention centers in the country. Many of the questions that he fields in the online discussions excerpted have little to do with juvenile crime. Instead, these queries express concerns such as: How can I raise my child with a strong sense of faith? What school is best for my child? What is the best way of disciplining my child? How can I convince my child not to get an art degree?

Q. I have a question in regard to my son who is now fourteen years old. My concern is that he doesn't have friends at his public school. He is a very nice, socialized, and easy to be loved boy. We moved him from school to another searching for a better one. He feels so lonely and sometimes he asks me, "Why don't I have friends?" This question hurts me a lot and I really don't know what to do. I talked to him and encouraged him to try his best and to be more friendly. He told me that this is not the problem and that it is the attire that attract young boys at this age and nothing else. Of course, he doesn't wear loose jeans. . . . He is very respect[able], but he has a sense of humor and very nice. Is there particular advices for him? Please help.

A. Dear sister, we feel for you and your son, and we know how lonely it can be without friends at school. You are correct when you say that it is the dress/attire that makes a kid "cool." It is not necessarily a bad thing that your son doesn't fit in with the cool kids who dress a certain way, they are usually not the type of kids you would want your son to be around. Three pieces of advice: (1) Get your son involved in an extracurricular activity (sports, journalism club, drama club, etc.) after school or during lunch time. In a social setting your son is more likely to develop friendships because of the small group setting. (2) The best companionship is righteous companionship. Have your son seek out other Muslims at school. If there aren't any or he just doesn't make a connection, enroll him in the youth group at your local mosque. This will fulfill part of his social need and he may even meet somebody from his school. (3) You may want to re-evaluate your son's wardrobe. He doesn't need to dress like the other kids in clothes that you don't approve of; however, at the same time, you don't want your son to be labeled as a "nerd" just because of the way he dresses. Find a happy medium. Lastly, remember, that just one good friend at school should fulfill his social needs at school. May Allah grant your son with righteous companionship.

Q. What is the best way to make *da'wa* [missionary outreach] with non-Muslims? Some non-Muslim parents asked me for a play date with their children and mine. This is the first time for me to do it and I was wondering how should I deal with this mother. What should we talk about? Excuse my innocent question, but I really didn't try talking to them before and I am not used to it.

A. This is a situation that all Muslim parents come across at some point in their lives when living in this country. This is a great opportunity for you to give a non-Muslim a favorable impression of Islam. All you have to do is be yourself. Talk to her as you would talk to any of your Muslim sisters. Share with her your concerns re: your children. Discuss with her your hopes and goals for your children. Insha'Allah [God willing], by doing this, she will come to realize that your concerns as a Muslim mother are not much different than hers, and she may even open to you in time and begin to ask you questions about Islam.

Q. Should I tell my friends at school about Ramadan? Should I talk to them about fasting? It is hard to explain that to them. Please advise.

A. You should definitely tell your friends at school about Ramadan. Why? Three reasons: (1) A real friend always knows what's going on in the life of his friend. Ramadan is something very important to you as a Muslim and your friends should know that. (2) It is important that you as a young Muslim man exemplify what it is to be a good Muslim. One of the ways you do that is by taking these types of opportunities to explain your religion. (3) It will increase the amount of respect that your friends have for you. Challenge any of them to fast for a whole day with you and see what they say. Lastly, fasting is easy to explain, don't use that as an excuse. Be proud of being Muslim and never be afraid of what others may say about you.

Q. I don't feel comfortable to send my daughter to a public middle school. I am so worried of doing so. Her older brothers are in public schools. But I worry she might suffer with her *hijab* [scarf]. The problem is that there are no other options. We don't have Islamic middle or high schools in our area. What do you suggest?

A. We love to hear about young sisters who carry themselves as upright Muslims from a young age. The younger our children practice Islam, the stronger their Islam will develop as they grow older. This is something that you as a parent should be pleased with. At some point, sister, all of our daughters must step out into an environment where they will stick out because of their dress. On a positive note, we have numerous young girls who have gone to public schools in our community and have reported very few problems. More likely than not, your daughter will fit right in and make friends and these friends will be there to stand up for her if she ever does have any problems. Also you, as the mother, should always follow up with your daughter to see how things are going at school. There is a lot she will not tell you if you don't ask. It is possible that your daughter will be looked at differently because of the *hijab*. But this is what we want, we want the general public to know a Muslim woman when they see one and we don't want our women to be looked at the way other women are looked at (i.e., sex objects, etc.). It may also happen that she will be treated differently, possibly made fun of, etc. I don't say these things to scare you or your daughter, but only to get you mentally prepared for what you may or may not face as she begins middle school. After saying all that, you should take this as an opportunity to teach your daughter a very valuable life lesson. And that is that we do our best to follow the commandments of Allah and after that we leave the results up to

Him and after taking all of the necessary steps, we leave ourselves under His protection.

Q. I would like to hear your opinion concerning the home schooling. Do you recommend this idea for our daughters? My husband insists on moving our daughter to home schooling believing that he is protecting her from the outside society, which could affect her in a negative way. I feel that by doing so, my daughter will lose a lot and her chance for a better education will decrease. This is in addition to the other side effects, such as isolating her from the outside society, community and friends. Please help me because I am so confused.

A. Dear Sister, you have raised an issue that almost every Muslim family struggles with; that is, "What type of school should I send my children to?" The options include public, private, Islamic, and home schooling. Home schooling is the least frequently chosen option. I am personally not a big proponent of home schooling. I believe that a child's full potential can be brought out best in a regular school setting where the child can interact with teachers, other students and other school staff. Cooperative learning is becoming a more commonly used method in teaching, and this is something that cannot take place in a one-on-one teacher/student relationship. Also, there are valuable social and life skills that are learned in a regular school setting that cannot be taught in a home schooling situation. Besides, to be involved with and to interact with other people, is closer to the experiences of life after school and is not something that can be taught as theory but is something that must be experienced. Some people think they are shielding their children from certain negative elements in society by home schooling their children. They may be shielding them from certain elements for the time being, but what is going to happen when their children have to face these same negative elements after they leave the protective home environment? They will not have the same ability to cope with these issues as those who have encountered and learned to deal with these issues throughout their life. In addition, if home schooling is decided as the course a family is going to take with their children, all parties involved should be in *agreement* and *capable* for it to be an optimal learning situation. 95+% of the time the mother is the primary teacher when a child is home schooled and it can be an immense burden for her if she is not ready for the task. Therefore, she should be doing it of her own free will and she should be scholastically capable of teaching all the material that any regular teacher must have command of. The mother must also be capable of transforming her home into a school and providing a strict, compartmentalized daily schedule of study just as a regular school provides. Allah knows best.

Q. I allowed my son to get out with his non-Muslim friends to play. He is not a young kid and I trust him, but I feel that there is a bad influence. As a father, when I think about it, I feel that they don't have the same background and they can't meet at one point. I mean someone should be influenced by the other and would try to meet with the other in the middle. I don't want my son to sacrifice his principles for the sake of friendship, but meanwhile I feel sorry for him for not having friends. What do you think?

A. Dear Brother, we share your concerns that you have for your son. The parental instinct that makes you feel that there is a bad influence among his friends is not something that should be ignored because it is something that comes from Allah. Parents know their children better than anyone else, and Allah has endowed them with the ability to know when they are going astray. You are absolutely correct about the fact that when two people are involved in a relationship or friendship they influence each other. Usually, the stronger personality has a greater influence and in this case it sounds like your son is being influenced by these stronger influences. There are numerous steps you can take to try to improve your son's situation. First of all, you should invite your son's friends over so that you can see who they are and get to know them. Have a BBQ, or some other activity that your son's friends would enjoy. After this meeting, you can discuss your son's relationship with his friends and you will be able to better gauge the extent of his friendship with particular individuals. Also, make sure you know your son's whereabouts at all times. You are the father and must regulate when and where he goes. One other very, very important step you must take is to try and connect your son with other Muslim youth. You should look to a local youth group, try to find a local *halaqa* [an Islamic study group] or find some outlet where he can connect with other Muslim youth. There is nothing else that can guarantee your son staying on the right track more than having good Muslim companionship.

Q. As parents, we need to encourage our kids when they do good things, but sometimes we need to punish them. In this country it is too hard to use your hands with your kids, although it helps them learn and to never forget what they learned. Do you believe that we could raise our kids well without using our hands?

A. Thank you for bringing up a very important point. My answer: We can *definitely* raise good children without having to raise our hands towards them. In fact, I believe that it is best not to punish our children with our hands. There is much debate as to whether or not physical punishment should be used with children. Most of this research tells us that we are much better off having a discipline system that doesn't include physical punishment. Our Prophet, peace be upon him, was never known to raise his hand against any of his children, nor against anyone else in his household. He is our example in all aspects of life, including his role as a parent. Shouldn't we follow his example?

Q. Dear Respected Brother: I am father of two boys. My old son wants to be an artist. I tried to convince him to select medicine, engineering or law, but he doesn't accept. He is very talented, but art is not a job. He could draw whenever he has extra time, but our nation doesn't need artists at this time. The problem is that his mother doesn't see any problem with her old son being an artist. I know art is good as a talent, but not as a career. Could you give me some tips on how to convince him or whom could convince from our Muslim scholars?

A. Dear Brother, May Allah bless you and your family and may Allah make your children from among our future leaders. Ameen. This scenario that you bring forth is a common scenario that plays out . . . in this society. In this society, there are many opportunities in many different fields, which is in stark contrast to the opportunities that exist in many Muslim countries. At any given university, you can find up to one hundred different majors; educational opportunities are not just confined to law, medicine, teaching, and engineering, as they may be in certain Muslim countries. This same opportunity also plays itself out in the actual real world—the work world. There are many opportunities in many different fields. I advise you to do some research with your son. See what opportunities art may afford him. For example, in today's technological world, computer graphic art is a very respectable field into which many artists go into and do very well for themselves, may I add. Art is more than just drawing and painting pictures and, Allah knows best, there may be something out there for your son. Allah gives different talents and abilities to whomsoever he wishes. The good thing is that this society embraces creativity in the arts. At least, explore the possibilities and see if there are any viable avenues for him in this field. Three last comments: (1) Please look at my bio on the website and see what I got my bachelor's degree in (if you knew my ethnicity you would be even more surprised!). Even with that I was able to eventually find a field for myself in which now I do quite well for myself, *alhamdulillah* [praise be to God]! (2) We have enough Muslim doctors and engineers (there is an unfortunate need now for more Muslim lawyers though). It is about time Muslims started spreading themselves out into other fields. (3) At least he did not say that he wants to be an actor!

7. Islamic Medical Association of North America (IMANA), "Islamic Medical Ethics: The IMANA Perspective" (2005)

IMANA is part of the Islamic Society of North America umbrella. The self-defined mission of the association, which is headquartered in Illinois, is to "provide a forum and resource for Muslim physicians and other health care professionals, to promote a greater awareness of Islamic medical ethics and values among Muslims and the community-at-large, to provide humanitarian and medical relief, and to be an advocate in health care policy." The organization also holds conventions, grants study scholarships, and publishes a journal and newsletter. IMANA is operated by a board of regents, an executive committee, and numerous subcommittees, and its participating physicians are some of the best-known Muslim medical doctors in the United States. Its ethics panel, which approved the document excerpted below, offers IMANA's perspective on medical ethics, a view that might be described as modern, rational, scientific, and religiously conservative. To be sure, this guide does not speak for all American Muslims, and it should not be read as the final word on American Muslim medical ethics. Instead, it begins to suggest the vitality of discussions in Muslim communities both here and abroad about the meaning of Islam for modern healthcare and vice versa. Readers interested in the complete and most up-to-date version of the ethics guide should consult IMANA's Web site (www.imana.org).

Muslim physicians, ethicists, *imams* and scholars are asked questions by Muslim and non-Muslim patients, physicians and institutions as to what is Islam's position or opinion on certain medical dilemmas affecting the care and outcome of patients' illness and life. Some of these issues, such as termination of pregnancy, are time-honored situations while many such as transplantation, assisted reproduction and life support are products of advances in medical technology. Since these are new issues, Muslim physicians have dire need for recommendations from the guiding principles of the Glorious Qur'an, the tradition of Prophet Muhammad (peace be upon him) and opinions of past and contemporary Muslim scholars. The Qur'an says, "It is not fitting for a believer, man or woman, when a matter has been decided by God, and His messenger, to have any option about their decision. If anyone disobeys God and His messenger, he is indeed on a clearly wrong path" (33:36).

Thus, IMANA decided to make a position paper to provide to those who seek our opinion and enable them to pursue further reading on their own. The positions expressed in this perspective are only suggestions on behalf of IMANA and are not to be considered *fatwas* (religious decrees) which are religiously binding. The members of the ethics committee are not in a position to issue a *fatwa* on any of the issues which we are writing on behalf of IMANA. However, from time to time, on a needed basis, we do consult Muslim scholars to have their opinion. These positions will be revised from time to time as new questions arise from advances in medical technology. . . .

IMANA's Perspective on Important Ethical Issues

(A) CARE OF THE MUSLIM PATIENT

All patients irrespective of their faith should be treated with human dignity and respect. Muslim physicians are advised to treat all patients with loving care as if they are members of their own family. We suggest to all healthcare providers that they familiarize themselves with the basic teachings of Islam and Islamic moral values. It is easier for a healthcare provider to deal with the patient if he/she understands the faith, values, and culture of his/her patient. These are some of the specific guidelines for healthcare providers especially of other faith traditions for caring for their Muslim patients.

1. Muslim patients should be identified—if possible—as Muslim (or with the religion Islam) in the registration information so as to prevent any mistakes happening unintentionally in terms of violating dietary rules or privacy.

2. Their care providers should respect their modesty and privacy. Muslim patients, particularly women, may need a special gown to cover the whole body in order to avoid unnecessary exposure during physical examination. Some examinations may be done over the gown.

3. Provide Muslim patients Islamically-slaughtered meat. Muslim patients should not be served any pork, pork products, or alcohol in their meals. A Muslim patient's family may be allowed to bring food from home, as long as it is meeting the patient's dietary restrictions.

4. Make it easy for Muslim patients to perform Islamic prayers if they can.

5. Inform them of their rights as a patient and encourage an Islamic living will . . .

6. Take time to explain test procedures and treatment. Some of the more recently immigrated Muslims may have a language problem. Muslim women can give consent for any treatment or procedure.

7. Allow their *imam* (religious teacher) to visit them and pray for them. Clerics of other faith traditions can pray for or with Muslim patients with their permission, using non-denominational words like God.

8. Autopsy is permitted if medically indicated or required by law.

9. Organ donation is permitted with some guidelines and is encouraged.

10. Always examine a female patient in the presence of another female (chaperon) or a female relative (except in medical emergencies). Especially for labor and delivery, if the patient's obstetrician is unavailable and upon her request, provide a female healthcare provider, if feasible. Her husband is encouraged to be present during the delivery.

11. After the death of a Muslim patient in a healthcare facility, allow the family and *imam* to arrange for preparing the dead body for burial under Islamic guidelines. A corpse should be given the same respect and privacy as he/she was receiving while alive. Muslim relatives and friends of the dead are encouraged to stay in the room where the dead body is kept to recite Qur'an. Muslim corpses are not embalmed.

(B) DEFINITION OF LIFE AND THE RESPONSIBILITY OF MUSLIM PHYSICIANS TOWARDS HUMAN LIFE

Muslims believe that God is the Creator of life and life is a gift from Him. Muslims believe that all life is sacred and must be protected. The respect for life in Islam is common for all humans, irrespective of gender, age, race, color, faith, ethnic origin or financial status.

IMANA holds the position that biological life begins at conception while human life begins when ensoulment takes place. A verse from the Qur'an reads:

Man We did create from a quintessence (of clay); Then We placed him as (a drop of) sperm in a place of rest, firmly fixed; Then We made the sperm into a clot of congealed blood; then of that clot We made a (fetus) lump; then we made out of that lump bones and clothed the bones with flesh; then we developed out of it another creature. So blessed be God, the best to create! (23:12–14)

Ensoulment is believed to occur at 40 or 120 days after fertilization, according to different schools of thought. The rights of the human fetus in Islam is similar to the rights of a mature human being, including the right to life, the right to inheritance, the right of compensation when injured by willful acts and the right to penalize assailants.

IMANA extends the principles of medical ethics to the patient in a vegetative state. Until the death has been declared, the patient in a vegetative state is considered a living person and has all the rights of a living person.

(C) DEFINITION OF DEATH

Permanent cessation of cardiopulmonary function, when diagnosed by a physician or a team of physicians, is considered death. The concept of brain death is necessitated when artificial means to maintain cardiopulmonary function are employed. In those situations, cortical and brain stem death, as established by specialist(s) using appropriate investigations can be used. It is the attending physician who should be responsible for making the diagnosis of death. Thus a person is considered dead when the conditions given below are met.

1. The physician has determined that after a standard examination, a person's cardiopulmonary function has come to a permanent stop.
2. A specialist physician (or physicians) has determined that after standard examination, the function of the brain, including the brain stem, has come to a permanent stop, even if some other organs may continue to show spontaneous activity.

(D) MECHANICAL LIFE SUPPORT IN TERMINALLY ILL
PATIENTS OR THOSE IN PERSISTENT VEGETATIVE
STATE AND EUTHANASIA

The following verses in the Glorious Qur'an are some of the verses which address issues of life and death:

"It is He who gives life and death and when He decides upon an affair, He says to it: Be and it is" (40:68).
"No soul can die except by God's permission, the term being fixed by writing" (3:145).
"Every soul will have a taste of death. In the end, to Us, shall you be brought back" (29:57).
"It is He who gives life and Who takes it away and to Him shall you be brought back" (10:56).
"Nor take life which God has made sacred except for a just cause" (17:33).

IMANA does not believe in prolonging the misery of dying patients who are terminally ill or in a persistent vegetative state (PVS). PVS is defined as a sub-acute or chronic condition which usually follows severe brain injury and is characterized by normal sleep/wake pattern and total lack of cognitive function with preserved blood pressure, respiratory control, that persists for more than two months.

When death becomes inevitable, as determined by a team of physicians, including critical care physicians, the patient should be allowed to die without unnecessary procedures. While all ongoing medical treatments can be continued, no further or new attempts should be made to sustain artificial life support. If the patient is on mechanical support, this can be withdrawn. The patient should be treated with full respect, comfort measures and pain control. No attempt should be made to withhold nutrition and hydration. In such cases, if and when the feeding tube has been withdrawn, it may not be reinserted. The patient should be allowed to die peacefully and comfortably. However, no attempt should be made to enhance the dying process in patients on life support.

IMANA is absolutely opposed to euthanasia and assisted suicide in terminally ill patients by healthcare providers or by patient's relatives. Suicide and euthanasia are prohibited in Islam.

(E) ISLAMIC LIVING WILL AND ADVANCE DIRECTIVE

IMANA recommends that all Muslims have a "Living Will," "Advance Directive" and a case manger for their care, to help physicians to know their wishes, when he or she is unable to give directions (i.e. in a coma).

A sample of such proposed living will is provided here which can be modified by the patient after consulting with family and/or an attorney.

(Sample)

Declaration made this _____day of _____, 20__, _____, a Muslim of sound mind, willfully and voluntarily make known my desires that my dying shall not be artificially prolonged under the circumstances set forth below and I declare: If at any time I have an incurable injury, disease or illness certified in writing to be a terminal condition by my attending physician(s), and my attending physician has determined that the use of life-prolonging procedures would serve only to artificially prolong the dying process, I direct that such procedures be withheld or withdrawn, and that I be permitted to die naturally with only the provision of appropriate nutrition and hydration and the administration of essential medications and the performances of any medical procedures necessary (as determined by my physician) to provide me with comfort or to alleviate pain.

In the absence of my ability to give direction regarding the use of life-prolonging procedures, it is my intention that this declaration be honored by my family and physician as the final expression of my legal right to refuse medical or surgical treatment and I accept the consequences of the refusal.

_____ is my case manager to enforce my living will, if I am not physically able to give direction. I do not permit autopsy of my body unless my death occurred in a suspicious manner and it is important to know the cause of death or if it is required by the court of law. It is my desire that Muslims attending my dying process ensure that Islamic *shari'a* is practiced during preparation of my body for burial and that my body be treated with grace and privacy and buried with Islamic guidelines under the directions of my Muslim family, *imam*, or other qualified Muslims as soon as it is feasible.

Signed _____ Date _____

Place _____

The declaring person has been personally known to me and I believe (him/her) to be of sound mind. I did not sign the declaring person's signature above for or at the direction of the declaring person. I am not a parent, spouse, or child of the declaring person. I am not entitled to any part of the declaring person's estate or directly financially responsible for his/her medical care. I am competent and at least eighteen (18) years of age.

Witness (to the document) _____

Date_____

Witness (second) _____

Date_____

(F) ORGAN DONATION AND TRANSPLANTATION

We, at IMANA, understand that certain organs may fail in the human body while the rest of the body may still be functional. The current state of medical knowledge holds the view with scientific proof that, if the diseased organs are replaced by healthy organs and if accepted, the body machine can continue to function rather than die because of one diseased organ. Islam instructs all Muslims to save life.

Thus, on this basis, transplantation in general, both giving and receiving organs, is allowed for the purpose of saving life.

This has to be done under the following guidelines:

1. The medical need has to be defined.
2. The possible benefit to the patient has to be defined.
3. Consent from the donor as well as the recipient must be obtained.
4. There should be no sale of organs by any party.
5. No financial incentive to the donor or his relatives for giving his organs, but a voluntary gift may be permitted. On the other hand, there should be no cost to the family of the donor for removing the organ.
6. Any permanent harm to the donor must be avoided.
7. Transplantation of sex organs (testicles or ovaries) which would violate the sanctity of marriage is forbidden.
8. Cadaver donation is permitted but only if specifically mentioned in that person's will or in driving license.

Blood transfusion is permissible. Giving blood to or receiving blood from people of other faiths is permissible.

(G) ASSISTED REPRODUCTIVE TECHNOLOGIES
AND SURROGACY

We believe infertility is a disease and desire for a cure by an infertile couple is natural. However, in Islam, for an action to be permissible all means of achieving that action are also to be pure.

We believe in the sanctity of marriage and the importance of preserving lineage.

The Qur'an says: "And God has made for you mates (and companions) of your own nature, and made for you, out of them, sons and daughters and grandchildren, and provided for you sustenance of the best: will they then believe in vain things, and be ungrateful for God's favours?" (16:72).

The Qur'an says: "It is He who has created man from water: then has He established relationships of lineage and marriage: for thy Lord has power (over all things)" (25:54).

Based on these Qur'anic guidelines, IMANA holds the following positions:

1. All forms of assisted reproductive technologies (ART) are permissible between husband and wife during the span of their marriage using the husband's sperm and the wife's ovaries and uterus. No third party involvement is allowed.

We believe in the sanctity of marriage and that the death of the husband terminates the marriage contract on earth, thus frozen sperm from a deceased husband cannot be used to impregnate his widow.

2. Sperm, ova and embryo donation are not permitted.

3. Additional embryos produced by IVF between husband and wife can be discarded or given for genetic research, if not to be used by the same couple for a future attempt.

4. Surrogacy involving a third person is not permissible, as we believe that it exceeds the boundaries of the marriage contract and lineage.

5. Use of fertility drugs is permissible.

An infertile couple, if they cannot find a permissible cure, can care for an orphan or someone else's child as their own within the Islamic guidelines of adoption, not the legal adoption as practiced in the United States.

(H) CONTRACEPTION AND STERILIZATION

Islam prohibits sex out of wedlock.

1. Contraception

For married couples, contraception for several reasons, including health of the mother, social or economic reasons, etc., is permitted, provided that it is practiced by mutual agreement of the husband and wife and that the method used is reversible and not harmful. Withdrawal, prophylactics, birth control pills and other hormonal methods are allowed. Contraceptive methods which can lead to abortion are not allowed.

2. Sterilization

Sterilization, whether by vasectomy or tubal ligation, as a national policy for family planning or population control, is unlawful and should not be allowed.

On an individual level it is permissible provided that both husband and wife want it and:

- When there is a significant medical contraindication to the pregnancy, for example, if there is a significant risk to the wife's health if she conceives.
- When other methods of birth control have failed or are causing significant side effects.
- When a genetic disease of the husband or wife or both poses a high risk of being transmitted to the fetus, e.g., autosomal dominant or autosomal recessive conditions when both husband and wife are carriers.
- When it is done for family planning, i.e., the husband and wife are satisfied with the number of children they have, some scholars will permit it but it is *makruh* (disliked).

(I) TERMINATION OF PREGNANCY (TOP)

Abortion is the willful termination of pregnancy by artificial means: drugs, chemicals, mechanical or surgical procedures before the age of viability (23 menstrual weeks, i.e., calculated from the first day of the last menstrual period) for any reason. Chemical or mechanical means to prevent the formation of the zygote (fertilized ovum, which marks the beginning of human life) is not considered abortion. We believe that life begins at conception and unless interrupted by disease or artificial means, the fertilized ovum will continue to grow and become a viable mature human being. However, some scholars differentiate between biological life, which starts at conception, and human life, which starts after ensoulment.

The two Shaykhs (al-Bukhari and Muslim) relate on the authority of 'Abdullah ibn Mas'ud that God's Messenger (peace be upon him), has said:

> The creation of each one of you is brought in the belly of his mother for forty days, then for a similar period he is a germ cell, then for another forty days he is an embryonic lump, then an angel is sent to him and ordered to write down four words. He is told: "Write down his career, his livelihood, his life duration and whether he is to be miserable or happy, and the angel breathes spirit into him."

Further, the time of ensoulment according to this *hadith* is considered to be at 40 days after fertilization by some scholars, while others consider it to be at 120 days after fertilization.

IMANA's position on abortion can be classified as follows:

1. Elective abortion of a viable fetus in a healthy mother is prohibited.

2. Abortion is permitted if continuation of pregnancy may cause the pregnant woman to die or cause serious deterioration of her health, both medical and mental, if done before 120 days after fertilization, i.e., 19 menstrual weeks.

3. Fetal congenital malformations in which abortion can be sought and is permitted are lethal malformations not compatible with extrauterine life such as bilateral renal aplasia, Trisomy 13, 18, etc. But even in these situations it is preferable to do it before the 120th day after fertilization or 19 weeks of gestation, calculated from the first day of the last menstrual period.

4. In non-lethal malformations such as severe hydrocephaly, cervical meningomyelocele, chromosomal aneuploidies and unbalanced translocations, abortion may be permissible before the 120th day of conception after consulting Islamic scholars and medical experts in the field.

5. Pregnancy occurring because of rape, war crimes and incest may be a cause to seek abortion. In all cases in which abortion is sought, the

recommendation should be made by a team of Islamic scholars and medical experts in the field.

Prohibition of infanticide is mentioned in several Qur'anic verses. One of these verses is: "Kill not your children for fear of want: We shall provide sustenance for them as well as for you. Verily the killing of them is a great sin" (29:51–53).

(J) GENETIC ENGINEERING AND HUMAN CLONING

Genetic research and engineering to alter or delete diseased genes is allowed and genetic research using stem cells from products of miscarriages or surplus ova after IVF procedures is permissible. However, to conceive in order to abort the fetus and harvest and use its stem cells is not permissible.

We believe that each individual is born with unique qualities and genetic makeup. Islamically, a child should be born out of marriage between husband and wife and the lineage of the child should be maintained. Therefore, human reproductive cloning is not permitted in Islam.

Therapeutic cloning may be permissible within strict guidelines.

(K) CARE OF THE HIV INFECTED/AIDS PATIENT

HIV infection, in addition to being associated with homosexuality, is also known to be acquired through heterosexual acts, as well as intravenous drug use, blood transfusion and child birth. While Islam is opposed to the homosexual lifestyle, promiscuity, and drug abuse, IMANA is not opposed to the care of HIV patients. In fact, it instructs Muslim physicians to care for HIV patients with the same degree of compassion as they would for other patients.

We do not discriminate against any patient on the basis of their lifestyle. We do advise healthcare providers to take precautions for themselves while taking care of HIV patients.

(L) EXAMINATION OF PATIENTS OF THE OPPOSITE SEX

IMANA encourages but does not mandate same sex healthcare providers. Examination of a patient of the opposite sex is allowed in the presence of a third person of the same sex as that of the patient. In case of a minor, one of the parents' presences is desirable. Only necessary examination needs to be done. Pelvic examination must be done using gloves. Medical or nursing students may be allowed during examination of a female patient, but only with her prior consent and in the presence of a female nurse or relative.

(M) DRUG RESEARCH

Biomedical research involving double blind trials, controls and the use of placebos in drug research is allowed, but the patient must be informed and consent must be taken. Worsening of the disease while in drug research, either due to placebo or an ineffective dosage of the drug, must be carefully monitored and the trial should be ended for the safety of the patient.

8. Yahia Abdul-Rahman and Abdullah S. Tug, "Introduction to LARIBA Financing" (1998)

Many Muslims, like other persons of faith, do not confine their religion to weekends or special events. They want to live their faith everyday. For guidance on how to do so, some American Muslims turn first to the traditions of shari'a, or Islamic law and ethics, which discusses everything from what kind of food to eat to how one should bury the dead. The shari'a also advises Muslims on money. Many Muslims believe that the shari'a bans all forms of interest collected on a loan, called riba; other Muslims insist that the ban applies only to predatory lending. But for those who believe the former, a serious challenge is posed: How are American Muslims supposed to buy a house without taking out a loan? Various American companies, including Guidance Financial Group, Devon Bank, Reba Free LLC, and LARIBA American Finance House, offer Islamic alternatives.

The founder of LARIBA, which literally means "no interest," is Yahya Abdul-Rahman, the son of a former Egyptian government official who came to the United States to study chemical engineering in 1968. After earning his PhD, Abdul-Rahman went to work as a successful chemical engineer for Atlantic Richfield. He was later employed as a private banker for Shearson Lehman. But in 1987, in the room above his garage, he established LARIBA, an Islamic mortgage company that would offer shari'a-compliant financing. With the support of Fannie Mae, the federally backed company that helps to fund American home ownership, LARIBA financed properties and business worth over two hundred million dollars. Why and how the company did so is the subject of the paper, initially given at a Harvard Law School forum, excerpted below.

The instinct of owning a place to live in and to produce livelihood has produced a natural dream for every individual and family. The motor of economic development throughout history has been through helping people own a home and a means of transportation. . . . That is why the backbone of the major developed countries and societies has been the housing and automobile industries.

The development of mortgage financing in England, Germany, and the U.S.A. has helped propel the economies directly and indirectly: directly by increasing demand for the products, industries and services associated with building homes, and indirectly by satisfying the natural instinct of ownership in the citizen. Feeling that he/she owns a house, "a piece of the rock," makes the citizen proud of his/her citizenship, deepens the feeling of belonging to the country, enhances the real estate in general as owners strive to beautify their owned properties by continually maintaining and improving it. Finally, owning a home strengthens the feeling of responsibility towards the citizens' own families and the community at large.

That is why major economic policies in developed nations have been designed to essentially subsidize the mortgage industry and to a lesser extent the automobile industry. In the United States, a number of institutions were developed to act as a catalyst in the promotion and facilitation of owning a home. Examples are Federal National Mortgage, designed to provide ongoing assistance to the secondary market for residential mortgages by providing liquidity for residential mortgage investments, thereby improving the distribution of investment capital available for such mortgage financing; the Federal Loan Home Association, chartered by the U.S. Congress in 1970 to create a continuous flow of funds to mortgage lenders in support of home ownership and rental housing; . . . [and] the Government National Mortgage Association (GNMA). . . .

In fact, one of the important parameters used by the Federal Reserve System in its decision regarding interest rate and monetary policy is its impact on the housing industry.

Finally, in an effort to encourage Americans to own homes through mortgage financing, the U.S. government has made *riba* interest paid through mortgage financing tax deductible. It is now one of the few deductions left to the average citizen that helps in reducing taxes. . . .

Home Mortgages in the United States

Approximately 66% of the residential properties in the United States are owner occupied. They represent about $7,000 billion in value. In fact, housing is the single biggest investment in the dream of a family . . . [and] the mortgage payment is the biggest monthly liability of a typical American household.

The typical homebuyer borrows up to 85 to 90% of the purchase price of a home. A typical mortgage has a thirty-year term. Because of the mobility of the U.S. employment market and the continued needs of American families to move to larger and more modern homes in more attractive suburbs and neighborhoods, many of these mortgages are closed way before the end of thirty years. California Home Financing Association 1996 statistics on the characteristics of homebuyers and sellers in California indicate that the average number of years of owning a home is approximately 8 years. As the homeowner moves to another home, he/she closes the old mortgage, pays off the loan and applies for a new home mortgage. In addition, as interest rates have continued to decline in the past two years many homeowners have refinanced their homes more than once (sometimes once every 6 months to a year.)

The American Muslim Community and LARIBA (Islamic) Financing

Most Muslims in the United States have been integrated in the *riba* conventional banking system prevailing in the United States. Most take advantage of *riba* interest-based, FDIC-insured deposits in the banks, borrow money for buying homes using *riba* mortgages, use their credit cards, and sometimes extend its use as a source of *riba*-based credit and take home equity *riba*-based lines of credit. Most of the affluent members of the Muslim business community have used the institutional *riba* financing through the banking system in the U.S.A. and accumulated significant wealth through its use. . . . Most affluent and upper middle class members of the community have been used to the beneficiaries of *riba* system. So, it was unconvincing for many to try to make them change over even in a small way because of the *haram* (forbidden) issue. A number of justifications were used to allow members of the community to continue participating in *riba* activities. . . .

For a newly emerging alternative system to prevail and succeed it is an understatement to say that it is a very difficult uphill battle. Unless the individual is motivated deeply by the strict adherence to the *shari'a*, the Qur'an and the Sunna, we found it to be almost impossible to capture people's interest and imagination. It is interesting to report, based on our experience, that people thought that we are "silly" to try to bring a LARIBA [no interest] concept in a world run by *riba*. We even were ridiculed by the closest of friends.

In all fairness, it is our feeling, based on first hand experience and our in-depth knowledge at the grassroots level of the community, that a large portion of the Muslim middle-class households have accepted *riba* mortgages against their will. It is our feeling that many of these households would convert to LARIBA if available and competitive. There are many people, Muslims and non-Muslims, who feel disenfranchised by traditional methods of financing, or who feel—correctly or not—that they do not have adequate access to credit, or that the terms of the credit that is available to them are morally objectionable or economically unfeasible for them. We are reminded of the successes of the credit union industry among blue-collar workers in the U.S., many of whom simply cannot afford traditional bank accounts because they live from paycheck to paycheck and cannot maintain a minimum balance. . . .

LARIBA (Islamic) Mortgages—The Market

The first and foremost market segment, which should be addressed, is the small minority of American Muslims who refused to participate in *riba* under any circumstance. Many of these households have reasonable cash savings but not enough to buy a home. Their balance sheets are clean of any debt of any sort. It is the moral responsibility of the LARIBA (Islamic) bankers and investment/mortgage bankers to cater to the needs of this "Puritan" segment of the community. It is important to note that the term Puritan is used here in American LARIBA on purpose. The term "Puritan" conveys the core principles of American democratic freedom and virtue through industriousness and property ownership. . . .

They want to make sure of the validity of the LARIBA (Islamic) mortgage model and approach and they want to check it with their most respected and trusted religious scholar (usually back in Pakistan or other Muslim countries). The profile of this unique market segment is unique. They are extremely pious. They run cash-only households. They use the banks for safe deposits of funds and refuse to accept money market interest. They carry no debt. They pay their obligations on time. They fulfill their obligations. They are honorable and extremely successful and reputable. They do not show off their success and accumulated savings because of their training to be humble. . . . They are devout members of the community. They can be classified as the best credit worthy members of a community. They only can be recognized if those LARIBA (Islamic) bankers are true community workers on a grassroots level. . . .

The LARIBA Lease Purchase Model

The model is simple and straightforward. It consists of two parts.

The first is the return of capital. If the house price is $180,000, the client pays $60,000 and the balance is financed by LARIBA. In this case the client owns 33.4% of the house and LARIBA owns 66.6% of the house. The client agrees to buy back the share of LARIBA over a period of five years in monthly installments of $2,000 per month. The title of the house is transferred directly to the client to minimize costs and taxes. LARIBA becomes the lien holder. The client owns the house and handles his/her property in terms of maintenance, upkeep, and renovation in the same way a traditional mortgage holder would.

The second part is the lease of the house. The client agrees to lease the house for a period of sixty months, the term of the pay back. The lease is estimated based on comparable lease rates of houses in the neighborhood and is negotiated on an ad-hoc basis between the client and LARIBA. The lease income is distributed between the client and LARIBA. The client's portion of the lease is used in our computer model to expedite the buy back process.

The Strategic Approach to LARIBA (Islamic) Mortgages

A strategy is the art and wisdom of matching our goals with our available resources in light of the social, business, and political environment we live in. Our approach to achieving our goals is to wisely "start from the possible to achieve the impossible." The following is a summary of our strategy:

1. The Need for Grassroots Community Involvement. The primary market segment for LARIBA mortgages is large by the American Muslim community's humble means. A mere $200 million is a "drop in the bucket" by American banking and financing standards. LARIBA (Islamic) banking and financing system does not have a proven track record in the United States. We found from experience that relying on our local resources is a must. That means that we should rely on localized grass-roots community effort at every community center. So, in order to do this we must start small in order to achieve our ultimate goal. Also, we must have the flexibility and foresight in order to compete in the market.

2. The Laws of the Land. Based on our thirty-one-year experience as American Muslims we learned that it is difficult, expensive, and essentially impossible to change the laws of the land. We tried to do it regarding marriage contracts. We settled for abiding by the civil code to protect the rights of the married couple and performing the wedding according to the Islamic rites. We encountered the same experience in cases of divorce. We concluded that the Muslims do not have yet the "critical" mass and the ways and means even to attempt to change the laws of the land.

From a strategic point of view, we decided that changing the banking and finances laws of the United States to fit the Islamic *shari'a* is not our goal in this stage of the American Muslim community's experience. We believe that in the future the passing of the "Financial Services Modernization Act," will modernize the American banking industry and may soften the Glass Stiegel Act. . . . However, it will take a long time. We are aware that others have tried at huge expense only to dress up the regular *riba* financing contract to make it look and sound proper from the *shari'a* Islamic point of view. We respectfully disagree with the approach and wish those who have tried and are still trying it the best and pray for their success.

We therefore decided and in the same time strongly urge that in dealing with banking and financing matters in the United States strict adherence to the letter of the law is required. We also believe that respecting the laws of the United States and abiding by them is our responsibility to God, the future of the community, and the good of the alternative system we hope to lay the foundation of. We know from history that toying with financial, securities, and banking laws of America is dangerous. We also know that the punishment is instant, terminal, and irreversible. On the other hand, many components of the American system represent years of human experience that cannot be thrown away. We simply cannot reinvent the wheel. The Community Re-investment Act (CRA), the laws against usury, the equal lending opportunity laws, the Securities and Exchange Commission rules and regulations, the regulatory functions of the U.S. banking regulators and the laws regarding full and complete disclosures are laws and regulations that reinforce basic human and Islamic values. We also know that the American financial, monetary, and banking system is the most sophisticated and reliable in the world. It is our duty to uphold these laws. Our efforts should concentrate on providing an alternative not a substitute to that system. The reliability of that alternative system is, in fact, enhanced by the already tried and proven regulatory and legal system of America. We should abide by the Prophet Muhammad saying "God bestows peace and mercy unto those who know and who are realistic about their capabilities."

Conclusions

LARIBA financing is potentially in harmony with the best of American virtue and values. It offers many benefits for civil society and community in a world where many are excluded from credit and finance. LARIBA mortgage financing is feasible in the U.S.A. if done strategically to satisfy the laws of the *shari'a* and those of the United States. The initial market for LARIBA mortgage is that of the LARIBA Puritans who accumulated a sizeable down payment but are not able to afford the full price. The market size is crudely estimated to be 7,500 households in the USA. Involvement with the community on the grassroots level provides the safest way to finance and put in effect the "know your client" rule. Long term (fifteen or thirty year mortgages) may offer the buyer an easy monthly payment but it also indirectly enhances the clients going deeper in debt. It is the responsibility of the LARIBA banker to rid people of debt in order to live freely. The LARIBA model helps pay off the debt faster. It is the most suitable in the American mobile society that changes residences or refinances once every five to eight years. LARIBA mortgages and financing brings real life into the Community Reinvestment Act stipulated by the American banking regulations. A savings program for the future generations is needed to save a sizeable down payment for the children's first home. . . . LARIBA mortgage can best survive and grow under the protection and scrutiny of the American banking, monetary and financial laws.

9. Capital D, "Culture of Terrorism," from *Insomnia* (2004)

Many young American Muslims encounter God in the sometimes provocative, sometimes sublime lyrics of Islamic hip-hop, a musical genre which is popular not only among African Americans, but also among white, Latino/a, Arab, and South Asian American Muslims. Islamic hip-hop also crosses ideological and doctrinal lines. It is a phenomenon too big for any one group or artist to control. The social boundaries of various American Muslim religious groups are crossed and challenged as hip-hop themes and lyrics travel from the mouths and ears of Nation of Islam practitioners to Five Percenters, Sunnis, and listeners well beyond the borders of the United States. Some artists note the aesthetic similarity between the sound patterns of hip-hop and the sound patterns of the Qur'an, heard especially in the use of rhyme and alliteration. In addition, allusions to the Qur'an and Islamic history appear in the work of the Poor Righteous Teachers, Mos Def, Native Deen, Eve, JT the Bigga Figga, and others. Below, in the song lyrics by African American Sunni Muslim David Kelly, or Capital D, one finds references to the Dajjal, or Satan; the kuffar, or unbelievers; the Ansari, or God's helpers; and the scholar Bukhari, one of the great compilers of the words and deeds of the Prophet Muhammad. Like many of his fellow Muslim rappers, Capital D also stresses Islam's emphasis on social justice as a source of inspiration, and he has been deeply critical of the 2003 war in Iraq and unfettered American capitalism. Such political criticism is inspired, at least in part, by Kelly's religious outlook. His music is simultaneously religious and political, both socially engaged and spiritual. Kelly, who holds a law degree, is also a writer and a volunteer for the Chicago-based Inner City Muslim Action Network, which offers job training, health care, and prison outreach.

No introductions time be rushing like a renegade
disrupt the function put a cease to all these serenades
I'm breaking down the barricades and blurring the dividing lines
never shook just looking to Allah for His guiding signs
attack Columbus I ain't begging him to reparate
meanwhile Mugabe forces robbers to repatriate
let's set it straight I never glorify no terrorist
but nonetheless your pimping with the emperor is perilous
I'm strictly off limit to the cotton-soft scented type
who tip-toe and dread light and dread the sight
of a kufi-wearing kid who's kicking science
picking mental padlocks
I specialize in defiance
alliance of the havenots
bottled up energy's exploding out the bottle cap
cap smash the glass
y'all hold fast . . . now model that
replicate the detonation
spread across the nation to the Serengeti
but mentally I'm there already
I done drop Machiavelli with a bo shiver
smack Sun Tzu, I'm reading Lao Tzu
and douse crews with verbal gasoline
while average teens is unaware and living terrible
I yell out Geronimo and watch the falling dominos
the drama knows no end until the meek are equal on the earth
I unleash the pen to blow your speakers in for what it's worth
upset the status quo by smacking up ya master
til we smashing in his bottle caps I'm staying stuck on autosnap

I read Bukhari and the way of the Ansari for sure
while the kuffar be spending time on their Atari but yo
with these attachments and distractions can we see it's about
walking the path of many prophets that precede us
no doubt, we gots to train the mind to recognize and read the signs
redefine the inner til my outer shell is redesigned
maintain and motivate then watch the hours culminate
I cultivate my frame until it's firm enough to hold the weight

don't know the date but still the judgment day is closing in
a few are chosen but the most of men dozing and
the body's like a temple from my soul on to my mental
seeing with my inner eye the spiritual is quintessential
I perform my mind aerobics rising far before the dawn
give my soul a proper workout while I'm reading the Qur'an
to keep my mental sharp I tossed the TV out my crib
and now looking for my chance to jab Dajjal up in the jibs
And this land of bravery, wage slavery, ill imagery
yo peep the symmetry
they spending billions on global domination
while women and children got no accommodations
meanwhile my thugs is giving desires and savageness
just tryin' to survive and defy the law of averages
see two in three young bros ain't gon' make it
so once they see a little money they gon' take it
they got us living by a code that is makeshift
cause in our heart kid you too scared to break with
the system that dissed you and forgets you
refuses to fit you
it either seeks to enlist you or commits you
but never to permit or admit you

The American economy's surviving of arms
third world debt
closing down farms
promoting conflict and violent behavior
then using convicts for cheap slave labor
extending patents on the xy chromosome
pushing drugs from crack down to methadone
drones to the metronome marchalong to the rhythm
of the free trade and forced patriotism
now racism still gives a little bit of stature
to modern legacies of the former slave masters
all these factors then create factions
insulate the power from a unified action
across the map the rich be relaxing
and in former Burma you'll never hear no murmur

cause the dispossessed poor are in sweatshops
and if they get caught tryna unionize they get shot
on home soil leaders of the U.S.
map foreign oil determine who gets
temporary military so-called aid
And the neverending scheme of getting paid
as the rich get richer and the poor get poorer
it's a nonstop saga bringing worldwide horror
we fight, losing sight over what we warring over
as the rich get richer and the poor get poorer

10. Hamza Yusuf, Introduction to *Purification of the Heart* (2004)

Hamza Yusuf, born Mark Hanson in 1960, was raised a Greek Orthodox Christian but embraced Islam during his teenage years in Santa Barbara, California. In 1979, he left the United States for several years to study the classical Islamic religious sciences—including Arabic, Islamic law and ethics, and Islamic philosophy—in the Middle East, North Africa, and West Africa. After returning to the United States and earning a religious studies degree at San Jose State University, he helped to establish the Zaytuna Institute, an Islamic school based in Hayward, California, devoted to the revival of the classical religious sciences of Islam. Yusuf is a popular speaker, writer, and translator. In the piece below, Yusuf writes an introduction to a twelfth-century Islamic text called Purification of the Heart, *a guide to Islamic spirituality. Here, as in other writings and speeches, he shows his fluency not only in Islamic studies but also in European literature, American history, and even anatomy.*

Almost universally, religious traditions have stressed the importance of the condition of the heart. In the Muslim scripture, the Day of Judgment is described as "a day in which neither wealth nor children shall be of any benefit [to anyone], except one who comes to God with a sound heart" (26:88–89). The sound heart is understood to be free of character defects and spiritual blemishes. This "heart" is actually the spiritual heart and not the physical organ per se, although in Islamic tradition the spiritual heart is centered in the physical. One of the extraordinary aspects of the modern era is that we are discovering aspects about the heart unknown in previous times, although there were remarkable insights in ancient traditions. For instance, according to traditional Chinese medicine, the heart houses what is known as *shen*, which is spirit. The Chinese characters for thinking, thought, love, the intention to listen, and virtue all contain the ideogram for the heart.

In nearly every culture in the world, people use metaphors that directly or indirectly allude to the heart. We call certain types of people "hard-hearted," usually because they show no mercy and kindness. Likewise, people are said to have "cold hearts" and others yet who are "warm-hearted." We speak of people as wearing their "hearts on their sleeves" because they do not (or cannot) conceal their emotions from others. When someone's words or actions penetrate our souls and affect us profoundly, we say that this person "touched my heart" or "touched the core of my being." The Arabic equivalent for the English word *core* (which originally in Latin meant heart) is known as *lubb*, which also refers to the heart, as well as the intellect and the essence of something.

The most ancient Indo-European word for heart means "that which leaps," which is consonant with the idea of the beating heart that leaps in the breast of man. People speak of their hearts as "leaping for joy." People also say that their heart "skipped a beat" when they come upon something startling that elicited from them a very strong emotional response. When people fall in love, they speak of "stealing one's heart." There are many other metaphors involving the human heart, owing to its centrality in life. These phrases—however casually we may utter them today—have roots in ancient concepts.

The ancients were aware of spiritual diseases of the heart. And this understanding is certainly at the essence of Islamic teachings. The Qur'an defines three types of people: *al-mu'minun* (believers), *al-kafirun* (scoffers or atheists), and *al-munafiqun* (hypocrites). The believers are described as people whose hearts are alive and full of light, while the scoffers are in darkness: "Is one who was dead and then We revived [with faith] and made for him a light by which to walk among the people like one who is in darkness from which he cannot exit?" (6:122). According to commentators of the Qur'an, *the one who was dead* refers to having a dead heart, which God revived with the light of guidance that one may walk straight and honorably among human beings. Also, the Prophet Muhammad said, "The difference between the one who remembers God and one who does not is like the difference between the living and the dead." In essence, the believer is someone whose heart is alive, while the disbeliever is someone whose heart is spiritually dead. The hypocrite, however, is somebody whose heart is diseased. The Qur'an speaks of certain people with diseased hearts (self-inflicted, we understand) and, as a result, they were increased in their disease (2:10).

The heart is centered slightly to the left of our bodies. Two sacred languages of Arabic and Hebrew are written from right to left, toward the heart, which, as some have noted, mirrors the purpose of writing, namely to affect the heart. One should also consider the ritual of circumambulation or circling around the Ancient House (or Ka'ba) in Makkah during the Pilgrimage. It is performed in a counterclockwise fashion, with the left side of the worshipper facing the House—with the heart inclined towards it to remind us of God and His presence in the life of humanity.

The physical heart, which houses the spiritual heart, beats about 100,000 times a day, pumping two gallons of blood per minute and over one hundred gallons per hour. If one were to attempt to carry one hundred gallons of water (whose density is lighter than blood) from one place to another, it would be an exhausting task. Yet the human heart does this every hour of every day for an entire lifetime without respite. The vascular system transporting life-giving blood is over 60,000 miles long—more than two times the circumference or the earth. So when we conceive of our blood being pumped throughout our bodies, know that this means that it travels through 60,000 miles of a closed vascular system that connects all the parts of the body—all the vital organs and living tissues—to this incredible heart.

We now know that the heart starts beating before the brain is fully fashioned, that is, without the benefit of a fully formed central system. The dominant theory states that the central nervous system is what controls the entire human being, with the brain as its center. Yet we also know that the nervous system does not initiate the beat of the heart, but that it is actually self-initiated, or, as we would say, initiated by God. We also know that the heart, should all of its connections to the brain be severed (as they are during a heart transplant), continues to beat.

Many in the West have long proffered that the brain is the center of consciousness. But in traditional Islamic thought—as in other traditions—the heart is viewed as the center of our being. The Qur'an, for example, speaks of wayward people who have hearts "with which they do not understand" (7:179). Also the Qur'an mentions people who mocked the

Prophet and were entirely insincere in listening to his message, so God "placed over their hearts a covering that they may not understand it and in their ears [He placed] acute deafness" (6:25). Their inability to understand is a deviation from the spiritual function of a sound heart, just as their ears have been afflicted with a spiritual *deafness*. So we understand from this that the center of the intellect, the center of human consciousness and conscience, is actually the heart and not the brain. Only recently have we discovered that there are over 40,000 neurons in the heart. In other words, there are cells in the heart that are communicating with the brain. While the brain sends messages to the heart, the heart also sends messages to the brain.

Two physiologists in the 1970s, John and Beatrice Lacey, conducted a study and found that the brain sent messages to the heart, but the heart did not automatically obey the messages. Sometimes the heart sped up, while at other times it slowed down, indicating that the heart itself has its own type of intelligence. The brain receives signals from the heart through the brain's amygdale, thalamus, and cortex. The amygdale relates to emotions, while the cortex or the neocortex relates to learning and reasoning. Although this interaction is something that is not fully understood from a physiological point of view, we do know that the heart is an extremely sophisticated organ with secrets still veiled from us.

The Prophet of Islam spoke of the heart as a repository of knowledge and a vessel sensitive to the deeds of the body. He said, for example, that wrongdoing irritates the heart. So the heart actually perceives wrong action. In fact, when people do terrible things, the core of their humanity is injured. Fyodor Dostoyevsky expresses brilliantly in *Crime and Punishment* that the crime itself is the punishment because human beings ultimately have to live with the painful consequences of their deeds. When someone commits a crime, he does so first against his own heart, which then affects the whole human being. The person enters a state of spiritual agitation and often tries to suppress it. The root meaning of the word *kufr* (disbelief) is to *cover* something up. As it relates to this discussion, the problems we see in our society come down to covering up or suppressing the symptoms of its troubles. The agents used to do this include alcohol, drugs, sexual experimentation and deviance, power grabs, wealth, arrogance, pursuit of fame, and the like. These enable people to submerge themselves into a state of heedlessness concerning their hearts and the natural feelings found there. The pressures to do this are very strong in our modern culture.

One of the major drawbacks of being severed from the heart is that the more one is severed, the sicker the heart becomes, for the heart needs nourishment. Heedlessness starves the heart, robs it of its spiritual manna. One enters into a state of unawareness—a debilitating lack of awareness of God and an acute neglect of humanity's ultimate destination: the infinite world of the Hereafter. When one peers into the limitless world through remembrance of God and increases in beneficial knowledge, one's concerns become more focused on the infinite world, not the finite one that is disappearing and ephemeral. When people are completely immersed in the material world, believing that this world is all that matters and all that exists and that they are not accountable for their actions, they effect a spiritual death of their hearts. Before the heart dies, however, it shows symptoms of affliction. These afflictions are the spiritual diseases of the heart (the center of our being)—the topic of this book.

In Islamic tradition, these diseases fall under two categories. The first is known as *shubuhat* or obfuscations, diseases that relate to impaired understanding. For instance, if somebody is fearful that God will not provide for him or her, this is considered a disease of the heart because a sound heart has knowledge and trust, not doubt and anxiety. *Shubuhat* alludes to aspects closely connected to the heart: the soul, the ego, Satan's whisperings and instigations, caprice, and the ardent love of this ephemeral world. The heart is an organ designed to be in a state of calm, which is achieved with the remembrance of God: "Most surely, in the remembrance of God do hearts find calm" (13:28). This calm is what the heart seeks out and gravitates to. It yearns always to remember God the Exalted. But when God is not remembered, when human beings forget God, then the heart falls into a state of agitation and turmoil. In this state it becomes vulnerable to diseases because it is undernourished and cut off. Cells require oxygen, so we breathe, and the breath of the heart is none other than the remembrance of God. Without it, the spiritual heart dies. The very purpose of revelation and of scripture is to remind us that our hearts need to be nourished.

We enter the world in a state the Qur'an calls *fitra*, our original state and inherent nature that is disposed to accept faith and prefer morality. But we soon learn anxiety mainly from our parents and then our societies. The heart is created vulnerable to anxiety and agitation (70:19). Those who are protected from this state are people of prayer, people who establish prayer and guard its performance with a humble and open heart connected with God, the Lord of all creation. The highest ranks among people are those who do not allow anything to divert them from the remembrance of God. They are the ones who remember God as they are "standing, sitting, and reclining on their sides" (3:191).

The second category of disease concerns the base desires of the self and is called *shahawat*. This relates to our desires exceeding their natural state, as when people live merely to satisfy these urges and are led by them. Islam provides the method by which our hearts can become sound and safe again. This method has been the subject of brilliant and insightful scholarship for centuries in the Islamic tradition. One can say that Islam in essence is a program to restore purity and calm to the heart through the remembrance of God.

This present text is based on the poem known as *Mathartat al-Qulūb* (literally, *Purification of the Hearts*), which offers the means by which purification can be achieved. It is a treatise on the "alchemy of the hearts," namely, a manual on how to transform the heart. It was written by a great scholar and saint, Shaykh Muhammad Mawlud al-Ya'qubi al-Musawi al-Muratani. As his name indicates, he was from Mauritania in West Africa. He was a master of all the Islamic sciences, including the inward sciences of the heart. He stated that he wrote this poem because he observed the prevalence of diseased hearts. He saw students of religion spending their time learning abstract sciences that people were not really in need of, to the neglect of those sciences that pertain to what people are accountable for in the next life, namely, the spiritual condition of the heart. In one of his most cited statements, the Prophet said, "Actions are based upon intentions." All deeds are thus valued according to the intentions behind them, and intentions emanate from the heart. So every action a person intends or performs is rooted in the heart. . . .

If we examine the trials and tribulations, wars and other conflicts, every act of injustice all over earth, we'll find they are rooted in human hearts. Covetousness, the desire to aggress and exploit, the longing to pilfer natural resources, the inordinate love of wealth and position, and other maladies are manifestations of diseases found nowhere but in the heart. Every criminal, miser, abuser, scoffer, embezzler, and hateful person does what he or she does because of a diseased heart. If hearts were sound, these actions would no longer be a reality. So if we want to change our world, we do not begin by rectifying the outward. Instead, we must change the condition of our inward. Everything we see happening outside of us is in reality coming from the unseen world within. It is from the unseen world that the phenomenal world emerges, and it is from the unseen realm of our hearts that all actions spring.

The well-known civil rights activist Martin Luther King Jr. said that in order for people to condemn injustice, they must go through four stages. The first stage is that people must ascertain that indeed injustices are being perpetrated. In his case, it was injustices against African Americans in the United States. The second stage is to negotiate, that is, approach the oppressor and demand justice. If the oppressor refuses, King said that the third stage is self-purification, which starts with the question: "Are we ourselves wrong-doers? Are we ourselves oppressors?" The fourth stage, then, is to take action after true self-examination, after removing one's own wrongs before demanding justice from others.

We of the modern world are reluctant to ask ourselves—when we look at the terrible things that are happening—"Why do they occur?" And if we ask that with all sincerity, the answer will come resoundingly: "All of this is from your own selves." In so many ways, we have brought this upon ourselves. This is the only empowering position we can take. The Qur'an implies that if a people oppress others, God will send another people to oppress them: "We put some oppressors over other oppressors because of what their own hands have earned" (6:129). According to Fakhruddin al-Razi (a twelfth-century scholar of the Qur'an), the verse means that the existence of oppression on earth may be caused by previous oppression. By implication, often the victims of aggression were once aggressors themselves. This, however, is not the case with tribulations, for there are times in which people are indeed tried, but if they respond with patience and perseverance, God will always give them relief and victory. If we examine the life of the Prophet in Makkah, it's clear that he and the community of believers were being harmed and oppressed, but they were patient and God gave them victory. Within twenty-three years, the Prophet was not only free of oppression, but became the leader of the entire Arabian Peninsula. Those people who once oppressed him now sought mercy from him; and he was most gracious and kind in his response. Despite their former brutality toward him, the Prophet forgave them and admitted them into the brotherhood of faith.

This is the difference between someone whose heart is purified and sound and one whose heart is impure and corrupt. Impure people oppress, and the pure-hearted not only forgive their oppressors, but elevate them in status and character. In order to purify ourselves, we must begin to recognize this truth. This is what this book is all about—a book of self-purification and a manual of liberation. If we work on our hearts, if we actually implement what is suggested here, we'll begin to see changes in our lives, our condition, our society, and even within our own family dynamics. It is a blessing that we have this science of purification, a blessing that this teaching exists in the world today. What remains is for us to take these teachings seriously.

So let us go through what is explained here by this great scholar and learn of the diseases of the heart, examine their etiology (their causes), their signs and symptoms, and, finally, how to treat them. There are two types of treatments: the theoretical treatment, which is understanding the disease itself, and the practical treatment, which focuses on the prescriptions we must take in order to restore the heart's natural purity. If we apply the techniques that have been learned and transmitted by the great scholars of the vast tradition of Islam, we will see results. But just like medicinal prescriptions, the physician cannot force you to take it. The knowledgeable scholars of spiritual purification have given us the treatment, as they have gleaned it from the teachings of the Qur'an and the exemplary model of the Prophet. The teachings are available. They are clear, and they work. It is then up to us to learn and apply them to ourselves and share them with others.

Acknowledgments

One of the greatest pleasures of finishing a book is thanking all those who helped you along the way. I owe an enormous debt to many of the scholars mentioned in the "further reading" section of the book. They deserve no blame for my mistakes and errors of judgment, but their scholarly work has taught me a lot about Islam and Muslims in the United States. In addition to those scholars, I wish to thank colleagues who read and commented on the book's prospectus, including Amir Hussain, Bruce Lawrence, Karen Leonard, and Jane Idleman Smith. Other scholars offered advice or suggested possible documents for inclusion, among them Jon Brockopp, Carl Ernst, Barbara Metcalf, Vernon Schubel, Andrew Shryock, Laury Silvers, and Frances Trix.

I thank Philip Goff for first suggesting that I contact Wendy Lochner at Columbia University Press with my idea for this project. Going far beyond the call of collegiality, Professor Goff later convened the fellows of IUPUI's Center for the Study of Religion and American Culture to discuss my first full draft. I received wonderful comments and support from Indiana University–Bloomington professors Kathryn Lofton, Sylvester Johnson, and Candy Gunther Brown; Society for the Social Scientific Study of Religion officer Arthur Farnsley; IUPUI professors Rachel Wheeler and Peter Thuesen; and Christian Theological Seminary professor Scott Seay.

Debbie Dale typed many of these documents—her assistance was invaluable. The staff at the IUPUI University Library, especially Sharon Fish, Joe Harmon, and Karen Janke, worked hard to find many of the texts. Still others helped me acquire the permission to reprint them, including Zaheer Ali,

Saleemah Abdul-Ghafur, Susan Berman, Imam Mahdi Bray, Naheed Fakoor, Imam Shuajb Gerguri, Sharif Graham, Joanna Green, Muhammad Lateef Hayden, Bethany Johnson, Mariola Kalinska, Hosai Mojaddidi, Fahim Munshi, Bob Niegowski, Regina Sara Ryan, Zachary Twist, and Nathan Zezula. Special thanks to those authors who granted rights to reprint their work gratis; they made this book more affordable.

My students in classes on Modern Muslim Literatures and African American Islam convinced me that a documentary approach was an effective way to teach about Islam and Muslims in the United States. They deserve my thanks for enduring all those bad photocopies of old documents.

I am grateful to the School of Liberal Arts at IUPUI for its financial support of this project, but even more to my faculty colleagues for their congeniality and smart ideas.

Every effort has been made to trace copyright holders and give proper credit for all copyrighted material used in this book, which is printed below. I regret any oversights. The publisher will be pleased to hear from any copyright holders not acknowledged in this edition so that a correction might be made at the next opportunity.

Chapter 1

Omar ibn Sayyid, "The Autobiography of Omar ibn Sayyid" (1831), edited by John Franklin Jameson, *American Historical Review* 30, no. 4 (July 1925): 791–795. Used by permission of the American Historical Association.

Mohammed Alexander Russell Webb, *Islam in America* (New York: Oriental Publishing Co., 1893), 11–14, 23–26, 52–53.

Edward Wilmot Blyden, "Islam in the Western Soudan," *Journal of the Royal African Society* 2, no. 5 (October 1902): 24, 27–29, 30, 33.

George L. Root, *Ancient Arabic Order of the Nobles of the Mystic Shrine* (San Antonio, Tex.: Alamo Printing Co., 1916), 1–10.

Interviews with Mary Juma and Mike Abdallah, Works Progress Administration, North Dakota Writers' Project Ethnic Group Files, Series 30559, Roll 3, 1939.

Chapter 2

Pir Inayat Khan, "America: 1910–1912," in *The Sufi Message of Hazrat Inayat Khan*. Available online at http://wahiduddin.net/mv2/bio/Autobiography_1.htm. Last accessed on December 28, 2006. Used by kind permission of the Nekbakht Foundation and East-West Publications.

Moslem Sunrise, "I Am a Moslem" (October 1921); "True Salvation of the 'American Negroes': The Real Solution of the Negro Question" (April and July 1923); "Crescent or Cross: A Negro May Aspire to Any Position Under Islam Without Discrimination" (October 1923); and "Living Flora—And Dead" (January 1924).

Noble Drew Ali, *Holy Koran of the Moorish Science Temple* (Chicago, 1927), 1, 56–60.

Shaikh Daoud Ahmed Faisal, *Al-Islam: The Religion of Humanity* (Brooklyn, New York: Islamic Mission of America, 1950), 14–17, 48–51, 59–62.

Imam Vehby Ismail, "Youth's Pages: Our Prophet, Muhammad," *Jeta Muslimane Shqipetare (Albanian Moslem Life)* 8, no. 1 (September 1959): 58–62. Used by kind permission of the Albanian American Muslim Society.

Abdo Elkholy, *The Arab Moslems in the United States* (New Haven, Conn.: College and University Press Service, 1966), 17–18, 91–93, 102, 122–125, 129, 133–134.

Piri Thomas, "God, Ain't You for Everybody?" from *Down These Mean Streets* (New York: Random House, 1967), 275–283. Used by permission of Alfred A. Knopf, a division of Random House, Inc.

"What the Muslims Want" and "What the Muslims Believe," from Elijah Muhammad, *Message to the Blackman in America* (Chicago, 1965), 161–164.

Malcolm X, Interview with *Al-Muslimoon* (Geneva, 1965). Used by permission of Pathfinder Press.

Chapter 3

M. R. Bawa Muhaiyaddeen, "The Inner Qur'an," from *Islam and World Peace* (Philadelphia: Fellowship Press, 1987), 133–138. Material printed with the kind permission of the Bawa Muhaiyaddeen Fellowship.

W. D. Mohammed, "Historic Atlanta Address," *Bilalian News* (September 29, 1978): 16–17. By kind permission of Imam W. D. Mohammed.

Nation of Gods and Earths, "What We Teach," "Allah," and "Supreme Mathematics," from *The Word* 2, no. 1 (June 1992): 1, 3, 6; *The Word* 2, no. 3 (November/December 1992).

Frances Trix, prologue to *Spiritual Discourse: Learning with an Islamic Master* (Philadelphia: University of Pennsylvania Press, 1993), 1–5. Reprinted by permission of the University of Pennsylvania Press.

Minister Louis Farrakhan, "Million Man March Address," October 16, 1995. Available online at http://www.africawithin.com/mmm/transcript.htm. Last accessed on December 28, 2006.

Jeffrey Lang, *Struggling to Surrender: Some Impressions of an American Convert to Islam*, 2nd rev. ed. (Beltsville, Md.: Amana Publication, 1995), 7–16. Used by kind permission of Amana Publications.

Sally Howell, "Finding the Straight Path: A Conversation with Mohsen and Lila Amen about Faith, Life, and Family in Dearborn," in *Arab Detroit: From Margin to Mainstream*, edited by Nabeel Abraham and Andrew Shryock (Detroit, Mich.: Wayne State University Press, 2000), 243–254. Reprinted with the permission of Wayne State University Press.

Damarys Ocana, "Our Stories: A Leap of Faith," *Latina Magazine* (November 2004): 122–128. Used by kind permission of Latina Media Ventures.

"Matrimonials," from *Islamic Horizons* (March/April 2005): 59. Used by kind permission of *Islamic Horizons*.

Asra Q. Nomani, *Standing Alone in Mecca: An American Woman's Struggle for the Soul of Islam* (New York: HarperSanFrancisco, 2005), 3–11. Reprinted by permission of HarperCollins Publishers.

Chapter 4

Leila Ahmed, "From Abu Dhabi to America," in *A Border Passage: From Cairo to America—A Woman's Journey* (New York: Penguin, 2000), 291–296. Used by kind permission of Leila Ahmed, Victor S. Thomas Professor of Divinity, Harvard University.

Carol L. Anway, *Daughters of Another Path: Experiences of American Women Choosing Islam* (Lee's Summit, Mo.: Yawna Publications, 1996), 185–195.

Tarajee Abdur-Rahim, in Steven Barboza, *American Jihad: Islam After Malcolm X* (New York: Doubleday, 1993), 158–163, 168–172. Used by permission of Doubleday, a division of Random House, Inc.

Asma Gull Hasan, *American Muslims: The New Generation* (New York: Continuum, 2000), 35–37, 107–110, 133–137. Used by kind permission of Asma Gull Hasan.

Azizah al-Hibri, "An Introduction to Muslim Women's Rights," in *Windows of Faith: Muslim Women Scholar-Activists in North America*, edited by Gisela Webb (Syracuse, N.Y.: Syracuse University Press, 2002), 54–55, 57–60, 62–68. Used by permission of Syracuse University Press.

Amina Wadud, *Qur'an and Woman: Rereading the Sacred Text from a Woman's Perspective* (New York: Oxford, 1999), 34–42. Used by permission of Oxford University Press.

Khalida Saed, "On the Edge of Belonging," in *Living Islam Outloud: American Muslim Women* Speak, edited by Saleemah Abdul-Ghafur (Boston: Beacon Press, 2005), 86–94. Used by kind permission of Saleemah Abdul-Ghafur.

Imam Zaid Shakir, "An Examination of the Issue of Female Prayer Leadership," March 23, 2005. Available online at http://alghazzali.org/resources/femaleprayer.pdf#search = %22Zaid%20Shakir%20women%20prayer%22. Last accessed on December 28, 2006. Used by kind permission of the author.

Laury Silvers, "Islamic Jurisprudence, 'Civil' Disobedience, and Woman-Led Prayer," April 18, 2005. Available online at http://www.pmuna.org/archives/2005/04/laury_silvers_r_1.php. Last accessed on December 28, 2006. Used by kind permission of the author.

Ingrid Mattson, "Can a Woman Be an Imam? Debating Form and Function in Muslim Women's Leadership" (2005): 3, 4, 8–21. Available online at http://macdonald.hartsem.edu/muslimwomensleadership.pdf. Last accessed on December 28, 2006. Used by kind permission of the author.

Chapter 5

Council of American-Islamic Relations, "The Status of Muslim Civil Rights in the United States" (2005). Available online at http://www.cair-net.org/asp/2005CivilRightsReport.pdf. Last accessed on December 28, 2006. Used by kind permission of the Council of American-Islamic Relations.

Laila Al-Marayati, "American Muslim Charities: Easy Targets in the War on Terror," *Pace Law Review* 25 (2005): 321, 322, 324–326, 328–338. Used by kind permission of *Pace Law Review*.

United States District Court, Western District of Washington at Seattle, "United States of America v. Earnest James Ujaama." Available online at http://fl1.findlaw.com/news.findlaw.com/hdocs/docs/terrorism/usujaama82802ind.pdf. Last accessed on December 23, 2006.

Fiqh Council of North America, "Fatwa Against Terrorism," July 28, 2005. Available online at http://www.cair-net.org/downloads/fatwa.htm. Last accessed on December 23, 2006. Used by kind permission of Dr. Muzammil Siddiqi, Chair, Fiqh Council of North America.

Omid Safi, "Being Muslim, Being American After 9/11," in Michael Wolfe, *Taking Back Islam: American Muslims Reclaim Their Faith* (New York: Rodale, 2002), 67–75. Permission granted by Rodale, Inc., Emmaus, PA, 18098, (800) 848–4735, www.rodalestore.com.

Mustafa Tameez, Strategic Thinking, "Yaphett El-Amin for [Missouri] Senate District 4." Available online at http://elaminforsenate.com. Last accessed on December 28, 2006. Used by kind permission of the Hon. Yaphett El-Amin.

Khaled Abou El Fadl, "Islam and the Challenge of Democracy," *Boston Review* (April/May 2003): 2–6, 18–23. Available online at http://bostonreview.net/BR28.2/abou.html. Last accessed on December 28, 2006. Used by kind permission of Dr. Khaled Abou El Fadl, Omar and Azmeralda Alfi Distinguished Professor in Islamic Law, UCLA School of Law.

Shamim A. Siddiqi, "Islamic Movement in America—Why?" in *Muslims and Islamization in North America: Problems and Prospects*, edited by Amber

Haque (Beltsville, Md:. Amana Publications, 1999), 355–361. Used by kind permission of Amana Publications.

American Islamic Congress, "A New Guide to Muslim Interfaith Dialogue" (2006). Available online at http://www.aicongress.org/interfaith-guide.html. Last accessed on December 28, 2006. Used by kind permission of the American Islamic Congress.

Patricia S. Maloof and Fariyal Ross-Sherriff, "Challenges of Resettlement and Adaptation of Muslim Refugees," in *Muslim Refugees in the United States: A Guide for Service Providers*, Culture Profile No. 17 (Washington, D.C.: Center for Applied Linguistics, 2003), 15, 21, 24–25, 27. Reprinted with permission.

Chapter 6

Betty Hasan Amin, "Hajj in a Wheelchair," *Azizah Magazine* 1, no. 1 (Winter 2001): 39–41, 43. Reprinted with permission of *Azizah Magazine*.

Abdul Rauf, *Qur'an for Children*, edited by Laleh Bakhtiar (Chicago: Kazi Publications, 1995), 19–32. Used by kind permission of Kazi Publications.

Shakina Reinhertz, *Women Called to the Path of Rumi: The Way of the Whirling Dervish* (Prescott, Ariz.: Hohm Press, 2001), 86, 88–90, 92–95. Reprinted by permission of Hohm Press.

Tazim R. Kassam, "The Daily Prayer (*Du'a*) of Shi'a Isma'ili Muslims," in *Religions of the United States in Practice*, edited by Colleen McDannell (Princeton, N.J.: Princeton University Press, 2001), 2:32, 2:34–35, 2:37–43. Reprinted by permission of Princeton University Press.

Aminah McCloud and Frederick Thaufeer al-Deen, *A Question of Faith for Muslim Inmates* (Chicago: ABC International Group, 1999), 45–50, 56–61. Reprinted by kind permission of Aminah Beverly McCloud, Professor of Islamic Studies and Director, Islamic World Studies Program, and Frederick Thaufeer al-Deen Hajj, Imam, Oak Park Islamic community.

Suhail Mulla, Online Advice About Muslim Youth, October 21, 2004; November 2, 2004; December 7, 2004; December 28, 2004; and March 15, 2005. Available online at http://www.masnet.org/discussion_archive.asp. Last accessed on December 28, 2006. Used by kind permission of the Muslim American Society.

Islamic Medical Association of North America (IMANA), "Islamic Medical Ethics: The IMANA Perspective," May 15, 2005. Available online at http://data .memberclicks.com/site/imana/IMANAEthicsPaperPart1.pdf. Last accessed on December 28, 2006. Used by kind permission of Dr. H. E. Fadel, editor-in-chief, *Journal of Islamic Medical Association of North America*, www.imana.org.

Yahia Abdul-Rahman and Abdullah S. Tug, "Introduction to LARIBA Financing" (1998). Available online at http://www.lariba.com/knowledge-center/

articles/us-islamic-financing.htm. Last accessed on December 28, 2006. Reprinted by kind permission of Abdullah S. Tug and Yahia Abdul-Rahman, Chair, American Finance House LARIBA.

Capital D, "Culture of Terrorism," from *Insomnia* (Chicago: All Natural, Inc., 2004). Reprinted by kind permission of David J. Kelly.

Hamza Yusuf, introduction to *Purification of the Heart* (Starlatch Press, 2004), 1–10. Used by kind permission of the author.

Glossary of Islamic Terms

Most Islamic terms that appear here are taken from the Arabic language. Arabic has a different script than English, so these words have been *transliterated* into English—which means that the Arabic letters have been turned into English letters so that the reader can pronounce them. In transliterating words from Arabic into English, American scholars of Islam generally use a standard scheme endorsed by the Middle East Studies Association. This scheme, which includes lines drawn over certain letters and dots placed beneath other letters, is not used in newspapers or magazines or even by most English-speaking Muslims themselves. Most American students and general readers find it confusing. For that reason, I have chosen to use a simplified transliteration scheme. The only two "odd" letters that the reader encounters are the *'ayn*, rendered with an open quotation mark, and the *hamza*, rendered with a closed quotation mark—as in the word Qur'an.

In addition to offering definitions of the transliterated words, the glossary below includes a pedestrian guide to sounding them out. Of course, there is no one right way of pronouncing these words. As any speaker of English knows, English speakers from Scotland, India, and the United States can make the same words sound quite different. It is sometimes said that the Americans and the British are two peoples divided by a common language. The same is true for Muslims, in a way. Most Muslims are neither Arabs nor Arabic speakers. While they may share certain Islamic terms, often derived from the Qur'an or other Arabic sources, Muslims adopt local and regional pronunciations of these words.

In addition, because Muslims are so ethnically diverse and adhere to so many different religious interpretations of their faith, they disagree about the meaning of Islamic terms. In recognition of this fact, this glossary is offered with a bit of trepidation, with the proviso that the meaning of any religious idea is always tentative and changes depending on where and when it is used and who is using it.

Finally, I include a few Islamic names that are particularly important to know in the American context. Here, too, the reader should note that there is no one right way to spell or pronounce an Islamic name. In light of this, I have often erred on the side of "Americanizing" the name, which is the practice of many American Muslims.

ADAB (uh-duhb). Manners, courtesy, and respectful, appropriate behavior, as outlined in Islamic law and ethics.

ADHAN (uh-ZAHN, or uh-THAHN). The call to prayer, usually issued by a prayer caller, or *muezzin*, five times a day. "God is great, God is great," the *muezzin* calls. "I witness that there is no God but God . . . I witness that Muhammad is the Messenger of God . . . Come alive to prayer . . . Come alive to success." Shi'a *muezzins* add that Ali, the son-in-law and cousin of the Prophet, is the friend and proof of God.

AHMADIS (ah-MAH-dees, or ak-MAH-dees). Modern Muslim reform group, begun in 1889 in South Asia, whose members believe a man named Ghulam Ahmad was a *mujaddid*, or renewer of religion; the *mahdi*, or divinely guided figure; the *messiah*; and for some, a prophet. After his death, the group split into two but continued to attract a small but devoted number of followers around the world, including the United States. The movement advocates a peaceful form of Islam but is rejected by many Muslims and the government of Pakistan as heretical due to the claims of some Ahmadis that Ghulam Ahmad was a prophet.

AISHA (eye-EE-shuh). After Khadija's death, Muhammad married Aisha, whom many sources depict as his favorite wife. She was an important source of information of his words and deeds. Aisha also opposed the ascension of Ali to the caliphate in the Battle of the Camel.

ALHAMBRA (al-HAM-bruh). The fourteenth-century palace of a Muslim dynasty in Grenada, Spain. The interplay of water, light, and ornamentation makes the Alhambra one of the greatest examples of medieval Mediterranean architecture ever built. It is also a popular name in the United States for Shriner lodges.

ALI (ah-LEE). The son-in-law and cousin of the Prophet Muhammad, Ali is considered by Sunni Muslims to be the fourth caliph and by Shi'a Muslims to be the first Imam.

AL-AQSA (al-AHK-suh). The mosque that sits atop the Temple Mount, or Haram al-Sharif, in Jerusalem, important as the site from which Prophet Muhammad ascended into the heavens on his night journey.

AYATOLLAH (eye-uh-tuh-LAH, or eye-uh-TOE-luh). Literally a "sign of God," this is a high-ranking member of the Twelver Shi'a clergy accomplished in the interpretation of Islamic law and ethics.

BAY'A (bay-ah). An oath of allegiance to a leader.

BEKTASHIS (BECK-TAH-shees). The Bektashis (pl.) compose a mystical or Sufi order of Muslim practitioners originally established in Anatolia in the 1200s. They celebrate certain Shi'a holidays, are well known for their spiritual poetry, and stress the role of the spiritual director or guide in each believer's practice. While some Muslims have considered their lax adherence to Islamic legal traditions to be blameworthy and even heretical, others, especially in the Balkans, became Muslims under their tutelage.

CALIPH (KAY-lif). From the Arabic khalifa, this word is usually used to refer to the political leaders who succeeded the Prophet Muhammad as the leaders of the Islamic empire. The first four caliphs are known by many Muslims as the rightly guided moral and religious leaders of the Muslim community. The caliphs who succeeded them were dynastic rulers who did not command an equal degree of moral and spiritual authority. There is no caliph today.

DA'WA (DAH-wuh). Literally meaning "call," the word is used in modern contexts for Islamic missionary work.

DERVISH (DUHR-vish). Originally a Persian term that refers to Muslim mystics, or Sufis, who often devote their lives to prayer, meditation, or the performance of other rituals that bring them closer to God. Often ascetic in orientation, they eschew wealth and other impediments to a more spiritual life.

DHIKR (zik-er). Literally the "remembrance of God," dhikr is often ritualized through the use of prayer beads and/or supplicatory prayers. Muslims who perform dhikr may recite the ninety-names of God or chant other litanies. One frequently used formula is to recite, thirty-three times each in Arabic, "glory be to God," "praise be to God," and "there is no god but God." Sufi orders practice both individual and collective dhikr, which may assume musical, poetic, and other forms.

DIN (deen). Translated in modern contexts as "religion," din also refers to the human obligation to obey God and follow God's guidance. On the day of reckoning, or yawm ad-din, each soul will know what he or she has given and what he or she has held back.

EID AL-ADHA (eed-al-ud-ha). Festival of the Sacrifice, celebrating the end of the annual pilgrimage to Mecca. In memory of God's command to Abraham to sacrifice a ram in place of his son Ishmael, Muslims slaughter an animal and distribute food to the poor.

EID AL-FITR (eed-al-fih-ter). Festival of the Breaking of the Fast, marking the end of the month of fasting called Ramadan. Muslims often enjoy the company of family and friends, give gifts to their children, and donate money to charities.

AL-FATIHA (al-FAA-tee-hah). Literally "the opening," the first chapter of the Qur'an, recited in daily prayers, on special occasions, and during times of trouble. Its importance is similar to that of the Lord's Prayer in Christianity.

FATWA (fuht-wuh). A legal opinion or ethical ruling issued by one trained in Islamic law and ethics to an individual or group in response to a specific query.

FIQH (fihk). Often translated as "Islamic jurisprudence," *fiqh* is the human attempt to understand the *shari'a*, which is God's path or way for human beings. Traditionally, its sources or roots include the Qur'an, the traditions of the Prophet Muhammad and his companions, the consensus of scholars, and independent reasoning.

FITNA (fit-na). A "testing" or a "trial," *fitna* can also refer historically to the civil wars in the early period of Islam and to disorder in general.

HADITH (huh-DEETH). Reports of the sayings and deeds of the Prophet Muhammad and his companions. Originally oral reports, they were later written down. A *hadith* contains two sections: one section explaining the chain of transmitters (the persons who passed the story along) and one section with the actual text of the story or saying. The science of *hadith* criticism developed as a form of literary criticism meant to identify strong and weak *hadiths*. By the 800s, Muslim scholars produced several canonical collections of the reports. *Hadiths* constitute one of the important sources in the development of the *shari'a*, Islamic law and ethics.

HIJAZ (hih-JAZZ), also Hejaz. The western province of Arabia on the Gulf of Aqaba and the Red Sea. It contains Mecca and Medina.

HAJJ (hahj). The annual pilgrimage to Mecca, considered to be one of five pillars of Islamic practice, involves a series of rituals that, for many, results in strong feelings of God's mercy and human solidarity. Pilgrims enter a state of purity, circumambulate the Ka'ba, reenact sacred events, and pray God for the forgiveness of their sins, among other activities. Those who complete the ritual become known as *hajji* (m.) or *hajja* (f.).

HALAL (huh-LAAL). Permissible or lawful. Often used in reference to what food is permissible under Islamic law and ethics.

HARAM (hah-RAHM). Refers to an act forbidden according to Islamic law and ethics as well as to the areas around the holy cities of Mecca, Medina, and Jerusalem, inside of which no one may be hurt.

HIJAB (hih-JAAB). The "veil" or covering that may conceal a woman's hair, face, or body. Originally adopted as a sign of high status, the covering became a symbol of modesty and morality. In the modern era, it has multiple and contradictory meanings—for some, it is a sign of female subordination; for others, a symbol of resistance to Western hegemony; for still others, an ethnic fashion accessory; and for many women who wear it, it is a sign of their obedience to God and His Prophet.

HUDUD (huh-DOOD). Pl. of *hadd*, which means limit or prohibition. In the past, many Islamic legal scholars have considered theft, fornication, false accusation of fornication, drinking alcohol, apostasy, and banditry to be acts against God, requiring harsh punishments. Some Muslim conservatives propose the codification and state administration of such guidelines, while Muslim human-rights activists oppose their implementation.

'IBADAT (ih-ba-DAAT). Religious duties and acts of devotion and worship incumbent on Muslims, sometimes thought of as the rules that regulate humankind's relationship with God. Compare *mu'amalat*.

'ID (eed). See *Eid*.

IHRAM (ihh-RAHM). State of purity necessary to participate in the annual pilgrimage to Mecca, achieved by ritual cleansing and the donning of a simple two-piece, usually white garment for men and modest clothing for women.

IJTIHAD (ihj-tee-HAD). Reasoned interpretations of the Qur'an and traditions of the Prophet Muhammad often by a trained Islamic scholar, used historically as a source of Islamic law and ethics.

IMAM (ee-MAM, or ee-MOM). Though its literal meaning is "one who stands in front," this honorific title can refer to the person who leads congregational prayer or the head of a Muslim community or state. For Shi'a Muslims, the Imam is the Prophet Muhammad's successor, often regarded as infallible. In the United States, the imam, like a minister or rabbi, sometimes serves as the administrative and spiritual leader of a Muslim congregation.

IMAN (ee-MAN). Faith.

ISLAM (iss-LAHM, or iss-LAAM). Literally, "submission to God," *islam* is now used as a sociological category referring to a world religion. Persons who practice Islam are called Muslims.

ISLAMISM. A modern term, increasingly used to refer to a political ideology advocating the creation of Muslim states ruled in accordance with *shari'a*, or Islamic law and ethics. Some Islamists are violent revolutionaries while others hope to establish Islamic hegemony through peaceful and democratic means, including missionary work.

JIHAD (jee-HAD). A contested term in modern parlance derived from the Arabic word meaning to "struggle," "exert oneself," "strive," or "fight." Sometimes translated as "holy war," it is also used to indicate a moral struggle with one's own faults or peaceful protest against injustice.

KA'BA (KAH-bah). The sacred house of God, believed by many Muslims to be built by Abraham (Ibrahim) and Ishmael (Isma'il), located in Mecca, Arabia. Most Muslims pray in the direction of the cube-shaped building and walk around it during the pilgrimage to Mecca.

KHADIJA (ka-DEE-jah). The wife of the Prophet Muhammad, she became the first to follow his message. A wealthy merchant, she was older than Muhammad.

Khadija gave birth to Fatima and other children. She is a revered figure across the Islamic world, and her name is particularly popular among African American Muslims.

KHANQA (khan-kah). Persian term for a Sufi lodge or residence, where believers may meditate, pray, worship, learn, and study with a spiritual master, who sometimes lives there.

KHEDIVE (keh-DEEV). An honorary title used to refer to the governors of Egypt, descended from the line of Muhammad Ali, from 1867 to World War I.

KUFI (KOO-fee). A short, round cap worn on the top of the head, sometimes made out of kente cloth or yarn. Often worn by African American Muslim men in observance of an early Islamic tradition, the *kufi* is popular among non-Muslim African American men as well.

KUFFAR (koo-FAHR). Unbelievers, ingrates, or infidels.

MADRASA (MUH-druh-suh). "School," in modern times, either secular or religious. In the middle ages, the *madrasa* was a college where the advanced study of sacred texts, philosophy, Islamic law and ethics, and other Islamic subjects was pursued.

MAHDI (MAH-dee). A divinely guided figure, expected to appear before the end of the world to establish true justice and belief among all. Both Sunni and Shi'a Muslims subscribe to a wide range of beliefs and traditions surrounding this redeemer. Among them is the belief that he will appear along side the Prophet Jesus to fight the false Messiah or Antichrist.

MARABOUT (MARE-ah-boo). A French term derived from the Arabic for *murabit* (mur-ah-bit) that refers to Muslim mystics and saints who have a special connection to God. Used most often in North and West Africa. Traditionally, many Muslims visit the shrines of these holy people to gain blessings, though this practice is often criticized by modern reformers and so-called fundamentalists.

MASJID (MUHS-jihd). Mosque.

MASLAHA (MUHSS-lah-hah). Particularly important to modern interpretations of Islamic law and ethics, *maslaha* means the "public interest," and modern Muslim thinkers often argue for the creation of new laws and policies based on the idea that this practice will serve the public welfare.

MECCA. The hometown of the Prophet Muhammad and the most sacred city in Islam. Many Muslims pray in the direction of Mecca and yearn to visit it at least once in their lifetimes in order to perform the great pilgrimage.

MEDINA (muh-DEE-nah). The abbreviated name for the "city of the prophet," located north of Mecca, where the Prophet Muhammad and his followers were invited to move in 622 CE. Originally called Yathrib, Medina became the capital of the nascent Islamic polity established by the Prophet Muhammad. Known to many as the second holiest city in Islam, it is also the site of the Prophet's tomb, which is visited by Muslim pilgrims from around the world.

MEVLEVIS (mehv-lehv-ees). A Sufi order established by poet Jalal al-Din Rumi (d. 1273). Famous in the West as the whirling dervishes, followers use music, dance, and the recitation of poetry and prayers to gain a closer sense of God's presence. As the Ottoman Empire grew, the order grew with it, spreading to the eastern Mediterranean and southeastern Europe.

MIHRAB (mih-rahb). A niche, generally in the wall of a mosque, indicating the direction toward Mecca.

MOHAMMEDAN. An archaic European term used to refer to Muslims. Now considered offensive.

MOORS. Refers to the Northwest African persons who conquered Spain in 711 CE, or to American Muslims who are practitioners of "Moorish Science." Established by North Carolinian Timothy Drew, or Noble Drew Ali, in Chicago (some scholars say New Jersey), the Moorish Science Temple taught that Islam was the natural religion of black people or "Moors," who were Asiatic in race and Moroccan in nationality.

MU'AMALAT (moo-AH-muh-LAAT). The ethical and legal obligations implied in business exchanges and human interactions more generally. Islamic legal and ethical discourses generally treat this area of human behavior in a flexible manner, with an eye toward achieving the maximum good for society. Compare 'ibadat.

MUEZZIN (moo-AH-zin). A person who recites the call to prayer, chanting, among other phrases, "God is great, I believe that there is no god but God, I believe that Muhammad is the Messenger of God."

MUFTI (MUHF-tee). A highly trained scholar of Islamic law and ethics capable of issuing authoritative opinions on a broad range of legal and ethical questions.

MUJAHIDIN (MOO-jah-hih-DEEN). Persons engaged in *jihad*, or struggle. In American media outlets, it is generally used to refer to warriors, though the term could equally be applied to peaceful human-rights activists.

MUNAFIQUN (moo-naa-fee-koon). Hypocrites, those who profess Islam while working against its interests in secret.

MUJADDID (moo-JUH-did). A renewer or redeemer of the faith, whom many Muslims believe appears every century or on a regular basis to revive Muslim believers and correct any wrongs.

MURSHID. See *pir*.

MUSLIM (muhs-lim), also Moslem. A person who is a follower of the Islamic religion, variously defined, or a person who identifies culturally with Islamic civilization or societies.

NAFS (nuhfs). The "self" or "soul." In Sufi contexts, sometimes akin to Freud's id.

NAMAZ (nuh-MAHZ). See *salat*.

NEFES (neh-fes). A Turkish Sufi ritual chant or song sometimes accompanied by a three-stringed lute.

PIR (peer). Persian word for a Sufi master responsible for training students in the ways of a particular Sufi order. The *pir* directs the spiritual life of the student, providing spiritual exercises, liturgies, and lessons, and by discussing his or her development along the path toward truth.

QADI (KAH-dee). An Islamic judge.

QUR'AN (core-ann, or core-ahn). Literally the "recitation," revealed to the Prophet Muhammad of Arabia from approximately 610 to 632 CE, later collected and put into one volume. For most Muslims, the Qur'an is the word of God sent to guide all humankind. Muslims listen to and recite the Qur'an more often than reading it in silence.

QURAYSH (Coor-aysh). The tribe of the Prophet Muhammad, known for their success as merchants. At first opposed to the message of Muhammad, they eventually accepted Islam and became strong supporters of the faith.

RIBA (rih-bah). A disputed term meaning interest or usury. Some Muslims consider all forms of interest on loans and savings to be unacceptable, while others consider only certain forms of interest to be prohibited.

RAMADAN (RAH-mah-DON). Observant Muslims often fast from dawn to dusk during this sacred month, the ninth month of the Muslim lunar calendar. A time for religious renewal, family togetherness, and fun, Muslims abstain from food, drink, smoking, and sex during the day, and then break their fasts together after sunset. Only those who are able participate: the ill, the old, the young, women who are breastfeeding or menstruating, and travelers are excused.

RUMI (ROO-mee). Jalal ad-Din Muhammad Rumi is often praised as one the world's greatest poets; he is also the founder of a Sufi order and a significant figure in Islamic thought. Born in Afghanistan, Rumi eventually settled in Konya, Turkey. Among Rumi's most famous works is a multivolume work called the *Masnavi*. Though Rumi wrote in Persian, his poetry has been translated into several other languages, including English. Rumi died in Turkey in 1273 CE. His shrine became a major pilgrimage site for Muslims seeking to be in the presence of Mevlana, or "our master."

SALAFI (SAL-ah-fee). Taken from the Arabic word *salaf*, meaning the pious ancestors who lived during the time of the Prophet Muhammad, this adjective refers to modern movements, both socially conservative and socially liberal, which advocate a return to the fundamentals of Islamic practice and the systematic dismantling of inappropriate additions to Islam. Salafis (plural) are sometimes called "fundamentalists." Some of them, especially those covered by major American media outlets such as the Muslim Brothers in Egypt or the Jamaat-i Islami in Pakistan, are strong advocates of a political form of Islam and claim that Islam is both a religion and a state.

SALAMU 'ALAYKUM (sa-LAAM-oo ah-LAY-koom). Meaning "peace be upon you," it is a common Muslim greeting. The response is *wa 'alaykum salam* (wa ah-LAY-koom sa-LAAM), meaning "and unto you be peace."

SALAT (sah-LAHT). The second pillar of Islam, daily ritual prayers consisting of a prescribed set of motions including prostrations and several verses from the Qur'an. For Sunni Muslims, there are five daily: at morning, noon, mid-afternoon, evening, and night. Those performing the prayers prepare by ritually cleansing themselves and announcing their intention to pray. Also known in many places as *namaz*.

SHAHADA (shuh-HAA-duh, or shuh-HAH-duh). The "witness" or profession of faith that constitutes the first pillar of Islamic practice: "I witness that there is no god but God; I witness that Muhammad is the messenger of God."

SHARI'A (shuh-REE-uh). Theoretically, the *shari'a* is the path of God, a perfect expression of God's expectations regarding every aspect of human life. Practically speaking, it is a body of rules, including law, ethics, and etiquette, derived from human beings' interpretations of the Qur'an, the traditions of the Prophet Muhammad, and the views of Muslim jurists, lawyers, religious leaders, and scholars. A remarkable and dynamic intellectual and social achievement in the middle ages, the *shari'a* was supported by a vast network of schools, courts, charitable endowments, and merchants. Unlike modern law, it was not generally codified. In modern times, it has become the subject of great controversy as Muslims argue over whether to implement *shari'a* as a legal code in Muslim-majority nation-states.

SHAYKH (shake). Sometimes spelled *sheik*, *sheikh*, or *shaikh*, a *shaykh* is an honorific term that could mean village elder, religious scholar, head of a religious organization, judge, or preacher.

SHI'A (SHEE-uh). Shi'a Muslims, also called Shi'ite and Shi'i Muslims, historically believe that members of the family of the Prophet Muhammad are the rightful spiritual and temporal leaders of Muslims. Though they are said to account for only 10 to 20 percent of all Muslims worldwide, this means there are well over one hundred million of them. They constitute the Muslim majority in Iran, Iraq, Bahrain, and Azerbaijan. Today, Shi'a Muslims are divided into three major groups, including the Twelvers, the Isma'ilis, and the Zaydis.

SHURA (SHOO-ruh). "Consultation," especially among the believers, to decide the political course of a Muslim society or organization. Taken by many modern Muslims to be an endorsement of democratic means of governance.

SUFISM (SOOF-ism). An encompassing and generic term used to describe a range of both elite and popular spiritual practices and institutions in Islam that in one way or another seek a more immediate, mystical, intimate, or personal relationship with God. Sufis may come from any sect of Islam. Sufi rituals may include the recitation of Qur'anic verses, prayers, or poems, the regulation of the breath, or the performance of music or dance. Some of the great thinkers and writers of Islam have been Sufi in orientation, including the poet Rumi and the jurist al-Ghazali. In addition, Sufis have developed and maintained orders, or *tariqas*, organizations in which believers enter often to train with a spiritual guide, called a *shaykh* or *pir*. Though some modern Muslim reformers have opposed Sufism as backward and superstitious, its various manifestations, both local and global, continue to attract the devotion of millions of Muslims worldwide.

SULTAN (sool-TAHN). Used generically to refer to someone with authority and power, the term is best known in the West as the title given to the leader of the Ottoman Empire, which began in the fourteenth century and ruled parts of Asia, Africa, and Europe until 1923.

SUNNA (SOO-nuh). Literally meaning "custom" or "tradition," *sunna* generally refers to the practices, ideals, and life example of the Prophet Muhammad of Arabia, who for many Muslims represents the complete human, worthy of imitation. Orally transmitted by one generation of Muslims to another, the sunna is contained in the *hadith*, the reports of the sayings and deeds of the Prophet Muhammad and his companions.

SUNNI (SOO-nee). Often referred to as "orthodoxy," Sunni Islam is a label associated with the "people of tradition (of the Prophet) and the community." Sunni Muslims account for the vast majority of the world's Muslims, and while most of them share certain ritual practices and basic beliefs in common, they are also separated by deep ethnic, political, socioeconomic, national, and cultural divides. While early Western scholars of Islam stressed the legal and intellectual aspects of the Sunni tradition, more recent scholars have also emphasized the spiritual and popular practices of Sunni Muslims.

TAKBIR (TACK-beer, or TUCK-beer). The phrase *Allahu akbar*, which means "God is greater" or "God is greatest." In addition to being chanted as part of the call to prayer, the ritual prayers, and meditation, the phrase is sometimes used in lieu of applause, to express gratitude, support, or endorsement by a crowd of persons.

TARIQA (tah-REE-kah). Literally means the "path," generally referring to Sufi orders established by or in the memory of a great spiritual master. Students travel along the way toward truth aided by a guide, whose spiritual authority is often passed on to a family member or another member of the order from generation to generation. In addition to performing the regular ritual prayers, initiates often engage in extensive study, meditation, and devotional exercises. *Tariqas* were a major factor in the growth and spread of Islamic religion across Afro-Eurasia. Some had an influence not only on the religious life but also on the political and military fortunes of various Muslim regimes.

TEKKE (teh-KAY). Turkish term for a Sufi lodge or residence, where believers may meditate, pray, worship, learn, and study with a spiritual master, who sometimes lives there.

THOBE (thohb, or thawb). An ankle-length garment or robe, which can be worn by men or women, popular among some African American Muslims.

UMMA (oo-mah). The global community of Muslim believers.

Urdu (oor-DO). A national language of Pakistan, Urdu is a South Asian language also spoken by millions in India. Similar to Hindi, Urdu has influences from Arabic and Persian. It is an "Islamicate" language formerly used in the courts of the Delhi sultanate and the Mughal Empire.

usul al-fiqh (oo-SOOL al-fihk). The roots or sources of Islamic jurisprudence. See also *fiqh*.

Wahhabis (wuh-HA-bees). Religious and political reform movement established by the Arabian religious scholar Muhammad ibn Abdul al-Wahhab in the 1700s, who became an ally of the Saud family, the current rulers of Saudi Arabia. Wahhabis are known for their strict monotheism and their sometimes violent opposition to mystics, shrines, and tomb visitation, as well as to Shi'a Islam. Advocates of the moral renewal of Islamic societies, they are also active in missionary work.

wudu (wuh-DOO), also *wuzu* and *wudzu*. An ablution or act of ritual cleansing performed before the prayers, usually with water. The practitioner cleans his or her hands, mouth, nose, face, arms up to the elbows, head, ears, and feet.

zakat (zuh-CAT). The "poor-tax," "alms," or charity. It is one of the pillars of Islamic practice.

zikr (zih-ker). See *dhikr*.

Further Reading

General Overviews

Haddad, Yvonne Yazbeck, and Jane Idleman Smith, eds. *Muslim Communities in North America*. Albany: State University of New York Press, 1994.

Leonard, Karen Isaksen. *Muslims in the United States: The State of Research*. New York: Russell Sage Foundation, 2003.

Smith, Jane I. *Islam in America*. New York: Columbia University Press, 1999.

Chapter 1

Austin, Allan D. *African Muslims in Antebellum America: Transatlantic Stories and Spiritual Struggles*. Rev. ed. New York: Routledge, 1997.

Diouf, Sylviane A. *Servants of Allah: African Muslims Enslaved in the Americas*. New York: New York University Press, 1998.

Marr, Timothy. *The Cultural Roots of American Islamicism*. Cambridge: Cambridge University Press, 2006.

McAlister, Melani. *Epic Encounters: Culture, Media, and U.S. Interests in the Middle East Since 1945*. 2nd ed. Berkeley and Los Angeles: University of California Press, 2005.

Naff, Alixa. *Becoming American: The Early Arab Immigrant Experience*. Carbondale, Ill.: Southern Illinois University Press, 1985.

Sherman, William C., Paul L. Whitney, and John Guerrero. *Prairie Peddlers: The Syrian-Lebanese in North Dakota*. Bismarck, N.D.: University of Mary Press, 2002.

Chapter 2

Bilgé, Barbara. "Voluntary Associations in the Old Turkish Community of Metropolitan Detroit." In *Muslim Communities in North America,* edited by Yvonne Y. Haddad and Jane Idleman Smith, 381–405.

Curtis, Edward E. "Why Malcolm X Never Developed an Islamic Approach to Civil Rights." *Religion* 32 (2002): 227–242.

Elkholy, Abdo. *The Arab Moslems in the United States.* New Haven, Conn.: College and University Press Service, 1966.

Essien-Udom, E. U. *Black Nationalism: A Search for an Identity in America.* Chicago: University of Chicago Press, 1962.

McCloud, Aminah Beverly. *African American Islam.* New York: Routledge, 1995.

Nance, Susan. "Mystery of the Moorish Science Temple: Southern Blacks and American Alternative Spirituality in 1920s Chicago." *Religion and American Culture* 12, no. 2 (2002): 123–166.

Trix, Frances. *The Albanians in Michigan.* East Lansing: Michigan State University Press, 2001.

Turner, Richard Brent. *Islam in the African American Experience.* 2nd ed. Bloomington: Indiana University Press, 2003.

Chapter 3

Abraham, Nabeel, and Andrew Shryock, eds. *Arab Detroit: From Margin to Mainstream.* Detroit, Mich.: Wayne State University Press, 2000.

Eck, Diana L. *A New Religious America: How a "Christian Country" Has Become the World's Most Religiously Diverse Nation.* New York: HarperSanFrancisco, 2002.

Jackson, Sherman A. *Islam and the Blackamerican: Looking Toward the Third Resurrection.* New York: Oxford University Press, 2005.

Lawrence, Bruce B. *New Faiths, Old Fears: Muslims and Other Asian Immigrants in American Religious Life.* New York: Columbia University Press, 2002.

Marsh, Clifton E. *Black Muslims to Muslims: The Resurrection, Transformation, and Change of the Lost-Found Nation of Islam in America, 1930–1995.* 2nd ed. Lanham, Md.: Scarecrow Press, 1996.

Naim, Anjum. "Sufism in America." *Span* (May/June 2005): 50–54.

Nuruddin, Yusuf. "The Five Percenters: A Teenage Nation of Gods and Earths." In *Muslim Communities in North America,* edited by Yvonne Y. Haddad and Jane Idleman Smith, 109–132.

Webb, Gisela. "Tradition and Innovation in Contemporary American Islamic

Spirituality: The Bawa Muhaiyaddeen Fellowship." In *Muslim Communities in North America,* edited by Yvonne Y. Haddad and Jane Idleman Smith, 75–108. Albany: State University of New York Press, 1994.

Chapter 4

Aswad, Barbara C., and Barbara Bilgé. *Family and Gender Among American Muslims: Issues Facing Immigrants and Their Descendants.* Philadelphia, Penn.: Temple University Press, 1996.

Kugle, Scott Siraj al-Haqq. "Sexuality, Diversity, and Ethics in the Agenda of Progressive Muslims." In *Progressive Muslims: On Justice, Gender, and Pluralism,* edited by Omid Safi, 190–234. Oxford: Oneworld Publications, 2003.

Majeed, Debra Mubashshir. "The Battle Has Been Joined: Gay and Polygynous Marriages Are out of the Closet and in Search of Legitimacy." *Cross Currents* 54, no. 2 (2004): 73–81.

Rouse, Carolyn Moxley. *Engaged Surrender: African American Women and Islam.* Berkeley and Los Angeles: University of California Press, 2004.

Simmons, Gwendolyn Zoharah. "Are We Up to the Challenge? The Need for a Radical Re-ordering of the Islamic Discourse on Women." In *Progressive Muslims: On Justice, Gender, and Pluralism,* edited by Omid Safi, 235–248.

Webb, Gisela. *Windows of Faith: Muslim Women Activists in North America.* Syracuse, N.Y.: Syracuse University Press, 2000.

Chapter 5

Haddad, Yvonne Yazbeck, and John L. Esposito, eds. *Muslims on the Americanization Path?* New York: Oxford University Press, 2000.

Hussain, Amir. "Muslims, Pluralism, and Interfaith Dialogue." In *Progressive Muslims: On Justice, Gender, and Pluralism,* edited by Omid Safi, 251–269.

Leonard, Karen. "South Asian Leadership of American Muslims." In *Muslims in the West: From Sojourners to Citizens,* edited by Yvonne Yazbeck Haddad, 233–249. New York: Oxford University Press, 2002.

Nimer, Mohamed. *The North American Muslim Resource Guide: Muslim Community Life in the United States and Canada.* New York: Routledge, 2002.

Strum, Philippa, and Danielle Tarantolo, eds. *Muslims in the United States.* Washington, D.C.: Woodrow Wilson International Center for Scholars, 2003.

Chapter 6

Bakhtiar, Laleh. *Sufi Women of America: Angels in the Making.* Chicago: Kazi Publications, 1996.

Barboza, Steven. *American Jihad: Islam After Malcolm X.* New York: Doubleday, 1993.

Cooke, Miriam, and Bruce B. Lawrence, eds. *Muslim Networks: From Hajj to Hip-Hop.* Chapel Hill: University of North Carolina Press, 2005.

Dannin, Robert. *Black Pilgrimage to Islam.* New York: Oxford University Press, 2002.

Haddad, Yvonne, and Adair T. Lummis. *Islamic Values in the United States.* New York: Oxford Press, 1987.

Kahera, Akel Ismail. *Deconstructing the American Mosque: Space, Gender, and Aesthetics.* Austin: University of Texas Press, 2002.

Metcalf, Barbara Daly, ed. *Making Muslim Space in North America and Europe.* Berkeley: University of California Press, 1996.

Index